Refugee Rights

Refugee Rights

ETHICS, ADVOCACY, AND AFRICA

David Hollenbach, Editor

Georgetown University Press / Washington, D.C.

Georgetown University Press, Washington, D.C. www.press.georgetown.edu

Library of Congress Cataloging-in-Publication Data

Refugee rights: ethics, advocacy, and Africa / David Hollenbach, editor.
    p. cm.
   Includes bibliographical references and index.
   ISBN 978-1-58901-202-8 (alk. paper)
    1. Refugees—Africa. 2. Human rights—Africa. 3. Asylum, Right of—Africa.
I. Hollenbach, David.
HV640.R41836 2008
325'.21096—dc22

2007034412

⊗ This book is printed on acid-free paper meeting the requirements of the American National Standard for Permanence in Paper for Printed Library Materials.

15 14 13 12 11 10 09 08   9 8 7 6 5 4 3 2
First printing

Printed in the United States of America

Contents

Acknowledgments

This volume would not have come into existence without the major contributions of David Rothrock of Catholic Relief Services and John Guiney, SJ, of the Jesuit Refugee Service, both formerly based in Nairobi, Kenya. Both of these men brought their deep experience working with refugees and others who have suffered the consequences of war in Africa to the planning of the conference that led to this book. Both were key participants in the discussions that took place at the conference itself. I am deeply grateful for the opportunity to have worked with them both.

I am also grateful to others who helped plan and realize the project. Aquiline Tarimo and Agbonkhianmeghe Orobator, Jesuit colleagues at Hekima College in Nairobi, worked with me on developing the plans for the project. Elizabeth King of the Center for Human Rights and International Justice at Boston College provided much help with the editing of the volume and in conducting the conference. Wanjiru Magwa and David Gitari of CRS in Nairobi handled the logistics of the conference, with assistance from Jacques Randrianary, Kabamba Emmanuel Nshimbi, Fidele Ingiyimbere, and Magnus Ahamefula Kelechi from Hekima College. Jane Vecchi provided support at Boston College throughout the project. Jennifer Christian helped with editing.

The financial support of both an international foundation that prefers to remain anonymous and Catholic Relief Services, thanks to the interest and support of its president, Kenneth Hackett, made the entire project possible. I am most grateful for their confidence in what we have tried to do.

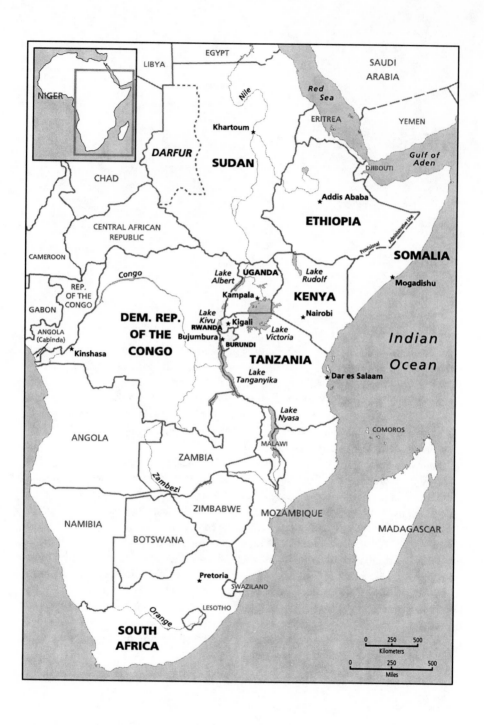

Introduction

Human Rights as an Ethical Framework for Advocacy

David Hollenbach

There are over thirty-three million refugees and internally displaced people in the world today.[1] A disproportionate percentage of these displaced people are in Africa. Most have been driven from their homes by the armed strife of both interstate and intrastate conflicts. Such coerced migration violates people's freedom, and most have been displaced into settings where conditions fall far short of what is required to live with basic human dignity. Such displacement, therefore, violates people's most basic human rights in multiple ways.

Human rights have played an increasingly important role in the assessment of international affairs since the proclamation of the Universal Declaration of Human Rights in 1948. The Universal Declaration was a response to the genocidal extermination of the Jewish people attempted by the Nazis and the destruction and displacement caused by World War II itself. This history thus ties contemporary human rights norms directly to the conditions faced by most refugees and internally displaced people today. In addition, the long-standing historical discussions of the ethics of war and peace in Western and non-Western traditions are also linked with key issues raised by forced migration. Both human rights norms and the ethics of war and peace, therefore, have direct relevance to the plight of displaced people and the way the world should respond to their needs.

Refugees and internally displaced people, however, are regrettably often the forgotten victims of human rights violations. The human rights issues raised by forced displacement have not been addressed in the same depth as other grave human rights issues, such as depriving people of their liberty for political reasons or the use of torture in gathering intelligence. Nor have the consequences of war for refugees received more than minimal attention in most legal and ethical analyses of armed conflict. We take it for granted today that intentionally killing civilians is a violation of the law and ethics of warfare. The displacement of millions from their homes, however, is not rejected nearly

1

as strongly as is the targeting of civilians in bombing raids. In practice, the displacement of refugees often seems to be accepted as a sad but inevitable consequence of war. The fate of the displaced fails to raise the concern, analysis, protest, and action for which their suffering calls.

In addition, neither public opinion nor the existing norms of international law adequately address the plight of internally displaced people—those who are not refugees in a strict legal sense because they have not been forced across an international border. This is particularly important in the African context, for about half of the more than twenty million internally displaced people in the world today are in Africa.[2] If human rights practitioners and policymakers are to address the needs of these populations more effectively, we need to reflect on both existing political practice and legal standards from a normative human rights standpoint. The *Guiding Principles on Internal Displacement* developed under the leadership of Francis M. Deng, representative of the UN secretary-general on internally displaced persons, provides a strong sense of the direction we need to move.[3] Deng's important leadership has led to the development of careful policy proposals to protect and aid the internally displaced. But in practice many of the internally displaced are still not being protected in a minimally humane way, nor are their most basic human rights secured.

This volume arose from a conviction that the human rights grounds for advocating change in practice and policy toward the displaced need to be addressed in greater depth, and that such examination is overdue. This book seeks to provide an analytic framework for a more vigorous and effective advocacy on behalf of refugees and internally displaced persons, so that more effective responses to their suffering are forthcoming in practice. Advocacy on behalf of the victims of humanitarian crises is increasingly seen as a key part of the work of the organizations that have traditionally provided them with direct aid and assistance. Both secular and religious nongovernmental agencies increasingly see their mission as including the advocacy of public policies that will alleviate and prevent the suffering of refugees.

For example, the Jesuit Refugee Service calls "advocacy" on behalf of justice for refugees and other forcibly displaced people one of its three overarching goals, along with accompaniment and service to the displaced.[4] Catholic Relief Services has adopted a "justice lens" to aid in focusing all of its relief and development work so it can advocate more effective response to the needs of vulnerable people both with the Catholic population of the United States and with the United States and other governments.[5] *Médecins Sans Frontières* (Doctors Without Borders) speaks of its obligation to bear witness (*témoinage*) when it encounters severe injustices in its work, rather than allowing its commitment to political neutrality to lead it to remain silent in the face of the causes of suffering.[6] Other humanitarian and relief organizations also see their roles as going beyond immediate response to the urgent needs of people in crisis situations. They aim to make more systematic responses that address the root causes and long-term consequences of humanitarian crises. Addressing these causes and consequences leads them to adopt stances of advocacy that address governments, intergovernmental bodies, and other sectors of civil society. For church-linked groups such as the Jesuit Refugee Service and Catholic Relief Services, such advocacy also addresses the larger religious communities in which they are based and seeks to influence the responses of these communities to the needs of the displaced.

Staff of these organizations, however, observe that they are often so caught up in response to crisis situations that they are unable to develop approaches to advocacy that are sufficiently grounded in empirical and normative analysis. In an effort to help provide a stronger framework for advocacy on behalf of displaced persons, the Boston College Center for Human Rights and International Justice, in collaboration with Catholic Relief Services and the Jesuit Refugee Service, organized a conference in Nairobi, Kenya, in October 2006, on the rights of refugees as a framework for advocacy. The chapters in this volume were initially presented at that conference. Some of them are descriptive case studies prepared by practitioners working directly with displaced people. These chapters reflect the direct experience of those working on the ground to bring assistance to people forcibly driven from home. Indeed, the first chapter in this book powerfully presents the personal experience of an Ethiopian refugee who has been living in camps for over fifteen years. Other chapters are more systematic analyses by scholars. At the conference, authors of both types of chapters engaged in a rich dialogue, and they have subsequently revised their presentations in light of this discussion. The dialogue led participants to some new insights into how to improve both theoretical analysis of the realities of displacement and practical responses to the plight of the displaced. It will be useful to highlight several of the key points that emerged.

There was agreement that advocacy will be more effective if it is grounded in the fundamental human rights of displaced persons, and if the conditions that impede or promote these rights are better understood through careful social and political analysis. The conference was also guided by a conviction that human rights are moral as well as legal norms, and that when existing legal standards fail to serve the human dignity of displaced persons, the law should be changed and developed in light of ethical requirements of humane treatment. Thus, the authors of this book's essays sometimes make ethical arguments for moving beyond existing international law. The authors do not hesitate to suggest changes in the international law of human rights and in humanitarian law when such changes are suggested by what is required if the displaced are to be treated in a way that is minimally humane.

Ethics, of course, is a domain of notable pluralism across cultures and religious traditions. The authors of the essays presented here are very much aware of this pluralism and want to respect its requirements. Pluralism, however, does not mean that anything goes in the treatment of the displaced. Pluralism is appropriately limited by the duty to respect and protect the basic human dignity of the persons whose lives and freedoms are threatened by the crisis of forced displacement. In other words, human rights set boundaries for legitimate pluralism.

Part I of this book addresses this issue of rights in the face of pluralism. The first essay, by Abebe Feyissa, with Rebecca Horn, describes the struggles and sufferings of one Ethiopian refugee over many years. This poignant narrative will lead most if not all people to say that no one should have to endure conditions like this. This is an ethical judgment similar to the response to the *shoah* and to the violence of World War II, which led to the formulation of the Universal Declaration of Human Rights. Despite the ethical diversity that characterizes our world, including the diversity of Africa, most people, including the authors writing here, are ready to conclude that the plight of refugees is morally problematic and that it is beyond the domain of the morally tolerable when it reaches conditions like those faced by Feyissa.

In chapter 2 William O'Neill builds a theoretical, philosophical argument for why the rights of refugees and internally displaced people should be affirmed by all of us, despite the diversity of our cultural and religious traditions. Indeed, O'Neill argues that all traditions that are broadly humanistic can affirm the fundamental rights of the displaced on grounds internal to their own traditions while they also respect the cultural differences of others. This applies to most African traditions as well as to the Catholic and Christian traditions that shape the approach of the organizations that sponsored this project. This approach is very much in line with the conviction, rooted in the natural law tradition, that the values embedded in Christian faith are compatible with reasoned reflection on human experience in many cultures. Thus, starting from the lived experience of the suffering of long-term refugees and moving through rigorous philosophical reflection, Part I makes a case for the validity of an ethic of human rights as the ground for advocacy on behalf of refugees and internally displaced people.

Part II addresses the issue of the right to the freedom of movement that is problematic for or denied to many refugees. All forcibly displaced people have been coerced to leave their homes, and so, by definition, their freedom of movement (or of nonmovement) has been violated. When they gain asylum in another country, their freedom of movement is often once again violated by being confined to camps. The essay by Feyissa in Part I describes this restriction vividly. Feyissa has been compelled to live in Kakuma Refugee Camp in northwestern Kenya for the past fifteen years. A camp is supposed to be a "temporary" refuge for the displaced, and the term "camp" does not even appear in the 1951 Refugee Convention. In actuality, however, the time spent in camps by displaced people frequently stretches to years, even decades. This leads the essay by the Joint Commission for Refugees of the Catholic Bishops of Burundi and Tanzania, chapter 3, to ask whether becoming a refugee means that one's human rights have become so "contingent" on circumstances that they are not really treated as genuine rights at all. Chapter 4 describes how internally displaced persons in Uganda have been confined to camps by the Ugandan government, supposedly for their protection against the attacks of the rebel Lord's Resistance Army (LRA). Whether this confinement has in fact improved their security can be debated, but it has surely limited their freedom. Similarly, in chapters 5 and 6 the situation of urban, "self-settled" refugees is discussed in two very different contexts: Kenya and South Africa. In Kenya most refugees are not supposed to be in the cities but are expected to live in camps far from urban settings. This restricts their freedom of movement and limits their access to many other human necessities, as Burton Wagacha and John Guiney describe. South Africa is more accommodating to refugees who settle in the cities, and Loren Landau makes an ethical argument for the basic resources to which they should have access.

Freedom of movement by refugees became one of the basic human rights that the conference identified as central to advocacy on behalf of the displaced. Many conference participants would join their voices to that of the U.S. Committee for Refugees and Migrants in challenging the protracted "warehousing" of refugees.[7] To be sure, conference participants recognized that camps can be a necessary way of responding to the needs of the displaced in the face of emergencies, and there was not full agreement on how long emergency encampment could be considered legitimate. But confinement to a camp is a serious diminishment of one's basic human dignity and a restriction of a fundamental human right. Thus, conference discussion highlighted several key norms that should govern restriction to camps:

- Confinement to camps should be imposed only when it is necessary for protection. It should be a last resort, used only when free movement by displaced people is not compatible with their protection or with the resources available to the host country.
- It should be temporary, lasting only as long as is strictly necessary to ensure protection of displaced people.
- It should be employed only when the harm that results from restricting people's right to freedom of movement is proportionately less than the harm they would face outside camps and less than the harm free movement by large numbers of refugees would cause to the host society.

Enabling refugees to exercise very basic rights such as those to freedom of movement and to obtain a livelihood can cost a lot more than very poor African countries can manage. If the human rights of displaced people are not contingent, therefore, richer countries have a fundamental responsibility to share the burdens of coming to the aid of the displaced. The burden should not fall exclusively on the very poor neighboring countries that are usually the first asylum for Africans forced from their homes. Pressing developed nations to assist in aiding the displaced find work and education for their children through development assistance for refugee-receiving countries in Africa should be a central emphasis of advocacy on behalf of the displaced today. Developing international institutions that will support and facilitate such assistance is also a key task. Thus, the rights to movement and to a livelihood help shape key points on an advocacy agenda that is very relevant to the African context.

Part III addresses the rights of women as criteria for a more adequate response to the struggle of refugees and the internally displaced. In chapter 7 Binaifer Nowrojee highlights some of the most egregious forms of violence to which displaced women are too often subjected. To be a refugee is to be in an extremely vulnerable situation, because the supportive frameworks of family, local community, and nation have been torn away. The internally displaced are often vulnerable to attacks by the agency that should be protecting them, namely their own national government. In these circumstances, women are often more subject to sexual and domestic violence than in other settings; thus, their rights to bodily integrity and even to life can be in severe danger. The major refugee-serving agencies have been developing standards and practices to protect displaced women from such abuse, and these efforts have shown some success where there is a concerted political will to implement them. There is urgent need, however, to deepen and broaden the commitment to implementation.

In chapter 8, Susan Martin notes that the challenge of cultural difference for universal human rights standards is particularly acute when traditional gender roles are at stake. The experience of forced migration itself also has complex effects on the roles of women. It not only subjects women to greater vulnerabilities and dangers but can also lead to role change that enhances women's autonomy, agency, and capacity for community leadership. Martin argues that there is no necessary conflict between protection of displaced women from violence or repression and respect for cultural traditions. How to balance these concerns, however, can be a delicate matter and can call for a great deal of concrete practical wisdom. The need for such practical wisdom also applies in human rights–based advocacy. Both the rights of women and the right to respect for one's culture are human rights, and these two sets of rights must be brought into an appropriate balance. Nevertheless, this call for practical wisdom should not be misunderstood as a call for timidity. The dignity of all human persons is the basis of both the rights of women and the right to respect for diverse cultures. Commitment to respect for this dignity means no attack on their dignity can be tolerated. Thus, violence against women, rape as a tool of war, and other serious violations of women's personal security must be challenged across cultures and wherever it occurs.

This suggests several further points for an advocacy agenda regarding displaced women:

- All refugee-serving programs and institutions should be assessed in light of their support for the equality and dignity of women. Practices that seriously violate that dignity should be challenged in the name of human rights. This may call for careful discernment of how to balance respect for cultural traditions with the protection of the rights of women.
- Despite the importance of respect for cultural traditions, protection of women's right to physical security and safety should always be a priority for refugee-serving programs.
- Active participation of women in the design and administration of programs aiding displaced populations is a key to protection of the rights of women.

Advocating the rights of refugees thus calls for strong advocacy on behalf of the rights of displaced women.

Part IV turns to analyses of war as the principal cause of displacement and how a human rights perspective can help frame a response to it. Africa is beset with numerous conflicts that have created many millions of refugees and internally displaced persons (IDPs). In chapter 9, Khoti Kamanga outlines the scope of the tragic displacement caused by war in the Great Lakes Region. Kamanga discusses legal norms concerning "crimes against peace" and norms outlawing the use of force for purposes other than self-defense. He also considers the Geneva Conventions' ban on forcible deportations and their standards of civilian protection. Both deliberate forcible transfers and the killing of defenseless civilians are serious crimes as well as being morally reprehensible. These are human rights issues that can help shape a framework of advocacy for the prevention of the kind of conflicts that are causing most displacement in Africa today. Kamanga notes that the implementation of these norms will depend on embedding these standards more deeply in public political will, national laws, and international institutions. Advocacy for such changes in opinion, law, and institutions will be important to reducing the causes of displacement in regions like the Great Lakes and elsewhere.

My own chapter 10 addresses what the 2005 UN World Summit called the "responsibility to protect"—the duty to safeguard populations from genocide, war crimes, ethnic cleansing, and crimes against humanity.[8] This responsibility is first the duty of each national government to protect its own citizens. Thus, national governments have the responsibility not to create humanitarian crises by committing grave evils such as genocide, ethnic cleansing, religious persecution, or any other form of attack that will compel people to flee from their homes. These duties raise serious questions about the behavior of the governments of a number of African countries like Rwanda, Liberia, and Sierra Leone in the 1990s and Sudan today. They also challenge the actions of nonstate actors like the LRA in northern Uganda. If national governments fail to protect their citizens from these abuses, the larger international community has a duty to come to their aid, even if this means intervening across national boundaries. Such interventions should initially take the form of efforts to sustain or build peace in ways that prevent displacement or other forms of humanitarian crisis. These preventative measures could be diplomatic or economic, depending on the need. In the face of grave abuses such as genocide, exercising this responsibility could take the form of military intervention by proportionate means as a last resort. The responsibility to protect can also call for efforts to rebuild a divided society in the aftermath of conflict. Such efforts are best carried out multilaterally, whether through the African Union, through regional agencies such as the Economic Community of West African States (ECOWAS), or on a global level through the United Nations.

In chapters 11 and 12, Lam Oryem Cosmas and Stephen Pope directly address the issue of how to pursue reconciliation and reconstruction in societies like Uganda that have been deeply divided by war, displacement, and grave human rights abuses. Reconciliation in the aftermath of a severe humanitarian crisis is probably the most problematic and elusive political objective that a society can pursue. If the cycle of conflict is to be broken, however, some effective steps toward healing social divisions are essential. Cosmas argues that reliance on the traditional justice systems of the people involved in the northern Uganda conflict can help them move toward reconciliation. Hybrids that blend traditional approaches with forms of international law familiar in the West may also make contributions to the needed reconciliation. In either case, there must be an acknowledgment of responsibility by those who have committed grave crimes and genuine assurance to the victims that the abuses will cease. Without such assurance of safety, the blurring of the distinction between self-defense and revenge can be expected to lead to continuing conflict.

Stephen Pope explores ways that reconciliation and rebuilding can facilitate the return of refugees and IDPs to their homes in the aftermath of conflict. He considers both the option of holding the perpetrators of grave abuses accountable for what they have done following standards of strict justice and the alternative option of seeking peace through amnesty or forgiveness. Pope draws on the experience of efforts to attain reconciliation in South Africa, Argentina, Chile, and El Salvador. In particular, he explores the current debate about whether a peace based on amnesty for LRA leaders should be the first step toward healing the wounds in northern Uganda, or whether justice through prosecution of LRA leaders in the International Criminal Court should come first. In effect Pope argues that neither justice without forgiveness nor forgiveness without justice can bring a lasting peace, and that truth about what has happened is an essential element of both justice and peace. Thus truth, justice, and steps toward forgiveness are all needed both to heal the conflicts that have driven so many people from home and to prevent repeat conflicts.

Thus, the conference discussions suggested the following conclusions on advocacy regarding conflict as a cause of displacement:

- Prevention of conflict is a key to avoiding much of the displacement that mars the face of Africa. Working to strengthen the commitment of public opinion, legal standards, and multilateral institutions to the prevention of conflict and its causes should be a principal focus of advocacy on behalf of refugees.
- Strengthening the recognition that national borders do not set limits to the scope of moral and legal responsibilities to protect the rights of human beings should be central to the work of refugee advocates.
- Healing the divisions of war-torn societies calls for a process that builds on truth, that requires the cessation of injustice, and that works toward reconciliation through a form of forgiveness.

Addressing the causes of refugee displacement and working to break the cycles of conflict that continue to drive people from home is of course a long-term goal. Some might even say it is utopian. Even incremental movement toward this goal, however, can itself save the lives of huge numbers of people and enable many to avoid the fate of long-term refugee status. Such incremental steps should be central to the work of refugee advocates.

In chapter 13, Agbonkhianmeghe Orobator addresses concrete human rights and ethical issues that arise for the humanitarian organizations, both religious and secular, that are so deeply involved in efforts to lift some of the burdens carried by refugees and internally displaced people. He explores the tension between the political neutrality that such agencies value and how they can come to be seen as political actors when they speak out on the injustices and human rights violations that displace people. He addresses the question of whether and how humanitarian agencies should relate to military forces that both oppress and seek to defend the displaced. He explores ways that refugee-serving agencies can be either empowered or compromised by the sources of their funding. And he considers the ethical standards that should govern the way NGO personnel relate to those they serve and the ethical norms for the kind of service they provide. This final chapter shows that the choices facing those who seek to serve refugees can be difficult and many-sided. But it also shows that there is a way forward if the well-being, dignity, and human rights of the displaced are kept in clear focus. The same is true for those who seek to be advocates on behalf of the displaced. Thus, this final chapter serves as a kind of conclusion for the volume as whole. It calls for practical wisdom, the moral virtue that aids in discerning how human rights norms should be pursued in practice. This wise discernment, as well as the moral virtue of courage, are equally needed in efforts to advocate refugee rights.

Notes

1. United States Committee for Refugees and Immigrants, World Refugee Survey 2006, Key Statistics, Table 1, http://www.refugees.org/data/wrs/06/docs/key_statistics.pdf (accessed May 22, 2007).

2. Internal Displacement Monitoring Centre and Norwegian Refugee Council, *Internal Dis-*

placement: Global Overview of Trends and Developments in 2006 (Geneva, 2007), 6, available from the website of the Internal Displacement Monitoring Centre, http://www.internal-displacement .org (accessed May 22, 2007). See the link under Resources, for IDMC Publications, Global Overview.

3. See the *Guiding Principles on Internal Displacement*, available from the website of the United Nations High Commissioner for Human Rights, http://www.unhchr.ch/html/menu2/7/b/ principles.htm (accessed May 22, 2007).

4. See Peter Hans Kolvenbach, S.J., "Accompany, Serve, Advocate Their Cause," address to JRS regional directors, June 23, 1997, in Jesuit Refugee Service, *Everybody's Challenge: Essential Documents of Jesuit Refugee Service 1980–2000* (Rome: Jesuit Refugee Service, 2000), 77–79.

5. For a description of the CRS "justice lens" approach, see Robin Gulick, "Justice," available from the CRS website, http://www.crs.org/our_work/what_we_do/CRS_themes/justice/index .cfm#background (accessed May 23, 2007).

6. See the description of the *Médecins Sans Frontières* mission of "Speaking Out to End Suffering," available from the MSF website under "About Us," http://www.doctorswithoutborders .org/aboutus (accessed May 23, 2007).

7. See U.S. Committee for Refugees and Immigrants, "Statement Calling for Solutions to End the Warehousing of Refugees," February 2007, which affirms that the basic human rights of refugees include "the rights to earn a livelihood — to engage in wage-employment, self-employment, the practice of professions, and the ownership of property — freedom of movement and residence, and the issuance of travel documents," http://www.refugees.org/uploadedFiles/Investigate/Anti _Warehousing/statement.pdf (accessed May 23, 2007).

8. United Nations General Assembly, *2005 World Summit Outcome Document*, September 16, 2005, no. 138, http://daccessdds.un.org/doc/UNDOC/GEN/N05/487/60/PDF/N0548760 .pdf?OpenElement (accessed May 23, 2007).

I

Displacement as a Human Rights Challenge

1

There Is More Than One Way of Dying

An Ethiopian Perspective on the Effects of Long-Term Stays in Refugee Camps

Abebe Feyissa, with Rebecca Horn

This chapter discusses the impact—moral, emotional, psychological, and behavioral—of long-term stays in refugee camps. It also attempts to identify those factors that lead refugees to stay for years at a time in camps and suggests some solutions, such as protecting their freedom of movement and enabling their speedier integration into host country economies.

We focus on refugees in the Kakuma refugee camp in northern Kenya. The camp was originally established for twelve thousand Sudanese minors who arrived in 1992, but since that time they have been joined by refugees of other nationalities as well as thousands more Sudanese. The camp now includes refugees from Somalia, Ethiopia, Democratic Republic of Congo, Burundi, Rwanda, and Uganda. Some have been resettled to third countries, such as the United States, Australia, and Canada, but many have been living in Kakuma for more than ten years. Those who came as children have been educated and have grown to adulthood in Kakuma; many children have been born in the camp and have never seen Sudan.

The opportunities for refugees in Kakuma to improve their lives are limited. Kenyan government policy dictates that refugees are not allowed to move freely, but must stay in one of two camps, Kakuma or Dadaab. In Kakuma, refugees are not allowed to keep animals, since this is likely to increase conflict between the refugees and the local Turkana people. The semi-arid environment is not conducive to growing crops. It is possible for refugees to start small businesses if the capital is available (either through a loan from a nongovernmental organization [NGO] or money sent by a family abroad). However, the market is finite because Kakuma is in a very isolated area and the majority of customers are other refugees, a small number of NGO staff, and local Kenyans. All NGOs in the camp "employ" refugees, but due to Kenyan laws prohibiting employment of refugees, they are engaged on a voluntary basis and then paid an "incentive," which is far lower than a wage would be for a Kenyan in an equivalent job.

The Ethiopian community in Kakuma camp will be used as an exemplar in this chapter. This is primarily because the author is himself an Ethiopian refugee who has stayed in Kakuma for twelve years and has lived in refugee camps in Kenya for the last fifteen years. As such, he is well acquainted with the effects that such long stays in camps have had on himself and his fellow Ethiopian refugees. In addition, he has been working as a counsellor for the Jesuit Refugee Service in Kakuma since 1994, and in this capacity has come into contact with refugees from all nationalities in the camp who are experiencing emotional distress. He is well-placed, therefore, to comment on the ways in which people are affected psychologically and emotionally by their lives as refugees in Kakuma, and on the ways in which people respond to their situation.

History of Ethiopian Refugees in Kenya

According to figures from the United Nations High Commissioner for Refugees (UNHCR), there are currently just under five thousand Ethiopian refugees living in Kakuma. The camp is organized into "communities," each of which has its own leaders and administration. Most of the Ethiopian refugees live in one community, which consists of several different Ethiopian ethnic groups. Many in the community are part of the group that fled to Kenya in 1991, while others left their country more recently; even now there are Ethiopians arriving in Kakuma claiming refugee status. The Ethiopian community in the camp includes people with good educational backgrounds, people with skills and professional qualifications. Some of these people are working for NGOs in Kakuma as "incentive workers," and others have established businesses such as shops and restaurants.

Ethiopians first sought refuge in Kenya in 1984. However, a significant group arrived in the country in 1991 following the overthrow of the Mengistu government. The new rulers implemented ethnic-based policies that favored one ethnic group over another and which brought about conflict between different groups in Ethiopia. The government itself also began oppressing those ethnic groups that were not working alongside the government. Opposition groups were not allowed to participate freely in politics. As a result of this situation, a large group of Ethiopians fled into Kenya in 1991.

Since 1991 the Ethiopian government has continued to implement ethnic-based policies, resulting in almost all administrative posts being held by people from the rulers' own ethnic group, all business activities being run by people from that group, and contracts being awarded to businesses established by members of the government. Those from other ethnic groups had difficulty in running effective businesses because it was difficult for them to get loans, impossible for them to obtain lucrative contracts, and not possible for them to compete with the government-supported businesses. Those who opposed the government were imprisoned without charge, and many disappeared. Even family members of opposition activists were arrested.

Due to international pressure, the first multiparty elections were held in Ethiopia in May 2005. Over two hundred international observers arrived to ensure that the elections were free and fair. The opposition party was voted into power, but the government claimed that the election had not been conducted properly and demanded that it be repeated. By the time this took place, the observers had left the country, and following the second vote, the government announced that it had been reelected. There were subsequently extensive protests throughout the country, and the government responded with violence, resulting in mass bloodshed. Since that time the government has continued to repress any opposition to or criticism of its activities, resulting in tens of thousands of people being imprisoned without access to their families or human rights activists. This continues to date.

The group of Ethiopians who fled their country in 1991 were initially located in Walda refugee camp, a provisional camp in northern Kenya, just 100 kilometers from the southern border of Ethiopia. These refugees remember very clearly a visit to the camp from the then-Kenyan president, Daniel Arap Moi. "Kenya is your second home," he said in comforting and heartwarming words to those refugees who found themselves in a strange land. For those who had been students in higher education institutes in Ethiopia, and those with professional skills, the visit of the president and his reassuring speech gave them hope that they would one day join Kenyan universities and have an opportunity to work in Kenya. This hope enabled them to survive in the camp.

However, as time went by there was no sign that the promise made by the president was going to be fulfilled. Refugees began to feel doubtful about the future. Nobody was sure whether tomorrow was going to be better than today. The situation was made worse by the proximity of the Walda camp to the Ethiopian border. It was relatively easy for the armed forces of the new, ethnic-based government of Ethiopia to cross the border and attack, kidnap, and kill refugees in the camp. Due to this insecurity, the period from 1991 to 1992 was a time of great suffering, unrest, and confusion for Ethiopian refugees in the Walda camp.

The newly built compound of the UNHCR was found in the middle of the refugee camp and was strongly fortressed by sandbags and barbed wire. This was understandable, since the gunfire that occurred at least twice a month threatened the lives of everyone. Yet as the fence of the UNHCR compound was increasingly reinforced and fortressed, the refugees felt increasingly distanced from those who were there to help and protect them. In practice, the refugees found that no member of the aid agency staff was available to hear their problems.

Throughout those two years in the Walda refugee camp, each moonlit night was a night of agony, as refugees were disturbed by the sounds of heavy gunfire. The following morning found more than one person dead. No one knew the killers. To be in a situation where you do not know your neighbor's killer and you do not know when your turn might come is by itself a form of death. It was astonishing and frightening to find that no humanitarian or government worker was willing to discuss the situation with refugees. Refugees had no access to UNHCR staff, except those who occasionally visited the camp to carry out sanitation awareness sessions. What was going on? What was coming next? Was there anyone who could have answered those questions? Did it occur to anybody on the staff that there might be refugees in the camp who were asking these questions? Those two agonizing years seemed an eternity for those Ethiopian refugees.

Thankfully, the Kenyan government, after thoroughly evaluating the ever-worsening security condition in the camp, transferred about eight thousand Ethiopian refugees to Kakuma refugee camp in 1993. Those refugees left Walda hopeful that their future would be better. Maybe it is a good thing they did not know that many of them would still be in Kakuma thirteen years later.

In the first few months of 1993, Ethiopian refugees in Kakuma camp had little contact with UNHCR staff, except when they collected their food rations or visited a clinic to get drugs to treat typhoid, malaria, or scorpion bites. Agencies did not seem to realize that the refugees needed more than food and medical care. They still lacked information about UNHCR's plans for them and there was no forum for them to express these concerns. This uncertainty was tormenting for many. None of the refugees had any idea what would happen in his or her future, except that they would be given food every fortnight.

Impact of Long Stays in Refugee Camps

I can confidently say that in the last fifteen years of my refugee life, the Ethiopian refugees have never been given adequate information about their fate. UNHCR has not afforded opportunities for refugees to express their concerns and to get concrete information from the authorities regarding those concerns. When community leaders meet with UNHCR officials, they frequently return with incorrect, incomplete, or misleading information due to the language barrier; it can be difficult for Amharic-speaking leaders to express themselves clearly in English or to understand the sometimes complex responses they receive.

What is amazing is the way a mind starved of information creates information of its own and then feeds on it. This was very evident in the Ethiopian community in Kakuma, especially during the years from 1995 to 1998, a time when various stories would pop up from nowhere every two or three months and would quickly reach everybody in the camp. The "news" would be related to the current concerns of refugees. For example, "The United States of America has requested to resettle all Ethiopian refugees and registration will soon start; Australia and Canada are arguing that those hard-working Ethiopian refugees are not to be resettled only by the United States; we must also have a share." This type of rumor spread like wildfire through the camp. Sometimes it would reach other communities, which would become concerned that only Ethiopians were being considered for resettlement. I still remember a time when UNHCR heard about a rumor spreading in the camp that the Kenyan government was planning to relocate the Kakuma refugee camp to Kitale. Kitale is a busy Kenyan town, many kilometers south of Kakuma and surrounded by very fertile land. This news was much discussed in the Ethiopian community. Mockingly, UNHCR officers came to the Ethiopian community administration to enquire about the exact date of departure.

When a refugee shares the news with a fellow refugee, he or she always talks of getting it from a dependable source. The one receiving the news does not bother to ask where the news really came from, or what the evidence might be for it. People starved of vital information about their future will devour anything they can obtain. The news then becomes a hot point of discussion and speculation for about a month, after which it disappears to nowhere, as it came from nowhere. And hopelessness and emptiness return, with fear and uncertainty filling the minds of those refugees who had such hope a few weeks earlier.

When am I going back home? Or being resettled? Or getting the freedom of movement that will allow me to work or pursue my education? Members of the Ethiopian community administration have been unable to discuss these matters with UNHCR, so the old unanswered questions still haunt the minds of Ethiopian refugees in Kakuma. This uncertainty, and a desire to take some control over one's situation after years of depending on agencies who do not seem to act, has led some refugees to take action themselves instead of waiting endlessly for "something to happen."

Refugee Daydreams

A number of Ethiopian refugees have started small businesses in the camp in anticipation of making and saving money. To refugees who left behind or lost all their property, refugees who lost their chance for higher education and job opportunities, refugees who have nothing to hope for, earning a lot of money can seem to be an alternative form of security for the future. However, not all who started businesses were successful, and many could not earn the amount of money of which they had dreamed.

There is a busy marketplace in the Ethiopian community in Kakuma, filled with small coffeehouses and restaurants, places showing the latest English Premier League football match and shops where almost anything can be bought. Visitors who occasionally come to the camp and see busy Ethiopian businesses or Ethiopians refugees enjoying coffee together while watching CNN news believe that Ethiopian refugees in Kakuma are contented and calm. But the truth is different. Ethiopian refugees have never been settled or content. Everyone's soul is traveling long distances looking for a change; only the body is in the camp. Everyone has gone for resettlement, everyone has completed their interrupted college studies, everyone has saved as much money as they want in the world of daydreams.

Ethiopian refugees in the camp live in a vicious cycle. In their daydreams they have everything they want, but when they wake up from these dreams, they find themselves with nothing. In the deep bitterness and disappointment that results, camp life becomes more painful than ever. To escape, the refugees sink deeper and deeper into their dreams, and the cycle continues. Life detached from reality breeds more and more emotional problems. Very many Ethiopian refugees show signs of emotional and psychological disturbance, including restlessness, irritability, and loss of concentration.

The cause of these problems is an inability or unwillingness to accept what one cannot change. If one is unwilling to accept the existing reality, one must either do something to change that reality or face some kind of emotional problem. A high number of refugees have not been able to change their reality, yet they are not willing or able to accept it, with the result that many refugees in the Ethiopian community are experiencing emotional and psychological problems.

Interpersonal Problems

The concentration of the refugees in one community results in interpersonal problems as well as individual ones. The ethnic division and conflict from which these people have fled now becomes an issue that brings conflict and unrest within the Ethiopian community. Tolerance of different political opinions among neighbors becomes very difficult. Often refugees fight each other for no reason at all. False allegations, backbiting, and even physical fighting are common. Maybe these conflicts give the mind something concrete on which to focus.

In contrast to other communities in the camp, ethnic conflicts in the Ethiopian community generally blow over without becoming too serious. Individual and domestic problems, in contrast, do not seem to settle so quickly. A husband who is embittered by his long refugee life releases his anger on his wife: "Why are you quiet?" "Why are you late?" "Who was that man you were with?" "Why is lunch late?" These are reasons enough to fight, use violence, and even obtain a divorce. A wife whose husband has no task other than to assist her in cooking and fetching water may feel she has good reason to despise and undermine him. He does not have a big shop or a resettlement process like others. She may desert him for another man. Children are punished for no reason other than playing with friends or watching TV programs. In the last fifteen years, 90 percent of allegations brought to the Ethiopian bench court stemmed from domestic problems.

I have also observed that their long refugee life has made many refugees chronically absentminded. Initially, this problem was a source of amusement. We commonly talked among ourselves about what we had forgotten today, such as going somewhere by bicycle and returning without it, looking for a flashlight with that very flashlight, locking doors while people are inside, and many other incidents that are surely laughable. However, it is of some concern to hear that some refugees do not remember which day it is, which month, or even which year it is. Some seem more affected by absentmindedness than they realize, talking to themselves and gesturing emotionally. Others are sleepwalkers. Many refugees absentmindedly leave their home at night and disappear. When persons disappear, it is customary to report the disappearances to the police and conduct searches for a day or two in the surrounding bush and cliffs. Then these persons are forgotten, without any confirmation of whether they are dead or alive.

There are distinct similarities among those refugees who are affected by absentmindedness: anxiety and the inability to make decisions. All of them are unwilling to spend one more day in the camp, yet they do nothing about it. And all of them are male.

Fleeing the Camp

As stated earlier, there are some refugees who, finding camp life and the ongoing uncertainty and dependency intolerable, decide to take action to change their situation. One way for many refugees to escape the long, agonizing camp life is to return back home on their own. That is difficult, however. For one thing, UNHCR has no formal repatriation process for Ethiopian refugees in Kakuma. For another, returning home would mean facing a life-threatening situation for many Ethiopians. Also, many believe that the Ethiopian government is not willing to receive returning refugees. Despite all of this, it is agonizing to spend years in a situation of complete uncertainty about everything, so if returning home means death at the hands of the refugees' persecutors, many say "it is better to die in your country than anywhere else."

Sebsibe Nigusie was a refugee who, like many others, was tired of camp life.[1] No matter what, he always talked of returning back home. He often fell sick of malaria, and during his illness he was disturbed by frightening nightmares every night. One night he disappeared from his home. After a two-day search he was found by local people about 40 kilometers from the camp and was said to be unaware of where he was going, or even in which direction. He was brought to the Kakuma police station, and after returning to the camp, Sebsibe seemed to be much improved. However, after a while he again began to behave strangely. He also heard strange voices. At that time there was no special clinic or professional to treat such mental illness. One morning, a friend of mine told me that Sebsibe had disappeared once more. Although I was shocked, it was not unexpected; many refugees had done the same before him. This time, in collaboration with locals, a wide and long search was conducted for days. After a few more mourning days he was forgotten. If he could reach home, well and good; if he died, may God rest his soul in peace, many said. Shockingly, after two weeks his remains were found by locals. It was confirmed that he was eaten by a wild animal. Whatever happened, now he rested, many said. Without believing it.

Ethiopian refugees seem to have a collective personality. The news of the death of a refugee is like a blow for all. Everyone is terrified. When returning from the burial place, everyone seems to have buried something of themselves. Everyone's head is down more than normally; everyone's face is a signboard of unspeakable sorrow. Everyone is crying, each weeping for himself or herself. Who is next? Afraid of the answer, everyone trembles. Maybe it is not the fear of death itself, but death as a refugee far from home.

An alternative for those refugees who are afraid of returning back home is fleeing to South Africa, because they believe that there they will have freedom of movement and job opportunities. However, many are unaware that this long journey across countries is far more dangerous and risky than the long camp life in Kakuma. Many refugees say that "monotonous camp life is more deadly than the risk of the long journey to South Africa." However, I know one thing; very many Ethiopian refugees are caught by the border police and deported back to Kenya after paying the money they painstakingly collected (up to four thousand dollars) to guides and to those who prepare false travel documents. Many who have tried to escape and failed more than once are now defeated beggars in Nairobi. Some might still suffer in the prisons found everywhere along the refugee road to South Africa.

Even though I cannot produce tangible evidence, there is a well-known story of a male refugee who was raped by soldiers on his way to South Africa. He was said to have somehow managed to reach South Africa but has become a crazy man who roams around.

Breaking Up Marriages to Escape

Many, many more Ethiopian refugees wounded by the refugee life are still on the run. Those refugees who dared not leave the Kakuma refugee camp seem to have other ways of dealing with the problem. Yet some of these ways are not actions of which one can be proud.

Yayeh Mamo was my neighbor. In the camp he sold tea and coffee with his wife. He was a fourth-year agriculture student at Alemay University back in Ethiopia. He had always dreamed of going abroad, completing his studies, and becoming a renowned scientist. His life in Kakuma was for him like life in the Dead Sea, where one cannot find a trace of life, where no natural phenomena exist, where one cannot swim out of it. Yayeh Mamo never stopped dreaming about his lifelong wish—to be an Ethiopian agronomist. His wife, Sara, was often sick, so it was mainly left to him to sell tea and coffee to buy her the extra food she needed. They loved each other. In 1997 Sara gave birth to a beautiful baby girl. Yayeh always told people how his dull refugee life changed completely after he got his baby girl. As she grew older, father and daughter became close friends with strong emotional ties. Apart from realizing his dream of obtaining higher education and being a scientist, Yayeh now had another concern: the future of his beloved daughter. One day his wife came home with "good news." A neighbor had volunteered to include Sara's name in his resettlement form as his wife, and Sara and Yayeh's daughter as his own daughter. This was great news, not only in Yayeh's household but to all their well-wishers. Yayeh told me that he did not care what happened to him in the camp, so long as his wife and child were safe somewhere. They might one day reunite. After one year, Yayeh's wife went abroad as the wife of another man, his daughter as the daughter of that man.

Some Ethiopian refugees wonder whether this type of solution to the problem of a long refugee life is immoral and humiliating. Husband and wife should be together through thick and thin, till death do them part. How can lovers do this to each other? What does marriage mean? What does it mean to their daughter? What does fatherhood mean? As many refugees pose such questions, many others say that in spite of its immorality, the action taken by Yayeh is of good intent. He was trying to save his wife and daughter from the hellish refugee life in Kakuma. It was the Devil's alternative. Sometimes, one type of death is better than the other.

As time went by, however, Yayeh found life without his wife and daughter more difficult than he had imagined. His loneliness was unbearable, and nothing could take the place of their voices. He was unhappy and depressed. The occasional letter he received from his wife was never enough to quench his longing for them. One day his wife wrote him a letter that made Yayeh deeply regret what he had done. The health of his daughter was deteriorating as she cried constantly for her beloved father. She was not sleeping well, not eating well. That was more than enough for Yayeh. Every day he was crying like his daughter. Ever since, all letters and phone calls have been about the deterioration of the health of his daughter. She even became a client of a child psychologist. Anxiety-stricken, Yayeh suddenly left Kakuma for Nairobi, where he could make cheaper international phone calls to at least hear the voice of his daughter. He never returned to Kakuma.

Still there are refugees who give away their wives to other men for the same reason. Some couples do not even care whether or not the man taking the wife is infected with HIV. They will do anything to escape from this Kakuma refugee life.

Fabricating Crises

Refugees in Kakuma know very well that anyone with a security problem in the camp can appeal for protection. It is also known that resettlement is more likely to be offered to those with security problems in the camp. Those without severe and obvious security problems in the camp feel they have no opportunity to make their case and explain their situation to UNHCR, and therefore they come to believe that the only way they will be heard is if they "create" an emergency situation. For example, a Somali woman marries an Ethiopian man. Soon problems occur. The family of the woman commonly attacks the man. Then an appeal is prepared to the UNHCR Protection Office by the man: "My wife is a Somali woman and now her family members and other Somalis are threatening to kill me." This staged drama sometimes creates conflict at a community level. An agreement is reached by the couple for their interethnic marriage to be dissolved once they are safely out of Kakuma refugee camp. Meanwhile, the children produced often suffer identity crises and communication problems, since they are split between two languages. Worst of all, they often are unloved by both parents. They are unwanted guests. They are the product of their parents' struggle to escape the never-ending camp life.

Such strategies do not work for long. Sometimes the problems fabricated by these marriage mates become unconvincing to the UNHCR Protection Office. And yet, this has never stopped refugees who are determined to end their long camp life. One couple agreed to go to the extreme. Mohamed Ali is an Ethiopian refugee. The owner of a small shop, he was about thirty-five years old at the time of the following incident. His wife was from the Somali community. He had many times appealed to the Protection Office that his life was in danger, but his claims did not convince the office. In the end, the couple devised a new idea. One night there was a shout of distress and a call for help. When neighbors arrived at the house of Mohamed Ali, his wife was rolling on the ground, burning all over with kerosene. Strangely enough, her husband was taking snapshots of his burning wife as evidence of conflicts that will lead to resettlement. How authentic will his "evidence" be? Why did it not occur to him that no one expects a husband to take photographs of his burning wife rather than trying to save her? The camera that was readily to hand at that particular time could also jeopardize the genuineness of the "case," but Mohamed never thought of this.

It is not surprising that Mohamed was unaware of the stumbling blocks in the way of his case being "acceptable." Refugees who spend years and years stagnating in a camp seem unable to think sensibly, or even sanely. They are impulsive, like an animal cornered by its predator. Refugees burn their houses on their own and accuse their neighbor of doing it; they wound their body with a knife and blame others for doing it because of ethnic differences. Women report being raped by their own neighbors to get protection, then resettlement, then freedom from the camp. This behavior leads to conflict, violent quarrels, and mutual mistrust among community members.

A simple solution to such problems would be for UNHCR to give any refugee the opportunity to explain their situation in the camp to a member of UNHCR staff and to ensure that refugees feel listened to and understood, instead of attending to a refugee's concerns only when a serious incident has already occurred. If refugees feel that they have been heard, then they are less likely to resort to creating situations that could cause serious harm to themselves and others just in order to be noticed.

The Frustration of Camp Teachers

In the Ethiopian refugee community, there are a good number of former students from institutes of higher education. Many of them fled Ethiopia in 1991 and later. Since 1993 almost all of them have been working as teachers in elementary and high schools in the camp, earning an "incentive" that is less than fifty dollars a month. Some of them are my friends. For the last twelve years they have taught hundreds of children from kindergarten up to high school. Some of those children, having grown up, are now in colleges and universities. Some of them are now inspectors and head teachers.

Sometimes I ask those teachers how they feel when they see their own students rising from kindergarten or first grade up to being the head teacher of the school in which they teach. They say they have mixed feelings. They are proud of their students' achievements, obviously. But they are also sad, very, very sad. "For the last fifteen years," one of the teachers said to me, "I was like a ladder standing against the wall. All of those students of mine climb on me and reach where they want to, as I continue standing forever more leaning against the wall."

Most of those teachers were college students when they fled from home in 1991. In this long camp life they seem to have lost everything they learned at college. There is no relevant work or activity in the camp that can stimulate their minds. For fifteen years they have been collecting their food rations and teaching in elementary school. The only thing to remind them of college is their report card, dated 1990. Their hair is graying. None of them believe they will have the chance even of completing their undergraduate degree in the future. They say time is against them. The prime time for study has been lost forever in the Kakuma refugee camp.

In 1991–92, when about eight hundred college students were living in Walda refugee camp, they founded a library with only six Amharic books of fiction collected from friends. At that time, about twenty people used to read for a few hours each day in a tent. In 1993, when all refugees were transferred to Kakuma, the library was also transferred. By then it had about one hundred books and a few magazines. In 2006 the library boasts of having more than fifteen thousand books (textbooks, reference works, and novels) and many, many magazines. It is the only library in the camp.

Interestingly, the volunteer librarian in the Walda refugee camp during 1992 is still the chief librarian in the same library, now earning incentive pay. He was a second-year student of library science at Addis Ababa University. He has been behind the emergence, expansion, and growth of the library, but he still feels unfulfilled. He sometimes looks at his student report card, from when he fled his homeland at the age of twenty. Today he is a graying man of thirty-five. He will soon retire before ever finishing his long-sought college studies.

In spite of the many emotional and physical problems that their long refugee life has brought, refugees have tried every way to free themselves from the bondage of the long camp life. Others, however, choose to give up, and they remain passive regardless of what happens to them. They do not care about either going back home or resettling. Neither happy nor sad, they have numbed their bodies and their minds, and their lives are a living death. Generally speaking, they have locked themselves up so as never to get hurt again.

Some refugees have gone further than that in taking action to deal with camp life, choosing what they might have thought was a "once and for all" solution. In the last fifteen years of camp life, at least seven refugees have committed suicide in the Ethiopian refugee community alone: six men and one mother of two children. Two of them died refusing to eat, while others hanged themselves.

I certainly believe that the terrible life of refugees can reduce one to act in a way that is degrading to oneself. One can be selfish and irresponsible toward oneself and other community members if one believes that he or she has been left to die in the camp. People who have lost the best years of their life in a refugee camp do not care for anything and do not think properly when making decisions. My observations of Ethiopian refugees after fifteen years of camp life have confirmed that beyond a doubt.

Causes of the Refugees' Problems

The psychological, emotional, social, and behavioral problems affecting Ethiopian refugees who have stayed for a long time in Kenyan camps have been outlined above. The following are relevant when considering the causes of these problems.

No Secure Protection Available

When Kakuma refugee camp was initially established in 1992, the first residents were Sudanese, numbering in the tens of thousands. In 1993 thousands of Ethiopian refugees joined the Sudanese in Kakuma. After that, Somalis, Congolese, Rwandese, Burundi, and Ugandans were added to the population of the camp. Now its official population is over ninety-three thousand.

At that time, there was no clear registration of refugees or determination of refugee status, at least in many cases. Most of those entering Kakuma in the early 1990s had been part of a great influx crossing the border into Kenya, and it may have been difficult to monitor their numbers and identities. However, no interview or determination of refugee status was ever done subsequently. Ever since, these Ethiopian refugees have only had their ration cards to indicate their refugee status.

Today, the number of Ethiopian refugees in Kakuma has been reduced to forty-seven hundred. That is because Ethiopian people living near the border of Kenya and displaced by the ethnic conflict have now returned home. The remaining Ethiopian refugees have no contact with UNHCR, except for collecting rations and showing up for an occasional headcount. They have no idea what refugee status is and how important it is. They do not know what an asylum seeker is or what a mandated refugee is. There is nobody to tell them.

Almost ten years after their arrival in Kakuma, some Ethiopian refugees who thought that knowing about these things was not only the right of refugees but a necessity for them, went to the UNHCR Protection Office. The response was, "Ethiopian refugees are economic refugees who in 1991 crossed the border in an influx." There is no Ethiopian refugee in Kakuma who would agree with that.

In fact, Ethiopian refugees had "prima facie" refugee status until August 2003. The term "prima facie" means that persons are deemed to be refugees without having to be interviewed or have their claim to refugee status assessed on an individual basis. It is normally granted to people fleeing war zones in large numbers, where it is generally accepted that they are refugees; they do not have to prove it through interview and assessment. This was the case for Ethiopians arriving in Kakuma until August 2003, after which time they were required to undergo an eligibility assessment.

There is a belief among the Ethiopian refugees in Kakuma that countries such as the United States, Australia, and Canada that are willing to resettle refugees within their borders tend not to be interested in prima facie refugees. Ethiopian refugees in Kakuma are unable to return home because of the continuing oppression of their government; have no hope of being resettled to a third country because, they believe, the UNHCR Resettlement Office is not interested in facilitating the resettlement of Ethiopian refugees; cannot move outside the refugee camp where they have been for twelve years, due to Kenyan refugee policies; and may have to continue their agonizing camp life for another fifteen years. The hopelessness and despair created by this situation exacerbates the psychological, emotional, and social problems already inherent in living as a refugee in a camp for so long.

Corruption of Officials

Around the year 2000, a problem suddenly erupted around the Nairobi UNHCR office. Some of the UNHCR staff were arrested for selling resettlement files that belonged to recognized refugees living in the camp. The picture on the file was torn off and replaced with the picture of someone who could pay four thousand or five thousand dollars. This crime was exposed by UN and Kenyan government officials, and the culprits were punished accordingly. However, refugees doubt that the problem has been completely eradicated. This incident caused refugees to lose confidence in UNHCR. It increased their sense of hopelessness and led to their belief that their problems could only be solved by refugees taking their destiny into their own hands; they do not feel able to rely on the agencies who are supposed to assist them. This means they continue to repeat the mistakes of those who earlier have attempted to free themselves from camp life on their own.

Inadequate Communication with and Access to Camp Staff

Many of the issues raised in this chapter relate to the lack of sufficient communication between UNHCR and the refugee communities in Kakuma. It is extremely difficult for any individual refugee to obtain access to a member of UNHCR staff to discuss her or his concerns; the UNHCR compound is closed to refugees, except those who have an official appointment letter. However, it is hard to obtain such a letter when you cannot access the people in a position to issue one. In an attempt to resolve this problem, UNHCR set up three field posts around the camp. The aim was to have staff from the different UNHCR departments and from other agencies present at the field posts on different days so that any refugee could go to the field post and discuss his or her concerns with a member of the staff present. This system would allow refugees from anywhere in the camp to access UNHCR staff. However, in practice, the field posts are frequently not staffed, and when staff are present, the number of refugees waiting to see them is far more than they could ever hope to serve. As a result, it is not uncommon for refugees to wait the whole day to see somebody who does not arrive at the field post or who has too many people to see, so that at the end of the day refugees have to return home unsatisfied and frustrated and still feeling that they are unnoticed and unheard.

The solution to this problem is simple. The idea of the field posts is a good one, and if the system were implemented as originally intended, all refugees would feel they had the opportunity to access staff from UNHCR whenever they needed to.

Failures in International Politics

The international community's opinion of some African countries, such as those from which Kakuma refugees fled, should also be considered when thinking of the problems and possible solutions for refugees who have stayed long in the camps. Let me take the Ethiopian government as an example.

This government was considered an exemplary democratic one that could be a model for many other African countries, and as such it was supported by Western powers. This meant that refugees fleeing from Ethiopia, and members of any opposition groups in Ethiopia, were not highly regarded by Western countries. Also, Ethiopia was seen as an ally of donor countries in the "war against terrorism."

Sadly enough, it took those Western countries fifteen years to understand that the Ethiopian government is not democratic. It took them fifteen years to see that the Ethiopian government was harassing, killing, and persecuting journalists, opposition leaders, and all others who entertained dissenting political opinions.

In the already-mentioned violence that followed the national election of May 2005, eighty-five innocent people were killed in less than half a day. Tens of thousands of opposition supporters have since been imprisoned all around the country. As a result of these oppressive actions, the international community, humanitarian organizations, and church groups are now actively advocating for the right to freedom of thought in Ethiopia and are denouncing and condemning the Ethiopian government. Some European countries have gone even further and stopped their financial aid to the government. However, the United States in particular, while acknowledging the inhumane and undemocratic rule of the Ethiopian government, is still supporting it. The reason is that a country like Ethiopia, which is a strong military power in East Africa, is considered to be a valuable partner in the war against terrorism.

Ethiopian refugees will be unable to go home until the Ethiopian government revises its policies to ensure that all ethnic groups have equal rights to participate in the decision-making process of their country; equal rights to participate in political activities; equal access to employment; and an equal chance to compete in the economy. There must be legal support for a multiparty system of politics to ensure that people are free to elect whomever they feel will truly represent them.

The most appropriate and least expensive way of helping Ethiopian refugees to find a durable solution to their fifteen-year-old problem would be for the Ethiopian government to establish democratic rule and freedom. There is little chance of this occurring until the United States and others reevaluate their foreign policy and stop supporting governments that are forcing their own people into exile. The fate of Ethiopian refugees is in the hands of the international community, and hope for Ethiopian refugees to return home will come only when the United States joins it in pressuring the government of Ethiopia to change its ethnic-based rule. The United States proclaims itself to be an advocate of democracy and human rights, but its relationship with the government of Ethiopia contradicts that assertion. Ethiopians expect the United States to live up to its claims.

Host Country Restrictions on Rights

The Kenyan government, in contrast to those of some other East African countries, is not one that forcibly deports refugees. All refugees living in Kenya are grateful to its government for respecting refugee rights, at least to a degree.

However, as has been made clear by the issues raised in this chapter, keeping refugees in camps for a prolonged period of time has severe negative consequences for their emotional, physical, and social well-being. The policy of encampment is dehumanizing and, as stated in other chapters in this volume, denial of the right to freedom of movement makes it impossible for other rights to be realized. The government of Kenya, which has shown such willingness to assist refugees, could usefully reconsider its response to those who have sought refuge in their country for the last fifteen years. All refugees fully understand the security concerns of the Kenyan government that cause its hesitation in passing a bill that allows refugees to obtain work permits, to move freely around the country, and above all to integrate into Kenyan society. However, refugees who have already lived in Kenya for fifteen years are not to be feared as such. Refugees who have been trained and educated during these years in the Walda and Kakuma camps can be an asset to Kenyan society. Slow integration of the refugees into Kenyan society would benefit both the refugees and Kenyans. It is clear that Kenyans are not in a position to provide employment for refugees, since so many nationals are without jobs. However, if given work permits, many Ethiopian refugees would be able to create their own jobs, by either setting up businesses or providing services (taxis and barber shops, for example). Some of the few Ethiopians who have been given permission to stay in Nairobi have already done this.

Clearly, this would not be a solution for all the refugees in Kakuma. The government of Kenya has previously suggested the possibility of granting refugees access to land for cultivation in the more fertile parts of the country. Refugees would not own the land, but would cultivate it to provide for their families and pay rent to the owners. This could be a desirable option for some refugees in Kakuma. There will be others, however, who have special vulnerabilities and would find it difficult to manage without the support of the agencies currently based in Kakuma. The needs of these people may have to be met in the camp or in other designated areas where services can be provided effectively.

Conclusion

All Ethiopian refugees strongly believe that the international community, which in the name of its "war against terrorism" supports oppressive governments, should review its policies and encourage such regimes to implement democratic systems that would enable their exiled citizens to return home. Otherwise, refugees who are able to work, and who would be self-sufficient if they were able to live freely in their own country, will be kept in camps, dependent on aid agencies for unjustifiably extended times.

Note

1. The cases described in this paper are real but the names have been changed.

2

What We Owe to Refugees and IDPs

An Inquiry into the Rights of the Forcibly Displaced

William O'Neill

At the cusp of the millennium, all the world's a market—a complex, globalized network of economic, social, and cultural interdependence.[1] And yet the millennial promise of a global household (*oikoumenē*) remains elusive. From Kigali to Kosovo, the recurrence of intrastate ethnic strife and regional instability has riven our global village. The UN's *State of the World's Refugees* (2006) estimates that there is a total of 9,236,000 refugees and 838,000 asylum seekers,[2] that is, "people who have left their own country to escape from persecution, armed conflict or violence."[3] Already victims of ethnic cleansing and mass expulsion, the majority of the world's refugees subsist in protracted refugee situations,[4] where "basic rights and essential economic, social and psychological needs remain unfulfilled after years in exile."[5] Living in camps "without any prospect of a durable solution to their plight," such refugees are increasingly perceived "not as victims, but as perpetrators of insecurity."[6]

Similar fears of uncivil strife betray the weakness of customary international refugee law, as potential asylees are forcibly repatriated (*refoulement*), for example, in the Great Lakes Region of Africa.[7] Effective protection is likewise denied the vast majority of the world's 25 million internally displaced persons (IDPs), only 5,428,000 of whom fall under the official purview of the United Nations High Commissioner for Refugees (UNHCR).[8] In the Darfur region of Sudan, for instance, internecine conflict has uprooted at least two million persons, including the two hundred thousand Sudanese who fled into the deserts of eastern Chad, where international assistance was slow to arrive.[9] So, too, more than three million Congolese, Burundians, and Rwandans remain displaced in the Great Lakes Region.[10]

According to demographic data relating to about 7.5 million persons of concern to UNHCR, "children and adolescents under the age of 18 account for nearly half this number, with 13 per cent of these children under the age of five." (In Africa, where half of the refugee population "consists of females and half are children and adolescents,

27

roughly a quarter of the refugee population is composed of girls under 18.") Such children, the UNHCR report concludes, "are particularly vulnerable to threats to their safety and wellbeing," including "separation from families, sexual exploitation, HIV/AIDS infection, forced labour or slavery, abuse and violence, forcible recruitment into armed groups, trafficking, lack of access to education and basic assistance, detention and denial of access to asylum or family-reunification programs."[11]

Still, the litany of suffering continues beyond official figures. The Convention Relating to the Status of Refugees (1951) and the Protocol Relating to the Status of Refugees (1967) exclude victims of general insecurity or economic deprivation, such as the systemic denial of basic subsistence rights. Fleeing famine, poverty, or ecological catastrophe, "economic refugees" lack a legal title to asylum.[12] Neither do the criteria stipulated in the 1951 Refugee Convention reflect the gender-specific persecution that women and girl children endure,[13] such as rape, genital mutilation, domestic abuse, and forced marriages.[14]

Yet mere wretchedness, Camus reminds us, is not tragedy.[15] Whether we "see" the suffering of the forcibly displaced as *morally* tragic or merely as an unimportant failure of global politics, depends, in large part, upon the interpretative perspective invoked.[16] Thus, in "the classical Westphalian regime of sovereignty,"[17] citizenship (membership in a territorially bounded polity) determines the allocation of rights as an "entailed inheritance."[18] States "regard cross-border processes as a 'private matter' concerning only those immediately affected."[19] Membership, too, determines ethnic, racial, or religious loyalties in a nascent, post-Westphalian order marked by *intra*-state conflict.

The developing *corpus juris* of international human rights law, by contrast, underwrites a transnational, universalist moral and legal perspective—one in which legitimate sovereignty is, in principle, tempered by adherence to the rule of law and democratic self-determination.[20] And yet, writes Hannah Arendt, the regnant liberal rhetoric of human rights exhibits its own perplexities. For it is precisely the "abstract nakedness of being nothing but human" that divests the refugee or IDP of "the very qualities which make it possible for other people to treat him as a *fellow*-man."[21] In these pages, I will first (a) consider the scope and limits of the prevailing liberal rights regime in seeing (recognizing and redeeming) the claims of the forcibly displaced.[22] I shall then offer (b), a reconstructive, communitarian interpretation of rights as a narrative grammar, drawing upon the interpretative resources of recent work in African philosophy and theology. Finally, in section (c), I will assess the distinctive role of religious attitudes and beliefs in reconfiguring our interpretation of the claims of refugees and IPDs, so as to restore their "place" (rhetorical *locus-topos*) in the world.[23]

Rival Rhetorics

Woven of disparate statist-communitarian and liberal cosmopolitan strands, the practice of states, writes Seyla Benhabib, suffers from both "moral and juridical ambivalence."[24] The primary right recognized in international refugee law is that of *nonrefoulement*: refugees cannot be forcibly repatriated to a country where there is a reasonable expectation of persecution. The Universal Declaration of Human Rights acknowledges that refugees have the right "to seek and to enjoy asylum"; yet neither the 1951 Refugee Convention nor the 1967 Protocol imposes a correlative obligation upon states to grant it.[25] As Michael Dummett observes, the "Convention Relating to the Status of Stateless Persons forbade any contracting state to expel stateless people lawfully resident on its territory, and required it to 'facilitate' their naturalisation; but it laid no obligation on any state to admit stateless people expelled from the country in which they were living."[26] All too often, as in the African Great Lakes Region, refugee protection is "governed by the vagaries of charity rather than viewed as a matter of rights."[27]

Unraveling these strands in favor of human rights, however, is far from a panacea. As Arendt remarked in 1951, the very year the Convention Relating to the Status of Refugees was adopted, "from the beginning, the paradox involved in the declaration of inalienable human rights was that it reckoned with an 'abstract' human being who seemed to exist nowhere." Deprived "of their place in the world," refugees are rhetorically effaced;[28] for it is precisely their "abstract nakedness" that renders victims of forced displacement effectively "rightless."[29] So it was, says Arendt, that the "conception of human rights, based upon the assumed existence of a human being as such, broke down at the very moment when those who professed to believe in it were for the first time confronted with people who had indeed lost all other qualities and specific relationships— except that they were still human." For the "world found nothing sacred in the abstract nakedness of being human."[30]

Even with subsequent ratification of the major instruments of modern refugee law, Arendt's critique remains germane. For our "right to have rights," that is, the *universal* human rights articulated in international law, depends on the *concrete* conditions of their redemption (membership in a specific moral community).[31] Refugees, to be sure, are no longer nominally "rightless" in international law. Under the aegis of UNHCR, the 1951 Convention, and the 1967 Protocol, states formally recognize obligations with respect to refugees. Yet a refugee is "still not considered to be a subject of international law, capable of enforcing his or her rights on the international plane."[32] As the plight of refugees and IDPs in the Great Lakes Region or Sudan attests, enforcing claim-rights typically remains bound to membership in a particular national, ethnic, racial, or religious community. For victims of uncivil strife, the "loss of home and political status" is often still tantamount to "expulsion from humanity altogether."[33]

The gravamen of Arendt's critique, I believe, rests precisely in the formal abstraction of rights discourse. In other words, human rights are attributed to a "generalized other," lacking a "place" (rhetorical *locus-topos*) in the world.[34] Emancipated from "all tutelage" of traditional mores, our regnant liberal philosophy ascribes natural or human rights to sovereign selves.[35] Indeed, for liberalism as a philosophic doctrine, the very irreconcilability of our local and ethnocentric conceptions of the (common) good leads us to cherish the "liberties of the moderns" as our foremost rights.[36] "The only freedom which deserves the name," writes J. S. Mill in a justly memorable phrase, "is that of pursuing our own good in our own way."[37]

Our liberty, in turn, is parsed as our several immunities or negative rights, limited principally by negative duties of forbearance by others. For we must, says Mill, respect others' liberty, neither depriving them of their own good, nor impeding "their efforts to obtain it."[38] Under the banner of negative freedom, heirs of the liberal tradition invoke

their individual liberties, while relegating positive delimitations of liberty, such as refugees' claim of rights to adequate nutrition, potable water, or health care, to an inferior
sphere, if not dismissing them as mere rhetorical license. Our negative liberties, says
Robert Nozick, "fill up the space of rights."[39] And so it is, with the apotheosis of the
sovereign self, social bonds that once derived from the ethical ideal of the common
good (the medievals' *bonum commune*) must now be constructed through exercise of
individual will—whether through Locke's fiduciary contract or Hobbes's imperious Le-
viathan. "Positive" obligations extend primarily to fellow citizens privy to the social
contract underlying the moral legitimacy of the state.

In such closed social systems, noncitizens are owed the duty of forbearance; but
as "aliens," they lack legal title to the primary good of citizenship and its attendant
claim-rights.[40] Even then, with the emergence of a global rights regime, the liberal "*jus
cosmopoliticum*" remains highly restricted.[41] Liberal respect for the "generalized other"
fails, in large part, to generate positive (imperfect) moral obligations of *provision*, that is,
of welfare rights. Neither is a positive obligation to *protect* potential victims against systemic deprivation generally recognized. Nations such as Sudan are rightly condemned
for abetting massive human rights violations; but such violation fails to disturb our
undogmatic slumbers. Strategic considerations of national self-interest again prevail,
so that, as in protracted refugee situations, the "alien" becomes, not the exemplar of
humanity in general, but "a frightening symbol of difference as such."[42]

The implications of these perplexities are particularly onerous for victims of forced
migration. With respect to the *object and nature* of human rights claims, as we noted
above, the restrictive definition of refugees in international law neglects the basic security claims of IDPs, as in Sudan or the Democratic Republic of Congo (DRC). Yet
suffering does not respect borders, as the vulnerability of northern Uganda's "night
commuters"—children subject to abduction and sexual slavery—attests.[43] So too,
dismissing (or derogating) positive human rights to nutrition, potable water, or basic
health care further limits the legal title of "refugee," obscuring the mutually implicative
character of basic human rights.[44] And yet, as we saw in the Great Lakes Region, forced
migration results not only from persecution, but also a witches' brew of generalized
violence, famine, and disease.[45]

In a similar vein refugees, especially those in protracted refugee situations, are often
systemically deprived of subsistence rights to which they are legally entitled. Here too,
denying such rights to adequate nutrition, potable water, education, health care, and
so forth, or rendering their satisfaction dependent upon charity, threatens both refugees' security and civil liberty. Seeking firewood for sustenance, often at considerable
distances, women in refugee camps are put at risk of rape or other forms of gender and
sexually based violence. This vulnerability is only exacerbated by a denial of their positive freedom, that is, their civil-political rights to participate effectively in the design
and implementation of policies affecting them and their dependents.[46]

With respect to the *subject* of claim-rights, even for those legally accorded the title
"refugee" or "asylee," Arendt's paradox persists. The *specific* rights accorded refugees
or asylees as such derive precisely from the violation of their *general*, human rights.[47]
Indeed, the status of refugees and IDPs testifies to victims' deprivation of basic civil
liberties and security rights. It points to a systemic failure of the "negative" duty of

forbearance and, a fortiori, of "positive" duties to protect, especially the most vulnerable. Refugees or asylees possess rights as refugee or asylee, that is, in their "abstract nakedness," precisely because they are antecedently dispossessed of their rhetorical "place" (*locus*) in the world. Here, then, appears in most egregious form what Jack Donnelly describes as the "possession paradox" of "'having' (possessing) and 'not having' (not enjoying) a right at the same time, with the 'having' being particularly important precisely when one does not 'have' it."[48]

Finally, with respect to the *respondent* or *recipient* of human rights claims, far from redressing the resultant state of deprivation, the duties correlative to such *specific* claim-rights remain, as we have seen, in large part negative. In the absence of generally recognized positive duties of *provision, protection,* and *redress* (such as rescue, restitution, and reparation for the forcibly displaced), claims of forbearance are all too often nugatory. As Gil Loescher observes, "there is no mandate [generally recognized by states] to provide protection and assistance to refugees; almost all aid is voluntary and discretionary."[49] Recurring budget shortfalls in UNHCR funding are particularly biased against Africa, imposing even greater strains on host countries like Tanzania.[50] Indeed, as primary respondents of human claim-rights, states often summarily dismiss asylum claims, even though *nonrefoulement* remains a nonderogative right. Interdiction in international waters, "extraterritorial processing," and indefinite detention further erode potential asylees' basic security.

Even the granting of asylum is no guarantee of enjoying basic rights. "Barred from engaging in political activities," refugees confined to camps are often likewise denied rights to "engage in agricultural, wage-earning and income-generating opportunities." Lacking "access to land" and prospects of long-term residency rights or naturalization, they are not permitted to enter "the labour market, they cannot take out loans and restrictions on their freedom of movement make it difficult for them to engage in trade."[51] And, as we noted above, with the loss of traditional means of protection, women and children in camps, especially those unaccompanied, remain vulnerable to exploitation in the form of domestic abuse, rape, sexual exploitation, and so on.[52]

Such protracted refugee circumstances, moreover, engender regional insecurity as camps become sites of armed resistance, as with the Hutu *interahamwe* (those who fight together).[53] Forfeiting even limited legal protection in the camps, urban refugees similarly suffer discrimination in education, housing, employment, access to financial services, and other matters.[54] The UNHCR may, of course, officially demur. Yet despite its laudable accomplishments, the agency itself, in Loescher's words, suffers from "structural disharmony." For effective protection of refugee rights remains not only subservient to the policies of powerful donors, but operationally dependent on national governments for permission to establish and maintain camps.[55]

Rights Revisited

What, then, do we owe to the forcibly displaced—not essentially, but rather as forcibly unencumbered of home and political status? For, as we saw above, it is the very condition of being "claimed" by a particular people or state that secures our "right to have [claim] rights."[56] But in what sense can our rights talk fittingly become a place (rhetorical *locus*) of redeeming claims, if membership, and the shared conception of the good that inspires it, remain bounded by citizenship or discrete, narrative identity?

Let me sketch an initial reply in the form of seven theses, drawing upon the wisdom of African theory and practice.[57] For in African tradition, says Bénézet Bujo, the uniqueness of moral persons rests not in abstracting the Individual from the ensemble of social relations, but precisely in "the communitarian dimension of life."[58] The discourse of human rights, in Bujo's words, must reflect the natural "interdependence between the individual and society."[59] And it is just this interdependence in "cosmopolitan solidarity" that lets us "see" the morally tragic character of victims' suffering[60]—those whose "abstract nakedness" constitutes what Engelbert Mveng terms "anthropological poverty."[61]

Rights and Rhetoric

Bentham famously dismissed natural or human rights as "rhetorical nonsense,—nonsense on stilts."[62] And yet it is precisely their rhetorical use, for example, in the South African Truth and Reconciliation Commission (TRC), that lets us make sense of rights.[63] Indeed, the TRC provides an exemplary instance of rights as what Jean-Marc Éla calls a "pedagogy of seeing" or witness.[64] For here, rights appear not as properties of abstract, sovereign selves, but rather as the "grammar" of victims' testimony. Rights, in the words of Chinua Achebe, become a "mouth" with which victims "tell of their suffering."[65]

Blinded in a brutal attack by police in Cape Town and later tortured, Lucas Baba Sikwepere testified in the Human Rights Violations Committee of the TRC: "I feel what—what has brought my sight back, my eyesight back is to come back here and tell the story. But I feel what has been making me sick all the time is the fact that I couldn't tell my story. But now I—it feels like I got my sight back by coming here and telling you the story."[66] Under the rubrics of human rights, such "telling" becomes testimony (persuasive speech).[67] Indeed, for Baba Sikwepere, what "brought my sight back" is not merely "telling the story," but the "uniquely public" character of the *hearings*, that is, our seeing his story as testimony.[68]

The Narrative Embodiment of Dignity

In the hearings, "what we do"[69] in invoking human rights implicitly affirms "the dignity and humanity of those" who, in Desmond Tutu's words, "were cruelly silenced for so long."[70] Just as torture aims not only at denying the victim's voice, her claim, but her very capacity to "make" a world as agent,[71] so, writes Tutu, victims' public testimony in the TRC sought to restore "the civic and human dignity" of those "who for so long had been consigned to the edges of society as voiceless and anonymous."[72]

Victims' testimony thus exhibits, in a performative or illocutionary fashion, the unique, irreplaceable "value and dignity of human life."[73] As R. J. Vincent observes,

> Not only are [human] rights an important part of the language of morals, but they have, too, a unique role within that language. It is to denote a particular moral at-

titude. The demeanour of someone claiming his or her rights is not that of begging or pleading, and the response if the claim is met is not one of gratitude. Equally, if the claim is not met, the response is not one of disappointment but of indignation. This is because rights are insisted on as part of one's status as a person. They are not favours done by the holders of power to those beholden to it.[74]

Generalized Respect for the Concrete Other

As Paulin Hountondji of Benin remarks, it is here that the discursive reference of the word "we" ("what *we* do" in invoking rights) is extended in its *concrete* universality.[75] He says that "what varies, not only from one culture to another, . . . but also within one culture from one period to another and from one class or social group to another, are the forms of this indignation, the modes of expression of this universal demand for respect and, consequently, the details of the rights considered to be essential and inalienable. But in no society is awareness of dignity truly absent, perhaps because in no society, alas, has this dignity ever been fully respected."[76]

The proper response to the systemic violation of Baba Sikwepere's rights *is* indignation; we "see" his suffering as morally tragic. Yet tragedy is never generic. Even in apartheid or genocide, the victims are legion, but always ineluctably particular. In Baba Sikwepere's story, rights are neither an abstract metanarrative of the "generalized other" nor one of many concrete local narratives, but rather a grammar embedded or embodied in the telling. In Baba Sikwepere's testimony, or the new civic narrative constructed of victims' public testimony before the TRC, *basic human rights exhibit a generalized respect for the concrete other.*

An Overlapping Consensus

The universal demand for such respect is attested in the principal instruments of international positive law (the international "Bill of Rights"). Thus, the Preamble of the United Nations' Universal Declaration of Human Rights (1948) solemnly recognizes our "common faith" in "the inherent dignity" and "equal and inalienable rights of all members of the human family."[77] A consideration of the justificatory grounds for such "common faith" exceeds the bounds of the present essay. Yet might we not say, with Wittgenstein, "this is simply what [we] do" when we have "exhausted the justifications"? After all, to say our "justifications have run out" is not to succumb to rhetorical anomie, but rather, simply to say that no *further* justification is necessary.[78] As for the drafters of the Universal Declaration,[79] what John Rawls calls the "overlapping consensus" of our common faith suffices to warrant recognition of our basic claim-rights.[80]

Basic Human Rights

Now, such common faith in agents' inherent dignity (the status of the subject or rights claimant) permits us to specify, in Hountondji's words, which rights are "essential and inalienable" (the nature and object of basic human claim-rights). For respecting the concrete other *as* a practically rational, discursive agent implies *respect* for the necessary conditions of her or his exercising agency, that is, *recognition* of claims, not only to basic civil-political liberties, but to subsistence and basic security as well. Inasmuch as these conditions, or more precisely agential capabilities, are presumed in exercising practically rational agency, they are mutually implicative.[81] The Universal Declaration thus recognizes the interdependence of civil liberties, security, and welfare rights. For Simeon O. Ilesanmi as well, an African reconstruction of rights rhetoric serves to overcome the putative dichotomy between "so-called negative rights and positive rights."[82] Indeed, as Henry Shue has shown, threats to any basic human right imperil the enjoyment of all such rights, so that "trade-offs" at this basic level—sustenance for security (suffered by women in camps) or security for freedom of movement (as urban refugees experience in Nairobi)—become morally impermissible.[83]

Correlative Duties

As we saw earlier, the universal demand for respect, parsed in recognition of agents' basic claim-rights, must be embodied concretely.[84] This will be typically through the allocation of correlative duties in what Rawls calls "a people's political culture and its constitutional principles."[85] The culturally fitting communitarian embodiment of a basic rights regime through the legal-juridical recognition of claim-rights thus emerges as a structural imperative. Indeed, we may speak of inscribing the grammar of (universal) rights as an implicit aim (*telos*) of citizens' public reasoning.

In a similar vein, the duties correlative with recognizing such fundamental claim-rights are not restricted to "negative" obligations of forbearance, as in classical liberal thought.[86] For even the most negative of rights, such as freedom of speech, entails positive duties of institutional protection (against what Shue calls "standard threats") and of provision where fitting.[87] As Ignacio Ellacuría argues, rights rhetoric is reduced to an "abstract, mystifying formality" if we fail to secure the real structural "conditions which make them possible."[88] Such conditions, of course, vary historically; yet the structural realization of an integral and comprehensive rights regime—redeeming what Arendt calls our "right to have rights"—remains a common good that extends analogically to national, subnational, and supranational communities. For as we have seen in our communitarian account, it is the primary (common) good of membership in such communities, whether as citizens or legal persons, that underwrites the recognition, and hence redemption, of our claim-rights.

The common good, conceived in terms of such "cosmopolitan solidarity," is thus neither the mere aggregate of individual goods (as in philosophical liberalism) nor the good of a suprapersonal "total organism" (as in ethnocentric or patriarchal conceptions of the "Volk"). Rather, the common good "is basically a union of structural conditions" that, in Ellacuría's words, preserves and protects "the personal good and thus . . . the rights of the person."[89] The ideal of the common good is conceived distributively, as a good that all share in common, yet not en masse: "What is proposed, then, is a common good which transcends each one of the individuals, but without being extrinsic to them. It is a common good, moreover, which surpasses each one considered individually, but in the same way that each one surpasses himself or herself in his or her communitarian and social dimension."[90] Citizenship, in this sense, surpasses or transcends itself in implicit recognition of basic human rights, including, a fortiori, the claim-rights of the forcibly displaced. Indeed, human rights warrant a state's democratic self-constitution precisely inasmuch as they render its borders porous.[91]

Taking the Victim's Side

The very rubrics of the *common* good, enjoining an indiscriminate regard of agents' equal rights within and across our narrative traditions and polities, demand a discriminate response to the "concrete other."[92] Dignity is always in local garb. Our moral-legal entitlement to equal respect and recognition justifies preferential treatment for those whose basic rights are most imperiled.[93] In Camus's phrase, it justifies our taking "the victim's side."[94] Not only must basic rights, as morally exigent, be redeemed before less urgent claims, such as property rights; the duties correlative to such mutually implicative rights generate institutional imperatives to protect those whose basic rights are most threatened, that is, those who, like Baba Sikwepere, "were cruelly silenced for so long." Indeed, the systemic denial of basic *human* rights, as in the case of refugees or IDPs—gives rise to an ancillary set of *specific* rights and duties, such as the rights and correlative duties of redress, including reparation, restitution, rescue, and so forth.[95]

Precisely the "communitarian dimension," the recognition of the concrete other in the politics of human rights, warrants the privilege of the poor—including the epistemic privilege of those "who for so long had been consigned to the edges of society as voiceless and anonymous," such as displaced women and children specially vulnerable to exploitation. Redeeming the rights of such victims *as* agents, including, a fortiori, their rights to effective, civic participation in the design and implementation of refugee-IDP policy regarding asylum, leadership in the camps, effective redress of gender-specific violence, and so on thus emerges as a touchstone of the legitimacy of *our* prevailing institutional arrangements. Only thus do rights truly become a "pedagogy of seeing," not only in the international refugee-IDP regime, but in local policies and practices.

Rights of the Dispossessed

Decrying "official propaganda against asylum seekers," Dummett recalls Luke's parable of the Good Samaritan: "When Christ reiterated the Old Testament commandment to love your neighbour as yourself, his listeners asked him, 'Who is my neighbour?' He responded by telling the story of the good Samaritan. Is it not time for both politicians and public to ask the same question?"[96]

Our theses provide an initial, schematic response to Dummett's question. For the grammar of rights lets us see the *morally* tragic character of what Walter Benjamin called the suffering and "passion of the world."[97] Let us, then, briefly consider the implications of our critique in unraveling the foregoing perplexities. Lest these remarks seem merely notional, however, I will look to the embodiment of (universal) rights in one particular tradition: modern Roman Catholic social teaching.[98] As we shall see, the global (universal) import of our particular religious traditions redresses the inherent limitations of a statist approach to redeeming rights. (Such narrative traditions are, a fortiori, themselves subject to rights; Catholic teaching must likewise be learning for the Church.)[99]

The Object and Nature of Rights

The graduated urgency of basic, mutually implicative human rights claims (see above) establishes the relative (lexical) priority of victims' claims (the object and nature of rights). The legal-juridical recognition of such claims, in turn, extends the "title" refugee to all who flee their countries because of a grave, systematic violation of their basic human rights, whether these be negative or positive, such as generalized insecurity or famine. As in modern Roman Catholic social teaching, the legitimate sovereignty of states in regulating immigration subserves the global common good, so that states are morally bound to respect and promote the basic human rights of both citizen and resident alien, especially the most vulnerable—and of these, in particular, women and children.[100] The Catholic Church thus recognizes the right of persons to change nationality for social and economic as well as political reasons, for in view of the "common purpose of created things" (and the mutually implicative character of basic rights), "where a state which suffers from poverty combined with great population cannot supply such use of goods to its inhabitants . . . people possess a right to emigrate, to select a new home in foreign lands and to seek conditions of life worthy" of their common humanity.[101] Just so, the "new home," even where temporary, must provide for the equitable provision and protection of such basic human rights.

The rhetoric of basic human rights leaves many questions unresolved. Yet recognizing the graduated urgency of human rights and correlative duties does serve to indicate the lineaments of an equitable policy in domestic and international law, namely, that law should take due cognizance of the moral priority of relative need (the gravity and imminence of harm); particular vulnerabilities of women and children; familial relationships; complicity of the host country in generating refugee flows;[102] historical or cultural affiliations such as historic patterns of migration; and a fair distribution of burdens among countries offering asylum. The last consideration applies domestically as well, for the burdens of local integration or resettlement should not fall disproportionately upon the most vulnerable citizens. Indeed, where humanitarian, "charitable" assistance may pit refugee against citizen or engender dependency, an integral and comprehensive account of rights locates refugees' claims within the systemic, structural imperatives of equitable development and regional security.[103] As we have seen earlier, a consequentially sensitive realization of a rights regime militates against *any* trade-offs of basic rights, such as sacrificing security for subsistence or mobility for security and limited legal protection in the camps.

So too, the basic rights of IDPs become morally and legally exigent: internal displacement does not render victims "rightless." On the contrary, the mutually implicative character of basic rights underscores the particular vulnerability of the IDPs of the Darfur region in Sudan. Fleeing from genocidal violence abetted by the state, they likewise fall victim to chronic hunger, illness, and general insecurity. No less than their sisters or brothers who fled to Chad, their plight reveals the limits of the prevailing statist rights regime.

The Subject of Rights

As we noted above, a further perplexity arises inasmuch as "the abstract nakedness of being nothing but human" divests the refugee or IDP of "the very qualities which make it possible for other people to treat him a fellow-man." Respect of the "generalized other" without recognition, for example, of gender, is empty, while recognition of citizens or members of racial, ethnic, and religious groups without respect is blind. Yet, as we saw earlier, generalized respect for the concrete other as subject of rights lets us chart a critical *via media* between liberalism and communitarianism, adumbrating a different root metaphor: neither "members or strangers," nor "abstract citizens," but near and distant *neighbors*.

In the words of the Second Vatican Council's *Gaudium et spes*, we must "make ourselves the neighbor to absolutely every other person."[104] The narrative embodiment of basic rights and duties inscribes respect and recognition of the "concrete other" within the "latent wisdom" of citizens—a rhetorical *locus communis* restoring victims' "place in the world." Recognition of the "stranger" or "alien" *as* neighbor, and thus as a juridical person or claimant attests to our common "faith in fundamental human rights, in the dignity and worth of the human person"[105]—a faith underwritten by, even as it is expressed within, our differing comprehensive religious traditions. Passing to "the victim's side," as did the Samaritan in Luke's parable, appears, then, as the touchstone of the legitimacy of prevailing institutional arrangements, local, national, and global. Indeed, a "well-formed" narrative tradition, far from being merely patriarchal or ethnocentric, will, in Hountondji's words, recognize the fitting "modes of expression of this *universal* demand for respect." Consonant with an analogical interpretation of the common good and as affirmed by Pope John XXIII, the loss of citizenship "does not detract in any way from [one's] membership in the human family as a whole, nor from [one's] citizenship in the world community."[106]

Respondent of Rights

Finally, the duties correlative to recognizing the rights of victims of forced migration impose "positive" obligations (general and specific correlative duties) upon persons, states, and other transnational actors. Typically, such positive duties of provision, protection, and redress are mediated institutionally; indeed, for Catholic social teaching, their concrete recognition underwrites the legitimacy of state sovereignty.[107] For, as we argued above, it is not, *pace* Hobbes, finally sovereignty that defines legitimacy, but rather the converse. As David Hollenbach has eloquently argued, our particular institutional arrangements, including citizenship in a particular polity, are legitimate only if they subserve the global common good and our "moral citizenship" in a world community.[108] Yet it is just this cosmopolitan citizenship that is mediated in and across our concrete, particular polities, so that victims of forced migration, even if undocumented, are never rhetorically effaced, never "rightless."

Pope John XXIII's 1963 encyclical letter, *Pacem in terris*, thus properly affirms not only the commonly recognized right to emigrate, but also the specific right to immigrate as well, for, "when there are just reasons for it," every human being has "the right to emigrate to other countries and to take up residence there." In a similar vein, Pope Paul VI urges acceptance of "a charter which will assure [persons'] right to emigrate, favor their integration, facilitate their professional advancement and give them access to decent housing where, if such is the case, their families can join them."[109] In a world ever more interdependent, citizens must seek a "continual revision of programmes, systems and regimes" in revising the international refugee regime, so as to guarantee the full and effective implementation of the basic human rights of the most vulnerable, including those condemned to stateless existence in camps of first asylum, and of these, in particular, women and children.[110] Such guarantees, we have seen, must provide effective legal-juridical redress of gender-specific forms of violence, including rape and genital mutilation. As Binaifer Nowrojee argues, recognizing women's basic human rights requires implementation of the UNHCR guidelines for refugee protection.[111]

The virtue of solidarity with both near and distant neighbors enjoins equitable policies of voluntary repatriation, reintegration, rehabilitation, and reconstruction (with particular attention to legal rights of widows or unaccompanied women); hospitable treatment of those seeking to change nationality, whether through local integration in the host country or resettlement in a third country; assistance in their integration to a new homeland; respect for their cultural heritage; and recognition of the benefits of hosting, and the contributions of, migrants. Above all, there is no "place" for warehousing refugees or incarcerating those seeking asylum, the criminalization of displacement. Wealthier states must bear an equitable share of the burden disproportionately borne by the poorer countries of first asylum, for example, through UNHCR's Development Assistance for Refugees and Development through Local Integration.[112] And where domestic laws and practices infringe upon refugees' basic rights, the priority of natural or human rights justifies provision of sanctuary. So too, citizens' responsibility extends to fitting support of global and nonstate actors such as UNICEF, the International Committee of the Red Cross, the International Organization for Migration, Amnesty International, Human Rights Watch, Catholic Relief Services, the Jesuit Refugee Service, and so on.[113]

Finally, Catholic social teaching seeks not only to protect and extend the legal (general and specific) rights of refugees, IDPs, and their families in positive international law, but to redress the "oppression, intimidation, violence and terrorism" that impel them to migrate against their will.[114] The duties falling upon states and NGOs to aid and protect refugees and IDPs presume the antecedent duty of preserving an international social order (the global common good) in which the basic rights of the most vulnerable, like Uganda's "night commuters," are recognized.[115] Indeed, as David Hollenbach argues, the duty to protect grounds the subsidiary duty to rescue, whether through diplomatic initiatives, sanctions, or, in extremis, humanitarian intervention in the case of genocide or mass atrocity.[116]

Yet might one not object that such teaching, if not quaint, is excessively utopian? For is there not a legitimate fear that a people (or state) might be submerged by an influx of "alien" refugees or asylum seekers? Our communitarian construal of rights lets us respond. For universal rights must be concretely instantiated in "a people's political culture," just as culture is leavened by rights. Indeed, the plight of the forcibly displaced is exacerbated by the loss of just such a political culture. Would our residual "right not to be submerged" be threatened by recognizing the rights of refugees or asylum seekers? For the United States or European democracies, that would seem fanciful indeed. "Submergence," writes Dummett, "has threatened only those ruled by imperial powers or annexed by expansionist ones," for example, as "China is doing in Tibet."[117] Moreover, the duty of assistance through effective development strategies arises precisely because the greatest burden of providing haven is already borne by the poorest countries, such as Tanzania, Kenya, or Chad.

A Concluding Theological Postscript

I have argued that only where the stranger is treated as neighbor will the scriptural promise of solidarity be redeemed as "the indispensable basis for authentic justice and the condition of enduring peace."[118] Tempering our "latent wisdom" by rights remains, though, a regulative ideal of citizenship, a narrative *telos* perpetually threatened by Hume's "circumstances of justice," that is, a paucity of both resources and altruism.[119] History, after all, bears ample testimony to partial or hegemonic uses of rights rhetoric, such as illegitimately invoking a "right not be submerged." Just as in Jesus' parable, "taking the victim's side" goes against the statist grain, so redeeming the biblical metaphor of neighbor is always a dangerous memory. Lest our rhetoric be empty or blind, we must, then, invoke the critical force of rights. In the words of Edward Said, we must venture "interpretations of those rights in the same place and with the same language employed by the dominant power," but disputing "its hierarchy and methods." We must elucidate what this power has hidden and pronounce "what it has silenced or rendered unpronounceable."[120] Now, our religious traditions at their best, as in the TRC or the American civil rights movement, play this critical role, bequeathing us alternative political metaphors, such as "neighbor," to remedy our moral myopia.

But the biblical parable, as kindred stories from our religious traditions, also inspires. In Luke's story of the Good Samaritan, for instance, impartial regard for my neighbor's rights justifies preferential attention for my neighbor in distress. Luke's narrative reveals the boundless, universal scope of love precisely in demanding a moral solidarity with those who suffer—my "neighbor, the masses."[121] There is thus a surplus of religious meaning not exhausted by rights talk.[122] The grammar of rights, we saw, implies that citizens precisely in realizing the primary good of citizenship must "take the victim's side," recognizing the "stranger" or "alien" as neighbor. Yet for the citizen of *faith*, justice is ordered by love.[123] To "walk humbly with our God" (Micah 6:8) demands not only "seeing" the nameless, half-dead stranger on our way; the disciple must, as the Samaritan of Jesus' parable, "see and have compassion" (Luke 10:33). As John Donahue observes, "Luke subtly alters the thrust of the parable," for Jesus does not so much answer the lawyer's question as "describe what it means to be a neighbor which then becomes the substance of [his] counterquestion."[124]

The lawyer's response, "the one who showed mercy," is richly ironic, since it is the despised schismatic—the stranger—who reveals the meaning of the law to the lawyer.[125] And so, with salvific irony, Jesus bids him, "Go, and do likewise!" Jesus answers the lawyer's first question, "What must I do to inherit eternal life?" in reversing the second.[126] For the command to "love the Lord your God, with all your heart, and with all your soul, and with all your strength, and with all your mind; and your neighbor as yourself" (Luke 10:27) is fulfilled not in this or that particular deed of love,[127] but in one's "selving" *as* neighbor to the stranger.[128] And, as modern-day martyrs like Ellacuría attest, this is the work of love.

"What I must do to *live*" is, then, to "turn" to the world of the poor, of the half-dead stranger. In the martyred Archbishop Oscar Romero's words, this means "becoming incarnate in their world, . . . proclaiming the good news to them," even to the point of "sharing their fate."[129] For Christians, the disciple is, in Christ, always already in communion with the suffering stranger. To remember the Covenant implies not merely taking the victim's side (the "essential" requirement of ethics, to use Karl Rahner's word), but taking the victim's side as one's own (the "formal, existential" demand of love).[130] "To be a Christian," says Gustavo Gutiérrez, "is to draw near, to make oneself a neighbor, not the one I encounter in my journey but the one in whose journey I place myself."[131]

In the words of Simone Weil, the disciple must cultivate a compassionate "way of looking . . . attentive" to the refugee "in all his truth." She or he must come to see the refugee "not only as a unit in a collection, or a specimen from the social category labeled 'unfortunate,' but as a man, exactly like us, who was one day stamped with a special mark by affliction."[132] In solidarity with victims of forced migration—those who in their "abstract nakedness" are "nothing but human"—disciples "see and have compassion" (*esplanchnisthe*).[133] This signifies being moved in one's inmost heart, even as compassion becomes a way of seeing. Compassion, then, not only guides them in the fitting application of universal, essential norms, such as the rights of refugees or IDPs, but gives rise to existential, personal, and ecclesial imperatives. Only thus do disciples walk humbly with Jesus, the Good Samaritan, who, as Augustine wrote, comes to the aid of wounded humanity: what I must do to live is "go and do likewise" (Luke 10:37).

Notes

1. See, inter alia, Ronald Robertson, *Globalization: Social Theory and Global Culture* (London: Sage, 1992); Anthony Giddens, *The Consequences of Modernity* (Stanford, CA: Stanford University Press, 1990); David Held et al., *Global Transformations: Politics, Economics, and Culture* (Stanford, CA: Stanford University Press, 1999); Joseph S. Nye and John D. Donahue, eds., *Governance in a Globalizing World* (Washington, DC: Brookings Institution Press, 2000).

2. UNHCR, *The State of the World's Refugees 2006: Human Displacement in the New Millennium* (Oxford: Oxford University Press, 2006), 10. UNHCR includes an additional 1,455,260 stateless persons and 597,000 "others" under its "total population of concern."

3. A refugee is one who "owing to a well-founded fear of being persecuted for reasons of race, religion, nationality, membership of a particular social group or political opinion, is outside the country of his nationality and is unable or, owing to such a fear, is unwilling to avail himself of the protection of that country; or who, not having a nationality and being outside the country of his former habitual residence, is unable or, owing to such fear, is unwilling to return to it." "Convention Relating to the Status of Refugees" (Geneva: United Nations High Commissioner for Refugees, originally adopted 1951).

4. Gil Loescher and James Milner, *Protracted Refugee Situations: Domestic and International Security Implications* (London: International Institute for Strategic Studies, 2005), 7. In identifying

such situations, the UNHCR applies the "crude measure of refugee populations of 25,000 persons or more who have been in exile for five or more years in developing countries" (ibid., 13). Also see UNHCR, Executive Committee of the High Commissioner's Programme, "Protracted Refugee Situations," Standing Committee 30th Meeting, UN Doc. EC/54/SC/CRP.14 June 10, 2004, 2. Globally, sub-Saharan Africa hosts the greatest number of protracted refugee situations, involving a total of some 2.3 million refugees.

5. UNHCR, "Protracted Refugee Situations," 1. Cf. U.S. Committee for Refugees, *World Refugee Survey 2005*, Table 1; *World Refugee Survey 2004*, 2.

6. UNHCR, *The State of the World's Refugees 2006*, 64. Cf. Loescher and Milner, *Protracted Refugee Situations*, 23–34.

7. Ibid., 34. "In 2002, in the Great Lakes Region of Africa, tens of thousands of refugees from the Democratic Republic of Congo were returned to their country of origin under conditions that were far from secure." Cf. U.S. Committee for Refugees, *World Refugee Survey 2005*, Table 1; *World Refugee Survey 2004*, 1.

8. UNHCR, *The State of the World's Refugees 2006*, 10, 17.

9. Ibid., 17. See UNHCR, "Chad/Darfur Emergency," available from www.unhcr.org (accessed December 19, 2006). The UNHCR notes the "dire humanitarian situation facing some 232,000 Darfur refugees and 90,000 displaced Chadians as well as another 48,000 Central African Republic refugees in the south." On September 8, 2006, the UN High Commissioner for Refugees, António Guterres, spoke of "deteriorating security" facing "some two million internally displaced people inside Darfur," http://www.unhcr.org (accessed December 19, 2006).

10. UNHCR, *The State of the World's Refugees 2006*, 68.

11. Ibid., 20, 22. Globally, women comprise c. 50% of those forcibly displaced in regions hosting large displaced populations.

12. Definitions that are more inclusive are accepted by the Organization of African Unity (OAU) Convention Governing the Specific Aspects of Refugee Problems in Africa (1969); the Cartagena Declaration on Refugees (1984), endorsed by the Organization of American States (OAS); and in the operational practice of the United Nations High Commissioner for Refugees (UNHCR). See United Nations High Commissioner for Refugees (UNHCR), *The State of the World's Refugees: In Search of Solutions* (New York: Oxford University, 1995), 57–94.

13. Micheline R. Ishay, *The History of Human Rights from Ancient Times to the Globalization Era* (Berkeley: University of California Press, 2004), 299ff. Patriarchal domination, genital mutilation, child marriage, etc., militate against the enjoyment, assertion, and enforcement of women's basic human rights. Girl children are particularly vulnerable to exploitation. Cf. UNHCR, *The State of the World's Refugees 2006*, 66–67.

14. For detailed analysis of the particular vulnerability of displaced women to rights violations, see Binaifer Nowrojee, "Sexual Violence, Gender Roles, and Displacement," and Susan F. Martin, "Justice, Women's Rights, and Forced Migration," both in this volume.

15. Camus writes that "it is the failing of a certain literature to believe that life is tragic because it is wretched." Albert Camus, *Lyrical and Critical Essays*, trans. Ellen Conroy Kennedy (New York: Knopf, 1968), 201.

16. For the constructive, nonpejorative use of "prejudice," see Hans-Georg Gadamer, *Truth and Method*, 2nd rev. ed., trans. Joel Weinsheimer and Donald G. Marshall (New York: Crossroad, 1989), 277–307.

17. Seyla Benhabib, *The Rights of Others: Aliens, Residents, and Citizens* (Cambridge: Cambridge University Press, 2004), 40ff.

18. Cf. Edmund Burke, *Reflections on the Revolution in France*, in *Works*, vol. 2 (London: Bohn's British Classics, 1872), 305–6, 412; cf. Burleigh Taylor Wilkins, *The Problem of Burke's Political Philosophy* (Oxford: Clarendon Press, 1967), 59–60, 109–10.

19. David Held, "Law of States, Law of Peoples," *Legal Theory* 8 (2002): 4.20. Benhabib, *The Rights of Others*, 41.

21. Hannah Arendt, "The Perplexities of the Rights of Man," in *The Origins of Totalitarianism* (New York: Harcourt, Brace, & World, 1966), 300. Emphasis added.

22. Victims of forced migration comprise all those displaced due to systemic violation of their basic human rights, i.e., refugees and asylum seekers (under international law); IDPs; and victims of famine, general insecurity, or unbearable poverty. "The immediate causes of forced displacement may be identified as serious human rights violations or armed conflict. But these causes often overlap with, or may themselves be provoked or aggravated by, economic marginalization and poverty, environmental degradation, population pressure and poor governance." (*The State of the World's Refugees 2006*, 24, cf. 9ff.)

23. I am particularly indebted to my earlier collaboration with William Spohn and to David Hollenbach's incisive criticism. See O'Neill and Spohn, "Rights of Passage: The Ethics of Immigration and Refugee Policy," *Theological Studies* 59 (1998); also, Hollenbach, *The Common Good and Christian Ethics* (Cambridge: Cambridge University, 2002), and *The Global Face of Public Faith: Politics, Human Rights, and Christian Ethics* (Washington, DC: Georgetown University Press, 2003).

24. Benhabib, *The Rights of Others*, 29.

25. Other rights enumerated by international convention, yet often overridden or infringed upon, include entitlements to freedom of religion, education, social security, public assistance, work, and limited travel documents. See Guy S. Godwin-Gill, *The Refugee in International Law*, 2nd ed. (Oxford: Clarendon, 1996).

26. Michael Dummett, *On Immigration and Refugees* (London: Routledge, 2001), 29.

27. Human Rights First, "International Refugee Policy: Refugees in East Africa," 1–2, http://www.humanrightsfirst.org/intl (accessed September 18, 2006).

28. See the International Convention on the Protection of the Rights of All Migrant Workers and Their Families, adopted by the General Assembly of the UN, Resolution 45/158 (December 18, 1990).

29. Hannah Arendt, "The Perplexities of the Rights of Man," in *The Origins of Totalitarianism* (New York: Harcourt, Brace, & World, 1966), 300, 293.

30. Ibid., 299. My concern, then, is less with the formal articulation of rights in international law than with the underlying "pre-judices," i.e., the liberal "prejudice against prejudice," that tacitly governs the rhetorical use of rights. See Gadamer, *Truth and Method*, 265–77.

31. As Michael Walzer observes, "The primary good that we distribute to one another is membership in some human community. And what we do with regard to membership structures all our other distributive choices: it determines with whom we make those choices, from whom we require obedience and collect taxes, to whom we allocate goods and services." Michael Walzer, *Spheres of Justice: A Defense of Pluralism and Equality* (New York: Basic Books, 1983), 31. Cf. Michael Walzer, "The Moral Standing of States," *Philosophy and Public Affairs* 9 (1980); Michael Walzer, "Nation and Universe," *The Tanner Lectures on Human Values XI* (Salt Lake City: University of Utah, 1990). For a comparative analysis of Rawls and Walzer on admissions policy, cf. Mark Gibney, *Strangers or Friends: Principles for a New Alien Admission Policy* (New York: Greenwood Press, 1986), 3–34.

32. Godwin-Gill, *The Refugee in International Law*, 134.

33. Arendt, "The Perplexities of the Rights of Man," 297, 301.

34. See Seyla Benhabib, "The Generalized and the Concrete Other: The Kohlberg-Gilligan Controversy and Feminist Theory," in *Feminism as Critique*, ed. Seyla Benhabib and Drucilla Cornell (Minneapolis: University of Minnesota Press, 1987), 85; cf. George Herbert Mead, *Mind, Self, and Society from the Standpoint of a Social Behaviorist*, ed. Charles W. Morris (Chicago: University of Chicago Press, 1962), 152–64, 379–89.

35. Ibid., 290.

36. Benjamin Constant, "De la liberté des anciens comparée à celle des modernes," in *Oeuvres Politiques de Benjamin Constant* (Paris, 1874), ed. C. Louandre.

37. J. S. Mill, *On Liberty*, ed. Gertrude Himmelfarb (New York: Penguin Books, 1974), 72.

38. Ibid.

39. Robert Nozick, *Anarchy, State, and Utopia* (Oxford: Basil Blackwell, 1974), 238.

40. See John Rawls, *Political Liberalism*, rev. ed. (New York: Columbia University, 1996), 41. Cf. the more cosmopolitan liberalism of Joseph H. Carens, "Aliens and Citizens: The Case for Open Borders," in *Theorizing Citizenship*, ed. Ronald Beiner (New York: SUNY Press, 1995), 229–55; Carens, "Who Belongs? Theoretical and Legal Questions about Birthright Citizenship in the United States," *University of Toronto Law Journal* 37 (1987): 415; Carens, "Immigration and the Welfare State," in *Democracy and the Welfare State*, ed. Amy Gutmann (Princeton, NJ: Princeton University Press, 1988), 215; Bruce Ackerman, *Social Justice in the Liberal State* (New Haven, CT: Yale University Press, 1980); Charles R. Beitz, "Cosmopolitan Ideals and National Sentiment," *Journal of Philosophy* 80 (1983); Beitz, *Political Theory and International Relations*, rev. ed. (Princeton, NJ: Princeton University Press, 1999).

41. See Benhabib's analysis of Kant's "cosmopolitan right" in *The Rights of Others*, 25–48; cf. Immanuel Kant, *Perpetual Peace, and Other Essays on Politics, History, and Morals*, trans. Ted Humphrey (Indianapolis, IN: Hackett, 1983).

42. Arendt, "The Perplexities of the Rights of Man," 297, 301.

43. See Lam Oryem Cosmas, "Internally Displaced Persons in Northern Uganda: A Challenge for Peace and Reconciliation," and Lucy Hovil and Moses Chrispus Okello, "The Right to Freedom of Movement for Refugees in Uganda," in this volume.

44. See Henry Shue, *Basic Rights: Subsistence, Affluence, and U.S. Foreign Policy* (Princeton, NJ: Princeton University, 1980), 5–87; Alan Gewirth, *Human Rights* (Chicago: University of Chicago, 1982), 41–78. Cf. Alan Gewirth, *The Community of Rights* (Chicago: University of Chicago, 1996), 31–70.

45. See Khoti Kamanga, "Human Rights, the Use of Force, and Displacement in the Great Lakes Region: Reflections on a Troubling Trend," in this volume.

46. See Nowrojee, "Sexual Violence, Gender Roles, and Displacement," and Martin, "Justice, Women's Rights, and Forced Migration," both in this volume.

47. Though grounded in general human rights discourse, specific rights of refugees (or IDPs), i.e., to provision, protection, and redress, presume a juridical determination of status.

48. See Jack Donnelly, *Universal Human Rights in Theory and Practice*, 2nd ed. (Ithaca, NY: Cornell University Press, 2003), 9, 12.

49. Gil Loescher, *Beyond Charity: International Co-operation and the Global Refugee Crisis* (New York: Oxford University Press, 1993), 139.

50. Loescher and Milner, *Protracted Refugee Situations*, 20.

51. UNHCR, *The State of the World's Refugees 2006*, 47–48.

52. Traditional forms of mediation must themselves be tempered by rights as a "pedagogy of seeing." Patriarchal bias may limit recognition and effective redress of rights violations suffered by women, e.g., rape and domestic abuse.

53. Loescher and Milner, *Protracted Refugee Situations*, 35–65.

54. UNHCR, *The State of the World's Refugees 2006*, 50. See Abebe Feyissa's eloquent testimony in "There Is More Than One Way of Dying: An Ethiopian Perspective on the Effects of Long-Term Stays in Refugee Camps," with Rebecca Horn, in this volume. Cf. John Burton Wagacha and John Guiney, "The Plight of Urban Refugees in Nairobi, Kenya," also in this volume.

55. Loescher, *Beyond Charity*, 138.

56. Michael Sandel, *Liberalism and the Limits of Justice* (Cambridge: Cambridge University

Press, 1982), 54, 94. Cf. Michael Walzer, *Thick and Thin: Moral Argument at Home and Abroad* (Notre Dame, IN: University of Notre Dame Press, 1994), 21–25.

57. See William O'Neill, "The Children of Babel: Reconstructing the Common Good," in the *Annual of the Society of Christian Ethics* (1998): 161–76.

58. Bénézet Bujo, *The Ethical Dimension of Community: The African Model and the Dialogue between North and South*, trans. Cecilia Namulondo Nganda (Nairobi, Kenya: St. Paul, 1997), 147–48; cf. Bujo, *African Theology in Its Social Context*, trans. John O'Donohue (Nairobi, Kenya: St. Paul, 1986). Cf. Elochukwu Uzukwu, who argues that "African anthropology . . . parts company with . . . modern Western [individualism] to insist that communicability is of the very essence of the person. The autonomy and rights of the individual subject are enjoyed in relationship, in communication." (*A Listening Church: Autonomy and Communion in African Churches* [Maryknoll, NY: Orbis, 1996], 41, 44). Cf. the OAU's more expansive definition of refugee in note 12.

59. Bujo, *The Ethical Dimension of Community*, 147–48.

60. Cf. Benhabib, *The Rights of Others*, 21. "Cosmopolitan citizenship," says Benhabib, "entails the reclaiming and the repositioning of the universal—its iteration—within the framework of the local, the regional, or other sites of democratic activism and engagement" (ibid., 23–24, cf. 171–212).

61. Engelbert Mveng, "Impoverishment and Liberation: A Theological Approach for Africa and the Third World," in *Paths of African Theology*, 158; cf. Laurenti Magesa, "Christ the Liberator and Africa Today," in *Paths of African Theology*, 151–63; Jean-Marc Éla, "La Foi des pauvres en acte," *Telma* 35 (July–September 1983).

62. Jeremy Bentham, *Anarchical Fallacies*, in *Works*, vol. 2 (Edinburgh, U.K.: William Tait, 1843), 523.

63. Subjective rights are warranted claims to social goods, e.g., liberties, security, subsistence, which we may legitimately enjoy, assert, or enforce against other social actors (persons, institutions). Cf. Shue, *Basic Rights*, 13ff. The schema distinguishing the subject, nature, object, respondent, and justifying basis or ground of claim-rights is drawn from Alan Gewirth's *Reason and Morality* (Chicago: University of Chicago Press, 1978), 65, and *Human Rights*, 2–3.

64. Jean-Marc Éla, "Christianity and Liberation in Africa," in *Paths of African Theology*, p. 143 (emphasis in original); cf. Laurenti Magesa, "Christ the Liberator and Africa Today," in *Faces of Jesus in Africa*, ed. Robert J. Schreiter (Maryknoll, NY: Orbis.1991), 151–63.

65. Chinua Achebe, *Things Fall Apart* (New York: Ballantine Books, 1959), 162. Achebe's title is drawn from William Butler Yeats's poem, "The Second Coming."

66. Testimony of Lukas Baba Sikwepere at the Human Rights Commission's hearing in Heideveld, Cape Town; as reported in Antjie Krog, *Country of My Skull* (Johannesburg, South Africa: Random House, 1998), 31; cf. *Truth and Reconciliation Commission of South Africa Report* (New York: Grove's Dictionaries, 1999), vol. 5, chap. 9, par. 9.

67. Cf. Chaim Perelman, *The Realm of Rhetoric*, trans. William Kluback (Notre Dame, IN: University of Notre Dame, 1982). Perelman defines rhetoric as speech aiming "at persuasion and conviction" (5).

68. Wilhelm Verwoerd, "Continuing the Discussion: Reflections from within the Truth and Reconciliation Commission," *Current Writings* 8, no. 2 (1996): 70.

69. See Ludwig Wittgenstein, *Philosophical Investigations*, trans. G. E. M. Anscombe, 3rd ed. (New York: Macmillan, 1958), pt. 1, par. 217.

70. Desmond Mpilo Tutu, *No Future without Forgiveness* (London: Rider, 1999), 32–33.

71. See Eileen Scarry, *The Body in Pain: The Making and Unmaking of the World* (New York: Oxford University Press, 1985), 30.

72. Ibid., 87.

73. See Brian Tierney, *The Idea of Natural Rights: Studies on Natural Rights, Natural Law, and*

Church Law, 1150–1625, Emory University Studies in Law and Religion (Atlanta: Scholars Press), 347.

74. Vincent, *Human Rights and International Relations*, 17. Cf. Alexis de Tocqueville's observation, "There is nothing which, generally speaking, elevates and sustains the human spirit more than the idea of rights. There is something great and virile in the idea of right which removes from any request its suppliant character, and places the one who claims it on the same level as the one who grants it." Quoted in K. R. Minogue, "Natural Rights, Ideology, and the Game of Life," in *Human Rights*, ed. Eugene Kamenka and Alice Ehr-Soon Tay (London: Duckworth, 1977), 34.

75. Pace Richard Rorty, human rights exhibit a concrete universality. Rights talk, like edifying discourse generally, would, says Rorty, be "relative to the group to which we think it is necessary to justify ourselves—to the body of shared belief which determines the reference of the word 'we.'" See Richard Rorty, "The Priority of Democracy to Philosophy," in *The Virginia Statute for Religious Freedom: Its Evolution and Consequences in American History*, ed. Merrill D. Peterson and Robert C. Vaughan (New York and Cambridge: Cambridge University Press, 1988), 259.

76. Paulin J. Hountondji, "The Master's Voice—Remarks on the Problem of Human Rights in Africa," in *Philosophical Foundations of Human Rights*, ed. Alwin Diemer et al. (Paris: UNESCO, 1986), 325.

77. *United Nations Declaration of Human Rights*, UNGA Res. 217A (III), 3(1) UN GAOR Res. 71, UN Doc. A/810 (1948). The *Convention against Torture and Other Cruel, Inhuman or Degrading Treatment or Punishment*, A/Res/39/46, December 10, 1984, recognizes explicitly that "the equal and inalienable rights of all members of the human family . . . derive from the inherent dignity of the human person." Cf. Mary Ann Glendon, *A World Made New: Eleanor Roosevelt and the Universal Declaration of Human Rights* (New York: Random House, 2001), 173–91.

78. Cf. Wittgenstein, *Philosophical Investigations*, pt. 1, par. 217.

79. See Glendon, *A World Made New*, 221–33.

80. See Rawls, *Political Liberalism*, 15, 39ff., 150–54; Rawls, "The Idea of Public Reason Revisited," in *The Law of Peoples* (Cambridge, MA: Harvard University Press, 1999), 172–74.

81. See the refined understanding of needs, capabilities, and functionings as defining the moral minima of agency in the analyses of Amartya Sen and Martha C. Nussbaum in *Women, Culture, and Development*, 259–73, 61–115, and 360–95, respectively. For a perceptive application of capability theory to forced migration, see Loren B. Landau, "Protection as Capability Expansion: Practical Ethics for Assisting Urban Refugees," in this volume.

82. Simeon O. Ilesanmi, "Civil-Political Rights or Social Economic Rights for Africa? A Comparative Ethical Critique of a False Dichotomy," in *The Annual of the Society of Christian Ethics* (1997): 210–11. Cf. Ilesanmi, "Human Rights Discourse in Modern Africa: A Comparative Religious Ethical Perspective," *Journal of Religious Ethics* 23, no. 2 (1995): 309–16; Harvey Sindima, "The Community of Life," *Ecumenical Review* 41, no. 4 (1989): 543–49; and Kwasi Wiredu, "An Akan Perspective on Human Rights," in *Human Rights in Africa: Cross-Cultural Perspectives*, ed. Abdullahi Ahmed An-Na'im and Francis M. Deng (Washington, DC: The Brookings Institution, 1990), 243–60; Aquiline Tarimo and William O'Neill, "What San Salvador Says to Nairobi: The Liberation Ethics of Ignacio Ellacuría," in *Love That Produces Hope: Essays on the Thought of Ignacio Ellacuría*, ed. Kevin Burke, SJ, and Robert Lassalle-Klein, 237–49 (Collegeville, MN: Liturgical Press, 2006).

83. Shue, *Basic Rights*, 35–64.

84. See Kant, *Critique of Practical Reason*, 68–71. Kant describes the schema of a concept as "a rule for the synthesis of the imagination," i.e., a rule linking concepts (a posteriori or a priori) to perception. (Ibid., 135, B 81.) In Kant's Second Critique, the synthetic role of a schema is played by the "type" of pure, practical judgments, i.e., a realm or kingdom of ends. By analogy, the ideal of a well-formed narrative schematizes the grammar of rights by specifying correlative duties

and hence generating particular, properly circumstantial action-descriptions. Construed thus, the kingdom of ends is not a type for the abstract, ahistorical subject, but is historicized concretely in social narrative.

85. See Rawls, *The Law of Peoples*, 39.

86. To a limited degree, the Banjul Charter on Human and Peoples Rights, adopted by the Organization of African Unity (OAU) on June 27, 1981, offers such a "communitarian" interpretation. Cf. H. O. W. Okoth-Ogendo, "Human and Peoples' Rights: What Point Is Africa Trying to Make?" in *Human Rights and Governance in Africa*, ed. Ronald Cohen et al. (Miami: Florida University, 1993), 76.

87. See Alan Gewirth, *The Community of Rights*, 32. Cf. Henry Shue, *Basic Rights: Subsistence, Affluence, and U.S. Foreign Policy* (Princeton, NJ: Princeton University Press, 1980), 18–34.

88. Ignacio Ellacuría, "Human Rights in a Divided Society," in *Human Rights in the Americas: The Struggle for Consensus*, ed. Alfred Hennelly and John Langan, trans. Alfred Hennelly (Washington, DC: Georgetown University Press, 1982), 59.

89. Ibid., 56.

90. Ibid., 57.

91. Cf. Benhabib, *The Rights of Others*, 120, 211, 221.

92. Appealing thus to concrete universality permits us to make moral sense of contingency, e.g., the variable conditions of provision, protection, and redress, without assuming that moral claims (human rights) are themselves contingent.

93. See Gene Outka, *Agape* (New Haven, CT: Yale University Press, 1972), 20. Cf. Ronald Dworkin, *Taking Rights Seriously* (Cambridge, MA: Harvard University Press, 1978), 227.

94. Albert Camus, *The Plague* (New York: Knopf, 1960), 230.

95. See Stephen Pope, "Justice and Peace: Reintegration and Reconciliation of Returning Displaced Persons in Postconflict Situations," in this volume. For an analysis of the role of basic human rights in social reconciliation, see William O'Neill, "Imagining Otherwise: The Ethics of Social Reconciliation," in *Journal of the Society of Christian Ethics* 22 (2002): 183–99.

96. Ibid., 45.

97. Walter Benjamin, *The Origin of German Tragic Drama*, trans. John Osborne (London: Verso, 1998), 166.

98. See David Hollenbach, "A Communitarian Reconstruction of Human Rights: Contributions from Catholic Tradition," in *Catholicism and Liberalism: Contributions to American Public Philosophy*, ed. R. Bruce Douglas and David Hollenbach (Cambridge: Cambridge University, 1994), 127–50. Other religious traditions, of course, could make analogous claims.

99. My argument is not that Catholic practices are always exemplary, but rather that the grammar of *universal* claim-rights may be embodied in *particular* narrative traditions: our multiple narrative identities permit us to transcend statist membership in our public reason without thereby denying the moral-legal significance of citizenship. For an illustration of such a religious use of public reason, see the Joint Commission for Refugees of the Burundi and Tanzania Episcopal Conferences, "The Presence of the Burundian Refugees in Western Tanzania: Ethical Responsibilities as a Framework for Advocacy," in this volume.

100. For magisterial teaching on the moral status of migrants and refugees, see especially Leo XIII, *Rerum novarum*, 47; Pius XII, *Exsul familia*; John XXIII, *Mater et magistra*, 45; *Pacem in terris*, 11, 25, 94–108; Vatican Council II, *Gaudium et spes*, 27, 66; Paul VI, *Populorum progressio*, 66–69; Sacred Congregation of Bishops, *Instruction on the Pastoral Care of People Who Migrate*; Paul VI, *Octogesima adveniens*, 17; Synod of Bishops (1971), *Justice in the World*, 20–24; John Paul II, *Laborem exercens*, 23; *Sollicitudo rei socialis*, 24, 38; *Redemptoris missio*, 37, 82; *Centesimus annus* (18, 57–58); and Pontifical Council for Pastoral Care of Migrants and Itinerant People, *The Love of Christ towards Migrants*. For an analysis of the implications of Catholic social thought

in the American context, see Office for the Pastoral Care of Migrants and Refugees, National Conference of Catholic Bishops and the Department of Education, United States Catholic Conference, *Today's Immigrants and Refugees: A Christian Understanding* (Washington, DC: U.S. Catholic Conference, 1988); *Who Are My Sisters and Brothers? Reflections on Understanding and Welcoming Immigrants and Refugees* (Washington, DC: U.S. Catholic Conference, 1996); "Love One Another As I Love You" (1996); *Welcoming the Stranger among Us: Unity in Diversity* (Washington, DC: National Conference of Catholic Bishops, 2000); the pastoral letter issued jointly by the bishops of Mexico and the U.S., *Strangers No Longer: Together on the Journey of Hope* (Washington, DC: National Conference of Catholic Bishops, 2003); and Pontifical Council for the Pastoral Care of Migrants and Itinerant People, *Erga Migrantes Caritas Christi* (Vatican City Libreria: Editrice Vaticana, 2005).

101. *Instruction on the Pastoral Care of People Who Migrate*, 7, n.14.

102. Cf. Walzer, "The Distribution of Membership," 20.

103. See Loescher and Milner, *Protracted Refugee Situations*, 67–84. Loescher and Milner favor a comprehensive framework integrating humanitarian, developmental, and peace and security policies and programs.

104. *Gaudium et spes*, n. 27. Cf. *Catechism of the Catholic Church* (Liguori, MO: Liguori Publications, 1994), nn. 1825, 2196, 2443–49.

105. Universal Declaration of Human Rights, Preamble.

106. *Pacem in terris*, n. 25.

107. David Hollenbach proposes an imaginative application of the "Kew Gardens principle," assigning responsibility in terms of the displaced person's relative need, the respondent's proximity to the need; her or his relative capability to respond; and the determination of last, reasonable resort. (David Hollenbach, "Internally Displaced People, Sovereignty, and the Responsibility to Protect," in this volume. Cf. Hollenbach, "Humanitarian Crises, Refugees, and the Transnational Good: Global Challenges and Catholic Social Teaching," a paper presented at the Katholieke Universiteit Lueven Centre for Catholic Social thought, Leuven, Belgium, September 9–11, 2004.) Cf. Loescher, *Beyond Charity*, chaps. 7 and 8; Arthur C. Helton, *The Price of Indifference: Refugees and Humanitarian Action in the New Century* (New York: Oxford University Press, 2002).

108. See Hollenbach, *The Common Good and Christian Ethics*, 65-86, 212–44.

109. Paul VI, *Octogesima adveniens*, n. 17, in *Catholic Social Thought: The Documentary Heritage*, ed. David O'Brien and Thomas Shannon (Maryknoll, NY: Orbis, 1992), 271.

110. John Paul II, *Dives in misericordia*, n. 17.

111. Nowrojee, "Sexual Violence, Gender Roles, and Displacement," in this volume. Nowrojee proposes several revisions of the guidelines in accordance with the basic rights of women refugees and IDPs. Cf. Martin, "Justice, Women's Rights, and Forced Migration," in this volume.

112. Such programs encourage refugees' self-reliance, linking their welfare to broader development strategies. See *The State of the World's Refugees 2006*, 129–51. "Most forced displacement — whether caused by human rights abuses, natural disasters or development projects, or in the form of trafficking or abduction—takes place in poor countries, and has the greatest impact on the poorest and most vulnerable people in those societies" (29). Over two-thirds of the world's refugees have fled to developing countries (31, 70).

113. See Agbonkhianmeghe E. Orobator's illuminating assessment in "Key Ethical Issues in the Practices and Policies of Refugee-Serving NGOs and Churches," in this volume.

114. John Paul II, *Redemptor hominis*, n. 17. Cf. Drew Christiansen, "Movement, Asylum, Borders: Christian Perspectives," *International Migration Review* 30, no. 1 (Spring 1996): 7–17.

115. Paul VI, *Octogesima adveniens*, n. 17, in *Catholic Social Thought*, 271.

116. See Hollenbach, "Internally Displaced People, Sovereignty, and the Responsibility to Protect," in this volume. The complex ethical considerations posed by humanitarian intervention

in light of the UN Charter are addressed in Kenneth Himes, "The Morality of Humanitarian Intervention," *Theological Studies* 55 (1994): 82–105; Himes, "Intervention, Just War, and the U.S. National Security," *Theological Studies* 65 (2004): 141–57. Cf. International Commission on Intervention and State Sovereignty, *The Responsibility to Protect* (Ottawa: International Development Research Centre, 2001); Jonathan Moore, ed., *Hard Choices: Moral Dilemmas in Humanitarian Intervention* (Lanham, MD: Rowman and Littlefield, 1998).

117. Dummett, *On Immigration and Refugees*, 51.

118. Paul VI, *Octogesima adveniens*, n. 17, in *Catholic Social Thought*, 271.

119. See David Hume, *A Treatise of Human Nature*, bk. III, pt. II, sec. ii, and *An Inquiry Concerning the Principles of Morals*, sec. III, pt. I; cf. Rawls, *Political Liberalism*, 66–71.

120. Edward Said, "Nationalism, Human Rights, and Interpretation," *Raritan* 12, no. 3 (Winter 1993): 45–46. Cf. Antonio Gramsci, *Selections from the Prison Notebooks*, trans. Quentin Hoare and Geoffrey Nowell Smith (New York: International Publishers, 1971), passim.

121. M. D. Chenu, "Les masses pauvres," in *Eglise et pauvreté*, by Georges Cottier et al. (Paris: Cerf, 1965), 169. Schrage, *The Ethics of the New Testament*, 78, 81.

122. Ilesanmi, "Civil-Political Rights or Social Economic Rights for Africa?" 210–11.

123. See John R. Donahue, "The Bible and Catholic Social Teaching: Will This Engagement Lead to Marriage?" in *Modern Catholic Social Teaching: Commentaries and Interpretations*, ed. Kenneth R. Himes (Washington, DC: Georgetown University Press, 2004), 9–40.

124. John Donahue, "Who Is My Enemy? The Parable of the Good Samaritan and the Love of Enemies," in *The Love of Enemy and Nonretaliation in the New Testament*, ed. Willard M. Swartley (Louisville, KY: Westminster/John Knox, 1992), 144.

125. The lawyer's response, "The one who showed him mercy" (Luke 10:37), says Donahue, "alludes to the prophetic tradition of Hosea 6:6 and Mic. 7:8, whose authority was not recognized by Samaritans." Not only, then, "is the Samaritan a neighbor but he acts according to those scriptures which the lawyer himself recognizes as authoritative." "Who is My Enemy? The Parable of the Good Samaritan and the Love of Enemies," 145.

126. So Kierkegaard: "Christ does not speak about recognizing one's neighbor but about being a neighbor oneself, about proving oneself to be a neighbor, something the Samaritan showed by his compassion." Søren Kierkegaard, *Works of Love*, trans. Howard and Edna Hong (New York: Harper and Row, 1962), 38.

127. See Karl Rahner, "The 'Commandment' of Love in Relation to the Other Commandments," in *Theological Investigations*, vol. 5, trans. Karl Kruger (New York: Seabury, 1966), 453; cf. "The Theology of Freedom," in *Theological Investigations*, vol. 6, trans. Karl Kruger and Boniface Kruger (New York: Seabury, 1974), 178–96, and Rahner's observation that "freedom is not simply the capacity to do this or that but (formally) a self-disposing into finality" ("Reflections on the Unity of the Love of Neighbour and the Love of God," in *Theological Investigations*, vol. 6, 240).

128. See Gerard Manley Hopkins, "'As kingfishers catch fire, dragonflies draw flame,'" in *Poetry and Prose*, ed. Walford Davies (London: J. M. Dent, 1998), 70.

129. Oscar Romero, "The Political Dimension of the Faith from the Perspective of the Option for the Poor," in *Liberation Theology: A Documentary History*, ed. Alfred T. Hennelly (Maryknoll, New York: Orbis Books, 1990), 298.

130. Rahner, "On the Question of a Formal Existential Ethics," 217–34. Cf. Gustavo Gutiérrez' observation that "commitment to the poor means entering, and in some cases remaining, in that universe with a much clearer awareness." Such solidarity, he writes, "can therefore only follow an asymptotic curve," i.e., an ever richer "seeing and having compassion." (*We Drink from Our Own Wells: The Spiritual Journey of a People*, trans. Matthew J. O'Connell [New York: Orbis, 1984], 125–26.)

131. Gustavo Gutiérrez, "Toward a Theology of Liberation," in *Liberation Theology: A Documentary History*, 74.

132. Simon Weil, "Reflections on the Right Use of School Studies with a View to the Love of God," *Waiting for God*, trans. Emma Craufurd (New York: G. P. Putnam's Sons, 1951), 115.

133. Benjamin, *Illuminations*, 253ff. Cf. Thomas McCarthy, *Ideals and Illusions: On Reconstruction and Deconstruction in Contemporary Critical Theory* (Cambridge, MA: MIT Press, 1991), 205–10.

II

Camps, Settlement, and Human Rights

3

The Presence of the Burundian Refugees in Western Tanzania

Ethical Responsibilities as a Framework for Advocacy

Joint Commission for Refugees of the Burundi
and Tanzania Episcopal Conferences

> *In migration faith discovers once more the universal message of the prophets,*
> *who denounce discrimination, oppression, deportation, dispersion and*
> *persecution as contrary to God's plan. At the same time they proclaim*
> *salvation for all, witnessing even in the chaotic events and contradictions*
> *of human history, that God continues to work out his plan of salvation*
> *until all things are brought together in Christ* (cf. Eph 1:10).[1]

The Wound of Displacement

In his June 25, 1982, letter addressed to the United Nations High Commissioner for Refugees, Pope John Paul II described the problem of refugees as a "shameful wound of our time."[2] The peoples of the Great Lakes Region (GLR) of Africa have witnessed firsthand this wound. In the last fifteen years alone, the civil wars in Burundi, the Democratic Republic of Congo (DRC), and Rwanda, along with the genocide in Rwanda, have forced millions of people to flee their homes, often to unfamiliar and sometimes inhospitable surroundings. Those who flee to neighboring countries as refugees are often gathered, sometimes forcefully, into large camps or settlements, where they become dependent on others for their survival. The hostilities that led to their flight are the product of many complex political, socioeconomic, and moral factors in which the refugees themselves are not always only innocent victims.

A Protracted State of Transition

What is perceived by all as a temporary phenomenon often drags out into many years in a constant state of transition, where status and rights remain unclear. The frequent turnover among those aiding the refugees exacerbates this feeling of transition, making it very difficult to address the deep divisions and long-term problems within the refugee community itself and between them and those who remained behind in their country of origin. Proposed long-term solutions may change with each new administrative team. Expatriates rarely have an in-depth knowledge of the host country's language or culture. Host country nationals, who often make up the majority of those called upon to aid the refugees, may be resentful of the expatriates' presence and envious of the aid they receive. Leaders within the refugee community are often ignored or discounted by those aiding them and by the governments of the host country, the country of origin, and the international community. And few people, whether refugees, host country nationals, or those coming from the international community have sufficient experience to prepare them to address the complex psychosocial dynamics, the ethical dilemmas, and the practical difficulties of working with refugee communities.

The Tanzanian Context

Since its independence, Tanzania has been particularly gracious in granting asylum to countless refugees from neighboring countries. Many past and current leaders of those countries at one point lived as refugees in Tanzania. This has not been without sacrifice and difficulty for Tanzania, especially with respect to its legitimate concerns for security, the environment, and the socioeconomic welfare of its citizens. Tanzania has also devoted considerable diplomatic efforts to bringing about negotiated peace agreements in Burundi, beginning with the Arusha Accords, and more recently with the cease-fire accord negotiated in May 2005 between the current government of Burundi and the Forces Nationales pour la Libération, the sole remaining armed opposition party. Therefore, we would be seriously amiss if we did not express our sincere gratitude to the people of Tanzania and their government for the asylum they have granted to the refugees currently resident in Tanzania. Perhaps the greatest tribute to Tanzania's hospitality to its neighbors in their time of danger and desperate need was the awarding of the UNHCR's Nansen Medal in 1983 to then President Julius Nyerere. During the awards ceremony, President Nyerere made an offer of permanent citizenship and land grants to those refugees facing permanent exile, an offer that has since been accepted by thousands.[3]

In the 1990s, however, the massive waves of refugees who entered Tanzania fleeing the violence and upheaval in the neighboring countries of Burundi, the DRC, and Rwanda taxed its traditional hospitality to the breaking point. It is useful to review these past years in light of Tanzania's history of hospitality to those in need and in view of the commitments that Tanzania has taken upon itself as a signatory to various international conventions on human rights. Similarly, because of the responsibility entrusted to the Catholic Church for the pastoral care for the refugees, we would be equally amiss if we failed to express our concerns on behalf of the refugee community.

Scope and Methodology

This chapter is a descriptive report on the situation of the refugees in western Tanzania and the ethical issues inherent therein. The refugees primarily under consideration are those from Burundi who have been gathered into large camps or settlements in the Kigoma, Rukwa, Rulenge, and Tabora regions of Tanzania. They currently number 187,000 among a total of 329,000 refugees living in UNHCR-sponsored camps.[4] Also considered are another 200,000 long-term refugees from Burundi estimated by the Tanzanian government to be living in other settlements, primarily in the Tabora and Rukwa regions.

The problems of refugees represent a challenge for any responsible conscience, and they appeal for an advocacy that transcends positive law and calls for a broader sense of ethical or moral responsibility. This chapter is meant to be a humble response to that challenge. It presents an ethical reflection that draws on the years of pastoral experience of the Catholic Dioceses of Kigoma and Rulenge in western Tanzania serving the refugee communities from Burundi, the DRC, and Rwanda. It draws also on the experience of the Joint Commission for Refugees (JCR) formed by the Burundi and Tanzania Episcopal Conferences to advise them on matters concerning refugees and internally displaced persons (IDPs) and to oversee their pastoral programs for the Burundian refugees in Tanzania and the IDPs in Burundi. Finally, it draws on the personal experience as refugees of several members of the JCR, including its current co-president, Bishop Joachim Ntahondereye of Muyinga Diocese in Burundi.

First, we describe the situation of the refugees in several camps and settlements within which we are working and the extent to which their human dignity and rights are being respected. This description starts with the principle that exile does not cancel one's human rights. Second, we examine the treatment of the refugees to see if it goes beyond merely offering them physical protection. Third, we propose that the testimony of what the JCR has been trying to do is illustrative of ethically based advocacy.

The Right to Asylum in Relation to Rights in Asylum

> *Protection is not a simple concession made to the refugee: he is not*
> *an object of assistance, but rather a subject of rights and duties. Each*
> *country has the responsibility to respect the rights of refugees and assure*
> *that they are respected as much as the rights of its own citizens.*[5]

In theory, under international law the right to asylum is intended to augment the existing rights that a refugee possesses under other international conventions, such as the United Nations Universal Declaration of Human Rights.[6] In practice, however, when refugees are granted asylum, particularly in prima facie cases where refugee status is granted en masse, significant restrictions are placed on their other rights and freedoms. Nowhere is this clearer than in the contrast between the treatment granted a person who crosses the border into Tanzania from Burundi with his or her passport and visa or residency permit and that granted a person who, having fled the conflict in Burundi to Tanzania without such documentation, is granted prima facie status as a refugee. The former moves about freely in Tanzania for the duration of his or her visa or residency permit with little or no overt restrictions placed upon his or her other rights; however, the latter is obligated to live in a refugee camp where significant restrictions are placed upon his or her freedom of movement, which in turn seriously curtail the enjoyment of other fundamental rights.[7]

A Contingent View of Refugee Rights

These restrictions are placed on a refugee's rights in view of the government of Tanzania's concerns for security, the protection of the environment, and the socioeconomic well-being of the Tanzanian people. However, this results in a contingent view of a person's rights that is captured in the following excerpt from the Tanzanian National Refugee Policy (NRP), promulgated in 2003: "Similarly, the government [of Tanzania] is committed to treat all refugees in a humane way. However, there may be crisis situations in other countries whereby considerable numbers of refugees arrive at the Tanzanian borders, or cross the borders within a relatively short period of time. As it will be appreciated, the pressure of the needs in such crises, together with practical limitations, can make it impossible to meet the standards which should be applied in light of international instruments and protection principles."[8]

There is also a risk that emergency measures may become the norm, leading to routine infringements on refugee rights and freedoms. Similarly, this contingent view of refugee rights invites many encroachments, both large and small, that in effect make refugee rights dependent upon the willingness of government officials to recognize these rights.[9] For example, administrative procedures for granting permission to refugees to travel outside the refugee camps invite bribes. Refugees are not given identity cards to prove their refugee status, except for temporary travel permits. It has not always been clear which law should apply to refugees caught outside the camps without permission and the harsher penalties under illegal immigration laws (as opposed to refugee legislation) may sometimes be applied.[10] Recent prison statistics in the Kasulu district indicate that this is no longer the case, and the UNHCR has received clarification from the Tanzanian courts that the lesser penalties under the 1998 Refugee Act should apply in cases where refugees are found outside the camps without permission on a temporary basis. However, it is not clear that these changes have been implemented everywhere. For example, in Kigoma town itself there are recent reports of refugees imprisoned on immigration charges. While the UNHCR verifies refugee status and follows the cases of those arrested, often providing translators for the refugees, no formal legal representation, either from the UNHCR or from the Tanzanian government, is provided when the refugees are brought before the courts.[11]

Repatriation—To What Degree Voluntary?

This contingent view of refugee rights creates serious hardships for the refugees, which in turn may lead to a premature decision by them to return home even to a situation of continuing insecurity. At issue, therefore, is the fundamental stance of the UNHCR and the international community that repatriation must be voluntary and in safety and dignity. This is also recognized in the Tanzanian National Refugee Policy (NRP): "The need for international protection may cease when the circumstances [in the country of origin] . . . have fundamentally and durably changed and national protection can safely be resumed."[12] In a later point the NRP adds, "In cases where refugee status has ceased, any final settlement will be concluded in an essentially humanitarian way." [13] The questions, though, are who decides when conditions "have fundamentally and durably changed and national protection can safely be resumed" and what constitutes "voluntary" and "essentially humanitarian." In effect, decisions concerning whether conditions in the country of origin are such that repatriation can take place have been made by tripartite commissions consisting of representatives from the UNHCR and the governments of the host country and the country of origin. Once that decision is taken, measures using varying degrees of persuasion, including thinly veiled threats of dire consequences for those who delay in repatriating, are undertaken to convince the refugees to decide to voluntarily repatriate.

Here one must raise a concern about the role of the UNHCR as a "promoter" of repatriation while it also has a mandate to protect the refugees' safety and rights. The UNHCR has stated that repatriation is the preferred solution among the three durable solutions for refugees (the other two being local integration and resettlement to a third country). Therefore, the success or failure of its field officers in the eyes of the government of the host country and the UNHCR itself may be dependent on efforts to promote repatriation. This, in turn, may create a conflict of interest on the part of the field officers themselves.

Other measures that sound good in meetings or on the radio may take on a completely different form in local implementation. For example, in 1995–96, in response to the much-publicized presence of Interahamwe militias in the camps for the refugees from Rwanda, a campaign was undertaken in the camps in northwestern Tanzania to remove "intimidators." Obviously, this was a worthy goal. However, the program was often used to silence anyone expressing concerns about whether it was safe to repatriate at that time. This included the investigation of a missionary priest in the Karagwe camps for allegedly preaching against repatriation. In the end the allegations proved false, but it was clear that had the priest spoken out against repatriation, he would have been removed from his responsibilities as a pastor in the camps. Similarly, during the same period a program of cross-border visits was organized in the camps for the Rwandan refugees to promote repatriation. This program had many potential benefits, but in its implementation, refugees returning from the cross-border trips were pressed to speak at gatherings of their fellow refugees to inform them of the results of their visit. They were not allowed, however, to say anything negative about conditions in Rwanda. Those who declined to speak or who later did not themselves sign up to return to Rwanda were asked why they were reluctant in those matters.

More serious cases of infringement of refugee rights include forced repatriation. Following a dispute between the Tanzanian government, the UNHCR, and the international community over responsibilities for the care for the Rwandan refugees in the far northwestern corner of Tanzania, a mass forced repatriation of the Rwandan refugees was carried out by the Tanzanian government in December 1996. Individual cases of forced repatriations, particularly of released prisoners, continued to take place in the following years.[14] Periodic roundups of old caseload refugees of 1972 living in villages close to the Burundi-Tanzania border have been carried out, with those arrested being given a choice between returning to Burundi or moving to a refugee camp. In some cases, property of those arrested was looted. In cases of intermarriage between a Tanzanian and a Burundian, the Tanzanian was told that if he or she wished to remain together with his or her spouse, he or she must follow him or her either to Burundi or to a refugee camp.[15] Even Tanzanian citizens have been wrongly identified as refugees and forcibly sent to the DRC. Exorbitant residency permit and naturalization fees place legal residency of Tanzanian citizenship beyond the financial ability of all but a very few refugees. After more than thirty years in Tanzania, the 1972 refugees from Burundi living in the settlements of the Tabora and Mpanda regions still have to ask for permission to leave the settlements; such permissions are limited to two weeks. And the constant threat of repatriation hangs over the heads of these old caseload refugees.

Beyond Elementary Daily Needs to Full Humanity

> *"Conventional refugees" already have been offered some measure of protection; however, such protection must not be limited to a guarantee of physical integrity but must be extended to all the conditions necessary for a fully human existence. Thus, they must be assured not only food, clothing, housing, and protection from violence, but also access to education and medical assistance and the possibility of assuming responsibility for their own lives, cultivating their own cultures and traditions, and freely expressing their own faith. Likewise, since the family is the fundamental unit of every society, the reunification of refugee families must be promoted.*[16]

In many ways a refugee community is no different than any other. The members are people of all demographic characteristics: men and women; young and old; students and workers. They have the wide variety of backgrounds and skills found in any community: doctors, nurses, lawyers, ministers, teachers, skilled craftsmen and women, farmers, and day laborers. Among them are those who are recognized as leaders in various capacities and who are called upon by their fellow refugees to organize and represent their community. All of these people, with their respective skills, form the building blocks of a just and peaceful society. For them to be able to interact on an equal basis in a pluralistic, democratic society, they must be allowed to maintain and exercise these skills in developing a united and economically stable community and in educating the community's youth to carry on these tasks. If this is not recognized and respected, there is a risk of the refugees becoming permanent second-class citizens in their society of origin upon their return. Therein lies one of the seeds of future conflict.

Security Concerns and Refugee Rights

Unfortunately, providing refugees with appropriate skills and allowing them to exercise those skills may be seen as conflicting with the responsibility of the host country government to protect the security, the environment, and the economic well-being of its citizens and with its desire to promote a swift repatriation of the refugees. For example, legitimate security concerns of the host government can lead to strict limitations on the refugees' freedom of association for fear that refugee meetings may be used as a venue for political or even military planning. However, from our experience we note that the security concerns of the host country government are best addressed in conjunction with the leaders of the refugee community. This cooperation with the refugee community should be rooted in the belief that the vast majority of its members share with their hosts a respect and concern for law and order, along with the desire to live in peaceful coexistence. For example, research done by the University of Dar es Salaam on the impact of refugees in northwestern Tanzania shows that the percentage of the refugee population involved in serious crimes is no different from that of their Tanzanian hosts in the surrounding regions.[17]

Environmental Protection versus Refugees' Basic Needs

Refugees are given food rations that they must cook themselves; but because of a dispute between the district commissioner and the UNHCR, for more than six months in 2006 the Burundi refugees in the Kasulu district camps were prohibited from going to collect firewood, and the UNHCR was prevented from bringing firewood into the camps. This was obviously a policy that could not be strictly enforced because the result would have been the near starvation of the refugees. After many efforts by the UNHCR and the Tanzanian government to address this problem, it was resolved. However, for those months refugees caught bringing firewood to the camps were often forced to pay bribes to avoid arrest, and many of the refugees cited the lack of firewood as a determining factor in their decision to repatriate.

Refugee Self-Sufficiency versus Host Country Nationals' Economic Well-being

The Tanzanian National Refugee Policy recognizes that "adequate protection of refugees requires the attainment of a degree of self-sufficiency."[18] However, unemployment among the host country's population may be at unacceptably high levels, so gainful employment for the refugees may be viewed as taking opportunities from host country nationals. For example, the NRP states: "The employment policy, however, takes a look at the national employment growth potentials and reveals that the labour market is generally in crisis and faces many challenges. . . . As far as the refugees are concerned, the government will allow small income generating activities to be undertaken within the camps."[19]

However, the micro-projects promoted in the camps only help a small percentage of the refugee population. Most of the refugees are farmers by trade, but they are not permitted to cultivate plots of land outside the camps, nor are they permitted to go to the surrounding villages to seek day labor. The normal biweekly distribution of food aid that the refugees receive consists of a subsistence-level portion of corn kernels, which must be ground for flour, beans, salt, and a small amount of cooking oil. The cost of grinding the corn and of the matches to light the fire to cook their food must be paid for by the refugees themselves. Supplements to the meager food aid that they receive constitute another significant expense for them. Parents must buy clothes for themselves and for their children. The prohibition of firewood in the Kasulu camps made the cost of this essential commodity exorbitant for most of the refugees. To provide for these additional necessities for their families, the refugees have no choice but to seek work as day laborers in the surrounding villages. Those who are caught are often forced to pay bribes to avoid arrest.

We note also that the day labor that the refugees do in the villages around the camps is beneficial to their Tanzanian hosts, with the latter coming to the camps to seek out refugee workers for their farms. The increased produce generated by the refugee day laborers helps to supplement the Tanzanian families' food supplies as well as giving them a surplus to sell.[20]

For those refugees fortunate enough to find employment with the aid agencies or as teachers in the camps, the financial incentives given to them are intentionally kept significantly lower than the salaries received by their Tanzanian colleagues doing the same work.[21] Ostensibly it is because the refugees receive aid, but the aid given hardly accounts for the difference between the Tanzanians' salaries and the refugees' incentive payments.[22]

Secondary School Education

Even the provision of secondary school education can be a matter of concern. The UNHCR does not provide assistance for secondary school education in the Burundian and Congolese refugee camps. Instead, the post–primary school education provided is primarily through the initiative of the refugee parents and teachers, with intermittent aid provided by some of the NGOs and churches, as well as from fellow refugee workers. The Tanzanian government for its part recognizes the importance of education in its National Refugee Policy: "As for post primary school education, the government will encourage the international community through UNHCR and other agencies to establish special schools and institutions in the camps."[23] However, under its implementation strategies, the policy states, "On post primary school education emphasis shall be put on vocational training in order to facilitate self-employment upon their return to their countries of origin."[24] Our concern is that this emphasis on vocational schools may be interpreted so as to neglect normal secondary school education. Without the latter, returning youth are placed at a serious disadvantage relative to the youth who remained behind in their country of origin and who have received a normal secondary school education.

Health Care

Similarly, the UNHCR does not provide either dental or eye care in the Burundian and Congolese refugee camps, except in urgent and life-threatening cases. This constitutes a great shortcoming in the health care for the refugees themselves and also for their Tanzanian hosts in the region of the camps, as the latter are given free access to, and are dependent upon, the treatment provided in the camps.

Refugee Women and Girls

In addition to experiencing the same difficulties as their male counterparts, refugee women and girls face specific protection issues. Birth rates are often higher in refugee camps than outside. Incidences of rape, abuse, domestic violence, and prostitution are often higher also. Women often are the ones to travel long distances in isolated areas looking for firewood. Sexual demands may be placed on them before they are granted aid to which they are entitled. Single mothers, divorced or widowed women, and unaccompanied female adolescents are particularly vulnerable to sexual assault. And women may find themselves the sole provider of their families' needs, thus bringing about a change in traditional family roles that may lead to conflict with their husbands.[25]

Church Attempts to Respond to Its Ethical Responsibilities toward Forced Migrants

> *The way of solidarity demands on the part of everyone the overcoming*
> *of selfishness and of fear of the other; it demands a long range action*
> *of civic education which by itself can contribute to the elimination of*
> *some of the causes of the tragic exodus of refugees.*[26]

As can be gathered from the above discussion, refugees face a daunting array of difficulties in exile. In addition, fear and mistrust often prevail between them and their compatriots back home and even among the refugees themselves. Refugees are also often the object of prejudice and fear in the host country.[27] The perceptions that the international community have of them may or may not be sympathetic. In the turmoil of armed conflict, flight, and life in exile, the social structures and leadership of the refugee community often break down. Many go for years without news of their loved ones left behind. The refugees themselves may be divided with respect to how to address their own plight and the situation in their country of origin.

Negative Perceptions of Refugees

In the research cited above on the impact of the refugees in northwestern Tanzania, Boniventure Rutinwa and Khoti Kamanga found that the Tanzanians canvassed commonly perceived refugees as

- Threats to external security as a result of strained relations with the countries of origin,
- Threats to internal security (increase in criminal activities),
- Sources of environmental degradation,
- Sources of destruction of physical and social infrastructure,
- Excessive burdens on local governance and administration, and
- Retardants of economic development in refugee-affected regions.

These researchers concluded by noting that "despite our best endeavours, we could hardly find a story on the positive impact of the presence of refugees in Western Tanzania."[28]

In the eyes of many people in Burundi, the refugees in Tanzania were routinely seen as rebels, murderers, and bandits. Upon return, the refugees find that being reinserted and reintegrated into their society of origin is a difficult task. In addition, the hundreds of thousands of Burundian refugees who fled their country in 1972 have grown up in Tanzania and now have families of their own. Their livelihoods are based in Tanzania. Thousands of others stayed in Rwanda and the DRC for many years before arriving in Tanzania. Many of these long-term refugees were educated under the Tanzanian curriculum; many are more comfortable speaking Swahili than Kirundi; and many do not know French. Most of their children have never set foot in Burundi. When those who fled die, their children do not even know where their families' homes and farms are located. And under Burundian law the legal claim to land abandoned expires after thirty years.

Formation of the Joint Commission for Refugees by the Church

In light of the above, it is very difficult for the refugees, left on their own, to defend their rights whether in the host country or in their country of origin. Similarly, it is very difficult for the refugees to overcome internal divisions and conflict within their own community. And, as is true with most parties to a conflict, it is often difficult for the refugees to be objective enough to recognize their own hand in the hostilities that led to their flight. There is also a great need to help the refugees reestablish their relationships with their fellow Burundians at home. Returning refugees must work together with their brothers and sisters who remained behind to overcome the fear and mistrust, the bitterness and anger that remain between them after so many years of hostility and of war in which all sides have been guilty of human rights violations.

From the beginning of their ministry with the refugees, the pastoral agents appointed by the Catholic dioceses of Kigoma and Rulenge realized that efforts to help the refugees could not be taken in isolation. Instead, everything done in the camps has its counterpart in the refugees' country of origin. This begins with the basic need for liturgical and catechetical materials. But it extends to advocacy on their behalf and to the more difficult and long-term process of healing and reconciliation. This reality is recognized in *Refugees: A Challenge to Solidarity* (1992), published by the Pontifical Council for the Pastoral Care of Migrants and Itinerant People: "In the work of pastoral care of refugees, cooperation between the Churches of the countries of origin, temporary asylum and permanent resettlement is now more necessary than ever."[29] For that reason, in the latter half of 2001 Bishop Paul Ruzoka of Kigoma Diocese extended an invitation to the Catholic Church of Burundi to visit its people in the refugee camps in Tanzania.

In response, a delegation from Burundi headed by Archbishop Simon Ntamwana of the Archdiocese of Gitega, then president of the Burundi Episcopal Conference, met in January 2002 with a delegation from the refugee-hosting dioceses of Kigoma and Rulenge hosted by Bishop Severine Niwemugiz of Rulenge Diocese, then president of the Tanzania Episcopal Conference.[30] As a result of that meeting, the JCR was formed. It has since been designated by the Burundi and Tanzania Episcopal Conferences to advise them in refugee- and IDP-related matters and to coordinate their pastoral programs for the Burundian refugees in Tanzania and the IDPs in Burundi.

JCR Meetings and Visits

The JCR currently meets three times per year, alternately in Burundi and Tanzania. Bishop Joachim Ntahondereye of Muyinga Diocese, president of the Economic and Social Affairs Commission of the Burundi Episcopal Conference (BEC), is the current copresident of the JCR on the Burundian side, while Bishop Paul Ruzoka of Kigoma Diocese, president of the Justice and Peace Commission of the Tanzania Bishops Conference, is the current co-president of the JCR on the Tanzanian side.

To date the JCR has visited all the Burundian refugee camps and settlements in the Tanzanian dioceses of Kigoma, Rulenge, and Mpanda and the Archdiocese of Tabora; it has also visited numerous IDP settlements in Burundi. The JCR acts as a liaison between the refugees in Tanzania, the IDPs in Burundi, and the Burundian people as a whole, bringing news from all sides together with a message of forgiveness and reconciliation in its efforts to help build a lasting peace.

JCR Advocacy

Among the advocacy activities undertaken by the constituent members of the JCR on the Tanzanian side was a seminar on refugee law held June 18–19, 2004, in Kigoma in which representatives from the Tanzanian government and various NGOs participated. In addition to a review of pertinent international refugee and human rights law, concern was raised that a proper balance should be maintained between the legitimate national interests of the Tanzanian government and the rights of refugees.[31]

With respect to education, the JCR advocates that opportunities for all types of education be promoted so as to prepare the refugee youth to assume all the various responsibilities at all levels of their society of origin. We have also stressed the importance of ensuring that certification of educational achievements in exile is recognized in the country of origin and in the international community.

A position paper titled *The Way Forward to Peace and Security, Good Governance and Development in the Great Lakes Region*[32] was prepared by the Tanzanian contingent of the JCR on behalf of the Tanzanian bishops and was submitted to the UN–African Union International Conference on Peace, Security, Democracy, and Development in the Great Lakes Region, held in Dar es Salaam, Tanzania, in November 2004. Included in this document were the results of a survey conducted of refugees in camps within the Kigoma and Rulenge dioceses, giving their views on the state of affairs in their countries of origin at the time and their views concerning the way forward to peace.

Through personal contacts with important actors in both Tanzania and Burundi, as well as in its press releases, the JCR continues to advocate on behalf of the refugees and IDPs, particularly with respect to their rights in exile and for a voluntary, gradual, and well coordinated return home and reintegration into their communities of origin. While the refugees remain in Tanzania, we advocate that they be permitted to procure what they need for daily life, including firewood and materials to build adequate housing. They should be able to seek an adequate level of self-sufficiency, including fair wages for those working for the aid agencies, plots of land to farm, or mutually beneficial productive activities in the villages surrounding the refugee camps; to educate their children; to participate in decisions affecting their community; and to travel to carry out their legitimate affairs without being subjected to onerous burdens such as the require-ment of police escorts or bribes. With respect to travel and work outside the camps, the issuance of identity cards for refugees would help protect them from arbitrary arrests.

The JCR also advocates that, in accordance with the Tanzanian National Refugee Policy, "In cases where refugee status has ceased, any final settlement will be concluded in an essentially humanitarian way."[33] This would include special consideration to be given to the long-term refugees who have no land to which to return; for them, the JCR advocates for their local integration in the host country or their resettlement to third countries. The former option would include assistance from, for example, the UNHCR in paying residency permit and naturalization fees that are beyond the financial capa-bilities of the refugees themselves.

Church-Sponsored Seminars on Women's Rights and Concerns

The UNHCR has long recognized the particular vulnerability of refugee women and girls; therefore, it has undertaken significant preventative and corrective measures to protect their rights. Various church actors have joined in these efforts by offering semi-nars on psychosocial counseling and trauma healing, along with gender and develop-ment training both for refugees themselves and to aid agency personnel.[34] The Catholic churches in the Kasulu and Kibondo camps require three-month preparation classes for couples wishing to marry in the church, in which issues of women's rights, domestic violence, and AIDS are addressed. The age of those girls asking to be married is verified, and separate interviews are conducted with them to ensure they are not being forced to marry because of bridewealth or pregnancy. Counseling is offered for married couples having difficulties, and the churches work together with camp social services represen-tatives in cases of domestic violence. Women's rights and dignity within the society and in the family are frequent topics of homilies, especially those for wedding celebrations.

Overcoming Divisions within the Refugee Community

The need for recognition of the refugees' own contribution to the conflict in their coun-try, as well as the need for forgiveness and reconciliation, is frequently stressed in our homilies and retreats. We have also given peace education seminars for refugee leaders. In a practical way we have tried to overcome the divisions within the refugee com-munity itself through biennial elections of church leaders down to the street and zone level within the camps, who in turn call our church members to work together on proj-ects like church construction, reception of guests, and campwide celebrations of feast days. We believe that joining together in such church and community projects, working shoulder to shoulder, helps people to realize that they have much more in common than the differences that have separated them. In fact, significant research indicates that the direction of efforts to help communities devastated by war to heal and recover should be towards the restoration of their social structures.[35] For example, in his article "The Impact of War and Atrocity on Civilian Populations: Basic Principles for NGO

Interventions and a Critique of Psycho-social Projects," Derek Summerfield argues that in non-Western societies, "what is fundamental for Western relief interventions is to aim to augment efforts to stabilize and repair the war-torn social fabric and to allow it to regain some of its traditional capacity to be a source of resilience and problem solving for all."[36] Similarly, in her article, "War and Children in Mozambique: Is International Aid Strengthening or Eroding Community-based Policies?" Nazneen Kanji found that the most important government policy for assisting children was helping families and communities stay together by providing the land and resources necessary to reinitiate production and reestablish their lives. Community and political organizations, as well as health and education services, are all promoted. School is considered vital in providing normal structure and hope in the lives of children affected by war.[37]

Dialogue between Conflicting Parties

At its September 2005 meeting in Kirimbi parish of the Archdiocese of Gitega in Burundi, the JCR brought together selected representatives from among returned refugees, IDPs, and those who had remained behind in their communities of origin.[38] In the animated discussion that followed, each group spoke of the wrongs done to them, but it was also recognized by all sides that there was a need to acknowledge the wrongs committed by one's own group. No one said it was impossible to live together again in peace; instead, all spoke of the need for increased interaction to overcome the fear and mistrust that remains between the groups.[39] Their responses reflect our own experience, related above, that common projects help overcome the differences that divide a community.

The issues discussed at Kirimbi were in turn discussed in selected refugee camps in Kigoma, together with the responses from their brothers and sisters in Kirimbi in what has been an ongoing discussion of peace and reconciliation in the Advent 2005 and Lent 2006 retreats. In August 2006 a youth gathering was held in the Kasulu district refugee camps at which the Ubuntu organization from Burundi gave presentations on Ubuntu (basic African values) and on peace and reconciliation. Selected youth representatives of different ethnic origins from several dioceses in Burundi attended the gathering in the camps and shared with the more than fifteen hundred refugee youth present news of youth gatherings for peace and reconciliation held in their respective dioceses in Burundi.

The Need for Cooperation

In all these efforts to visit the refugees, to offer seminars and training, to rebuild the social structures of the refugee community, and to provide opportunities for cross-border exchanges, coordination and cooperation between church-based actors, camp authorities, and the NGO community is essential. For example, permission must be granted by the camp authorities for refugees to travel outside the camps, for visitors to enter the camps, and for large-scale gatherings in the camps. NGOs can help by making available transport, chairs, tables, and meeting tents for special occasions. The churches of all denominations in turn make available their facilities for primary school classes during the week because the number of students exceeds school facilities. NGOs for their part need to provide water and sanitary facilities for the students studying in the churches.

Similarly, with respect to advocacy by church actors, there needs to be an openness on the part of the government and aid agencies to listen to their concerns, as the faith-based communities have deep roots among their people. For that reason, refugees are frequently more at ease in expressing their concerns to the religious leaders than to government authorities or agency personnel.

JCR's Focus and Mission

All of the above activities reflect the decision taken by the JCR at its September 2005 meeting in Gitega to focus increasingly on bringing together representatives from conflicting groups to work for peace and reconciliation as an important aspect of the reintegration of returning refugees and IDPs and in ensuring a durable and just peace. The JCR will work with the UNHCR and the Tanzanian and Burundian governments to continue promoting intercultural exchange activities for women, youth, cultural, and student groups.

Recognizing that peace in one country is dependent on peace prevailing in all the Great Lakes Region's countries, the JCR has also taken steps to broaden its membership.[40] In 2005, delegates from the dioceses of Uvira and Bukavu in the DRC began attending JCR meetings and related events. A formal invitation was subsequently extended to the DRC Episcopal Conference to send an official delegation to the JCR meetings. A similar invitation has been extended to the Episcopal Conference of Rwanda, which has indicated its interest in joining the JCR.

The JCR cooperates and networks with other important actors such as the Catholic Justice and Peace Commissions, Caritas units, other pastoral agents and services from both the Catholic church and other denominations and religions, civil society, governments, international organizations, and other relevant persons and institutions in order to fulfill its mission in an effective and efficient way. For example, the JCR has proposed a Great Lakes Region conference on peace and reconciliation as a follow-up to the Third Annual International Conference of the Catholic Peacebuilding Network held July 23–28, 2006, in Bujumbura, Burundi.

This broader scope of the JCR's work with refugees, IDPs, and others for peace and reconciliation in the Great Lakes Region was expressed by delegates to the September 2005 JCR meeting in Gitega in the JCR's new mission statement:

- To strengthen the cooperation of the churches in the Great Lakes Regions in view of peace and reconciliation, development, and security in the region. This includes working for a common understanding between the churches of the GLR on the root causes of conflicts, violence, and wars in the region;
- To become a resource organ of the church by serving as a think tank for peace and reconciliation; and
- To cooperate closely with other relevant actors (government, UN, NGOs, academics, and so on) as a guiding principle.

Implications for Action and Advocacy

Today there is an inescapable duty to make ourselves the neighbor of every man [and woman], no matter who [s]he is, and if we meet him [her], to come to his [her] aid in a positive way, whether [s]he is an aged person abandoned by all, a foreign worker despised without reason, a refugee, an illegitimate child wrongly suffering for a sin [s]he did not commit, or a starving human being who awakens our conscience by calling to mind the words of Christ: "As you did it to one of the least of these my brethren, you did it to me" (Matt. 25:40).[41]

In this chapter we have cited examples of the many problems faced by refugees. Underlying a great number of their difficulties is a contingent understanding of refugee rights that invites frequent infringements. These restrictions cause many hardships and deprivations in the refugees' daily lives that in turn may result in a premature decision by refugees to repatriate to their home countries. As a result of its mandate from the Burundi and Tanzania Bishops Conferences to oversee their programs for the pastoral care for refugees and the IDPs, the JCR has undertaken many efforts, of both a legal and pastoral nature, to advocate on the refugees' behalf, including joining with them in the difficult work of peace and reconciliation that they face together with those who remained behind in their communities of origin.

Need for Additional Advocacy and Research

There are many additional needs for advocacy on behalf of refugees. For example, longer-term needs for advocacy include lobbying efforts to urge the host government to incorporate the provisions of international covenants on human rights into national and local laws. Churches and NGOs can coordinate seminars on refugee rights as a part of the training that the Tanzanian government has requested for its law enforcement personnel.[42] Also, greater efforts at advocacy on behalf of refugee prisoners remains a crying need because they are particularly vulnerable to violations of their rights. Continued efforts must be made to protect women and girl refugees' rights and to secure their vulnerabilities, especially in ways that effectively address traditional cultural practices which result in abuse. For example, the need to involve men directly in such efforts is essential in overcoming the perception that women's rights is solely a women's issue.

Similarly, more research like that done by the University of Dar es Salaam, as reported in *The Impact of the Presence of Refugees in Northwestern Tanzania* (2003), needs to be done to help dispel misconceptions and prejudices against the refugees and to focus attention on real issues of concern. For example, some of the significant findings of the University of Dar es Salaam's research included the statistics cited above that show that the rate of criminality among the refugees is no higher than that of the host population in the surrounding regions. The researchers also noted that the Tanzanian people themselves have benefited from improvements in health, education, roads, and transport as a result of the increased aid entering their region because of the refugees. The researchers also noted a greater awareness and receptivity to the development needs of the region itself because of the attention that the international assistance community focused on the region as a consequence of the refugees' presence.

Forced Encampment

For national and international policymakers, we ask that serious consideration be given to the question of forcing refugees to stay in refugee camps despite the obvious problems inherent in that policy. Many of the rights violations and infringements cited above, as well as many of the concerns expressed by the Tanzanians regarding refugees in the research by the University of Dar es Salaam noted previously, can be directly traced to the policy of confining refugees in camps. For example, large numbers of young men without education or employment provide fertile recruiting grounds for rebel groups. Similarly, if one compares a refugee camp of one hundred thousand people to a small village of five thousand, by sheer virtue of numbers one can expect a greater incidence of crime in the camp, even though the rate of crime may be the same among the refugees as among the host population. Nor, as Lucy Hovil and Moses Chrispus Okello note, do camps necessarily result in better security for the refugees themselves.[43] When there is a large concentration of people in a limited area who have no other way to cook their food than with firewood and no other way to build their homes than with wooden poles, then a negative environmental impact is inevitable. The administrative burden on both the host government and the agencies assisting the refugees will obviously increase relative to the number of people under their care.

The detrimental effects of forced encampment and the accompanying restriction of freedom of movement on the rights and life of refugees are clear. Perhaps the title of Abeye Feyissa and Rebecca Horn's chapter in this volume, "There Is More Than One Way of Dying: An Ethiopian Perspective on the Effects of Long-Term Stays in Refugee Camps," best captures the serious concerns raised by forced encampment. In contrast, Hovil and Okello note in this volume the positive contribution that self-settled refugees make to the host country's economy and development.[44] Legal documentation in the form of formal identity cards for refugees, which are recognized and respected by the host country's authorities and aid agencies, is a key to the protection and socioeconomic welfare of refugees who venture outside the confines of the refugee camps. At the same time, we need to avoid creating systems of protection and assistance for refugees separate from those directed toward the needs of host country nationals.[45]

Perhaps the greatest hurdle to the self-settlement of refugees, with the possibility of long-term local integration leading to naturalization, are the frequently expressed concerns that host countries will lose their ability to monitor and control the movements and activities of refugees in their country. The host countries fear that refugees will abuse their hospitality by pushing the hosts' already-overburdened socioeconomic structures to the breaking point. Paradoxically, cross-border ethnic, cultural, and linguistic affinities of refugees coming from neighboring countries exacerbate host country fears that the problems of the refugees' country of origin will become those of the host country. Therefore, if self-settlement is to be accepted by the host country, these concerns and fears must be addressed in a credible manner, and creative ways to meet the socioeconomic needs of both refugees and host country nationals and to enable them to live together peacefully must be explored as a part of burden sharing on the part of the international community.

With respect to encampment, we join with the Pontifical Council for the Pastoral Care of Migrants and Itinerant People in the following appeal: "Since life in [refugee] camps is artificial and imposed, even traumatizing, a long stay in them makes refugees still more vulnerable. Camps must remain what they were intended to be: an emergency and therefore temporary solution."[46] Here it is good to recall that the first assistance given to the large numbers of refugees in Europe in the wake of World War I was the Nansen document, in effect a passport, which enabled refugees to cross international boundaries and seek their own way. In East Africa, efforts to expand the East African Economic Community include freer movements of people to promote economic development. The freedom of movement now readily granted to those traveling with passports could be expanded to include those received as refugees by issuing them formal identity cards. However, it must be recognized that, particularly in Burundi and Rwanda, land pressures are cited as one of the underlying causes of conflict.[47] Those most vulnerable to land shortages are subsistence-level farmers whose land continues to be divided into ever-smaller plots among subsequent generations. These people, who would constitute the majority of those seeking alternative, self-supporting possibilities in neighboring countries, are the least capable of paying for visas or residency permits. Therefore, efforts to address the problem of land shortage must look beyond the traditional scope of regional agreements on economic integration and cooperation that focus more on providing opportunities for business and trade.

The Church's Role

In matters of advocacy and working for peace and reconciliation, the church has a unique role to play.[48] The church's special concern for the poor calls it to take the part of those who are oppressed and discriminated against in society. This is an essential part of the church's prophetic role in speaking out against the evils in society and presenting an alternative way to that of force in settling disputes. As a part of this prophetic role, the church must also call the refugee community itself to recognize its own contribution to the hostilities that its members fled and to the difficulties they face in exile. Similarly, the church is called by Christ to be a peacemaker in his name; therefore, it has a responsibility to bring people from all parties to the conflict to work together with people of good will from the international community in seeking its peaceful resolution. All of these roles of the church are played out in the country of asylum, in the country of origin, and in the refugee community itself.

However, the members of the church itself can be affected by the discrimination and hostility that led to the conflict in the country of origin, and they too may hold the prejudices against refugees in the host country. Also, the church often tries to work behind the scenes in quiet diplomacy, but there is a risk that quiet diplomacy can become silent complicity, especially in the eyes of those who are most in need of the church to speak out on their behalf. Therefore, the church must take special measures to protect its impartiality in its ministries of advocacy and peace and reconciliation, and it must be ready to take strong positions against the policies of the government when necessary.

Here the observations of the Commission on Justice and Peace of the Catholic Church in Germany are helpful: "The Church's talk of reconciliation and of dealing with a violence burdened past and present hence takes place not from a position of a passer-by, of a supra-historical observatory, but from a position of consciously being a contemporary. . . . Hence the need for a constant self-critical examination of our activities is one of the essential lessons we can learn here."[49]

Advocacy by Concerned Actors in the International Community

In countries where democracy has firmly taken root, the forum for advocacy is in the legislative bodies and the courts, in public demonstrations, and in the mass media. But in countries that are still ruled by oppressive governments or that are still struggling to overcome an oppressive history, the forum for advocacy of one's rights is often in prison or in other places where information is needed for effective advocacy. In the former setting one's weapons are words and their ability to persuade others of their truthfulness and righteousness. But under an oppressive regime, the weapons of those in charge are often instruments of torture and their ability to enforce fear and silence. Even in young democracies, efforts to speak out against government abuses can result in sanctions, imprisonment, or deportation.

Therefore, for those people of good will in well-established democracies who are ready to advocate on behalf of those living in less than fully open societies, it must be remembered that the well-being and even the lives of those on whose behalf they are advocating may easily be put in jeopardy by the information the refugees themselves provide. There is also a question of perceived authority that is attributed to someone coming from the international community such that those with whom they speak may feel they have no choice but to answer questions posed to them. This is particularly true in refugee communities.[50] Obviously, in all these matters, caution and discretion are of great importance. However, all that being said, someone coming from outside can say things that otherwise could not be said by local actors and the parties to the conflict. For example, where local actors are unable to speak out directly for concern about their own well-being and safety, a discrete intervention by external actors to protect the rights of refugees can be very helpful. Similarly, where the parties to the conflict are bogged down in inflexible positions, someone from the outside can pose new, previously unconsidered alternatives.[51]

Broader efforts at advocacy to change laws and policy at the local, national, and international levels normally exceed the sphere of influence and resources of local actors. Here concerned actors in the international community can play a significant role by working with local actors to help create a regional forum offering seminars and training, as well as by making available personnel with influence and expertise to lobby governments and international agencies like the UNHCR and to provide specialized training. International human rights conventions, for example, are sometimes seen as culturally inappropriate restrictions placed on the government's flexibility to respond to the problems it confronts. This is particularly true with respect to refugees' and women's rights. Therefore, there is a need for ongoing dialogue that translates human rights language into nationally and culturally relevant issues and concerns.

A Long-Term Presence in a Transitory Setting

We close by again noting that while the exile of refugees is frequently viewed by all concerned as a temporary state, all too often it drags on for many years in what constitutes a constant state of transition. There is a great need for those called to minister to refugee communities to be a symbol of constancy. This is particularly important in addressing the most difficult problems the refugees face. Those serving refugees must first learn what the problems of the community are, while at the same time working to gain refugees' trust. They must work to establish contacts within the church and with other important actors in the government and NGO community, both in the country of asylum and in the country of origin. In a setting where all too often those who offer assistance to the refugee community come and go every year or two, some of those who minister to the refugees need to be a long-term presence. They need to be given sufficient time to move from the role of welcomed guest working on the perimeter of the refugee community to trusted partner helping refugees to preserve their religious beliefs and traditions, to reaffirm and protect their God-given dignity and rights, to rebuild their churches and social institutions, to tell their stories and bring the truth to light, and to begin the long journey toward peace and reconciliation.

Notes

1. Pontifical Council for the Pastoral Care of Migrants and Itinerant People, *Erga Migrantes Caritas Christi* (Vatican City, 2004), no. 13.

2. Pope John Paul II, "Letter Addressed to the High Commissioner for Refugees," June 25, 1982, in Pontifical Council for the Pastoral Care of Migrants and Itinerant People, *Refugees: A Challenge to Solidarity* (Vatican City, 1992), Introduction.

3. UNHCR, "A Change of Direction for Tanzania," *Refugees* 110 (December 1997): 14.

4. UNHCR, "Monthly Statistics as of 1 August 2006," report distributed monthly by UNHCR within Tanzania.

5. Pontifical Council for the Pastoral Care of Migrants and Itinerant People, *Refugees: A Challenge to Solidarity*, no. 11.

6. See, for example, the preamble to the 1951 Refugee Convention, where it is stated that: "[The UN] endeavoured to assure refugees the widest possible exercise of fundamental rights and freedoms, as affirmed by the principle under the Charter of the United Nations and the Universal Declaration of Human Rights, that all human beings shall enjoy fundamental rights and freedoms without discrimination."

7. In East Africa and other parts of the continent, governments follow a similar policy of mandatory encampment of refugees with accompanying restrictions on freedom of movement. See other essays in this volume: Abebe Feyissa and Rebecca Horn, "There Is More than One Way of Dying: An Ethiopian Perspective on the Effects of Long-Term Stays in Refugee Camps"; Lucy Hovil and Moses Chrispus Okello, "The Right to Freedom of Movement for Refugees in Uganda"; and Loren B. Landau, "Protection as Capability Expansion: Practical Ethics for Assisting Urban Refugees." Hovil and Okello give a particularly insightful argument on the importance of freedom of movement to the enjoyment of other rights, and on the legal basis of freedom of movement in international and Ugandan law.

8. United Republic of Tanzania, Ministry of Home Affairs, *The National Refugee Policy* (Dar es Salaam, 15 September 2003), no. 12.

9. At question here is a fundamental tension between the rights of citizens by virtue of their membership in their own society versus the rights to be granted to refugees as stranger or alien. For an excellent legal, philosophical, and moral argument against considering the rights of citizens and refugees in terms of the categories of member and stranger, see William O'Neill, "What We Owe to Refugees and IDPs: An Inquiry into the Rights of the Forcibly Displaced," in this volume. Using the parable of the Good Samaritan from Luke's Gospel, O'Neill argues that citizen and refugee should be looked upon as near and distant neighbors, both of whose claims to respect of their rights are rooted in a common faith in the cosmopolitan, transnational, and nondiscriminatory nature of human rights witnessed to by the signatories to the Universal Declaration of Human Rights. From this perspective, the rights of citizens are viewed as a specific incarnation of universal human rights in which refugees share. In effect, O'Neill argues that the respect granted to the rights of citizens draws its moral force from the recognition of human rights regardless of citizenship; moreover, to the extent that the latter are concretely enforced in the particular cases of those whose rights are most threatened, like refugees, respect of citizens' rights is, in turn, strengthened. Citing Ignacio Ellacuria, O'Neill warns that without this concrete recognition of the rights, particularly of those most vulnerable to denial of their rights, the whole human rights discourse risks becoming an "abstract, mystifying formality" (Ignacio Ellacuria, "Human Rights in a Divided Society," in *Human Rights in the Americas: The Struggle for Consensus*, ed. Alfred Hennelly and John Langan, trans. Alfred Hennelly [Washington DC: Georgetown University Press, 1982], 59). Similarly, O'Neill argues that implicit in granting the fundamental right of asylum to a refugee is a recognition of the subsidiary rights to subsistence and basic security. Thus, one can begin to speak of positive rights claims like freedom of movement and choice of domicile, freedom of association, the right to work, and the right to education that are called for under international rights covenants and which, in turn, must be embodied in the social structures through which the refugee exercises her or his right to asylum.

10. See, for example, Boniventure Rutinwa and Khoti Kamanga, *The Impact of the Presence of Refugees in Northwest Tanzania* (Dar es Salaam, Tanzania: Centre for Study of Forced Migration, University of Dar es Salaam, September 2003), 16; this research showed that as of June 2002, 65% of the refugees held in Kasulu prison were jailed for immigration or administrative offences. A typical sentence given at that time was six months' imprisonment under immigration laws instead of the three days' confinement within the camp compound or the 5,000 Tanzania shillings fine provided for under the Refugees Act of 1998, sec. 18, subsec. 3 and 4.

11. For example, the advocacy agency ARTICLE 19, in its report by Richard Carver, *Voices in Exile: African Refugees and Freedom of Expression* (London: Article 19, 2001), 14, stated that "a magistrate in Kibondo [a district of Kigoma] told ARTICLE 19 that he would be prepared to raise a number of constitutional challenges related to existing practices of the government and of the agencies in the camps, but complained that UNHCR did not bring such cases."

12. Government of Tanzania, "National Refugee Policy," signed by Omar Ramadhan Mapuri, Minister for Home Affairs, September 15, 2003, no. 5.

13. Government of Tanzania, "National Refugee Policy," no. 11.

14. For example, after being released from a court appearance in Kasulu, four refugees were taken directly to the Burundi border where they were turned over to Burundian officials. One escaped to report that news, and his three compatriots were later discovered by the UNHCR in a military prison in Burundi.

15. See, for example, Human Rights Watch, *Tanzania: In the Name of Security–Forced Round-Ups of Refugees in Tanzania* (New York: Human Rights Watch, July 1999).

16. Pontifical Council for the Pastoral Care of Migrants and Itinerant People, *Refugees: A Challenge to Solidarity*, no.12

17. Rutinwa and Kamanga, *The Impact of the Presence of Refugees in Northwest Tanzania*, 16.

18. *National Refugee Policy*, no. 17.

19. Ibid.

20. Hovil and Okello (in this volume) cite similar benefits to the local economy from the productive efforts of self-settled refugees in Uganda.

21. Feyissa and Horn (in this volume) note a similar policy in Kenyan refugee camps of paying incentives to refugees that are significantly lower than the wages paid to nationals for the same work.

22. Aside from the subsistence level food assistance they receive, the only other aid they get on a regular basis is medical care, which is also available free of charge to Tanzanian residents living in the vicinity and working in the camps. One or two articles of clothing may be given every year or two, typically to women, children, and students, and plastic sheeting for roofing has been distributed once in the last seven years. Houses are constructed by the refugees themselves. Primary school education is free for the refugees, as is the case for the Tanzanians, but secondary school education has been largely provided through the contributions and efforts of the refugees themselves.

23. *National Refugee Policy*, no. 16.

24. *National Refugee Policy*, no. 31.

25. For a more in-depth treatment of the problems of women and girl refugees, see Binaifer Nowrojee, "Sexual Violence, Gender Roles, and Displacement," and Susan Martin, "Justice, Women's Rights, and Forced Migration," both in this volume.

26. Pontifical Council for the Pastoral Care of Migrants and Itinerant People, *Refugees: A Challenge to Solidarity*, no. 24

27. Khoti Kamanga notes an increasing tendency "the world over . . . to 'securitise' international migration and deal with migrants with the legislative and institutional tools designed to address criminals."

28. Rutinwa and Kamanga, *The Impact of the Presence of Refugees in Northwest Tanzania*, 9.

29. Pontifical Council for the Pastoral Care of Migrants and Itinerant People, *Refugees: A Challenge to Solidarity*, no. 30.

30. Archbishop Ntamwana was accompanied by the late Bishop Bernard Bududira of Bururi Diocese, Burundi, and delegates from numerous dioceses in Burundi. Attendees on the Tanzanian side included Bishop Paul Ruzoka of Kigoma Diocese and Bishop Damian Dallu of Geita Diocese, together with delegates of the pastoral workers from the Kigoma and Rulenge refugee camps.

31. It was suggested that this balance could be found in the Tanzanian government's own stated firm commitment in its NRP to act proactively "in preventing and eradicating all phenomena that lead to refugees being created" (*National Refugee Policy*, no. 22). We noted that this commitment begins in the host country with respect for the refugees' rights, thus avoiding a premature repatriation, resulting from unfavorable conditions in the host country, that could endanger the refugees themselves and destabilize the country of origin. Such a commitment to refugee rights in exile would also inculcate a respect for human rights that the refugees would carry with them upon their return home.

32. Tanzania Episcopal Conference, *The Way Forward to Peace and Security, Good Governance and Development in The Great Lakes Region*, submitted to the UN–African Union International Conference on Peace, Security, Democracy, and Development in the Great Lakes Region, Dar es Salaam, November 2004 (Dar es Salaam: TEC, May 2005).

33. *National Refugee Policy*, no. 11.

34. For example, psychosocial counseling is offered in most of the refugee camps in Kibondo district by the Good Counsel Sisters, working with the Jesuit Refugee Service. Caritas Kigoma, on request, offers gender and development training to the Congolese women in the Nyarugusu and Lugufu refugee camps, including components such as gender justice, gender analysis, HIV/AIDS

awareness, group formation, leadership, and savings and credit procedures. Caritas Kigoma also offers counseling on a walk-in basis to refugee women in transit. The Justice and Peace Office of Kigoma Diocese offered training in psychosocial counseling and trauma healing for UNHCR key staff working in the camps. This training focused on the vulnerability of refugee women and girls, women's rights, the empowerment of women, and an increase in the power of resilience. However, despite plans to extend selected training, for example, to the Burundian women refugees in the Kasulu district camps, the needs exceed the available capacity.

35. See Paul Flamm, "Refugee Ministry: Towards Healing and Reconciliation," *Mission Studies,* April 1998, 104–17.

36. Derek Summerfield, "The Impact of War and Atrocity on Civilian Populations: Basic Principles for NGO Interventions and a Critique of Psycho-social Projects," *Network Paper 14, Relief and Rehabilitation Network,* April 1996, 29.

37. Nanzeen Kanji, "War and Children in Mozambique: Is International Aid Strengthening or Eroding Community-based Policies?" in *Community Development Journal* 25, no. 2 (1990): 103, 107, 108.

38. Each group responded to three questions: (a) What in your history and traditions would help you to promote peace and reconciliation?; (b) What obstacles remain to peace and reconciliation?; and (c) What still needs to be done to promote peace and reconciliation? These questions were, in turn, used in subsequent discussions in the Kasulu district refugee camps

39. The following Sunday, Archbishop Simon Ntamwana of Gitega celebrated an open air mass in Mwurire, the commune of origin of those who participated in the meeting at Kirimbi parish. During the mass, a mixed Hutu and Tutsi couple, who had been forced to separate because of the hostility between their two ethnic groups, brought their infant to be baptized in a highly symbolic gesture of their desire to return to normal Christian life together. Bishop Ntahondereye presented a gift of rice and beans, as well as a cassette with songs on peace and reconciliation from the refugees in the Kasulu region camps in Tanzania to the people of Bugendana, the IDP settlement near Mwurire, signifying their desire to join together with Bugendana people in working for peace and reconciliation. Songs from the cassette were later played, and the message accompanying the gifts was read, on the Burundi national radio.

40. For example, David Hollenbach insists in this volume that "the responsibility to take positive action that will resolve and prevent displacement calls for significant efforts to strengthen the regional and global institutions that address this issue. . . . Nongovernmental groups, such as humanitarian NGOs, church-related agencies, and indeed whole churches and religious communities also have essential roles to play in building up these new networks of cooperation." David Hollenbach, "Internally Displaced People, Sovereignty, and the Responsibility to Protect," in this volume.

41. Vatican II, "Gaudium et spes," no. 27, in *Vatican Council II: The Conciliar and Post Conciliar Documents,* rev. ed., ed. Austin Flannery, O.P. (Boston: St. Paul Books and Media, 1992).

42. *National Refugee Policy,* no.18.

43. "The Right to Freedom of Movement," in this volume.

44. Feyissa and Horn, "There Is More Than One Way of Dying," in this volume.

45. Landau, "Protection as Capability Expansion," in this volume.

46. Pontifical Council for the Pastoral Care of Migrants and Itinerant People, *Refugees: A Challenge to Solidarity,* no.15.

47. See, for example, P. M. Kamungi, J. S. Oketch, and C. Huggins, "Land Access and Refugee Repatriation: The Case of Burundi," *Eco-Conflicts* 3, no. 2 (September 2004); and ACTS and Chris Huggins, "Preventing Conflict through Improved Policies on Land Tenure, Natural Resource Rights, and Migration in the Great Lakes Region," *Eco-Conflicts* 3, no. 1 (January 2004).

48. See, for example, Orobator, "Key Ethical Issues in the Practices and Policies of Refugee-Serving NGOs and Churches," in this volume.

49. Deutsche Kommission Justicia et Pax, *Memory, Truth, Justice: Recommendations on Dealing with a Burdened Past* (Bonn, Germany, September 2004), 33.

50. See, for example, Flamm, "Refugee Ministry," 102.

51. See Orobator, "Key Ethical Issues," for a good description of the roles various actors play at different levels in advocating for refugee rights.

4

The Right to Freedom of Movement for Refugees in Uganda

Lucy Hovil and Moses Chrispus Okello

Refugees who are restricted to camps clearly do not enjoy freedom of movement as envisaged in international law. Yet the policy of encampment continues to be viewed as the right approach to managing large numbers of refugees in many countries across the world, including Uganda. Sacrificing freedom of movement, it is argued, is a necessary compromise in order to care better for the needs of refugees and their hosts. By keeping refugees in camps, security concerns are addressed, refugees are easier to "manage," and the temporary nature of their exile is accommodated. In order to challenge such assumptions, this chapter argues that freedom of movement is a basic human right that is, in turn, vital to the enjoyment of numerous other rights, so that by denying refugees the ability to move freely, their quality of life is jeopardized.

Arguments against the settlement policy will be made at two levels: first, the chapter will demonstrate that denying refugees freedom of movement does not make empirical sense, and second, we will show that this denial contravenes international law and for that reason is unacceptable. For the first argument, this chapter draws upon six years of research carried out in Uganda by the Refugee Law Project (RLP), which investigated the lives of refugees living in settlements, those who have opted out of the settlement structure and have decided to "self-settle," and their Ugandan hosts.

Encampment in Uganda: An Overview

In 2007 Uganda is host to 261,580 officially registered refugees from Rwanda, the Democratic Republic of Congo (DRC), and Sudan, the majority of whom have lived in exile for well over a decade.[1] Indeed, despite some recent progress made toward ensuring stability within the region, particularly in Sudan and the DRC, it is quite possible (and in the case of the DRC evident) that many of the region's conflicts could persist and that, therefore, population movement across borders and within the countries of the Great Lakes Region could continue for many years to come.[2] Yet despite both the duration and scale of displacement within and into Uganda, durable solutions continue to remain elusive for the majority of displaced persons. In the meantime, a de facto policy based on the encampment of refugees is pursued. Uganda's legal framework for the protection and assistance of refugees reflects this fact: refugees are confined to living in designated and enclosed geographical locations,[3] and receiving assistance is contingent upon living in such a settlement.[4] Most significantly, no refugees are technically allowed to leave the settlement unless they have obtained a permit from the camp commandant (a representative of the Office of the Prime Minister, Department for Disaster Preparedness and Refugees), who is the administrative head of the settlement.[5] This situation is sustained by UNHCR's conspiracy of silence, constituting tacit approval, of the policy of confining refugees in settlements, even when UNHCR says it supports the pursuit of "all feasible opportunities for durable solutions."[6]

However, despite the arguments used by policymakers to justify the maintenance of refugees in camps, RLP research has demonstrated the extent to which refugees do not experience physical security or adequate livelihood opportunities within the settlement structure.[7] For instance, refugees have been vulnerable to attacks by armed rebel groups, including the Lord's Resistance Army (LRA), the now-defunct West Nile Bank Front (WNBF), and the Uganda National Resistance Front (UNRF). Indeed, as RLP Working Paper No. 5 demonstrates, settlements actually create an easy collective target for rebel groups.[8] For example, in July 1996 LRA rebels attacked the Achol-Pii refugee settlement, killing at least one hundred refugees and wounding several others. Despite early warning of this attack, there was little government response and, in August 2002, the rebels launched another attack on the same settlement, killing at least eighty refugees and wounding and abducting several others. Although the settlement has now been closed, the refugees have since been relocated to other settlements within the war-stricken greater northern region, which remains vulnerable to attack.

This insecurity is not limited to settlements in northern Uganda. Research conducted in the northern Uganda districts of Yumbe and Adjumani in 2005 and 2006, respectively, reveals multiple incidences of secondary displacement to other parts of these districts induced by the activities of rebel groups. Indeed, in Adjumani such threats to life, caused by LRA rebels operating around the Zoka forest belt, have led to large-scale involuntary relocation of refugees from some settlements into areas towards the center of the district. Some of the settlements abandoned by these refugees have since been reoccupied by internally displaced people (IDPs), who now have to assume the risks previously faced by refugees. As UNHCR recently admitted, "the threat of military infiltration into settlements is of continuing concern."[9] As such, threats to life associated with camps and settlements are not only limited to refugees and IDPs; they also point toward a broader problem regarding the conceptualization of threats to state security or the lack thereof.

At the same time, few refugees living in the settlements are able to reach the degree of self-reliance expected of them while their freedom of movement continues to be restricted. For instance, the fact that they are prevented from readily accessing markets impairs their ability to engage in the local economy, and self-reliance within the settlement structure has become a contradiction in terms. Furthermore, given the often-protracted nature of displacement, it is becoming increasingly questionable whether the emphasis on controlled settlements, as opposed to integration, is justifiable.[10]

Self-settlement

Owing to the hardships and restrictions associated with living in settlements, thousands of refugees in Uganda have chosen to opt out of the settlement structure and "self-settle"; they are now scattered in rural and urban areas all over the country because of a combination of factors, including the economic and security hardships associated with living in camps and the bureaucratic barriers to obtaining movement permits.[11] There are no reliable statistics on the numbers of self-settled refugees in Uganda. At best, they have an ambiguous legal status. A significant section of this population consists of refugees who migrated in the late 1950s and the 1960s and who have since been "integrated" among the national population. They therefore enjoy a status equivalent to that of Ugandans but have never had their legal status in the country reviewed or formalized. The ambiguity regarding the legal status of this population emanates in part from Article 12 of the 1995 Constitution of Uganda, which does not provide clear guidance for registration as a citizen. This is due, in part, to its narrow understanding of what should constitute durable solutions.

While the government of Uganda claims to use the 1951 Refugee Convention as guideline for determining refugee status and for the protection of those granted asylum, in practice only those who live in settlements are considered to be refugees.[12] This narrow definition of refugees was established in the Control of Alien Refugees Act of 1960; the provision has since been pasted into the new Refugee Act of 2006. Thus, not only do the self-settled forego assistance by opting out of the settlement structures, they also "lose" their status as refugees (although, clearly, this is not the case under international law.)

Despite these limiting factors, Refugee Law Project research has shown the extent to which, while encamped refugees are characterized by the word "burden," self-settled refugees suggest an alternative in which refugees engage in the local economy and live among the national population. For instance, a refugee living in Uganda's West Nile district talked of why he had chosen to opt out of the settlement structure:

> I knew that if I went to a camp, it would be difficult for me to make enough money for my children to go to school. When I arrived these Ugandans here had been with us in Kajo Keji. So when I asked them to assist me with some land, they gave me land. Since then I've been staying with them. I dig cassava, groundnuts and cotton. I also have a retail business selling beer and *waragi* [gin] . . . I pay tax because I stay with the citizens. I very much want to be able to move freely. That's why I pay tax. If I'm in a camp, I have to wait for permission from the Camp Commandant and this would affect my business.[13]

Indeed, it is clear that, given the right conditions, refugees can participate and contribute to the country's development.[14] Findings have also shown that refugees who have chosen to self-settle are widely accepted within local government structures, pay taxes, contribute to the local economy, and have better coping strategies for eventually returning to their home country when the time arises, if they so choose.[15] As the findings conclude, "Rather than being a burden, [refugees] are an asset to the communities in which they live. They are able to make decisions about their own security, and have been able to use skills and knowledge that they brought with them. Most importantly, they are planning for the day that they can return to their homeland."[16]

Legal Framework

Empirical data on both the problems associated with refugee camps and the corresponding opportunities exploited by those who have chosen to self-settle are reinforced by a legal framework in which freedom of movement is seen not only as a vital protection issue during all phases of displacement but also as a freedom that, when exercised, obtains durable solutions. The right to freedom of movement is, however, one of the first rights to be sacrificed during the reception of asylum seekers and for an extended period after refugee status determination. According to Ann Schmidt, "even though the cases where refugee movement outside designated areas is strictly impossible are rare, legal restriction and even lax and arbitrary enforcement have large implications for refugee livelihoods."[17] On his part, Jamal Arafat has noted that "camps may serve an important emergency protection function but, in the long run, they deny refugees the freedoms that would enable them to lead productive lives."[18]

Protections of Refugees' Freedom of Movement under International Law

Many sources of international human rights and humanitarian law—both global and regional—provide broad protections for individuals' freedom of movement. In most cases these conventions do not discriminate between citizens and aliens and implore states, by implication, to include refugees within the ambit of these general protections. The most authoritative source from which this can be derived is the Universal Declaration of Human Rights. Article 13 of the Universal Declaration states clearly that "everyone has the right to freedom of movement and residence within the borders of each State."[19] The rights conferred by the Declaration—including freedom of movement—are universally applicable, without discrimination. Article 2 states, "Everyone is entitled to all the rights and freedoms set forth in this Declaration, without distinction of any kind, such as race, colour, sex, language, religion, political or other opinion, national or social origin, property, birth or other status."[20] Accordingly, the rights conferred under Article 13 must extend to refugees.

In particular, international (refugee) law accords asylum seekers and refugees protection through three interrelated subcomponents of freedom of movement, which correspond with the different phases of displacement: in deciding whether or not to flee the country of origin (the freedom to leave or remain in one's country); in the country of asylum (the right to move within the borders of a state, to choose a place of residence and to *nonrefoulement*); and at the end of asylum (the right to voluntary return, which includes access to accurate and objective information regarding the conditions in the country of origin).

With respect to international human rights law, the International Covenant on Civil and Political Rights (ICCPR), in Article 2, has laid down the lowest common denominator for the enjoyment of the right to freedom of movement by all without discrimination. This article has been interpreted by the Human Rights Committee of the United Nations, in General Comment No. 15, as requiring, as a general rule, that "the rights of the Covenant must be guaranteed without discrimination between citizens and aliens. Aliens receive the benefit of the general requirement of non-discrimination in respect of the rights guaranteed in the Covenant, as provided for in article 2 thereof. This guarantee applies to aliens and citizens alike."[21]

In this general comment, the Human Rights Committee tackles the broader question of the position of aliens under the ICCPR and provides some useful information about their right to freedom of movement. The general rule is that each one of the rights of the Covenant must be guaranteed without discrimination between citizens and aliens.[22] While countries may restrict aliens' entry across their borders, "once aliens are allowed to enter the territory of a State party they are entitled to the rights set out in the Covenant."[23]

More specifically, Article 12 of the ICCPR accords every individual lawfully present in a state's territory the right to liberty of movement and choice of residence.[24] This article has been elaborated upon by the Human Rights Committee's General Comment 27,[25] which describes "liberty of movement" as "an indispensable condition for the free development of a person."[26] Indeed, in the general debate on protection of refugees' rights, scholars have long concluded that freedom of movement is a fundamental prerequisite for the enjoyment of other human rights found in general and specific human rights treaties and conventions.

The committee has further elaborated that once aliens are lawfully within the territory of a state, their freedom of movement within and their right to leave that territory may only be restricted in accordance with Article 12, paragraph 3. In this regard, however, differences in treatment of aliens and nationals, or between different categories of aliens, even if justifiable under national law, have to be necessary and reasonable, since such restrictions must, inter alia, be consistent with the other rights recognized in the Covenant. A state party cannot, by restraining an alien or deporting him to a third country, arbitrarily prevent his return to his own country, according to Article 12, paragraph 4.[27]

Thus, the Human Rights Committee has declared that any restrictions on movement must be carefully tailored in several important ways: "Permissible limitations . . . must not nullify the principle of liberty of movement, and are governed by the requirement of necessity provided for in article 12, paragraph 3, and by the need for consistency with the other rights recognized in the Covenant."[28] Article 12, paragraph 3 states that the *only* legitimate restrictions on freedom of movement are those that "are provided by law, are necessary to protect national security, public order (*ordre public*), public health or morals or the rights and freedoms of others, and are consistent with the other rights recognized in the present Covenant."[29]

According to Khoti Kamanga, while the wording of Article 12, paragraph 3 is fairly ambiguous and therefore can be interpreted widely, courts of law in jurisdictions such as the European Community have elaborated on the content so as to eliminate any controversy regarding its meaning. Granted, the drafters of the ICCPR did not accord freedom of movement nonderogable status, implying that there are circumstances, as demonstrated above, under which it can be restricted. According to the Human Rights Committee, however, restrictions notwithstanding, the overarching right to free movement must be preserved.[30] Moreover, the committee has denounced unnecessary "bureaucratic barriers" on free movement, including "provisions requiring individuals to apply for permission to change their residence or to seek the approval of the local authorities of the place of destination, as well as delays in processing such written applications."[31]

According to past RLP research, a number of the same "bureaucratic barriers" prohibited by the Human Rights Committee are currently curtailing refugees' freedom of movement and choice of residence. For instance, in order to leave settlements, refugees have to obtain permission from the settlement commandant, who is in most cases several kilometers away from the refugees' places of residence within the settlement. Because of this system, which does not allow for decentralization of the process for obtaining permission to travel, refugees often have to make a double journey—to seek permission and then to organize the proposed travel—and have to meet the financial implications of this process themselves. The requirement for centralization of refugee registration, if only to track movements for purposes of protection, may be a matter of erring on the side of caution. However, to do so in a way that contravenes refugees' rights is clearly to contravene international obligations to refugees.

Moreover, refugees' freedom of movement is accorded additional protection under refugee-specific conventions and treaties. The Refugee Convention extends the enjoyment of freedom of movement to refugees.[32] Article 26 stipulates, "Each Contracting State shall accord to refugees lawfully in its territory the right to choose their place of residence and to move freely within its territory, subject to any regulations applicable to aliens generally in the same circumstances."[33] According to the 1951 Convention, the phrase "in the same circumstances" implies that "any requirements (including requirements as to length and conditions of sojourn or residence) which the particular individual would have to fulfil for the enjoyment of the right in question, if he were not a refugee, must be fulfilled by him, with the exception of requirements which by their nature a refugee is incapable of fulfilling."[34] In other words, the movement of refugees may not be restricted to any greater degree than for other aliens.

Within the African continent, the African Charter on Human and Peoples' Rights (ACHPR), the very article that grants the right to seek and obtain asylum also guarantees everyone "the right to freedom of movement and residence within the border of a State provided he abides by the law."[35] Just like the ICCPR, the ACHPR grants refugees the right to freedom of movement and at the same time limits it. As noted above, however, both instruments emphasize the fundamental nature of this freedom, and in addition to the explicit safeguards outlined above, international sources of law incorporated in the ACHPR guarantee multiple rights and freedoms whose full exercise would be substantially curtailed without a baseline level of mobility. Although the Organization of African Unity Convention on the Specific Aspects of Refugee Problems in Africa (henceforth the 1969 OAU Convention) does not have provisions explicitly granting refugees freedom of movement, it nonetheless recognizes the necessity to resort to the positions of other regional and international bodies regarding the protection of refugees in interpreting this right of refugees. Such interpretation implies respect for the principles embodied in, and the explicit provisions of, the ACHPR and the Universal Declaration on Human Rights.

Clearly, therefore, the right to freedom of movement and choice of residence is protected under multiple sources of international law, ranging from the universal to the regional. Although these conventions, especially the ACHPR, grant states wide interpretive discretion, any restrictions must be carefully tailored so as to prevent discriminatory treatment, to preserve enjoyment of the broader principle of free movement, and to restrict movement only in the event of necessity. This principle is embodied in Human Rights Committee's General Comment No. 15, which not only requires states to treat all individuals equally within its borders but also to carefully justify any restrictions on the movement of aliens: "Once an alien is lawfully within a territory, his freedom of movement within the territory and his right to leave that territory may only be restricted in accordance with article 12, paragraph 3. Differences in treatment in this regard between aliens and nationals, or between different categories of aliens, need to be justified under article 12, paragraph 3. . . . Such restrictions must, inter alia, be consistent with the other rights recognized in the Covenant."[36]

Uganda's Refugee Act of 2006

On May 24, 2006, the Ugandan government repealed the obsolete Control of Alien Refugees Act (CARA), until then the legal foundation for the protection and assistance of refugees, replacing it with a new Refugee Act of 2006.[37] Until its nullification, the Office of the Prime Minister, UNHCR, and other practitioners had long distanced themselves from the CARA, arguing that they relied upon international refugee and human rights law in their practice and programming. As noted in the new Refugee Act, the CARA was substantially, institutionally, and procedurally flawed in its assumptions and provisions. The intention of the Refugee Act of 2006, therefore, was to bring refugee law and practice into conformity with the Bill of Rights in the Constitution of Uganda, give effect to international law conventions, and to incorporate the act into Uganda's domestic policies, practices, and procedures regarding Refugee Status Determination and guidelines for the delivery of humanitarian assistance.[38] Part V of the Refugee Act entitles refugees to the rights conferred through the Geneva Convention of 1951 and the OAU Convention of 1969 and any other conventions relating to the rights of refugees, subject to reservations entered by the government to international conventions regarding the protection and assistance of refugees.[39]

Uganda's government has made several reservations, understandings, and declarations to the 1951 Convention but none on freedom of movement, implying that the framers of the act recognize the significance of freedom of movement and that granting refugees the right in question does not contradict the obligation to preserve *ordre public*, public health, and indeed national security. In theory, therefore, the act provides that recognized refugees should receive "at least the same treatment as is generally accorded to aliens under the Constitution and any other law in force in Uganda; and be entitled to privileges that may be granted under the laws of Uganda by any administrative agency or organ of government."[40]

Yet the new law, lauded on the African continent as a progressive piece of legislation, stands at odds with some of its stated objectives and, in fact, refrains from rectifying or amending some of the misguided assumptions in the CARA. In its repeal and transitional provisions, the new act allows for some provisions of the CARA to remain in force insofar as they do not conflict with each other. One such provision might be section 14 of the CARA, which makes it an offense for anyone, other than a refugee, to enter settlements without "special" or "general" permission from authorized officials. Indeed, such restrictions on entry by outsiders and exit for refugees define the negative and restrictive manner in which settlements have been viewed.

Moreover, the legislation retains the settlement policy and places undue restrictions on the right of refugees to free movement. For instance, under section 44 (1) b, the act enjoins the responsible minister to "designate places or areas on public land to be transit centres or refugee settlements for the purposes of local settlement and integration of refugees." While section 44 (2) grants refugees the option of staying outside the "designated places or areas," such an application is incumbent upon the discretion of the minister or other authorized official and is not guaranteed. Although in practice some refugees have generally been able to self-settle, the criteria for refugee assistance exclude those who choose this option from being helped and indeed requires them to prove self-sufficiency before they are allowed residence outside settlements.

The assumptions embedded in this encampment policy are entrenched in section 30 (1) of the act, which grants refugees the freedom to move but subjects such freedom, in section 30 (2), to "Reasonable restrictions specified in the laws of Uganda, or directives issued by the commissioner, which applies to aliens generally in the same circumstances, especially on grounds of national security, public order, public health, public morals or the protection of the rights and freedoms of others."[41] Such limitations on the freedom of movement do not cease when refugees opt to stay out of the "designated place or area": a refugee authorized to stay somewhere other than a designated place may be required to report from time to time to the authorities of his or her new area of origin.[42] This restriction does not apply to other Ugandan nationals or indeed to aliens more generally. In other words, refugees who are able to move out of the settlement remain under surveillance and are still duty bound—albeit permissively—to account for their activities and movements.

The "laws of Uganda" as defined in section 30 include the Constitution as well as the Immigration Act. The Immigration Act does not provide clarification on the notion of "aliens generally in the same circumstances" in the Refugee Act, nor does it specify the rights of aliens generally. Presumably, this implies that aliens in fact enjoy all rights conferred under the Constitution, with the exception of those restricted to Ugandans. The Constitution of Uganda, however, limits the enjoyment of freedom of movement to Ugandans to the exclusion of aliens generally and indeed refugees.[43] This implies that refugees, just like aliens, may have their freedom restricted from time to time. As noted above, however, one of the objectives of the Refugee Act is to bring Uganda's refugee law into conformity with the Constitution and to give effect to international conventions relating to the treatment of refugees. The dual objectives of the act thus bring Article 29, section 2 of the Constitution into direct conflict with the obligations freely assumed by Uganda when signing international treaties. Obviously, the Constitution, being the fundamental basis of the Ugandan legal system, takes precedence over any conflicting subsidiary legislation, including the Refugee Act. This suggests no conflict between the act and the Constitution but a real tension between the Constitution and international refugee law.

Moreover, since the act does not provide guidance as to the meaning of the phrase "reasonable restrictions," officials have generally interpreted it to include confinement in camps—a situation that is analogous to detention. Moreover, just like the CARA, and as noted by UNHCR, "the Refugee Act and international instruments are not yet well understood and hence not properly implemented."[44]

In order for the act (and indeed the Constitution) to be consistent with the international treaties it incorporates, "reasonable restrictions" must be precise and rise out of substantial "necessity." Even if settlements successfully dealt with security concerns, those concerns would have to be sufficiently grave so as to rise to the level of necessity in order to warrant restrictions. Moreover, the RLP has highlighted how substantial security risks for refugees living in camps drive many of them to leave the settlements. Integrating refugees into host communities rather than segregating them into camps, the RLP has argued, will bring substantial benefits both to refugees and to local Ugandan communities rather than posing a heightened security threat.[45] As it currently stands, therefore, the refugee settlement policy and its attendant restrictions on freedom of movement have not achieved the standards required under international law, and consequently, Uganda has breached the rights of refugees under international refugee and human rights law.

Freedom of Movement: A Legal and Moral Imperative

Given the extent to which international refugee law has been flouted in practice, debates on the subject gravitate around a stricter refugee protection regime that potentially includes a second protocol to the 1951 Convention or indeed drafting a new convention which plugs the holes in the current one. This, while desirable, is nonetheless a needless imperative. There is no necessity for another refugee convention that will inevitably take years to negotiate and that will no doubt encounter stiff resistance from states and other actors now more concerned with state security and so have further mystified refugee protection and assistance by linking it to the "war on terror." Indeed, in the current environment, violations of additional refugee rights have emerged, particularly through the manipulation of international law to allow for detention without trial—perhaps the most severe means of limiting freedom of movement—of refugees, asylum seekers, and other "undesired" aliens. This has been done through the creation of new legal categories such as "illegal combatants" and the expansion of the notion of "exceptional circumstances" to allow the state a wide "margin of appreciation" in the treatment of refugees.

Yet this is not to suggest that international refugee law and international human rights and humanitarian law is not developed fully enough to safeguard, in addition to freedom of movement, human rights in general as well. Indeed, as noted above, through the use of only a few conventions, most if not all subcomponents of international law—international human rights and humanitarian law, international refugee law and international criminal law—have come of age and therefore provide a vast array of protections for refugees, including criminalization of the very fact of displacement.[46] The International Bill of Rights, more specific human rights conventions, and particularly regional apparatus for the protection of human rights provide a sophisticated infrastructure from which to discern the full range of mechanisms in place. Indeed, by allowing refugee rights to be enforced through national, regional, and international jurisdictions, the problem is no longer a lack of conventions but rather the absence of the will to abide by or enforce their provisions. Moreover, it is evident that refugee rights are in fact human rights and that regardless of their status, refugees are first and foremost human beings, who are only due additional protections because of the specific circumstances in which they find themselves. In other words, the question of the protection of refugees' freedom of movement is no longer only a legal issue; it is a moral and ethical imperative.

Ethical Implications

In addition to the persuasiveness of the legal framework, issues of freedom of movement touch upon the very essence of human dignity. Regardless of the extent to which such freedoms are enshrined in law, the need for human beings to make their own choices is fundamental to every other aspect of their lives. Conversely, refugees who are not allowed freedom of movement are, effectively, locked-up members of society. This form of repression relates to all other aspects of their lives: by being confined to camps they are unable to realize their worth as human beings, and the lack of dignity entailed in having to flee one's home in the first place is perpetuated throughout exile.

As the first section of this chapter outlined, what this means in reality is that refugees are given a small plot of land on which to farm—regardless of whether or not they were farmers before they fled their homes—and are told to become self-reliant over a period of time set by the government or UNHCR. Without access to markets, they are unable to sell any surplus produce they have, and when the land becomes fallow—normally after four years, which is also often the moment when their rations have been completely stopped—they have no mechanisms to cope. Not only are they unable to move, either officially through the government's restriction on self-relocation to new sites within a settlement or other settlements, or to an alternative place that might offer them better opportunities; they have also often become so reliant on the assistance structures that they no longer have the courage or will to make their own decisions.

Thus, restrictions on freedom of movement become increasingly problematic as exile moves from the initial emergency phase to a more protracted situation, indeed lasting over the course of a search for durable solutions. The need at times to have reception centers or camps for the purpose of receiving large numbers of refugees when they first arrive in the country is reasonable. But that does not mean that this should become the status quo in the long term. The transition from emergency to development needs to be acknowledged; by warehousing refugees year after year and keeping them reliant on sporadic assistance, the government and UNHCR simply ensure that, rather than alleviating the situation, they simply prolong and even exacerbate it. They ensure that refugees are suspended in a perpetual emergency, unable to return to their homeland and unable to attain a decent quality of life in exile.

Thus, while it is acknowledged that exile is, by definition, suboptimal, it is unnecessarily exacerbated by the structures that are then forced upon the lives of refugees. Furthermore, the restrictions placed on their lives become self-perpetuating as refugees lose the ability to dictate their own circumstances. In recognition of this fact, the RLP has deliberately used research methods that incorporate refugees' voices in situations where their rights and voices are otherwise stifled. Furthermore, by returning repeatedly to the same places, we have sought to ensure a "deep understanding" of how refugees interpret their circumstances, working to assure that our research is accurate and, thus, ethical. Analyzing our findings through a human rights lens then reinforces this methodology.

Similarly, advocating for the freedom of movement for refugees in an environment crowded by multiple actors—the governments of both the host country and the country of origin, UNHCR, Implementing/Operational Partners (IPs/OPs), the donor community, and refugees themselves—invariably implies confronting competing, and sometimes conflicting, institutional mandates. An illustration involving just two of these organizations demonstrates the complexity of the problem. Whenever UNHCR is confronted regarding its support for the encampment policy, it rightly argues that policymaking is the prerogative of the host country's government. On the other hand, however, the Office of the Prime Minister in Uganda has often argued that UNHCR will not provide assistance to refugees who are not in a settlement. Clearly, such a situation can be perpetuated only by a lack of interest in the situation of refugees and the implication of such stances.

Needless to say, it is important to understand the legal, political, and economic context within which policymakers operate and the constraints on making certain decisions at a national and international level. However, it is also ethically imperative to keep the lives of our clients at the front of every decision and not to imperil the livelihoods of thousands of individuals in order to fulfill century-old bureaucratic rules. Understanding the context—which includes the mandates of organizations within the country, the political environment of the country, and international pressures such as diplomacy—might require adopting less doctrinal or adversarial mechanisms for advocating for all rights of refugees and adopting "soft," more persuasive approaches. In contexts such as Uganda, however, unofficial and less public mechanisms have been used to play these domains of possible action against each other. The net outcome is the abdication of all from legal and political obligations entered into in relation to refugees.

Curiously enough, debate regarding refugee freedom of movement is never as impassioned concerning exile as such as it is in the course of discussions of the search for durable solutions. In other words, free movement is only genuinely free in the context of conditions under which repatriation can take place, a setting in which our moral and legal obligations towards assistance and protection of refugees are perceived to be diminishing or vanishing. The numerous programs adopted in order to enhance refugee return—for instance, "go-and-see-visits," initiatives stressing "voluntary return," and the provision of country-of-origin information to help refugees make "informed" decisions—are a clear manifestation of the double standard involved in the refugee protection regime.

It is hoped that policymakers will come to see refugees as individual human beings rather than as a homogenous group with a surfeit of needs. While it is vital to advocate for change within the legal structures, the empirical data speaks for itself concerning the harsh conditions placed on refugees. Regardless of the legal structures, from an ethical point of view it is hard to justify confining refugees to camps, as it robs them of the most basic aspects of human dignity.

Conclusion

This chapter has shown that confining refugees to camps is unacceptable from both a legal and empirical point of view. Given that freedom of movement is fundamental to refugees' ability to enjoy numerous other rights, it is legally and ethically questionable to confine them within designated settlements. From extensive research into the lives of refugees, it is clear that settlements offer refugees neither the economic opportunities nor the physical security that are supposed to justify encampment. At the same time, the lives of self-settled refugees demonstrate the possibility of local integration; they offer an alternative approach to exile that cannot be ignored. As demonstrated above, the legal regime for the protection of refugee rights in general has enough safeguards; they merely lack integration into programming activities, sometimes by default but more often by design. Moreover, the enthusiasm with which free movement is emphasized during the course of return is a clear manifestation that the problem of free movement is not unsolved for want of a feasible alternative to the settlement structure, but rather for a lack of creative application of and, therefore, adherence to existing local and international laws. As some have argued, the settlement structure was designed to encourage "orderly repatriation" and that therefore observance of the right of freedom of movement is only encouraged during the "end of exile."

Notes

We gratefully acknowledge the assistance of Aliza Cover, who in the course of her internship with the Refugee Law Project, did background research for this chapter.

1. See United Nations High Commissioner for Refugees, Global Appeal 2007, available from http://www.unhcr.org/static/publ/ga2007toc.htm.
2. In a recent Update, UNHCR noted that "following the fighting between FARDC and Nkunda

rebel forces on Saturday, December 16, 2006, three thousand Congolese crossed into Kisoro district (in Western Uganda)." See United Nations High Commissioner for Refugees (UNHCR) Update, Congolese Refugees Influx into Uganda, January 2007. While the UNHCR has noted that many of these refugees have returned to the DRC, the situation in the DRC remains critical and can allow only for cyclical population movement.

3. The only official exceptions to this are the 219 refugees currently on UNHCR's "urban caseload" in Kampala, who received limited assistance. See Jesse Bernstein, "Drop in the Ocean": Assistance and Protection for Forced Migrants in Kampala, Refugee Law Project, Working Paper no. 16, May 2005, available from http://www.refugeelawproject.org/resources/papers/workingpapers/index.htm.

4. The term "settlement" is often used interchangeably with that of "camp" as, in effect, there is little difference between the two.

5. See, for instance, Lucy Hovil, Free to Stay, Free to Go? Movement, Seclusion, and Integration of Refugees in Moyo District, Refugee Law Project, Working Paper no. 4, May 2002, available from http://www.refugeelawproject.org/resources/papers/workingpapers/index.htm..

6. See UNHCR, Global Appeal 2007, 142

7. See, for example, Refugee Law Project Working Papers nos. 2, 3, 4, 7, 14, and 18, available from http://www.refugeelawproject.org/resources/papers/workingpapers/index.htm.

8. See Lucy Hovil and Alex Moorehead, War as Normal: The Impact of Violence on the Lives of Displaced Communities, Refugee Law Project Working Paper no. 5, June 2002, available from http://www.refugeelawproject.org/resources/papers/workingpapers/index.htm.; and Emmanuel Bagenda and Lucy Hovil, "Sudanese Refugees in Northern Uganda: From One Conflict to the Next," Forced Migration Review 16 (January 2003).

9. See UNHCR, Global Appeal 2007.

10. For a critique of the self-reliance strategy, see Sarah Dryden Peterson and Lucy Hovil, "Local Integration as a Durable Solution: Refugees, Host Populations, and Education in Uganda," UNHCR, New Issues in Refugee Research, Working Paper no. 93, September 2003.

11. See Working Paper no. 18.

12. CARA 1960, sec. 8.

13. Interview with refugee man, Metu Village, Moyo district, May 29, 2004, as quoted in Lucy Hovil, "Self-settled Refugees in Uganda: An Alternative Approach to Displacement?" Journal of Refugee Studies 20, no. 4 (December 2007): 599–629.

14. See Lucy Hovil, "Self Settled Refugees in Uganda," and Refugee Law Project Final Narrative Report to the John D. and Catherine T. MacArthur Foundation, October 2005.

15. Ibid.

16. Ibid.

17. Anna Schmidt, FMO Thematic Guide: Camps versus Settlements, Oxford, UK, University of Oxford, 2005, CD-ROM.

18. Arafat Jamal, "Camps and Freedoms: Long-term Refugee Situations in Africa," Forced Migration Review 16 (January 2003). Arafat goes on to note that protracted refugee situations exist for political reasons (4).

19. Universal Declaration of Human Rights, Art. 13, para. 1.

20. Ibid., Art. 2.

21. Human Rights Committee, General Comment 15, "The Position of Aliens under the Covenant" (Twenty-seventh session, 1986), Compilation of General Comments and General Recommendations Adopted by Human Rights Treaty Bodies, UN Doc. HRI\GEN\1\Rev.1 at 18 (1994).

22. Human Rights Committee, General Comment 15, paras. 1–2, "The Position of Aliens under the Covenant" (Twenty-seventh session, 1986), Compilation of General Comments and

General Recommendations Adopted by Human Rights Treaty Bodies, UN Doc. HRI\GEN\1\ Rev.1 at 18 (1994), http://www1.umn.edu/humanrts/gencomm/hrcom15.htm (accessed April 19, 2007).

23. Ibid., para. 6.

24. International Covenant on Civil and Political Rights, Art. 12, para. 1.

25. Human Rights Committee, General Comment 27, Freedom of movement (Art. 12), UN Doc CCPR/C/21/Rev.1/Add.9 (1999), http://www1.umn.edu/humanrts/gencomm/hrcom27 .htm (accessed April 19, 2007).

26. Ibid., para. 1.

27. Human Rights Committee, General Comment 27, Freedom of Movement (Art. 12), UN Doc. CCPR/C/21/Rev.1/Add.9 (1999).

28. Ibid., para. 2.

29. Ibid., Art. 12, para. 3.

30. Ibid., para. 13. "States should always be guided by the principle that the restrictions must not impair the essence of the right . . . ; the relation between right and restriction, between norm and exception, must not be reversed. The laws authorizing the application of restrictions should use precise criteria and may not confer unfettered discretion on those charged with their execution."

31. Ibid., para. 17.

32. The guarantees of the 1951 Convention are made applicable to present-day refugees through the 1967 Protocol.

33. Convention Relating to the Status of Refugees, Art. 26. Adopted on July 28, 1951, by the United Nations Conference of Plenipotentiaries on the Status of Refugees and Stateless Persons convened under General Assembly resolution 429 (V) of December 14, 1950, entry into force April 22, 1954, in accordance with Article 43 (hereinafter "1951 Refugee Convention").

34. 1951 Refugee Convention, Article 6.

35. See Article 12 of the African Charter on Human and Peoples' Rights (henceforth the African Charter or ACHPR), adopted on June 17, 1981, by the Eighteenth Assembly of the Heads of State of Government of the Organization of African Unity and entered into force on October 21, 1986.

36. Ibid., para. 8.

37. While the Refugee Act of 2006 assented to by the president of Uganda on May 24, 2006, is the de facto law regulating the protection of refugees in Uganda, the minister for disaster preparedness and refugees is yet to indicate the date on which it will come into effect as required by Part I (2), providing for the date of commencement of the Act.

38. Ibid., Preamble.

39. Ibid., sec. 28.

40. Ibid., sec. 29 (d).

41. Ibid., sec. 30 (2).

42. Ibid., sec. 44 (3).

43. Constitution of Uganda, 1995, Article 29 (2)(a).

44. UNHCR, Global Appeal for Uganda 2007, available from http://www.unhcr.org/home .org/home/PUBL/455443a1b.pdf.

45. Moses Chrispus Okello, Noah Gottschalk, and Katinka Ridderbos, *There Are No Refugees in This Area: Self-Settled Refugees in Koboko*, RLP Working Paper No. 18 (November 2005), available from http://www.refugeelawproject.org/resources/papers/workingpapers/index.htm.

46. See, for instance, Article 7 of the Statute of the International Criminal Court, which elaborates on the elements of "crimes against humanity" and "war crimes."

5

The Plight of Urban Refugees in Nairobi, Kenya

John Burton Wagacha and John Guiney

Many urban refugees—refugees who flee to urban areas—live in dangerous and inhumane conditions. An example of the extreme danger that confronts some refugees is the incident of the two Rwandan children, aged nine and ten, who were murdered on the night of April 17, 2002, at a "secure residence" run by the Office of the United Nations High Commissioner for Refugees (UNHCR) in Nairobi, Kenya. Their throats were slit; their mother was injured. The attack occurred one day after they had been accepted for resettlement.[1]

Few refugees living in Nairobi face such serious danger and loss of life, but many do cope with a devastating plight. They have fled conflict and persecution, only to be met with further insecurity. Largely unacknowledged by the government and underassisted by UNHCR and other agencies, urban refugees in Nairobi frequently live in extreme poverty, enduring squalid housing conditions and often lacking access to food, clean water, medical care, jobs, or education. Women and children often are subject to sexual abuse, and most refugees in Nairobi have to deal constantly with police harassment and arbitrary arrests.

The Historical Context

A brief overview of the historical refugee context in Kenya provides background and insight to the urban refugee reality. Prior to 1991, Kenya hosted a refugee population estimated to be fifteen thousand, mostly from Uganda, Ethiopia, southern Sudan, and the Great Lakes Region. They mainly lived in small camps in northern Kenya (Mandera, El Wak, and Walda) and in urban settings such as Thika, Nairobi and Mombasa.[2] However, at the height of the refugee influx in 1991 that resulted from the collapse of Somalia and the fall of the Ethiopian government, the number of refugees rose drastically to an estimated 370,000 to 700,000.³ The majority of refugees were Somalis, who were assigned prima facie refugee status, as provided by the Organization of African Unity (OAU) Refugee Convention of 1969.

Kenya was signatory to all the main international conventions on refugees: the Geneva Convention Relating to the Status of Refugees of 1951, the Protocol Relating to the Status of Refugees of 1967, and the OAU Convention Governing the Specific Aspects of Refugee Protection in Africa of 1969. Nevertheless, the country had no administrative and domestic legal framework nor the capacity to handle the rapidly changing situation.⁴ Before 1991 the Kenyan government used an ad hoc administrative refugee status system to recognize refugees. Generally, refugees were allowed to integrate locally and enjoy the rights to work, to an education, and to freedom of movement. However, with the increase of regional conflicts and the massive influx of refugees beginning in 1991, the Kenyan government surrendered its role in refugee status determination to UNHCR. Even with emergency support from UNHCR and international NGOs, the high number of refugees strained social services, creating competition and conflict between refugees and the local population over food, relief, housing, health care, and security.

Fear of insecurity and instability permeated government circles in Kenya as a consequence of major domestic political changes that were occurring. At the time of the new influx of refugees, Kenya was experiencing drought and internal unrest accompanied by cries for a multiparty system, growing tribalism, and increasing corruption. These resulted in a withdrawal of donor funding and increased demands by the World Bank and the international community for greater accountability, transparency, and freedom of the press.⁵ Porous borders, increased trade in small arms, and widespread banditry existed in northeastern Kenya, where Kenyan Somalis ordinarily resided. From the 1960s to 1990, a state of emergency existed in that area of Kenya.

An ideology for a greater Somalia was embraced by many Kenyan Somalis who sought a country of Somalia that would extend to all areas occupied by Somali-speaking communities in Kenya and Ethiopia.⁶ This added to the fear within the Kenyan government that since Somalis' first loyalty was to the Somali state, they posed a security risk to the nation-state of Kenya. In 1992 another influx of refugees began in the northwest of Kenya with the arrival of "the lost boys and girls" from southern Sudan.

Coping with the great influx of Somali refugees and the accompanying fear of increased insecurity, the Kenyan government adopted a general encampment policy. In 1993 the government designated Dadaab and Kakuma as the only refugee camps in the country. By 1997 the Kenyan government had closed all other camps on the coast and in other parts of Kenya, and most refugees were transferred to these two camps. The government of Kenya enhanced its policy of "light security intervention" by adopting measures to deal with ongoing banditry attacks and any other insurgence.

As the refugee influx continued, significant problems arose. For instance, in 1992 the United States Committee for Refugees (USCR) charged that UNHCR and Kenyan officials deliberately withheld assistance at two remote camps in northeast Kenya as part of a policy to encourage the seventy thousand Somali refugees living in these areas to move to the designated refugee camps. In 1993 the policy of "light intervention" at the two camps of Mandera and El Wak allegedly resulted in at least two thousand avoidable deaths.[7] This so-called El Wak Massacre has since then remained a major political issue in the North-Eastern Province and in Kenya as a whole, as no Kenyan government has shown a commitment to investigating and unravelling the extent of the human rights abuse and deaths that resulted.

Encampment in Kenya

Encampment became the operative policy in Kenya. Prior to the massive influx of refugees in the early 1990s and UNHCR's taking on responsibility for status determination, refugees received alien identity cards from the Kenyan government, which enabled them to live and work legally outside the camps. Since then, the government has followed the more conventional approach of putting refugees in camps. The majority recognized as refugees under UNHCR's mandate have been referred to live in one of the two designated camps.

The camps of Dadaab, hosting primarily Somali refugees, and Kakuma, hosting primarily Sudanese refugees, are located in the remote, arid areas of northern Kenya close to the borders of Somalia and Sudan, respectively. The local populations perceived the land on which the camps were established as their "soil," a soil that had been invaded by outsiders with the assistance of the government. The locals resisted any attempts by refugees to carry out activities in pursuit of a livelihood.

Two key problems with the locations of these camps were (and still are) the proximity to the borders of the embattled countries, making the locations dangerous for many refugees, and the very harsh, hot, and arid environment, which has caused physical and mental health problems for a good number of refugees and precluded any kind of sustainable farming. Refugees have been forced to rely completely on humanitarian relief. Such conditions may be endured for short periods of time, but refugees have been living in these hostile regions for years on end.

While most refugees reside in the designated camps, a crucial question is what happens when refugees feel that refugee camps are too dangerous. Some decide not to go to the camp in the first place but remain in the urban areas where they initially settled. Others leave the camp for urban settings due to increasing insecurity; the harsh environment; and inadequate and, at times, worsening services. For instance, Tutsi and Hutu refugees have frequently made the active choice not to reside in Kakuma camp due to either real or perceived dangers there. As refugees from the Great Lakes Region, they were expected to live alongside each other in Kakuma camp, despite the fact that they fled their own countries due to the politically engineered ethnic hostility and violence between them.

Between 2000 and 2002, the only two Tutsis who lived in Kakuma camp were threatened to such an extent that UNHCR placed then in a protected area. Finally, after two years of living in this situation, both were resettled to Australia for reasons of protection. Refugee camps, considered safe havens, sometimes have increased the risk for refugees. One refugee scholar noted, "It is very well-known that congregating refugees in camps can actually create insecurity."[8]

Urban Refugees

Refugees come to urban areas, and particularly to Nairobi, for a variety of reasons. Many arrive in Nairobi directly from their own countries, where they faced persecution or violent conflict. Others leave Kenya's refugee camps and come to Nairobi due to inadequate humanitarian aid; general insecurity; and insufficient educational services, medical care, or job opportunities.[9] Some possess skills and a professional background, which enable them to take up employment more likely to be available in an urban setting.

Studies on urban refugees in different parts of the world associate refugee choices to live in urban or camp settings with their living conditions at home. If refugees are used to urban settings and a particular standard of living, they may avoid remote refugee camps. For instance, Louis Pirouet has noted that urban refugees mainly consist of people from the middle- and upper-income classes of their countries of origin.[10] Some refugees have said that outside a camp they have a little more control over their lives and a greater sense of their own self-worth and dignity.

Refugees have moved to the city in order to keep in touch with relatives and friends in diasporas, to follow up for resettlement with embassies,[11] or simply to escape the monotonous and at times dangerous life of the camps, where there is little to do other than depend on humanitarian assistance.[12] Somali refugees moved to the city and settled relatively easily among the Kenyan Somalis, while Sudanese refugees have been known to settle among earlier groups of Sudanese refugees in Ruiru and other peri-urban areas.

Although the Kenyan government has at times denied the presence of a large urban refugee population, UNCHR reports estimate it to be over twenty thousand.[13] However, the number of refugees living in Nairobi is more commonly estimated at sixty to one hundred thousand or higher.[14] In 2005 the Nairobi Urban Refugee Inter-Agency Joint Participatory Assessment found that many newly arriving refugees opted not to register with UNHCR for fear of being told to go to Kakuma. As a result, an increasing number of urban refugees are not registered and lack documentation. Others are without legal permission to live outside the camp. Tens of thousands live in Nairobi without legal protection and material support. The urban refugee population has steadily increased despite the fact that refugee life in the urban setting is not much easier than residence in the camps and, in some cases, may even be worse.

The Plight of Urban Refugees

Most urban refugees are invisible. For years UNHCR and the Kenyan government have denied the existence of large numbers of urban refugees. The limited outreach work by UNHCR has meant scarce information about the profile, status, and location of refugees, apart from those who approach UNHCR regularly. The dispersion of refugees throughout Nairobi and the surrounding environs and the lack of a central refugee area may have hidden them and perhaps given rise to the impression that urban refugees are few and have successfully integrated. The dearth of information and research about urban refugees in Nairobi and the inadequacy of the forums through which these refugees can voice their problems and concerns create a dangerous scenario for them. They frequently face insecurity and human rights abuse while living with their basic needs unmet.

Though UNHCR and other agencies, such as Jesuit Refugee Services (JRS), Refugee Consortium of Kenya (RCK), Mapendo International, and Hebrew Immigrant Aid Society (HIAS), have urban refugee programs, the extent of these services is limited. UNHCR only assists a few urban refugees who have been issued with a mandate letter "with full assistance," enabling them to live in Nairobi for documented reasons, such as special health concerns or security problems in the camps. Other organizations provide limited and usually short-term assistance to new arrivals and those identified as the most vulnerable.

The majority of refugees with convincing justification for living outside the camp are more often issued a mandate letter with a "no assistance" clause, meaning that the holders of these letters must meet all their own needs outside of the designated camps, whether food, shelter, medical, livelihoods, and protection. Although this document is proof of refugee status, receiving such a letter from UNHCR can take longer than a year, and the process has to be renewed yearly. Even when the document has been received, the Kenyan police often either ignore or destroy it when they encounter and harass refugees.[15]

The reality is that most refugees in Nairobi do not have any legal documentation, which increases their vulnerability and leaves them without any human rights protections. A number of cross-cutting problems, identified by all nationality groups, result from the lack of legal documentation. Some of these include police harassment, arrest, and detention; lack of access to basic services; and lack of livelihoods, which add to the difficulties of obtaining food and shelter.[16] These challenges have varying impact on refugees depending on age, gender, and nationality and lead to diverse coping mechanism, both legal and illegal.

Protection Issues

Numerous security and protection issues confront urban refugees. The lack of and delays in obtaining documentation are at the root of much of the insecurity and many of the human rights violations faced by urban refugees. Nairobi refugees appeal for some kind of documentation in order to deal with harassment and arrest by police. Almost all the refugees interviewed during the participatory assessments narrated their ordeals with police and discussed how they have to pay bribes to police to secure release once arrested. At times, the churches and mosques raise funds to bail out arrested refugees.

Lack of identification documentation commonly prevents refugees from accessing national medical services. Restrictive documents state that refugees can only receive assistance in designated camps. In camps, refugees are often charged double the local rates according to Kenyan policy.

The absence of a proper refugee law and legal framework in Kenya for so many years has been partly to blame for many of the injustices and evils faced by refugees. However, the lack of capacity and the bureaucratic procedures of UNCHR, the agency mandated to protect refugees, as well as more insidious problems, are also to blame. In 2001 a UNHCR corruption scandal surrounding refugee resettlement was exposed in the media. The UN's subsequent investigation found a systematic breakdown and failure to protect urban refugees.

Even now, with this scandal in the past, other problems hamper UNHCR efforts. Some refugees interviewed during the participatory assessment discussed how they had waited over two years, with frequent appointments, before UNHCR finally completed the refugee status determination process. For many refugees this is a matter of grave concern, as in the meantime they went through appalling abuse at the hands of police for being in the country illegally. Many slept in inhuman jail cells for days; others were taken to court and charged with being in the country illegally.

Ethiopian and Somali women have reported that police harass them by taking them to dark corners in the dangerous Eastleigh section of Nairobi, sometimes abusing them physically and raping them. One technique used by police is the "walkabout," where police officers walk refugees around for hours, taking them closer and closer to the police station until money exchanges hands.[17] Many refugees narrated how they stayed hungry to save KSh100 (US$1.45) just in case they should meet with police. Others remained indoors during the day and only walked out to look for food at night for fear of police arrest. Frequently, when refugees are arrested, other offenses are added to their cases.

The ever-increasing cross-border trade in small arms has generated deeper problems for many innocent and vulnerable refugees. The host population often views urban refugees as a security threat. Such sentiments are used as excuses for further police harassment and violence towards refugees, so evident in recent instances of intense searches carried out by police for small arms in Eastleigh. Such action has been interpreted by Muslims as religious discrimination by non-Muslim authorities, which has led to street demonstrations and further violence. Unsafe housing or the lack of it entirely have increased fear, attacks, robberies, and rapes. The first weeks in Nairobi are often the most risky for asylum seekers as they look for shelter and try to situate themselves. Some have been targets of violence and rape while sleeping outside. Other refugees live in constant fear and risk because of inadequate shelter and because, having fled their native country without other family members, they must live alone or with strangers.[18]

Complicated ethnic and military alliances, which have characterized conflicts in Ethiopia and the Great Lakes Region, have crossed borders. Refugees in Nairobi often experience threats, abuse, and harassment by other refugees from their own country and must choose carefully which slum, informal settlement, or section of Nairobi to live in. For example, Tutsis and Hutus tend not to live in the same areas of the city. A Banyamulenge refugee felt that several groups of refugees in Nairobi were openly hostile to him. Several Ethiopian refugees have described the ethnic tensions that have developed in exile between them and the Oromo refugees.[19] Frequently, refugees have reported, and UNHCR and other NGOs have acknowledged, that refugees living in Nairobi have been targeted by alleged security agents, and occasionally by Kenyan police, for their activities in their countries of origin.[20] Refugees have been trailed and harassed, even abducted and murdered. Safe houses and protected areas in camps often have proven to be no safer than the Nairobi slums and streets.

Livelihoods

Earning an income to obtain food, pay the rent, and meet health needs is a major challenge. Since the 1990s, the Kenyan government has not issued work permits to documented urban refugees. As a result, it has become more difficult for most refugees to find work to sustain themselves. Refugees suffer some of the worst conditions to be found in Nairobi, in the poorest and least safe areas. Many live in rectangular sheds constructed of corrugated iron sheets, divided into a single row of several rooms, each with a door to the outside; either mud, wood, or tin divide the rooms. Entire refugee families or groups occupy a single room. Often there is only a communal pit latrine for all living in the entire row of rooms.

The various refugee communities have different methods of survival, including receiving financial remittances from their home regions, sharing rent and food among themselves, moving from house to house because they are unable to make the monthly rent payments, and prostitution. A majority of those who have lived in Nairobi for more than two years are self-employed through petty trade. Only JRS and ARTES (African Refugees Talents) are known to have programs aimed at developing the skills and talents of urban refugees and facilitating market access for their local crafts. After securing shelter, the rest of the time is spent trying to obtain food and other material assistance for survival.

The most vulnerable groups are unaccompanied minors (UAMs), minority groups, and child-headed and female-headed households. It is not uncommon to find a teenager looking after younger siblings from five to twelve years of age, and the distributions of aid through churches or humanitarian agencies are not sufficient to meet their actual needs. The Ethiopian and Somali UAMs are known to move from house to house to obtain food and shelter, while the Congolese and Sudanese UAMs sometimes have established arrangements, where refugees of the same age and gender take care of each other.[21] Sexual exploitation is of greatest concern where a minor or a woman has sole responsibility for the household. Minority groups, those of small clans, and those of mixed ethnicity such as Ethiopian-Eritrean or Tutsi-Hutu are especially isolated and vulnerable in Nairobi. Their livelihood support comes only from within the clan or particular ethnic group.

Health

Only a few asylum seekers and refugees are eligible for medical treatment through a referral system from UNHCR and its implementing partners. Most often refugees remain at home and use traditional or generic medicines. If refugees have funds, they are able to access private and public health care, although in some cases at higher fees than Kenyans pay. The urban refugee lifestyle is often of a transient nature, refugees being forced to move from one place to another due to police harassment, lack of funds for rent, or the search for food and safety. This lessens their ability to obtain medical care, especially with regard to HIV/AIDS. Many in treatment for diseases like tuberculosis miss their DOT medicine due to limits on their movement.[22]

The Kenyan government has put significant effort towards ensuring patient access to antiretroviral (ARV) medicine. But the conditions of eligibility—including a judgment that one is prepared to continue taking medicine, has the motivation to keep taking it, has a means of livelihood, and has a permanent residence to which one can be traced if one defaults—can lead to urban refugees being denied access to treatment. Some HIV-positive refugees in urban areas continue to languish and die due to their inability to access the life-prolonging ARVs. Others are prevented from obtaining adequate access to services and health information in general, as the awareness information is presented in the languages of English and Kiswahili, neither of which is understood by some refugee groups. The "hide and seek" game refugees are forced to play with police makes it difficult for the country as a whole to achieve certain public health goals like disease control and eradication through high immunization coverage.

Very limited data are available on women and their access to sexual and reproductive health services, especially for emergency cases of sexual and gender-based violence such as rape and domestic violence. From various reports and testimonies, it is evident that most victims of sexual and other forms of violence do not get the treatment, medical care, and counseling they require.[23]

Education

Denial of children's right to basic education is one of the many human rights violations that some urban refugees face. Kenyan government policy constrains refugees' access to education except for the "convention status refugees." Refugee children whose families do not have proper registration documentation have difficulty accessing the Kenyan primary education system, largely because an identification of the child's guardian or parent and the child's birth certificate are requirements in the schools' registration process.

According to refugees, the right to free primary education in Nairobi is somewhat dependent on where one resides. Schools in some areas welcome refugees; in other areas, an "admission fee" is requested. Sudanese refugees, it has been found, educate their children through city council, private, or informal schools. Ethiopian and Somali children attend madrassas, or Islamic religious schools. Many Congolese and other French-speaking refugees prefer to educate their children in French and in their own countries' curriculum. Some have begun their own schools; internal exams are given or the children are taken to Tanzania for final exams.[24] Refugee access to secondary and tertiary level education is even more limited.

Vulnerable Groups of Refugees

Besides being exposed to the horror of poverty in Nairobi slums and informal settlements, some groups of refugees are of special concern because of their particular vulnerability. Single women and mothers and unaccompanied children continue to be the most at risk. Many refugee women are subjected to sexual and gender-based violence by other refugees and law enforcers. Police and local thugs who assault female refugees often go unpunished because many refugees lack the means, support, and knowledge of services to obtain treatment and to address these human rights violations. They also fear the consequences of seeking out law enforcement agencies. Others get involved in commercial sex work for survival due to a lack of other viable livelihoods. The increased number of refugee commercial sex workers, especially among Ethiopian refugee women in the Eastleigh and Hurlingham areas of Nairobi, is of great concern as it predisposes the women to HIV/AIDS, as well as to human rights abuses.

Unaccompanied, separated, orphaned, and trafficked children seem to be lost and struggling to survive. A significant number of Congolese, Ethiopian, and Somali adolescents and children have been found living in Nairobi. Refugee children orphaned by AIDS are heading households, searching for food and rent money. Young girls within the Ethiopian and Somali communities, who seem to be unaccompanied or separated, work as housemaids. They have no opportunities for education or vocational training and face considerable risk of sexual exploitation and abuse.[25]

The prolonged stay of refugees in Kenya has created additional vulnerability and rights issues for urban refugees. Some who came young, healthy, and productive have been slowly falling back into a state where they need for humanitarian support due to old age, chronic disease, the HIV/AIDS pandemic, or the difficult economic situations that have made previously thriving businesses collapse. The most affected are elderly women and men without accompaniment, as there are no social support systems for the elderly among urban refugee populations. The scenarios faced by the refugees' children, who are maturing yet have no income or anywhere else to go, generate an increasing number of refugee street families, especially around Westlands and the city center toward Uhuru Highway.

Conclusion

Refugees living in Nairobi suffer greatly from the poverty and violence that afflict many Kenyans. However, the situation of refugees is worse than that of poor Kenyan citizens for many reasons. They lack legal and material as well as social and moral support for their protection and basic survival. The encampment policy is still in place in Kenya, and the arbitrary arrests of refugees living outside the camps by police, even when they have some identification documents, violate the right to movement and deny access to social services. Lack of sufficient opportunities for higher education and the inability to procure a work permit from the government have violated refugee rights to self-reliance, livelihood, health care, and education, and by extension the right to life with dignity.

The diffuse settlement of refugees in urban areas makes assistance more difficult. The absence of centralized living areas makes it is more challenging for refugees to form social support groups. At the same time, the plight of refugees in urban areas has not been taken seriously enough, perhaps, in part, because they are so invisible and thus unlikely to draw significant media attention.

The needs of urban refugees are diverse, yet the economic and developmental potential for urban refugees is great. A Refugee Consortium of Kenya study of 2005 has documented the great talents and potential of urban refugees that, if efficiently tapped, could contribute to national economic growth through the refugees' business and other skills.[26] There is a continual need to further awareness among the government agencies and Kenyans about issues refugees face. It is imperative, therefore, to persist in advocating for sufficient and effective implementation of Kenya's Refugee Act of 2006 (passed on December 30, 2006, and published January 2, 2007). Implementation would help promote the rights of refugees and aid in educating the community and law enforcers about refugee rights.

The encampment of thousands of young and potentially productive refugees in the camps for over fifteen years is not only unethical and inhuman, but also a major economic burden to the international community. Humanitarian aid continues to flow into refugee camps for "care and maintenance" purposes, yet this aid does not benefit refugees in ways that would help them move forward with their lives. There are also thousands of undocumented refugees whose children have been born, educated, and socialized in an urban Kenyan society. They do not know home and have little prospect or even desire of ever returning home, particularly those who have fled interethnic conflict. They are a lost generation seeking a home.

As the UNHCR has reminded us, "In many cases, today's neighbour is tomorrow's refugee. They have lost their homes, jobs, community and often family. They are not a threat, but they do need temporary help until they can establish their lives. The greater majority of people wish to return to their own homes once the situation there normalizes. But if a refugee does stay for whatever reason, he or she can often become a valuable asset to a community. A Who's Who of the world's leading businessmen, artists and politicians includes many former refugees."[27]

Notes

1. For testimonies and reports of various protection problems, see Human Rights Watch, *Hidden in Plain View: Refugees Living without Protection in Nairobi and Kampala* (New York: Human Rights Watch, 2002). Also available at http://www.hrw.org/reports/2002/kenyugan/kenyugan.pdf (accessed April 16, 2007).

2. UNHCR, *Information Bulletin: Kenya Refugee Emergency* (Nairobi, Kenya: UNHCR, July and November 1992).

3. Ibid.

4. Patricia Daley, "Situation of Refugees in East Africa," paper for the Fourth International Research Advisory Panel Conference, Oxford, 1995; Human Rights Watch, *Kenya: Taking Liberties, an Africa Watch Report* (London: Human Rights Watch, 1991).

5. United Nations, *Consolidated Inter-Agency Appeal: Kenya, Special Emergency Program for the Horn of Africa (SEPHA)* (Geneva, 1993).

6. Duncan Ndegwa, *Walking in Kenyatta Struggles: My Story* (Nairobi: Kenya Leadership Institute, 2006).

7. United States Committee for Refugees, *World Refugee Survey* (Washington, DC, 1993).

8. Barbara Harrell-Bond, "Are Refugee Camps Good for Children?" *Journal of Humanitarian Studies, New Issues in Refugee Research*, Working Paper No. 29, August 2000, available from http://www.jha.ac/articles/u029.htm.

9. Human Rights Watch, *Hidden in Plain View*, 27–28.

10. Louis Pirouet, "Refugees in and from Uganda in the Post Colonial Period," in *Uganda Now*, ed. Holger Bernt Hansen and Michael Twaddle (Nairobi, Kenya: Heinemann East African Studies, 1988).

11. Cindy Hosrt, *Transnational Nomads: How Somalis Cope with Refugee Life in the Dadaab Camps of Kenya* (Oxford and New York: Berghahn Books, 2006), 141.

12. Mapendo International, "Un-Met Needs of Urban Refugees in Nairobi," Nairobi, Kenya, unpublished report of Mapendo International, 2005.

13. Human Rights Watch, *Hidden in Plain View*.

14. Refugee Consortium of Kenya, "Self-Settled Refugees in Nairobi: A Close Look at Urban Refugees Coping Strategies," (Nairobi: Refugee Consortium of Kenya, 2005). The report is also available at http://www.rckkenya.org/research.html, under link for Urban Refugees in Nairobi (accessed April 19, 2007).

15. Human Rights Watch, *Hidden in Plain View*, 27.

16. "Participatory Assessment: Age, Gender, and Diversity Mainstreaming," Nairobi, Kenya, unpublished report of assessment exercise carried out among Nairobi refugees by UNHCR and Nairobi-based NGOs, 2005, 9.

17. Ibid., 14.

18. Human Rights Watch, *Hidden in Plain View*, 36 ff.

19. Ibid., 38–39.

20. Ibid., 39 ff.

21. "Participatory Assessment," 14.

22. John Wagacha Burton, "Socio-Economic Factors that Militate against Tuberculosis Control among the Somali Community in Eastleigh Section of Nairobi, Kenya" (master's thesis, University of Nairobi, 2006).

23. Human Rights Watch, *Hidden in Plain View*, 32–34.

24. "Participatory Assessment," 14.

25. Ibid., 10.

26. Refugee Consortium of Kenya, "Self-Settled Refugees in Nairobi," 36.

27. UNHCR, *Helping Refugees: An Introduction to UNHCR* (Geneva: UNHCR, 2003).

6

Protection as Capability Expansion
Practical Ethics for Assisting Urban Refugees

Loren B. Landau

Until recently, urban refugees rarely appeared on the agendas of many donor governments, aid agencies, scholars, and advocates, all actors accustomed to assisting refugees
in camps and settlements.[1] But as Africa's cities grow and displaced people face the
prospect of ever-longer periods in restrictive rural camps, refugees and other forced
migrants are becoming increasingly evident in the continent's urban centers.[2] Reflect-
ing the lack of a coherent approach to issues of urban displacement, responses to urban
refugees have been almost as diverse as the refugees themselves. In Egypt and South
Africa, government has actively promoted urban self-settlement through policies that
neither restrict refugee mobility nor provide purpose-built refugee settlements. Other
countries, including those practicing "zonal assistance schemes," tolerate refugees in urban areas but place some restrictions on refugees' mobility and the points at which they
can access aid. However, in East Africa and elsewhere, refugees need clearance before
coming to cities. Even semipermanent relocation is typically allowed only for reasons
of health or education. Anyone else caught outside of designated settlements areas can
be prosecuted and may forfeit some or all of their rights as refugees. Despite these prohibitions, the potential benefits of urban life (especially compared to an interminable
camp-based existence) motivate people to leave the camps or bypass them altogether
to find their way into and through the continent's towns and cities. What almost all instances of urban refugee settlement in Africa—both organized and spontaneous—have
in common is the lack of protection for refugees.

Effective protection in cities first means understanding the nature of urban settlement. Whereas purpose-built settlements and camps isolate refugees from host communities—although alienation is never total—urban refugees are necessarily involved
in host countries' economic, social, and political affairs. For many, such de facto integration fosters relative freedom and opens avenues for education and employment. But
with these opportunities also come risks of exploitation, abuse, and marginalization. It

103

is in this context that the United Nations High Commissioner for Refugees (UNHCR) is currently revising its policy on urban refugee areas in an attempt to implement what will undoubtedly remain a contested definition of protection.[3] Much of the debate will undoubtedly center on the practicability of the UNHCR's approach. However, some critics will likely point to a lack of clarity on what kind of protection urban refugees *should* receive. What is already evident is that an effective approach to refugee protection must explicitly consider broader urban development politics, processes, and social configurations. Working from that perspective, this chapter delineates a normative framework for urban refugee protection.

This chapter takes many of its cues from legal principles—particularly the Refugee Convention of 1951 and interpretations thereof—but derives its specific ethical obligations and guidance for action from the principles informing the "capability approach," a framework most notably and articulately promoted by Amartya Sen and Martha Nussbaum. This approach—discussed in more detail below—is at once universalistic and highly contextualized. In all instances, it is dedicated to expanding agency—the ability to choose different ways of living—while ensuring that fundamental prerequisites for survival are never compromised.

My ambitions here are both pragmatic and theoretical. The most immediate objective is to provide a general framework for protecting refugees in urban areas that includes guiding principles but is neither overly prescriptive nor universalist. Doing so will help to address host communities' concerns of "cultural imperialism" that, rather than assisting refugees, only harden attitudes against them.[4] For the same reasons, I carefully avoid explicitly nonsecular ethical bases. Such care is especially important given the de facto integration of urban refugees into host communities, a condition requiring an approach that is sensitive to heterogeneous values, economic environments, and institutional capacities and explicitly provides space for what Nussbaum terms "cooperative critical discourse."[5]

For these and other reasons, I hope this chapter can move the discussion of refugee protection beyond the legalistic and welfarist frameworks in which it is most often discussed. There are three reasons why I deviate from a solely legalistic approach. Most obviously, despite more than fifty years of legal deliberation on refugee protection, there is still no clearly justiciable definition of specific obligations.[6] Moreover, while it is important to develop pro-protection legal and policy frameworks, in most places across Africa, law only weakly determines anyone's behavior.[7] This should not be read as disparaging or dismissing the power of law or rights, as the approach outlined here is compatible with individual and collective rights. However, even in environments where law's autonomous status is relatively secure, fixating on law can distract us from the other, more powerful reasons for protecting refugees. Unlike purely legal strategies, this approach sees the promotion of rights as one of many potential approaches for expanding human freedom.

Welfarist approaches, including the recently developed Sphere standards, provide an alternative for protection and assistance that is not based exclusively on law- and rights-based frameworks.[8] In such cases, the emphasis becomes technical and outputs based, usually measured in lives saved, nutritional status achieved, children educated, and so forth. There is undeniable value in making such calculations in emergency situations where a population is unknown and information is generally scarce. Such outputs are also critical in convincing donors that their money is well spent. Despite its value, there is a danger that such welfarist approaches ultimately treat people as sites of action or as outputs. A well-nourished refugee becomes the goal, regardless of that person's aspirations, frustrations, or abilities. As David A. Crocker notes in reviewing Sen's capability model, "humans are not only experiences or preference satisfiers; they are also judges, evaluators, and doers. Agency and well-being are, for Sen, two fundamental and irreducible dimensions of being human."[9] The capability approach, by emphasizing the need to ensure refugees have the right to choice and to control their own environments, helps to avoid a kind of commodity fetishism characteristic of many humanitarian programs and welfarist treatments of assistance.

Lastly, this chapter intends to extend the capability approach's applicability to new areas of study and action. To date, almost all work undertaken within the framework addresses perennial poverty among populations residing in their country of citizenship. This chapter challenges this work in two ways. First, it suggests that the capability approach should not be limited to stable, systemic problems, but may also serve as a guide for addressing short- and medium-term concerns. Second, and more importantly, this chapter moves the discussion of capabilities beyond the Rousseauian social contract by considering the position of noncitizens and the obligations of international actors. While there may be moral and ethical reasons for institutional discrimination against noncitizens, this essay begins questioning the bases of such distinctions. I by no means reconcile these tensions—a commission that has eluded far greater authors—but by explicitly addressing the treatment of noncitizens, I hope to stimulate further, productive deliberation.

Before turning to the specific case of refugees in urban areas and detailing my definition of protection, I wish to make clear that this chapter is intended more as provocation than concrete plan. As such, I am not particularly concerned with strict ethical consistency in a theoretical sense or with representing the full subtlety of the ethicists and scholars cited here. Rather, it draws compatible and complementary insights and tools from various approaches broadly framed by the empirical research and efforts to expand human agency and freedom.

The Case for an Urban Distinction

Finding practical ways of applying the approach to protection outlined in more detail below means first understanding the context in which protection is to be promoted. There are strong arguments for developing international protection standards that apply to refugees regardless of their location or settlement pattern. To be sure, a minimum standard of protection must everywhere include protecting the sanctity of life, the possibility of a lasting solution, and "the social bases of respect."[10] However, there is danger in going much further with minimum standards in that we may settle on lowest common denominators or lapse into welfarism. Rather, what is most important is to identify broad principles for addressing the specific protection needs of refugees in urban areas.

Perhaps the most significant distinction between urban refugees and those in a camp setting is the degree to which they are, de facto, integrated with host populations. While camp-based refugees are never thoroughly isolated from prevailing socioeconomic configurations,[11] these are "exceptional" spaces where states have established rights—however problematical—to impose restrictions on mobility and livelihoods.[12] In urban environments, refugees may be marginalized through policy and socioeconomic practice, but such distinctions are often empirically blurred, almost impossible to enforce, and ethically difficult to justify. This muddiness has critical implications for protection. First, for the sake of ethical consistency, in instances where policies promote—as either explicit intention or logical outcome—refugees' integration into host communities, broader principles of justice mean equalizing rights and capabilities across those communities, whether they be rural or urban. More importantly, accepting refugees' de facto integration in host populations means that states' obligations to their own citizens generate responsibilities for refugees. If the socioeconomic or political marginalization of any group negatively affects all residents' well-being, allowing the marginalization or exploitation of refugees also constitutes a violation of commitments to citizens' welfare.[13]

The urban environment also shifts the modalities of assistance, protection, and advocacy. Whereas a system of specialized agencies and dedicated actors typically provide services to camp-based refugees, the social and spatial dispersion of urban refugees renders such specialized assistance unsustainable or simply untenable. The UNHCR and other agencies may have offices in urban areas supported by individual organizations' refugee-oriented programs, but there are unlikely to be the financial and human resources needed to assist all urban refugees. Moreover, international donors have proved reluctant to support urban refugee programs that they see as overly expensive and prone to abuse.[14] Instead of protecting, parallel systems may foster separation even more jealously among the host populations than they do in rural settings. Consequently, just as urban refugees must largely rely on existing land, labor, and job markets for their income, they too must rely on existing public, private, and nongovernmental institutions for their protection. This includes reliance on nonspecialized forms of protection (the police, legal services, and private security or vigilante groups) against violence and criminality.[15]

In addition to the institutional distinctions outlined above, case studies suggest a qualitative difference between the type of refugees settling in camps and those in urban areas. The latter are typically from urban backgrounds, better educated, disproportionately male, and more professionally varied.[16] Further studies will reveal whether these characteristics apply equally across time and space. While "pervasive human diversity"[17] is evident in rural areas and refugee camps, the heterogeneity of urban refugees and the urban economy requires a protection approach that affords a greater freedom in pursuing livelihood strategies and site of residence. Such an approach must, however, also recognize that people vary in their abilities to convert the same resources (financial, personal, social) into true capabilities.

Lastly, and perhaps most controversially, urban settlement is, de facto, a gateway to a durable solution or itself part of a durable solution. Camp-based refugees may remain in specialized settlements for many years, but few—refugees, humanitarians, or host governments—conceive of this as a permanent strategy for addressing the needs of affected populations. Many refugees settling in urban areas may eventually return "home" (however defined). But the majority may well move elsewhere or remain. Indeed, the integration necessary for survival in urban areas makes it far more likely that there will be emotional and economic "sunk costs" in residential sites that make return or onward movement less likely. Moreover, whereas states can more easily "force" refugees to repatriate when they are settled in densely populated camps—something Tanzania did in the mid-1990s—the use of force is considerably more difficult when facing populations dispersed throughout urban centers. When states attempt to "round up" urban refugees, the harm to the security and welfare of all urban residents may far outweigh the economic or political gains of such actions.[18] Recognizing that refugees are likely to remain in urban areas for extended periods may discourage some states from allowing urban settlement. However, a protection strategy for refugees in urban areas presupposes at least the tacit approval of relevant political authorities, which are aware that refugees may indefinitely remain. In this context, protection should be premised on promoting refugees' permanent or semipermanent inclusion in the cities in which they live.

Some will argue against the necessity of urban protection programs, given that in many instances urban refugees have chosen to forgo camp life and may be generally well-equipped for the urban environment, or that assistance in urban areas is relatively expensive. Although many urban refugees could find succour elsewhere, as long as they are recognized as refugees within a country's policy, they should not be denied protection simply for choosing to live outside restrictive camp structures. Moreover, while some refugees may independently overcome significant obstacles—a testament to their strength and creativity—significant numbers fail to best the challenges of resettlement and the hazards urban life.[19] Moreover, survival or prosperity may come at long-term costs to refugees and the communities in which they live. At the very least, refugees' economic activities often contravene existing laws and regulations. However absurd those restrictions may be, consistent violations can help erode the rule of law, heighten vulnerability, and generate economies of corruption and violence that subsequently diminish others' ability to expand their capabilities (including host populations and future generations of refugees). Such actions can also strengthen resentment against refugees labeled as scofflaws and unfair competitors. Certain activities, including transactional sex, also offer short-term economic gains but with long-term health and security risks. Faced with these dangers, there will always be a need for contextualized strategies to protect urban refugees.

I wish to make one important caveat before delineating the objectives and parameters of obligation for refugee protection: this approach applies primarily to instances where host countries use law, policy, or programming explicitly to promote or endorse the self-settlement of refugees in urban environments. Although there are clear ethical and legal reasons for protecting the rights of refugees (and other non-nationals) who violate prohibitions on urban residence—and there are strong reasons to protest policies limiting movement—domestic and international actors' obligations are less easily defined in such circumstances. While my own values go against this distinction, there are least two pragmatic reasons why I maintain—if only for present purposes—the distinction between "legally" and "illegally" settled urban refugees.

First, successful protection will only be achieved with the support of host communities. As John Rawls and others argue, individuals (including refugees) should not pursue ends that are inherently at odds with the idea of collective morality—or unduly limit what others see as important to their freedoms and capabilities.[20] This is ethically unjustified and will foster resentment, especially in instances where cultural preservation or the promotion of particular forms of moral, ethnic, or religious homogeneity is the value of a society. However, once states—if not their populations—recognize individuals' right to reside within a territory (or a specific part of it), the preferences of the former "outsiders" must immediately be included among the society's collective values.

Second, under international law and custom, states have limited rights to restrict the movement of noncitizens and refugees into and within their territory. Although freedom of movement is fundamental to human functioning, an approach explicitly denying states the right to restrict movements is unlikely to be embraced by both the people and the institutions whose support is needed for its success. Longer-term refugee advocacy may eventually promote a broader acceptance of the right to movement and erode the necessity for this distinction.

Due to the exclusion of "illegally" settled urban refugees, this chapter applies to a relatively narrow range of empirical cases. That said, the approach discussed here can provide a framework for considering urban refugee policies elsewhere and a framework for the protection of all self-settled refugees.

Protection as Capability Expansion

As Catherine Phuong notes, "everybody seems to talk about 'effective protection,' but without ever defining its precise meaning."[21] So while she can cite a UNHCR document arguing for a "shared understanding on the types of situations guaranteeing effective protection," the UNHCR offers only a vague definition of what protection means.[22] However, through careful reading of multiple documents, we can piece together what the agency sees as minimum protection standards. This includes ensuring that refugees are in environments where they are protected against persecution, *refoulement*, torture, and other cruel and degrading treatments; free of acute risks to life; able to ensure the unity and integrity of the family; and are ultimately able to access a truly durable solution.[23] Such a definition is a valuable start, but it provides little guidance for protecting self-settled refugees in cities or rural areas.

To develop a practical standard of protection in the contexts discussed here, we must augment the UNHCR's definition in at least three ways. First, more specific guidance is needed than merely suggesting that a person have "access to means of subsistence sufficient to maintain an adequate standard of living."[24] Second, a definition of protection cannot accept the division of assistance and durable solutions into two discrete phases as such distinctions are often empirically and ethically indistinguishable—all the more so in urban areas (see below). Third, and finally, the principles of protection must not focus exclusively on refugees. For the reasons discussed elsewhere, effective urban refugee protection is highly contextualized protection that also considers nonrefugee actors and their interests. Any approach unduly enforcing distinctions between refugees and hosts not only requires (expensive) parallel assistance structures, but may also foster political resentments that will ultimately undermine its sustainability.

By incorporating principles from international and domestic instruments and Sen's and Nussbaum's work on entitlements, capabilities, and "human functionings," this essay advocates for a kind of protection that can address the concerns raised above. I begin with Article 4(2) of the International Covenant on Civil and Political Rights (ICCPR), which argues that all people have the right to recognition as a person before the law. From the UNHCR's interpretation, protection is, inter alia, physical security, avoidance of torture or *refoulement*, and an adequate and dignified means of subsistence. Not only are these both basic capabilities central to human survival, but key to the exercise of agency. In the highly dynamic cities of the global South, a dignified means of subsistence is more than simple handouts or meeting basic nutritional needs, but also includes the flexibility to move, change employment, and invest in ways that can lead to a dignified life, or, at least, a life of comparable dignity to the lives of those around one.[25]

This flexibility also requires that we develop intervention strategies premised on individuals' skills and ambitions. The use of Sphere standards may help address basic needs and capabilities, but any kind of objective measure based on kilograms, liters, or square meters can only provide for humanity's basic animal functions. Past basic survival, they do little to expand freedom, protect dignity, or pave pathways to durable solutions. It is here that I turn to Nussbaum's and Sen's work on capabilities.

In the opening sentence of *Development as Freedom*, Sen writes that "development can be seen . . . as a process of expanding the real freedoms that people enjoy."[26] By replacing "development" with "effective protection," we take the first step in building a strategy for addressing the conditions of self-settled refugees. The measure of success is the ability of any intervention to expand progressively the opportunities (that is, capabilities) for people to achieve locally appropriate functionings (actions or states of being) that help achieve individuals' heterogeneous objectives. (Sen refers to someone's proven ability to act or do as their "functioning" and a capability as a person's ability to achieve a given functioning.)[27] Whereas utilitarian reasoning would evaluate the outcome of these functionings in easily measurable terms (income, happiness, nutrition), the emphasis here is on maximizing true opportunities for freedom and human agency. The success of protection ceases to be survival or physical integrity—although these remain important—but is to be judged by "a person's capability to achieve a functioning that he or she has reason to value."[28] This may frustrate those seeking predictable outcomes (for example, logframe-obsessed donors); the approach is premised on expanding people's ability to make substantive choices, not on the choices they actually make. This will not guarantee prosperity for refugees who, like all other people, have preference sets that include nonmaterial and nonpersonal objectives: assisting others, living peacefully with one's neighbors, experiencing aesthetic beauty, practicing religion, and promoting values.[29] By linking protection to agency and freedom, this approach first addresses the need for basic capabilities—necessary to sustain life and avoid poverty—while providing the bases for the achievement of higher-order capabilities linked to personal fulfilment and the full realization of people's human dignity.

This approach not only explicitly recognizes that people will make different choices with the freedoms they are provided, but also that they convert "raw materials" into functionings at different rates and in different ways. A person disabled by physical injury or trauma, for example, will need additional resources to achieve the same thing as others. People are also varied in their abilities to adapt to varied social challenges: learning new languages, speaking to strangers, or finding jobs.[30] Therefore, when we compare people's capabilities—or the level of protection—we must not only measure protection in cubic meters of water provided or kilocalories consumed, both markers of a welfarist approach to protection; we must also consider how well each individual can function with the resources they command. In practice, external interventions to promote the protection of capabilities means (a) ensuring there are resources available; (b) identifying external obstacles to the conversion of these resources into functionings; and (c) identifying personal factors affecting their conversion (internal constraints).[31]

External factors are the target of conventional protection measures: legal prohibitions, detention, violence, and so on. As Henry Steiner argues, the sources of constraints on one's capabilities do not include only intentional policies and prohibitions, but all kinds of human and environmental causes, whether or not an individual or institution can be held responsible for them.[32] These include a person's physical and mental health (including the ability to love and reason); education or qualifications; and an awareness of the options available for achieving a desired outcome. Despite Steiner's arguments to the contrary, these must also include "well-founded fears" or a well-founded threat—of violence, embarrassment, or denial of any capability. (As Michel Foucault's work illustrates, consistent exposure to coercion or prohibitions may result in the internalization of that prohibition in a way that limits action even when the original threat is removed.)[33]

This approach is valuable for a number of critical reasons. First, it responds symbolically and practically to an ever-growing pool of authors demanding that we move away from a disempowering or pathologizing protection model that sees refugee welfare as outputs and refugees as passive recipients.[34] Instead, it imagines refugees as effective agents in their own welfare who—like other potentially vulnerable groups—may require assistance to overcome internal and external obstacles limiting their capabilities. Second, this approach is not a generalized theory of justice nor does it establish the desirability of specific models of socioeconomic or political organization. As such, it remains compatible with a range of normative, religious, and political systems as long as those systems value individual choice and the expansion of every person's capabilities. Third, by establishing principles of individual freedom within a collective, it works from the ontological position that the gradual improvement of everyone's life will come from the gradual improvement of every individual's rights and freedoms. Doing so avoids utilitarian arguments that could justify the marginalization of minority populations (including refugees) while considering the interests of all affected parties: refugees and host communities.

For reasons discussed in more detail in the following section, the approach promoted here can only be effectively operationalized in terms of its progressive realization. That is because it is effectively impossible to recognize the full range of obstacles to protection until those obstacles are empirically evident.

Applying a Capability-Based Approach

In its purest form, intervention for the protection of refugees should be highly specialized in ways that consider the range of all relevant actors' interests and capabilities. More specifically, interventions and advocacy should be dedicated to addressing the specific challenges that refugees (or a refugee) face in overcoming internal and externally imposed obstacles to capability expansion. Such a standard of action is an effective guide but can also lead to paralysis, as it demands financial support for humanitarian assistance as well as data on newly arriving refugees, host communities, and institutional capacities. For these reasons, I recommend a two-phased approach to assisting refugees in urban areas. While all refugees are entitled to individualized attention, a *nonexclusive* set of priority areas can serve as an initial guide to early programmatic intervention. Such consideration builds on Sen's observation that "in dealing with extreme poverty in developing economies, we may be able to go a fairly long distance in terms of a relatively small number of centrally important functionings (and the corresponding basic capabilities, e.g., the ability to be well-nourished and well-sheltered, the capability of escaping avoidable morbidity and premature mortality, and so forth)."[35] In urban environments, there are a number of critical areas where early intervention will almost always result in expanding capabilities. Recognizing this, the two-phase approach outlined here is loosely informed by the distinction Sen makes between basic and other forms of capabilities. In this case, basic capabilities refer to the freedom to do some basic things that are necessary for survival and to escape abject poverty.[36] To some extent, the Sphere standards are intended to address these basic capabilities—to ensure what Sen terms "minimally adequate levels"—but in a way that is welfarist and not premised on the principle of expanding agency and freedom.[37] In this approach, ensuring that basic capabilities are met is not an end in itself, but a means to allow urban refugees to overcome a threshold that will allow them to gradually expand other capabilities. This leads to a second—much longer—phase involving monitoring, evaluation, and an expansion or specialization of protection activities in order to address specificities and continue expanding the capabilities of refugees and host populations. Through an initial phase dedicated to response on arrival that paves the way for longer-term integration, this approach explicitly considers the particularities of urban refugee settlement: economic diversity; that urban settlement is, de facto, a gateway to a durable solution; and the analytic and practical inseparability of refugees and hosts.

While based on a principle of expanding capabilities, in all instances refugee protection must also be pragmatic and flexible for at least three reasons. First, this approach is rooted in individual experiences, the diversity of which prevents the creation of universal protection standards. Second, and more important, it is pragmatic in the sense that John Dewey and others associated with pragmatist philosophy intend: in its actions and the issues it addresses, this approach is guided less by absolute principles than by emergent problems. Third, the limited availability of resources (financial, human, institutional) means that efforts to expand the capabilities of refugees will always be a commitment to "progressively realize" rights and "progressively expand" capabilities. This will generate contentious evaluation standards where it will always be unclear if various actors are fulfilling their respective obligations. These will generate debate, but no more so than discussions around the meaning of development or urban regeneration. As with these processes, there is a need for constant dialogue, compromise, and adaptations, something that legal principles do not readily allow. Such compromises must come from all actors involved in refugee protection: states and bureaucrats (at multiple levels); service providers; employers; domestic and international aid organizations (including the UNHCR); and refugees themselves.

This willingness to adapt as a result of research and critical engagement distinguishes this approach—even in its first phase—from Nussbaum's universalistic leanings (although, to be fair, she is also open to empirically informed reexamination). While I outline a series of more or less concrete steps to expand refugees' basic capabilities, I follow Sen in not reifying any of these as "objectively" or universally correct.[38] There may be a number of intrinsically valuable capabilities (such as living long; being well nourished; being able to read, write, and communicate), but the list proposed here is derived inductively through my own and others' empirical research. As with all lists of capabilities, these should be revised on the basis of continued research. But the only way to do this is to make an initial list explicit so the proposed capabilities can be discussed, defended, and ultimately reconfigured.[39]

Phase One: Basic Capabilities and Areas of Immediate Assistance

From what little we know about the experiences of refugees in urban Africa, the following action areas are intended to begin the process of enhancing urban refugees' capabilities. These are intended to address the need to protect basic capabilities while positioning urban refugees to make the choices needed to participate fully as members of the communities in which they live. As noted above, this is a nonexclusive list that can (and should) be modified based on additional data and analysis.

Documentation and legal status   In legalized environments where law structures the social interactions, legal status and documentation are critical to capability expansion. On the one hand, they enable bearers to make demands on those actors—public or private—who control access to social and financial services. They also act as a guard against abuse at the hands of police and exploitation at the hands of employers and landlords and prevent detention or deportation. Although legal status may initially make little difference in people's lives in the African context or elsewhere, advocacy efforts should nevertheless focus on ensuring the provision of adequate documentation, including travel papers, work permits, and photo identity cards.[40] Recognizing that the provision of documents is not enough, protection must also include training relevant officials to recognize and respect these forms of documentation and supporting disciplinary action against those who do not. Even when such documentation provides only limited protection or access to services, documentation can help promote an objective and consistent regulatory system that may ultimate enhance opportunities for all residents. Certainly, increased reliance on documentation can help fight corruption within the state and private bureaucracy.

An urban refugee starter pack   New arrivals anywhere—whether moving due to coercion or choice—incur significant financial liabilities in reestablishing their lives. Those who have been displaced over long distances, are newly urbanized, or move without the benefit of other family members or kin face additional challenges in accessing credit or emergency support to address these challenges.[41] Rather than provide ongoing financial support to urban refugees, protection efforts should include what, together with Karen Jacobsen, I term a locally appropriate urban refugee "starter pack."[42] This might include paying housing deposits, school fees, or providing small grants to acquire business tools or equipment. In other environments, it may include initial language training or other forms of short-term assistance needed to overcome the initial costs of movement.[43]

Qualifications and skills training   As noted earlier, many urban refugees have professional credentials and qualifications that are not recognized by national authorities or professional associations in asylum countries. For example, while South Africa faces an acute nursing shortage, hundreds of refugee nurses remain unemployed because they cannot prove their qualifications. In many instances, there are national qualifications boards that can convert existing certificates or training into a form that is recognizable by local employers. In other instances, training should be provided to allow refugees to upgrade or adapt their existing qualifications to enable them to pursue their choice of income-generation strategy. Where needed, such assistance may provide mentorship or internship programs. In line with the principle of compromise suggested above, refugees must also be encouraged to accept a (temporary) reduction in both wages and professional status.

Advocacy for practical labor rights   Protection should involve promoting the right to work for refugees and asylum seekers in accordance with Articles 17, 18, and 19 of the 1951 Refugee Convention. This effort should engage the government at a high level (the office of the prime minister or president) as well as relevant ministries or departments. Advocacy cannot, however, be limited to policy change. UNHCR and other advocates should also work with local lobbying organizations, unions, and others effectively to open labor markets to refugees. Legal action may be key to success in securing the right to work but is unlikely to be enough.

Multilevel awareness exercises   There is a need to work with local governments and businesses to help them identify their responsibilities to refugees and asylum seekers. With decentralization, local governments are increasingly responsible for primary health care, housing, policing, and economic development. These are critical components of refugee protection. This means that refugees ought to be included in such programs as both participants and beneficiaries. Advocates should help local governments to recognize that excluding refugees from key programs heightens social marginalization and fragmentation.

An emergency safety net   Not everyone is able to capitalize on the opportunities in the cities, including unaccompanied minors, single parents, the elderly and infirm, and people of rural origin. In line with protecting basic capabilities, urban assistance programs will, therefore, only be effective when complemented by initiatives that provide direct humanitarian assistance to those refugees who are unable to compete in the urban environment. Such programs might be located in geographically distinct areas, including purpose-built camps and settlements or designated zones of assistance. Ideally, however, such facilities will be voluntary and used only for those who self-identify as needing such assistance.

Political participation   The inability to participate in deciding who should govern and on what principles those who govern should follow represents a denied opportunity for capability expansion.[44] Political participation is not only a value in its own right but is critical to the universal expansion of capabilities. If we accept that urban refugees are, de facto, community members, then we must also accept that they should have a role in determining that community's policy directions. Although there will be protests against the influence of foreigners, such participation is critical for a number of reasons. First, policies formed without accurately assessing the interests and capabilities of all affected by them are unlikely to achieve their intended outcomes. For example, an urban regeneration strategy that assumes residents' desire for single-family housing will be counterproductive if most people wish to live as part of an extended family. Accepting that refugees are part of the community means that they must be included in determining what Rousseau would term its "general will."

Opportunities for political participation are also critical in fostering the sense of community needed to expand economic opportunities across the city. Exclusion from participatory processes can encourage refugees to cling to their outsider status, leading to conscious strategies for avoiding close personal or economic relationships with host communities.[45] While it is impossible to force people to identify themselves with the communities in which they live, many undoubtedly would if the option were available. Continued exclusion, however, means people will not dedicate themselves to acquiring fixed assets and may maximize immediate profits at the expense of long-term planning. Such exclusion also limits the ability of cities to capitalize on immigrants' valuable transnational connections.

Certain forms of political participation may be reserved for citizens (for example, the right to elect leaders), but refugees should be provided substantive opportunities to influence the policies directly affecting them. This should go beyond participation in community meetings and advisory or representative councils—although these are important—but an effective right to protest through the same channels open to citizens: letters; formal complaints; and, where necessary, public demonstrations. As in other areas, efforts to promote political participation must not only overcome legal prohibitions, but also exclusion based on ethnicity, language, patriarchy, intimidation, and internalized psychological barriers.[46] The political marginalization of refugees is not only an affront to dignity, but is also likely to compromise the capabilities of all urban residents. If the goal of government is to expand the capabilities of all urban residents—to provide services and to promote health, security, and prosperity—policies must be formulated with a comprehensive understanding of all urban residents.

Monitoring and evaluation   In order to generate the conditions necessary for the on-going expansion of capabilities (and durable solutions), it is necessary to monitor the effectiveness of existing interventions. Such monitoring should promote ongoing communication between host organizations, the United Nations, refugees, and government so as to better evaluate the continued obstacles to capability expansion and the full range of consequences stemming from refugee activities.

Wherever possible, protection efforts should avoid creating parallel structures such as special refugee credit organizations, schools, or clinics. Special structures for refugees may be necessary in the early assistance phase where the host country lacks such institutions. In such instances, efforts should be made to extend similar services to members of the host community. Developing a single system of service delivery and protection is ultimately intended to combat the kind of social fragmentation and exclusion that inhibits capability expansion of both refugees and hosts.

Phase Two: Evaluation and Expanding Freedom

Since what is offered here is effectively an empirically based approach to assistance, it demands that functionings and obstacles be revealed in order to develop appropriate protection standards and intervention strategies. As noted earlier, this approach makes it difficult to generate an "all at once" policy; instead, it relies on an initial approach designed to meet minimum standards and common obstacles. Periodic monitoring must then follow, along with, wherever possible, the expansion of what could, to borrow Nussbaum's terms, move from "basic" capabilities to internal capabilities and combined capabilities (internal and external).

Over the longer term (say, in the second year following the arrival of refugees), existing interventions should be evaluated for the degree to which they achieved the desired outcomes of expanding agency and ensuring basic capabilities. Where refugees are no longer arriving, initiatives dedicated to providing immediate assistance may be supplanted by efforts to foster longer-term economic and sociopolitical integration and greater control by refugees over how they live and what they do. These programs can capitalize on growing familiarity with the internal and external obstacles to capability expansion by further customizing interventions to specific populations and contexts. As the pool of available data expands—and expansion of accurate information will also be critical to effective protection—programs should be regularly reevaluated and adjusted. The specifics of the programs should not be pre-determined, but rather emerge out of a true process of organizational learning.[47]

Limits to Protection as Capability Expansion

Despite its considerable advantages over legalistic approaches or those privileging negative rights, an approach equating protection with capability expansion comes with hazards of its own. Perhaps most obviously, there are risks associated with a definition of protection that does not rely exclusively on a universal system of policies and jurisprudence risks. The focus on individual environments and individuals offers the potential of greater protection, but the peculiarities of such an approach may risk its integration with other programs and global (or even regional) advocacy strategies. Such an approach may also alienate or exclude UNHCR and human rights lawyers—both strong advocates for refugee protection—whose actions are defined (and curtailed) by formal policy and law. However, additional consideration of this approach may help develop points of intersection between legalism and an approach promoting capability.

A protection strategy dedicated to maximizing refugees' freedom and integration may also prove politically untenable in an era of such pronounced anti-immigrant hostilities. The demand that states recognize that urban settlement is a gateway to a durable solution (let alone a de facto durable solution in itself) will raise the ire of xenophobes and others who perceive such integration as threatening to their interests. However, disregarding these politics because of their unpalatability is not the solution. Rather, advocates must develop strategies to convince host communities (and governments) that refugees (and other non-nationals, for the distinctions are often missed) do not represent an inherent threat to them. This means developing media and publicity strategies that highlight the threats to law, welfare, and security that come from continued exclusion. By allowing states to "progressively expand" refugees' capabilities, advocates may also be better able to negotiate locally acceptable programmatic interventions.

In addition to the practicality of developing a unified approach to advocacy, there are more fundamental ethical challenges to the capability approach. In this chapter's introductory sections, I restrict the application of this approach to those cases where urban settlement is part of a conscious policy, which excludes the vast majority of Africa's urban refugees. Policies limiting refugees to particular (usually rural) settlements may violate the principle equating protection with capability expansion, but such restrictions do not in turn justify "illegal" settlement in urban areas. Such violations may provide short-term benefits but are likely to be counterproductive, as they may harden policies that result in reduced capabilities and protection for others. Moreover, by working outside of the law, refugees undermine the value of legal action as a form of protection. This does not, however, mean there are no ethical responsibilities for protecting urban refugees who are "illegally" in cities. This approach, though, does not (yet) outline what those obligations should be or how advocates should promote the right to settle outside of camps.

There are also risks associated with my repeated demand for compromise, as such an approach relies to a certain degree on a system of adaptive preferences. Sen highlights the danger that such an approach will result in the poor becoming accomplices in their own poverty by growing resigned to their objective deprivation.[48] Although the justifications offered for self-settlement usually include both saving costs and promoting individual freedom, refugees must nevertheless contextualize their preferences. Doctors trained in one environment may, for example, never be able to practice in another because upgrading medical qualifications is too costly. While every effort should be made to expand individuals' opportunities for choice, we must also recognize the need for resignation while at the same time not promoting a kind of "defensive adjustment of desires and expectations" following long-term exposure to grave deprivation.[49] As it now stands, this chapter does not adequately define the conditions under which refugees are expected to adapt their preferences. Nor does it adequately determine when such adaptations fundamentally denude an individual's dignity or self-worth.

This approach may also be criticized for trading a vague term like "protection" for the equally ill-defined term "capability." Indeed, even those sympathetic to Sen's approach recognize the difficulty of operationalizing it. Sabina Alkire argues that Sen has not adequately specified how the various value judgments within his approach should be ordered for its practical use.[50] She goes on to suggest that without a certain degree of specification—and simplification—the capability approach cannot be effectively used.[51] This is a legitimate concern, but also one that I have sought to address by providing "rules of thumb" for early intervention. This does not, however, fully address the issue of developing effective and contextualized standards of protection. Further research on individual cases and findings from additional cases will help develop both a set of areas for early intervention and better tools for evaluating successes and failures in expanding capabilities. Importantly, this research need not be only refugee-specific, although adaptations for displaced persons are important, but can draw on a growing body of empirical studies and policy interventions informed by the capability approach.

Lastly, this approach, as an empirically informed methodology, demands regular monitoring, evaluation, and analysis of obstacles, activities, and their impacts. Unfortunately, while Africa has one of the highest numbers of refugees per capita in the world, it is also woefully ill equipped for undertaking such analysis.[52] Moreover, to be most effective, analysis of refugee protection must be undertaken by those who have a holistic understanding of the socioeconomic and political environments in which they live. In the absence of reliable, objective, and regular information, a temptation will exist for states (and other actors) to rely permanently on a set of minimum standards or to continue indefinitely with early intervention programs that may not promote the progressive expansion of refugee capabilities.

Conclusion

By way of conclusion I wish only to suggest that effective refugee protection—for urban and rural areas—will only be achieved through the expansion of the number of people able to analyze the status of refugee protection in host communities. Given the growing scholarship inspired by Sen's capability framework, refugee advocates can capitalize on innovative and practical thinking done by those working in other fields. These efforts must, however, be translated into locally specific programs. Preparing people for this task means going beyond technical and legal training in ways that generate bureaucrats, NGO employees, advocates, and scholars ready to analyze and debate existing conditions and collectively plot a course towards better protection.

Notes

I am grateful for comments from other participants at the conference that led to this volume, and in particular, William O'Neill and David Hollenbach. The chapter has also greatly benefited from the insights of Valerie Reboud, resident capabilities expert and migration specialist at the Agence Française de Développement.

1. Marc Sommers, *Fear in Bongoland: Burundi Refugees in Urban Tanzania* (New York: Berghahn Books, 2001); Gaim Kibreab, "Eritrean and Ethiopian Urban Refugees in Khartoum: What the Eye Refuses to See," *African Studies Review* 39 (1996): 131–78.

2. Karen Jacobsen, "Refugees and Asylum Seekers in Urban Areas: A Livelihoods Perspective," *Journal of Refugee Studies* 19 (2006): 273–86.

3. At the time of writing, the UNHCR has developed a draft revision to its 1997 policy on assisting refugees in urban areas. Although the draft was the result of a broad consultative process, it has not yet been released to those outside of the UNHCR.

4. See, for example, Barbara E. Harrell-Bond, *Imposing Aid: Emergency Assistance to Refugees* (Oxford: Oxford University Press, 1996); Loren B. Landau, "Beyond the Losers: Transforming Governmental Practice in Refugee-Affected Tanzania," *Journal of Refugee Studies* 16 (2003): 19–43.

5. Martha Nussbaum, "Therapeutic Arguments: Epicurus and Aristotle," in *The Norms of Nature: Studies in Hellenistic Ethics,* ed. Malcome Schofield and Gisela Strikers (Cambridge: Cambridge University Press, 1986), 62.

6. See Jane McAdam, *The Refugee Convention as a Rights Blueprint for Persons in Need of International Protection,* New Issues in Refugee Research Paper no. 125 (Geneva: United Nations High Commissioner for Refugees, 2006); Catherine Phuong, "The Concept of 'Effective Protection' in the Context of Irregular Secondary Movement and Protection in Regions of Origins," *Global Migration Perspectives* 26 (2005); United Nations High Commissioner for Refugees, *The State of the World's Refugees: The Challenge of Protection* (Oxford: Oxford University Press, 1993).

7. See Jean-François Bayart, Stephen Ellis, and Béatrice Hibou, "From Kleptocracy to the Felonious State," in *The Criminalization of the State in Africa,* ed. Jean-François Bayart, Stephen Ellis, and Béatrice Hibou (Oxford: Oxford University Press, 1999); James Currey, Patrick Chabal, and Jean-Pascal Daloz, *Africa Works: Disorder as Political Instrument* (Oxford: International African Institute in Association, 1999).

8. See SPHERE, "Sphere, Humanitarian Charter and Minimum Standards in Disaster Response," http://www.sphereproject.org/.

9. David A. Crocker, "Functioning and Capability: The Foundations of Sen's and Nussbaum's Development Ethic," *Political Theory* 20 (1992): 600. See also Amartya K. Sen, "Well-Being, Agency, and Freedom: The Dewey Lectures, 1984," *Journal of Philosophy* 82 (1985):169–221.

10. John Rawls, "The Priority of Right and Ideas of the Good," *Philosophy and Public Affairs* 19 (1988): 257.

11. See Marc-Antoine Perouse de Montclos and Peter Mwanga Kagwanja, "Refugee Camps or Cities? The Socio-Economic Dynamics of the Dadaab and Kakuma Camps in Northern Kenya," *Journal of Refugee Studies* 13 (2000): 205–22; also Robert Chambers, "Hidden Losers: The Impact of Rural Refugees and Refugee Programs on Poorer Hosts," in *Refugee Aid and Development Theory and Practice,* ed. Robert F. Gorman (Westport, CT: Greenwood Press, 1993).

12. See Giorgio Agamben, *Homo Sacer: Sovereign Power and Bare Life* (Stanford: Stanford University Press, 1988); Loren B. Landau, "Immigration and the State of Exception: Security and Sovereignty in Refugee-Affected Africa," *Millennium Journal of International Studies* 34 (2005): 325–48.

13. For justification of the interrelationship between equity and development in urban environments, see Jenny Robinson, "City Futures: New Territories for Development Studies," in *Development and Displacement,* ed. Jenny Robinson (Oxford: Open University, 2002); Peter Evans, "Political Strategies for More Liveable Cities: Lessons from Six Cases of Development and Political

Transition," in *Liveable Cities? Urban Struggles for Livelihood and Sustainability*, ed. Peter Evans (Berkeley: University of California Press, 2002); Jo Beal, Owen Crankshaw, and Susan Parnell, *Uniting a Divided City: Governance and Social Exclusion in Johannesburg* (London: Earthscan, 2002).

14. Fedde Groot, deputy regional representative for Southern Africa, UNHCR, interview with author, Pretoria, July 13, 2005.

15. The hazards of such reliance are painfully evident in South Africa, where approximately thirty Somali shopkeepers, almost all of whom are refugees or asylum seekers, were murdered in Cape Town's peri-urban townships during August 2006. See Babalo Ndenze, "Somali Shopkeeper 'Critical' after Armed Attack in Delft," *Cape Times*, September 4, 2006.

16. Katarzyna Grabska, "Marginalization in Urban Spaces of the Global South: Urban Refugees in Cairo," *Journal of Refugee Studies* 19 (2006): 287–307; Sarah Dryden-Peterson, "'I Find Myself as Someone Who Is in the Forest': Urban Refugees as Agents of Social Change in Kampala, Uganda," *Journal of Refugee Studies* 19 (2006): 381–95; Elizabeth H. Campbell, "Urban Refugees in Nairobi: Problems of Protection, Mechanisms of Survival, and Possibilities for Integration," *Journal of Refugee Studies* 19 (2006): 396–413; Loren B. Landau and Karen Jacobsen, "Refugees in the New Johannesburg," *Forced Migration Review* 19 (2004): 44–46; Marc Sommers, *Fear in Bongoland: Burundi Refugees in Urban Tanzania* (New York: Berghahn Books, 2001).

17. Amartya K. Sen, *Inequality Reexamined* (Oxford: Oxford University Press, 1992), 117.

18. Loren B. Landau, "Immigration and the State of Exception: Security and Sovereignty in Refugee-Affected Africa," *Millennium Journal of International Studies* 34, no. 2 (2005): 325–48.

19. For discussions of urban refugees' often remarkable achievements, see Maja Korac, "The Lack of Integration Policy and Experiences of Settlement: A Case Study of Refugees in Rome," *Journal of Refugee Studies* 16 (2003): 398–421; Michela Macchiavello, *Forced Migrants as an Under-Utilised Asset: Refugee Skills, Livelihoods, and Achievements in Kampala, Uganda*, UNHCR, New Issues in Refugee Research, Working Paper No. 95 (Geneva: Evaluation and Policy Analysis Unit, United Nations High Commissioner for Refugees, 2003).

20. John Rawls, "The Priority of Right and Ideas of the Good," *Philosophy and Public Affairs* 19 (1988): 257.

21. See Catherine Phuong, "The Concept of 'Effective Protection' in the Context of Irregular Secondary Movement and Protection in Regions of Origins," *Global Migration Perspectives* 26 (2005): 2.

22. See ibid., 3–4.

23. Erika Feller, "Statement by Ms. Erika Feller, director, Department of International Protection" (address, Fifty-fifth Session of the Executive Committee of the High Commissioner's Programme, Geneva, Switzerland, October 7, 2004).

24. Lisbon Expert Roundtable, "Summary Conclusions on the Concept of 'Effective Protection' in Context of Secondary Movements of Refugees and Asylum-Seekers" (paper presented at the Agenda for Protection Lisbon Expert Roundtable, Lisbon, Portugal, December 9–10, 2002). See especially paragraph 15(g).

25. For discussion of mobility and cities, see Zygmunt Bauman, *Globalization: The Human Consequences* (New York: Columbia University Press, 2000); AbdouMaliq Simone, *For the City Yet to Come: Changing African Life in Four Cities* (Durham, NC: Duke University Press, 2004); Achille Mbembe, "Aesthetics of Superfluity," *PublicCulture* 16 (2004): 373–405.

26. Amartya K. Sen, *Development as Freedom* (Oxford: Oxford University Press, 1999), 3.

27. See Sen, *Commodities and Capabilities* (Oxford: Elsevier Science Publishers, 1985), 10; also Suhi Saith, "Capabilities: The Concept and Its Operationalisation," *QEH Working Paper Series* 66 (Oxford: Queen Elizabeth House, University of Oxford, 2001), 8.

28. Sen, *Inequality Reexamined*, 5.

29. Sen, *Commodities and Capabilites*, 18–20.

30. Ibid., 25–26; see also Sen, *Development as Freedom*, 70–71.

31. This perspective not only resonates with Sen's work on entitlements, but with broader debates over the indivisibility of positive and negative freedoms. See Isaiah Berlin, "Two Concepts of Liberty," in *Four Essays on Liberty* (Oxford: Oxford University Press, 1969).

32. Henry Steiner, *An Essay on Rights* (Oxford: Blackwell, 1994).

33. See Nikolas Rose, *Powers of Freedom: Reframing Political Thought* (Cambridge: Cambridge University Press, 1999).

34. See, for example, Karen Jacobsen, *The Economic Life of Refugees* (New York: Kumarian Press, 2005); Barbara E. Harrell-Bond, "The Experiences of Refugees as Recipients of Aid," in *Refugees: Perspectives on the Experience of Forced Migration,* ed. Alastair Ager (New York: Cassell, 1999); Giam Kibreab, "The Myth of Dependency among Camp Refugees," *Journal of Refugee Studies* 6 (1993): 321–49.

35. Sen, *Inequality Reexamined*, 44–45.

36. Amartya K. Sen, "The Standard of Living," in *The Standards of Living*, ed. Geoffrey Hawthorn (Cambridge: Cambridge University Press, 1987), 109.

37. Amartya K. Sen, "Capability as Well-Being," in *The Quality of Life*, ed. Martha Nussbaum and Amartya Sen (Oxford: Oxford University Press, 1993), 31.

38. Amartya K. Sen, *Resources, Values, and Development* (Oxford: Basil Blackwell, 1984): 497; see also David A. Clark, "The Capability Approach: Its Development, Critiques, and Recent Advances," *Global Poverty Research Group Working Paper*, GPRG-WPS-032 (2005), www .gprg.org.

39. See, for further discussion of the strengths and dangers of lists, Amartya K. Sen, "Capabilities, Lists, and Public Reasons: Continuing the Conversation," *Feminist Economics* 10 (2004): 77–81. Also, Ingrid Robeyns, "Sen's Capability Approach and Gender Inequality: Selecting Relevant Capabilities," *Feminist Economics* 9 (2003): 61–92; and Sabina Alkire, *Valuing Freedoms: Sen's Capability Approach and Poverty Reduction.* (Oxford: Oxford University Press, 2002), esp. chap. four. In this instance the list represents a critical review of a list of recommendations published in Karen Jacobsen and Loren B. Landau, "Recommendations for Urban Refugee Policy," *Forced Migration Review* 23 (2005): 52.

40. See Katarzyna Grabska, "Marginalization in Urban Spaces of the Global South: Urban Refugees in Cairo," *Journal of Refugee Studies* 19 (2006): 287–307, and Loren B. Landau, "Urbanization, Nativism, and the Rule of Law in South Africa's 'Forbidden Cities,'" *Third World Quarterly* 26 (2005): 1115–34.

41. See Michael M. Cernea and Chris McDowell, "Reconstructing Resettlers' and Refugees' Livelihoods," in *Risks and Reconstruction: Experiences of Resettlers and Refugees*, ed. Michael M. Cernea and Chris McDowell (Washington, DC: World Bank, 2000), 1–10.

42. Karen Jacobsen and Loren B. Landau, "Recommendations for Urban Refugee Policy," *Forced Migration Review* 23 (2005): 52.

43. Cf. Vaishali Mamgain, with Karen Collins, "Off the Boat, Now Off to Work: Refugees in the Labour Market in Portland, Maine," *Journal of Refugee Studies* 16 (2003): 113–46.

44. Sen, *Development as Freedom*.

45. See Baruti Amisi and Richard Ballard, "In the Absence of Citizenship: Congolese Refugee Struggle and Organisation in South Africa," *Forced Migration Working Paper No. 16* (2005), http://migration.wits.ac.za/AmisiBallardwp.pdf (accessed November 24, 2007); T. J. Araia, "Routes, Motivations, and Duration: Explaining Eritrean Forced Migrants' Journeys to Johannesburg" (master's thesis, University of the Witwatersrand, 2005); J. M. Mang'ana, "The Effects of Migration on Human Rights Consciousness among Congolese Refugees in Johannesburg" (master's thesis, University of the Witwatersrand, 2004).

46. See Gail Hopkins, "Somali Community Organizations in London and Toronto: Collaboration and Effectiveness," *Journal of Refugee Studies* 19 (2006): 261–380; Isaiah Berlin, "From Hope and Fear Set Free," in *Isaiah Berlin, Concepts and Categories: Philosophical Essays,* ed. Henry Hardy (London: Hogarth Press, 1978).

47. See Ernst B. Haas, *When Knowledge Is Power: Three Models of Change in International Organizations* (Berkeley: University of California Press, 1990).

48. Amartya K. Sen, "Justice: Means Versus Freedoms," *Philosophy and Public Affairs* 19 (1990): 111-121; see also Sen, *Commodities and Capabilities,* 82–83.

49. Sen, *Inequality Reexamined,* 9–10.

50. Alkire, *Valuing Freedoms.*

51. See also Ingrid Robeyns, "An Unworkable Idea or a Promising Alternative? Sen's Capability Approach Re-Examined," *Centre for Economic Studies Discussion Paper* (University of Leuven), no. 00.30 (2000): 26; Working Papers of the Human Development and Capability Association, http://www.capabilityapproach.com (accessed November 24, 2007).

52. Global Commission for International Migration, "Summary Report of the Regional Hearing for Africa" (paper presented at the Global Commission for International Migration, Cape Town, South Africa, February 28–March 1, 2005); Holly Reed, *The Demography of Forced Migration: Summary of a Workshop* (Washington, DC: National Academy Press, 1998).

III

Gender and the Rights of the Displaced

7

Sexual Violence, Gender Roles, and Displacement

Binaifer Nowrojee

Women who flee their homes in search of sanctuary from violence too often find that there is no meaningful refuge—they have simply escaped violence in war to face a different type of violence in the refugee camps. Suffering from their disadvantaged status, women face particular protection and security risks in refugee camps, aside from the challenges of heading households. Refugee women are vulnerable to rape, sexual assault, and other forms of sexual violence. Levels of domestic violence are also high in many refugee communities; in refugee settings, pressures regarding housing, food, security, and other resources often strain domestic situations and erupt in violence.

While the conflicts that cause women to flee often make news headlines, the plight of women who become refugees and displaced persons frequently remains unpublicized. In many cases, refugee and displaced women flee conflict after being terrorized by rape and other sexual and physical abuse. Although they seek refuge to escape these dangers, many are subjected to similar abuse as refugees. The former UN special rapporteur on violence against women, Radhika Coomaraswamy, found that "sexual violence against refugees is a global problem. Refugees from Bosnia, Rwanda, Somalia, and Vietnam have brought harrowing stories of abuse and suffering. It constitutes a violation of basic human rights, instilling fear in the lives of victims already profoundly affected by their displacement."[1] Refugee and displaced women, uprooted from their homes and countries by war, internal strife, or natural catastrophe are vulnerable to violence both as a result of the surrounding problem and because of their dependency on outsiders for relief provisions. The internally displaced are further at risk because the abuses they seek to escape are often being committed by the very government that should afford them protection. Moreover, because they have not crossed any international border to seek refuge or asylum, displaced persons can claim only minimal protection from international law. While the United Nations High Commissioner for Refugees (UNHCR) is tasked with the primary responsibility for ensuring protection and assistance to refugees, no similar organization exists within the United Nations system for internally displaced persons. The programs run by the UNHCR and the UN Development Program (UNDP) for the internally displaced operate only on an ad hoc basis.

Sexual Violence

The wide range of abuses against refugees and displaced persons frequently include rape and other forms of sexual assault. Women refugees are raped because they are refugees, because of their actual or perceived political or ethnic affiliations, and because they are women. The use of this gender-specific form of abuse frequently has political or ethnic, as well as gender-specific, components. In some cases, refugee and displaced persons' camps are relatively close to the site of the conflict that caused displacement. Women in such camps are often the object of attacks from factions that enter the camps in order to dominate and punish those refugees perceived to be supporting opposing factions. In other cases, persons who support different sides of a conflict or who even may be combatants on different sides may mingle with civilian populations within camps. The humiliation, pain, and terror that the rapist inflicts on an individual woman in this context is intended to degrade the entire ethnic or political group.

Rape and other forms of sexual assault are frequently gender-specific not only in their form but also in their motivation. Thus, refugee and displaced women and girls are raped because of their gender, irrespective of their age, ethnicity, or political beliefs. In host countries, local residents and even police, military, and immigration officials often view refugee women as targets for assault. They subject refugee and displaced women to rape or other forms of sexual extortion in return for the granting of passage to safety, refugee status, personal documentation, or relief supplies.

Fellow refugees may also target displaced and refugee women for sexual abuse. The dislocation and violence experienced by displaced and refugee populations often destroy family and social structures, and with them the norms and taboos that normally would have proscribed sexual violence against women. Moreover, the anger, uncertainty, and helplessness sometimes experienced by male refugees unable to assume their traditionally dominant roles are often translated into violent behavior toward women.

In many refugee camps, the task of fetching water, collecting firewood, or gathering vegetables falls on the women and girls. Often, women are liable to be attacked on the outskirts of the camps while carrying out routine, daily tasks such as these or searching for employment.

The injuries that refugee and displaced women sustain from being violently raped persist long after the incident. Refugee women frequently report ongoing medical problems, including miscarriages by women raped when pregnant, hemorrhaging for long periods, inability to control urination, sleeplessness, nightmares, chest and back pains, and painful menstruation. Moreover, refugee and displaced women who become pregnant as a result of rape are often unable to procure safe abortions because abortion is either illegal or too expensive.

For women who have undergone the practice of female genital mutilation, the physical injuries caused by rape are compounded. Female genital mutilation, also known as female circumcision, is the collective name given to several different traditional practices involving the cutting of female genitals. In the most extreme version, infibulation, the clitoris and inner vaginal lips are removed and the outer lips are stitched closed leaving only a small opening (sometimes the size of a match stick) for the flow of urine and menstrual blood. Sexual intercourse for women who have undergone this operation is painful unless the opening is gradually expanded over time or they are re-cut to widen the opening. Rape becomes excruciatingly painful for the refugee women who have undergone this procedure. Refugee women who had been circumcised often have their vaginal openings torn or cut by their attackers in the course of being raped. The healing process is exacerbated by the poor living conditions in refugee camps and the greater likelihood of infection.

Strong cultural stigma attached to rape further intensifies the rape victims' physical and psychological trauma. Women in refugee and displaced camps who acknowledge being raped may be ostracized, isolated, or even punished by their husbands and families. In some places, women who have been raped face not only the physical and psychological trauma of rape but also the likelihood of rejection by their families. UNHCR officials report cases in which refugee families have begged UNHCR officials to move their daughters to another camp after they have been raped because of the stigma on the family.

As a result, women survivors of sexual violence often are reluctant to seek medical assistance or to file police reports, because they do not want it known that they were raped. Most refugee women who have been raped go to a doctor only if they suffer other injuries from being beaten, knifed, or shot, and even then many do not mention that they were raped. Even when incidents are reported, however, effective responses may not be forthcoming, since international humanitarian organizations as well as countries of asylum often are not properly set up or equipped to handle such gender-related abuse.

Domestic Violence

Domestic violence is a leading cause of female injuries around the world. Women are often targets of domestic violence because of their unequal status in society. Domestic violence usually involves the infliction of bodily injury accompanied by verbal threats and harassment, emotional and psychological abuse, or the destruction of property, and it is usually employed as a means of coercion, control, revenge, or punishment of a person with whom the abuser is or has been involved in an intimate relationship. The assailant, in fact, frequently blames his violence on the victim and on her behavior and may use the violence to assert his control. As a result, the woman victim may become isolated, cut off from family or community support, and afraid to venture from her home. She may also be made to feel that her inability to avoid abuse at the hands of her intimate partner means that she is somehow inadequate, a failure, even deserving of abuse.

Many women refugees were victims of domestic violence long before they fled their country, but the special pressures, uncertainties, and indignities associated with their flight and the housing, security, food, and other problems that people tend to face in the camps exacerbate already frayed domestic situations, often leading to increased violence in the home. Women often experience severe violence in their homes, including rape, murder, assault, and battery—crimes that are prohibited by the criminal laws of virtually all countries. Yet when committed against a woman in an intimate relationship, these attacks are more often tolerated by law enforcement authorities as the norm than prosecuted as crimes, even when laws exist that specifically penalize domestic violence. In many countries, marital rape is not recognized as a crime. In a number of countries, those who commit domestic violence are prosecuted with less vigor and receive milder punishments than perpetrators of similarly violent crimes not committed in a domestic setting.

Not surprising, many refugee men feel that aspects of life in the camps challenge their traditional male role. In particular, male refugees complain that their role and standing in the home is effectively being usurped by UNHCR and relief organizations providing food and other necessities. This challenge to their traditional role as providers for their families tends to result in anger, frustration, uncertainty, and helplessness among male refugees, and sometimes this translates into violence against women in the refugee camps.

Within the refugee camps, systems that women had formerly relied upon to help address domestic violence—extended networks of family, neighbors, and community leaders—still exist, but in much weaker, more compromised, and less reliable forms. Consequently, battered women are often left destitute, with few means to obtain protection and few opportunities to hide from their abusers. Often, perpetrators are left free and go unpunished. This is due to a lack of effective legal mechanisms and to the reluctance of women victims to report their abusers to the police. Thus, abusers often remain free to further beat or torment their victims with virtual impunity.

Addressing the problem of domestic violence is a complex matter. Many women feel obliged to conceal the fact of their own abuse and to continue to live in violent relationships. The various reasons include a desire to maintain the higher status given to women who are married or have a male partner, religious convictions, a belief that their decision is better for their children, and the existence of emotional attachments.

Women abused by a spouse or intimate partner confront unique difficulties in bringing their attackers to justice and securing safety for themselves and other family members. They may, for example, be financially dependent on their abuser, reluctant to have their partners jailed or their families broken up, or fearful of condemnation by their families or communities should they pursue criminal charges. These and other factors often make women reluctant to bring charges in domestic violence cases or lead them to drop charges already filed. It is critical, therefore, to provide domestic violence victims with measures of support, such as mediation and counseling by community elders, family members, or friends. In many cases, women look to nonlitigation, community-based mediation, and counseling to resolve domestic violence disputes. Although mediation and counseling may work well in some cases, in others such alternatives can leave women vulnerable to further violence and with little meaningful protection.

The attitudes of law enforcement officials frequently serve the interests of the abuser, not those of the woman who is his victim. Women commonly face huge obstacles in seeking legal protection from domestic violence or in getting law enforcement authorities to take action against and prosecute their batterers and in obtaining protection from further violence. Laws against rape frequently exempt marital rape from criminal sanction. Police in some cases force women to withdraw complaints about domestic violence or simply refuse to charge men with domestic assault. Women who seek restraining or protection orders are often turned away by judicial authorities. In many countries, judges readily accept "honor" or "heat of passion" defenses by men who have murdered their wives, accepting a woman's adultery or other action as "legitimate provocation." Police and judicial authorities also dismiss domestic violence as a "private" matter rather than a crime that demands urgent state action.

Refugee women who are subjected to domestic violence are often reluctant to invoke the laws of the host country to address the abuse. They often face pressure from within their communities, and from their families and partners, not to report cases of domestic violence to the police. They may also feel intimidated and fear ostracization by their families and community or retaliation from their abuser. They may still be emotionally attached to their abuser or be dependent on him for their and their children's welfare. At home, women victims usually turn to community mediation structures, although these may not be adequate to provide protection, especially in male-dominated societies.

The Responsibility of Governments

International law imposes clear obligations on governments to prohibit rape and other forms of sexual violence. At a minimum, such abuses violate the right to security of the person.[2] Rape committed by or permitted by a state agent is torture under international law, which defines torture as any act "intentionally inflicted on a person for such purposes as obtaining from him or a third person information or a confession, punishing him for an act he or a third person has committed or is suspected of having committed, or intimidating or coercing him or a third person, or for any reason based on discrimination of any kind, when such pain or suffering is inflicted by or at the acquiescence of a public official or other person acting in an official capacity."[3] International human rights norms also require governments to ensure that all individuals within their territories, regardless of citizenship, enjoy the equal protection of the law.[4] In the case of refugees, the responsibility to protect "remains the primary responsibility of the countries where the refugees find themselves."[5]

Notwithstanding human rights standards, host governments often show little concern for the violence experienced by refugees, including rape of refugee women. Their indifference is demonstrated by ineffective security arrangements in the camps and by inadequate investigation and prosecution of rape and other forms of sexual violence against refugee women, even when the perpetrators are state agents tasked with refugee protection. The police often provide inadequate security around the camps and make no concerted effort to arrest or prosecute those responsible for rape. One reason for the failure to investigate and prosecute rape is law enforcement officials' refusal to treat such claims seriously.

Aside from international norms, the domestic laws of virtually all host governments also prohibit rape. However, the ability of refugee and displaced women actually to seek legal redress is undermined for a number of different reasons. They are often destitute; unable to speak the local language; fearful of dealing with authorities; or situated in remote areas, miles from the nearest police station or court. Where the local criminal justice system is unresponsive to allegations of rape, many refugee survivors of sexual violence consider legal redress futile. In particular, local police often are unwilling to investigate complaints against fellow police, military, or immigration officials. These factors, alone or in combination, effectively deny refugees who have survived rape access to justice.

The Responsibility of the Relief Community

The international relief community has been slow to address the problem of violence against women in refugee camps, although some progress has been made in the past decade. Guidelines have been developed to improve protection, but while these documents reflect enhanced awareness of the urgent plight of refugee women, they have not been properly or consistently implemented in all situations by UNHCR, host countries, or nongovernmental relief organizations. UNHCR—the lead UN agency for refugee relief and protection—has promulgated two sets of guidelines to deal with sexual assault of refugee women and to provide direction to staff on ways to better protect women refugees. However, these guidelines have not formed a routine and integral part of all UNHCR programs from the very first stage of any refugee crisis. Too often, women refugees have been left languishing in camps with little or no attention paid to their protection needs—and action is only taken after high rates of violence against women come to the attention of UNHCR and the host government.

In 1991 UNHCR promulgated the *Guidelines on the Protection of Refugee Women* to assist the staff of UNHCR in identifying and responding to the issues, problems, and risks facing refugee women. Almost four years later, in 1995, UNHCR issued *Sexual Violence Guidelines* to improve or initiate services to address the special needs and concerns of refugees who are at risk of or have suffered sexual violence.[6]

The *Guidelines on the Protection of Refugee Women* (hereafter *Protection Guidelines*) prescribe measures that "can" or "may" be taken to counter physical and sexual attacks and abuse of women during flight and in their countries of asylum.[7] They call for, among other things, changing the physical design and location of refugee camps to provide greater physical security, using security patrols, reducing the use of closed facilities or detention centers, training staff regarding the particular problems faced by refugee women and employing female staff to work with women refugees to identify their concerns, establishing mechanisms for law enforcement within the refugee camps, educating refugee women about their rights, giving priority to assessing the protection needs of unaccompanied refugee women, and ensuring women's direct access to food and other services, including whatever registration process is used to determine eligibility for assistance.

The *Sexual Violence Guidelines* supplement the *Protection Guidelines* by suggesting a range of preventive measures that can and should be taken to prevent sexual violence.

These steps include ensuring that the physical design and location of the refugee camps enhance physical security; providing frequent security patrols by law enforcement authorities and by the refugees themselves; installing fencing around the camps; identifying and promoting alternatives to refugee camps where possible; organizing interagency meetings between UNHCR, other relief organizations, and relevant government officials, as well as the refugees themselves, to develop a plan of action to prevent sexual violence; and assigning to the camps a greater number of female protection officers, field interpreters, doctors, health workers, and counselors.

Domestic violence has been much more difficult to tackle, and UNHCR has been reluctant to take it on. There is a significant gap in UNHCR's *Guidelines on the Protection of Refugee Women*: it does not substantively address the problem of domestic violence. In fact, the one reference to domestic abuse contained in the *Sexual Violence Guidelines* discourages staff from becoming involved in domestic rape cases. Section 3.5 of the *Sexual Violence Guidelines* reads, "Extreme caution should be exercised before any intervention is made on sexual violence in domestic situations. Concerned staff should be aware of the possible difficulties that may arise following intervention. In some situations, more harm may be caused to the victim and other relatives by becoming involved than had the matter been left alone."

Refugee Asylum Law

International refugee law protects the right of persons who have fled a country to seek asylum in another if they have a well-founded fear of persecution should they be returned to the country they have fled. However, refugee women who have suffered sexual violence have faced great difficulty in obtaining asylum elsewhere for three reasons.

First, the procedure to determine asylum eligibility is generally insensitive, and even hostile, to refugee women who have suffered sexual abuse or who for other reasons may have difficulty relating their claims. In this procedure, all refugees are required to describe the persecution they have suffered to asylum adjudicators. However, refugee women are often reluctant to disclose experiences of sexual violence, particularly if the asylum adjudicators are men, due to the stigma attached to sexual violence or as a result of trauma.[8] Other refugee women might refuse to detail the abuses they have experienced for fear of retribution against their family members or rejection by their communities. Asylum adjudicators who are not aware of such concerns have negatively interpreted women's reluctance to describe the sexual violence inflicted on them and incorrectly judged their testimony not credible.

Second, despite some progress, asylum adjudicators have tended to dismiss gender-specific violations experienced by refugee women as "personal" or "cultural" harms that do not qualify as political persecution. Often, accounts of rape and other sexual abuse perpetrated against refugee women for political purposes have been treated in a discriminatory manner by asylum adjudicators who have dismissed such persecution as "personal" harm and denied asylum.

Third, asylum adjudicators have presumptively excluded women asylum applicants on the grounds that gender-related persecution is not specifically listed in the UN

Convention Regarding the Status of Refugees. That convention requires states to grant asylum to refugees fleeing a well-founded fear of persecution on the grounds of "race, religion, nationality, membership of a particular social group, or political opinion."

Gradually, however, the international community is recognizing that gender-related persecution is a basis for asylum. The UNHCR has interpreted the refugee definition to include women asylum seekers with gender-related claims as members of a "particular social group." Two broad categories of gender-related claims have been identified: those in which the persecution constitutes a *type* of harm that is particular to the applicant's gender, such as rape or genital mutilation; and those in which the persecution may be imposed *because of* the applicant's gender, for example, when a woman has violated societal norms regarding women's proper conduct.[9]

Several countries and other political entities have taken actions that have contributed to the growing acceptance of gender-related persecution as grounds for asylum. In 1984 the European Parliament determined that women fearing cruel or inhuman treatment as a result of seeming to have transgressed social mores should be considered a "social group" for the purposes of determining their status. Both Canada and the United States have issued guidelines to their immigration officials to help them identify women who should be granted asylum because they suffered gender-specific forms of abuse used for political persecution in their homelands. These guidelines educate asylum adjudicators to recognize gender-specific forms of violence and provide them with procedures and methods to better evaluate whether individual claims meet the refugee standard. While these guidelines do not change the standard that women asylum seekers must meet, they do recognize that human rights abuses faced by women because of their gender can rise to the level of persecution.

Community Justice Mechanisms in Refugee Camps

Refugee women are also discouraged by other refugees, including their families, from taking complaints about sexual or domestic violence to the local police or the courts. Those women who do lodge cases often face recrimination and blame from within the refugee community for reporting on fellow refugees instead of seeking assistance from within the community. In most camps, refugees set up their own community justice machinery, based on customary or traditional mechanisms. Often, this entails the appointment by the community of a group of respected elders, mostly male refugees, to act as arbiter of disputes.

UNHCR's policy on the protection of refugee women encourages its staff to improve the standards of internal dispute resolution mechanisms within refugee camps to ensure that protection problems of women refugees are covered and that women have equal access to the remedies provided by these structures. Section 51 of the *Guidelines on the Protection of Refugee Women* charges UNHCR staff to "review legal codes and processes adopted in the camps to make sure that protection needs of women refugees are covered and that women have equal access to the remedies provided in these courts. Encourage adoption of rules governing these situations, encourage the participation of refugee women in these procedures, and provide training to those administering them."[10] These refugee-run structures are not state-sanctioned courts of law; rather, they operate as a community justice system run by refugees to resolve disputes among themselves.

Frequently, however, the lack of enforcement powers leaves the refugee-run system in no position to deliver justice to victims. Moreover, without monitoring or guidance and training on how to deal with cases, particularly serious cases of domestic and sexual violence, the refugee-run system tends not to meet the needs of women victims of violence in the camps. In cases of domestic violence in the Burundian refugee camps in Tanzania, husbands who beat their wives were required by the council to "apologize" formally by purchasing for them a piece of cloth or paying a small fine.

Women refugees who are victims of violence are often encouraged to seek redress through this refugee-run channel rather than lodge a report with the police. Involving the police or judicial authorities is done only as a very last resort and is often not viewed as a practical option due to discrimination against refugees by the local authorities as well as the distance to the nearest police station and the difficulties of travel. Also, seeking the intervention of such official judicial structures is perceived as bringing shame upon the family and is cause for a woman to be ostracized.

However, in many cases the traditional mechanisms do not constitute a satisfactory form of justice because the process is reconciliatory or because it minimizes women's claims. Domestic violence is largely regarded as a private matter rather than a crime that the state must prosecute and punish. Refugee women are often urged to reconcile with and return to their abusive husbands, sometimes placing them at great physical risk. To the extent that control of women's sexuality and physical integrity is regarded as a matter of family or community honor rather than personal autonomy and individual rights, refugee women still face enormous obstacles in their search for redress when they have suffered abuse committed in the name of custom or tradition. Throughout the world women are still relegated to a second-class status that increases their vulnerability to abuse and lessens their able to protect themselves from discrimination.

On occasion, if a rapist is identified as another refugee, the families settle the case through the elders, with the rapist's family paying a token amount (sometimes as little as a piece of material) in compensation for the crime committed. The settlement is usually negotiated on behalf of the woman by her male relatives, sometimes against her wishes, and the settlement money often remains with the male relatives.

Some refugees express the view that the traditional councils offered a better chance of securing some form of redress, compared to the often uncaring and inadequate criminal justice system. However, community-based mediation mechanisms do not have the power to enforce their judgments or to punish perpetrators and thus deter them from committing further acts of physical violence against women. Hence, they should not always be treated as an acceptable substitute for redress through the criminal justice system.

Conclusion

Notwithstanding some limitations, the *Guidelines on the Protection of Refugee Women* and the *Sexual Violence Guidelines* are important for raising the profile of refugee women throughout UNHCR's mission and ensuring that the needs of women are reflected at every stage of program planning. In particular, they draw critical attention to the widespread, but previously much ignored, problem of violence against women.

Over the past decade, some commendable efforts have been undertaken by UNHCR to initiate more systematic, careful, and effective efforts to address the problem of sexual violence.[11] In some camps UNHCR and its implementing partners have begun to put in place a stronger safety net for refugee women who are victims of violence by expanding and strengthening existing programs to combat such violence. These programs are aimed at raising community awareness of sexual and other gender-based violence; providing counseling for victims of sexual violence; following up rape cases with the police and courts to ensure that they are investigated and that perpetrators are prosecuted; and establishing food distribution systems to ensure women's access to food, particularly in situations of domestic violence or divorce.

Where UNHCR and host governments have made concerted efforts to address violence against women—such as in the Somali refugee camps in Kenya and the Burundian refugee camps in Tanzania—their efforts have not only demonstrated the difficulties of translating guidelines into practice, but have also yielded improvements for the period of time that attention was paid to this issue. This demonstrates that where there is political will to implement the guidelines, gains can be made. In addition to overcoming resource constraints, UNHCR and host governments can overcome apathy and discriminatory attitudes. Once the political will is there, much more can be done to create programs that better protect women.

Such developments show what can be achieved with political will and the appropriate allocation of resources. While it will clearly take some time for these measures to have their full effect, they appear to be a step in the right direction and, if ultimately successful, they could usefully be adapted and replicated in refugee settings elsewhere.

There still remains a clear need for both governments and UNHCR to take much more concerted and systematic action to prevent and punish sexual and domestic violence. Despite some progress in implementing both these sets of guidelines in UNHCR-run refugee camps, violence against refugee women is far from ended.

In many cases, implementation problems stem from the fact that refugee situations are crisis-driven, with relief workers often overwhelmed by a seemingly endless refugee flow. Aside from the exigencies of each situation, consistent implementation of the UNHCR guidelines remains an issue. The UNHCR itself has acknowledged that some of its staff may avoid confronting or remedying widespread sexual violence in refugee camps because of personal discomfort with addressing the issue or a perception that such acts are a private matter or "an inevitable by-product" of the conflict.[12] Additionally, underreporting of sexual assault always allows relief workers to deny the scale of such violence.

UNHCR employees and the staff of private relief agencies under contract to UNHCR must be made aware, through appropriate training, of the widespread sexual violence against refugee and displaced women, and all protection programs should address this issue. All new staff, including police deployed to refugee camps, should be trained on their duty to protect refugees from sexual and domestic violence and on the relevant law and services available for victims. Where possible, female staff should be employed to address the concerns of women refugees subjected to violence. Refugee workers should be trained to treat women victims of violence in a confidential and sensitive manner.

UNHCR should continue to step up its efforts for the full implementation of its guidelines in all refugee camps. These efforts should begin with setting up the camp to ensure physical security for women. Interagency cooperation among UNHCR, other relief organizations, and relevant government agencies, as well as involvement of the refugees themselves, should be utilized to develop a plan of action to prevent violence against women. In a timely and consistent manner, data on all reported incidents of domestic and sexual violence in the camps, showing the number of victims, their ages, and their gender, should be compiled in order to determine problem areas and design solutions. Priority should be given to the protection needs of unaccompanied refugee women and girls, who are often the most vulnerable groups.

In addition to preventive measures, steps should be taken to address responsive services for victims of violence. Appropriate medical care should be available for refugee women and girls, including psychological counseling and care for refugee women who have become pregnant as a result of rape. Where possible, health providers should be women, given cultural sensitivities that may inhibit a woman from seeking medical assistance from male health care workers. Health care workers should be sensitized to the fact that women will often be reluctant to speak of sexual assault. In areas where female genital mutilation is practiced, health care providers should be trained to address the specific medical complications that may occur to raped women who have undergone the practice. There may be a need to establish shelter homes in the refugee camps to provide victims of domestic violence with safe shelter when they need to hide from their abusers.

Refugee protection programs should integrally involve the refugee community. Women's experience of rape can be rendered even more traumatic by cultural or religious views within their community that blame the victim. Community education is necessary within refugee camps to protect rape and domestic violence survivors from further stigmatization, ostracism, or punishment by their own communities. Setting up community reporting mechanisms within refugee camps can help reduce the underreporting of sexual and domestic violence.

Notwithstanding the difficulties and obstacles to ensuring women's safety in refugee camps, it is possible to improve the situation. With adequate political will, resource allocation, and creative, committed programming, we can diminish the levels of violence to which refugee women are exposed.

Notes

This chapter is heavily based on work that Binaifer Nowrojee researched and wrote while she was at Human Rights Watch, particularly "Sexual Assault of Refugee and Displaced Women," in *The Human Rights Watch Global Report on Women's Human Rights* (New York: Human Rights Watch, August 1995), and *Seeking Protection: Addressing Sexual and Domestic Violence in Tanzania's Refugee Camps* (New York: Human Rights Watch, October 2000).

1. United Nations High Commissioner for Refugees, "Sexual Violence against Refugees: Guidelines on Prevention and Response" (Geneva, Switzerland: UNHCR, March 1995), foreword by Radhika Coomaraswamy, special rapporteur on violence against women.

2. International Covenant on Civil and Political Rights (ICCPR), adopted 1966, entered into force in 1976, Article 9.

3. Convention against Torture and Other Cruel, Inhuman, or Degrading Treatment or Punishment, opened for signature by General Assembly resolution 39146 of December 10, 1984, Art. 1. In addition, Article 7 of the ICCPR and the UN Code of Conduct for Law Enforcement Officials, adopted by the General Assembly by resolution 34/169 on December 17, 1979, also prohibit torture.

4. Article 2(1) of the ICCPR states: "Each State Party to the Covenant undertakes to respect and to ensure to all individuals within its territory and subject to its jurisdiction the rights recognized in the present Covenant, without distinction of any kind, such as race, colour, sex, language, religion, political or other opinion, national or social origin, property, birth or other status." Article 26 further provides that all persons are "equal before the law and are entitled without any discrimination to the equal protection of the law."

5. Report of the U.N. High Commissioner for Refugees, 38 UN GAOR Supp. (no. 12) p. 8, UN Doc. A/38/12 (1983).

6. UNHCR, *Sexual Violence against Refugees: Guidelines on Prevention and Response* (Geneva, Switzerland: UNHCR, March 1995).

7. UNHCR, *Guidelines on the Protection of Refugee Women* (Geneva, Switzerland: UNHCR, July 1991).

8. Victims of sexual violence may exhibit a pattern of symptoms referred to as post-traumatic stress disorder or rape trauma syndrome that makes it difficult for them to testify. These symptoms may include persistent fear, a loss of self-confidence and self-esteem, difficulty in concentrating, an attitude of self-blame, a pervasive feeling of loss of control, and memory loss or distortion. Nancy Kelly, "Guidelines for Women's Asylum Claims," *International Journal of Refugee Law* 6 (1994): 533–34.

9. Ibid., 517–34.

10. UNHCR, *Guidelines on the Protection of Refugee Women*, sec. 51.

11. For a fuller discussion, see Susan Martin, "Justice, Women's Rights, and Forced Migration," in this volume.

12. UNHCR, *Sexual Violence against Refugees*, ch. 1, sec. 1.4.

8

Justice, Women's Rights, and Forced Migration

Susan Martin

One of the most significant trends in migration has been the entry of women into migration streams that once had been primarily male. About half of the migrants in the world today are women. They include both international migrants, who move to other countries, and internal migrants, who relocate in other parts of their own countries. Most women move voluntarily, but a significant number are forced migrants who have fled conflict, persecution, environmental degradation, natural disasters, and other situations that affect their habitat and livelihood. Still other women have been trafficked to new locations for purposes of sexual and labor exploitation.

The mobility of women affects the roles of both female and male migrants, families left behind in the migration process, and the source and destination communities and countries of migrants. Each of these issues has an ethical dimension, affecting gender roles, women's rights, and justice for migrants.

Gender Equality and Cultural Relativism

The 2004 World Survey on Women and Development summarized the advantages of using a gender lens in examining migration:

> A gender perspective on migration addresses the limited attention given to the presence of migrant women and their contributions. It begins with the principle that gender is a core organizing principle of social relations, including hierarchical relations in all societies. It views the migration of women and men as influenced by beliefs and expectations about appropriate behaviours for women and men and between women and men, which are reinforced in economic, political and social institutions. A gender perspective acknowledges the influence of gender inequalities that

exist in both origin and destination countries and illustrates how these inequalities can empower women but can also handicap them in the migratory process.[1]

Until the mid-1980s, little of the research or analysis on forced migration trends focused on gender issues. With increasing recognition of the large number and proportion of female refugees, displaced persons, and trafficking victims and the changing role of women more generally, significantly more attention is being paid today to these issues by both researchers and policy makers. No longer can half of the world's forced migrants be ignored.

Yet addressing the challenges presented herein inevitably raises questions about ethics as well as rights. Cultural relativism still rears its head whenever debate turns to efforts needed to improve the rights of women, and when a population is highly dependent on international assistance, the ethics of purposefully challenging traditional gender roles is a legitimate area for discussion.

The ethical issue is the extent to which international actors should respect or challenge traditional notions of female roles and relationships in the recognition of refugees as well as in efforts to protect the rights of refugee and displaced women. While the universality of human rights, particularly in relationship to women's rights, need not necessarily conflict with respect for traditional values, the challenge is to change harmful practices that render women vulnerable to violence and repression when these are rooted in tradition. These practices may be the cause of women becoming refugees or displaced persons in the first place, and the practices may also disadvantage women seriously once they have been displaced.

Some scholars argue that "human rights can be safeguarded through international standards in a way that is muted by neither extreme cultural relativism nor a set of standards that is imperialistically imposed."[2] While the ethical ideal is to arrive at an appropriate balance between protection of the individual rights of women and cultural and traditional norms regarding the role of women, reaching such a balance is often difficult, particularly in the context of conflict, instability, and resulting displacement. Positive cultural and societal mechanisms for protection may be lost during conflict, and they may not be restored when refugees and displaced persons live for extended periods in camps or reception centers. In particular, the communal support systems for protection of widows, single women, and unaccompanied minors are often no longer present.

Moreover, migration itself profoundly affects gender relations, particularly the role of women in households and communities. The impacts are complex. In many respects, forced migration, as with voluntary migration, can enhance the autonomy and power of women. When women from traditional societies migrate, they become familiar with new norms regarding women's rights and opportunities. If they take outside employment, they may have access to financial resources that they never had until receiving compensation for their labor. Even if their pay is pooled with that of other family members, this new wage-earning capacity often gives women greater ability to direct household priorities. Similar changes may occur when women are the principal recipients of international assistance.

In other respects, migration can serve to reinforce traditional gender roles or place new burdens on women. This is particularly the case when women are expected to preserve cultural and religious norms that appear to be under attack. The nature of camp life puts these challenges into sharp relief. Women in refugee camps generally continue to be productive members of their families, responsible for such domestic activities as food, water, and firewood collection; preparation of meals; and other household chores. By contrast, men often find that they cannot fulfill their traditional productive role in agricultural or other employment. The frustrations experienced by men can result in increased domestic violence, depression, and alcoholism. These tensions may also reinforce the need to preserve traditional notions of female subservience, at least among male leaders.

Finding an appropriate balance between universal rights and cultural relativism is made more difficult because women have generally not had the power within their traditional societies to affect decisions regarding their own roles and responsibilities. In arguing for a weak form of relativism in his classic article, Jack Donnelly nevertheless noted that "appeals to traditional practices and values all too often are a mere cloak for self-interest or arbitrary rule."[3] Adding the inevitable power disparities between aid providers (largely Western agencies) and aid recipients only increases this tension. Moreover, ensuring the participation of refugees and displaced persons, including women, in decision making about access to humanitarian assistance and protection initiatives has proven extremely difficult during most crises.

This chapter will address both the opportunities for empowerment of women and the challenges and vulnerabilities women face in the context of migration and movement nationally as well as internationally. It raises a number of important issues to be considered in developing a framework for advocacy on forced migration:

- What are the factors that cause women to migrate internally and internationally?
- Which factors are of particular import in understanding forced migration?
- What has been the impact of forced migration on women's rights and gender roles and gender relations?
- In what ways does the status accorded to women who have been forced to migrate (for example, as refugee, displaced person, trafficking victim, or irregular migrant) affect their rights and opportunities?
- How best can women who have been forced to migrate empower themselves to participate meaningfully in decisions about their own lives?
- How best can the rights and safety of forced migrant women be protected, particularly from labor abuses, sexual exploitation, trafficking, involuntary prostitution, and other exploitable situations?
- How best can the economic and health status of forced migrant women be improved to enable them to support themselves and their families in dignity and safety?
- What statistics, data collection, and research are needed to improve understanding of women and migration?

This last question foretells a difficulty in assessing the full implications of migration for women. Statistics on migration, both internal and international, are notoriously poor. Data on certain categories of migrants, for example, those who cross borders without the authorization of host countries, are particularly difficult to collect. Many of these migrants without legal status are fearful of stepping forward for censuses and surveys. For the purpose of this chapter, a further difficulty is in obtaining accurate demographic breakdowns of the migrant populations in order to assess the situation of migrants by gender and age.

This chapter begins with a brief discussion of the various forms of migration occurring today and their implications for women. It places the discussion to follow in context by examining both voluntary and forced migration. The next sections address issues related to the rights of migrant women and their changing roles and relationships, with particular focus on Africa. In conclusion, the chapter addresses the ethical issues raised in this analysis and suggests specific areas in need of further discussion.

Trends in Internal and International Migration

Internal migration and movements across borders have increased since the 1960s, when the UN Population Division began collecting data. A number of factors contribute to this increase, particularly of international movements, including

- economic globalization and integration, which have linked the economies of source and destination countries together;
- trade agreements that contain provisions for mobility of international personnel, particularly but not exclusively in trade in services;
- the growth of multinational corporations that move their personnel across countries and across the globe;
- demographic trends, with many developed countries facing population stagnation and aging while developing countries continue to grow faster than their job markets can absorb new workers;
- the transportation revolution that has made migration affordable to millions of would-be migrants;
- the revolution in communications (Internet, cellular phones) that informs would-be migrants of opportunities outside of their home countries and allows them to keep in touch with families and communities left behind; and
- the growth in transnational communities, including growing numbers of persons with dual and multinational citizenship, which remain involved in the countries of their birth as well as their countries of destination.

In addition, in the past decade many countries, particularly those ending years of communist rule and restrictive emigration policies, have torn down their barriers to the movement of their nationals abroad. The changing geopolitical situation has also caused the formation of new states, particularly in the area of the former Soviet Union. Russia has become one of the largest recipients of international migrants, but many of those now counted in this category would have been internal migrants prior to 1990.

Internal Migration

Internal movements are caused by conflicts, violence, and human rights abuses. An estimated 23.5 million persons are now internally displaced because of these political events.[4] Additional persons are forced to leave their homes because of development projects such as dams that destroy their habitat. Others move because of environmental degradation. Mass migration may result from natural disasters. Human-made disasters also precipitate mass movements.

Internal trafficking of women and girls for sexual and other exploitation is a growing problem.[5] Human trafficking involves forced or coerced movements. Sometimes people are kidnapped outright and taken forcibly to another location. In other cases, traffickers use deception to entice victims to move with false promises of good paying jobs as models, dancers, domestic workers, and so on. Victims of forced prostitution usually end up in large cities, sex tourism areas, or near military bases, where the demand is highest. Victims of forced labor may be found throughout a country, in agriculture, fishing industries, mines, and sweatshops. Persons who have been internally displaced by conflict, violations of human rights, and natural or human-made disasters are more vulnerable to trafficking.

International Migration

The number of long-term international migrants (that is, those residing in foreign countries for more than one year) has grown steadily from an estimated 76 million in 1960 to an estimated 200 million today.[6] Most are voluntary migrants, but a significant number of refugees or others are internationally displaced because of conflict or insecurity. As of 2005, almost 50 percent of the world's migrants were women, up from 46.6 percent in 1960.

By most estimates, 70 to 75 percent of the world's refugee and displaced population is composed of women and their dependent children.[7] Children account for about half of all refugees, with adult women often outnumbering adult men. This picture varies, however, by countries of origin and refuge. It is particularly true when refugees flee conflict in one developing country and take refuge in another, usually a neighboring country.

International trafficking for sexual and labor exploitation is a further form of forced migration. It is estimated that the vast majority of those trafficked are women and girls.

Women and Forced Migration in Africa

Forced migration is a particular challenge for the women of Africa. This section begins with the scope of the problem and then discusses issues regarding legal protection, physical security, access to assistance and self-support, return and reconstruction. It gives special attention to human trafficking in Africa.

Numbers

According to the UN Population Division, in 2005 there were eight million female international migrants in Africa out of a total of seventeen million international migrants on the continent. UNHCR estimates that there were 2.6 million refugees in Africa, about half of whom are female. The Internal Displacement Monitoring Centre estimates that 12.7 million of the world's 24.6 million internally displaced persons are in Africa.[8] There are no reliable sex disaggregated statistics on IDPs, but it is assumed that the proportion of females is about the same as that of refugees. The numbers on trafficked persons are even less reliable.

Legal Protection

The basic structures and legal instruments to ensure the legal protection of refugees were established over forty years ago. The UN Convention Relating to the Status of Refugees was adopted in July 1951. The essential purpose of the Convention was to provide a general definition of who was to be considered a refugee and to define his or her legal status. The 1951 Convention was produced in the early days of the cold war, largely to resolve the situation of the millions of refugees who remained displaced by World War II and fascist and Nazi persecution. At its core, this treaty substitutes the protection of the international community (in the form of a host government) for that of an unable or unwilling sovereign. Defining refugees as persons who were unable or unwilling to avail themselves of the protection of their home countries because of a "well-founded fear of persecution based on their race, religion, nationality, political opinion or membership in a particular social group," the 1951 Convention was limited geographically to Europe and temporally to persons displaced before 1951. These limitations were lifted in the 1967 Protocol to the 1951 Convention, so that since 1967, the Refugee Convention has been a universal instrument, applying to refugees worldwide.

In addition, the Organization of African Unity (OAU) adopted a refugee convention in 1969 that expands the definition of a refugee. According to the OAU Convention, "the term 'refugee' shall also apply to every person who, owing to external aggression, occupation, foreign domination or events seriously disturbing public order in either part or the whole of his [or her] country of origin or nationality, is compelled to leave his [or her] place of habitual residence in order to seek refuge in another place outside his [or her] country of origin or nationality."[9] Gender is not included in the international definition of a refugee as a person with a well-founded fear of persecution on the basis of race, religion, nationality, political opinion, or membership in a social group. Yet women asylum seekers may be fleeing such gender-based persecution as rape, widow burnings, honor killings, domestic violence, forced marriages, and female genital cutting from which their home country governments are unwilling or unable to protect them.[10]

In 2002 UNHCR issued two guidelines to provide guidance for state parties and national refugee status determination (RSD) authorities on gender-sensitive assessment and processing of asylum claims. The *Guidelines on International Protection No. 1* and *No. 2* complement other UNHCR guidance on aspects of gender-related persecution. These guidelines provide legal interpretive guidance on ensuring gender-sensitive interpretation of the Convention and that RSD procedures do not marginalize or exclude gender-related experiences of persecution.

In its 2002 "Guidelines on Gender-Related Persecution," UNHCR noted that "though gender is not specifically referenced in the refugee definition, it is widely accepted that it can influence, or dictate, the type of persecution or harm suffered and the reasons for this treatment. The refugee definition, properly interpreted, therefore covers gender-related claims. As such, there is no need to add an additional ground to the 1951 Convention definition."[11]

Several governments have issued guidelines or regulations for asylum determinations in this area. Universities and nongovernmental organizations have supplemented these guidelines. In South Africa, for example, the University of Cape Town Legal Aid Clinic, as a member of the National Consortium on Refugee Affairs, developed gender guidelines on asylum proceedings for the South African government.

Some forms of persecution are in themselves gender-specific. The definition promulgated in the United Kingdom is generally applicable: "Gender-specific harm may include but is not limited to sexual violence and abuse, female genital mutilation, marriage-related harm, violence within the family, forced sterilisation and forced abortion."[12] The guidelines generally make a distinction as to the perpetrator of the persecution in determining whether the applicant is justified in her inability or unwillingness to accept the protection of her home country. In many gender-persecution cases, the harm is carried out by nonstate actors—family members, armed elements that are not sanctioned by the government, even community members seeking to hold up social norms. When nonstate actors are recognized as perpetrators of persecution, the asylum applicant must demonstrate a failure of the state to provide protection from the nonstate actor.

The most difficult issue to overcome in gender-based cases is the nexus between the harm suffered and any of the grounds for protection. These cases often try to tie the persecution to the applicant's "membership in a particular social group." UNHCR guidelines define "social group": "a particular social group is a group of persons who share a common characteristic other than their risk of being persecuted, or who are perceived as a group by society. The characteristic will often be one which is innate, unchangeable, or which is otherwise fundamental to identity, conscience or the exercise of one's human rights."[13]

The forms of persecution that refugees experience are often gendered. For example, a woman may face serious harm because she is unwilling to practice religion as the authorities of her country require. These cases generally involve a refusal by the woman to follow the behaviors that religious leaders say are required of all adherents—for example, wearing the veil or other garments deemed proper for women. In theocracies, opposition to these behaviors may also be, or be seen as, expressions of political opinion. In addition to opposition to social norms upheld by the state, women may be persecuted for their opposition to laws and practices that discriminate against them or make it difficult for them to support themselves and their children.

Women often face special problems in making their case to the authorities, particularly when they have had experiences that are difficult and painful to describe. The female victim of sexual torture may be reluctant to speak about it, particularly to a male interviewer. Rape, even in the context of torture, is seen in some cultures as a failure on the part of the woman to preserve her virginity or marital dignity. She may be shunned by her family and isolated from other members of the community. Discussing her experience becomes a further source of alienation.

Physical Security

Protection goes well beyond legal recognition. The protection of refugee and displaced women in conflict situations is particularly problematic. Civilians are increasingly the targets of attacks in civil conflicts. Articles 7 and 8 of the Rome Statute of the International Criminal Court include rape and sexual violence among the crimes against humanity and war crimes. Rape and sexual assault also occur during flight at the hands of border guards, government and rebel military units, bandits, and others. Women's safety may be no more ensured once in refugee and displaced persons camps or reception centers. For example, refugee and displaced women have faced serious threat of rape when they pick firewood, often the only source of heating and cooking fuel. Refugee women have been forced to provide sexual favors in exchange for obtaining food rations for themselves and their families. In some cases, only male heads of households receive documentation of their status, leaving their spouses vulnerable to harassment each time they leave their homes.

Revelations about sexual exploitation of refugee children in West Africa brought the issue to international attention in 2002. A study carried out by the UNHCR and Save the Children–UK interviewed refugee girls and adolescents in Liberia, Guinea, and Sierra Leone. Noting that the study was not intended to be as rigorous as would be required for a criminal investigation, the report cited numerous examples of sexual exploitation by staff working for international humanitarian organizations.[14]

Many factors contribute to the vulnerability of refugee and displaced women and girls to sexual violence and exploitation. Exploitation certainly occurs in the absence of alternatives for refugees and displaced persons. When a group is completely dependent on others for economic survival, members of the group are inherently vulnerable to such exploitation. In many camps, the physical facilities increase the likelihood of protection problems. Camps are often overcrowded. Unrelated families may be required to share a communal living space. A UN team investigating allegations of sexual abuse in West Africa found that "bathing facilities in a number of the camps consist of one building with one side for men and another side for women. The isolation and lack of separate and distinctly placed facilities, which would increase the cost, has caused the facilities to occasionally be the site of sexual violence."[15] When refugee and displaced women do not have documentation of their status, they are particularly vulnerable to abuse.

The Inter-Agency Standing Committee (IASC) has issued guidelines to prevent and respond to gender-based violence, developed training programs for staff, raised awareness, and taken other steps to prevent sexual exploitation and abuse.[16] UNHCR is committed to implementing its 2003 guidelines on prevention of sexual and gender-based violence (SGBV). However, the fundamental problem of dependency on humanitarian aid remains for many refugee and displaced women and children.

Security is generally inadequate as well. International humanitarian aid staff is often absent from camps, leaving operations to local national and refugee staff. Night patrols to ensure greater protection may be absent or infrequent. The responsibility for security generally rests with governments. Yet government authorities, particularly in poorer countries, usually do not have sufficient resources to fulfill the responsibility. In many cases of internal displacement, in particular, government authorities are hostile to the forced migrants. The refugees and displaced themselves may take on the responsibility for patrolling the camps, but their capacities are limited as well. In developed countries, the refugee reception facilities are often overcrowded and their staff not sensitized and equipped to combat SGBV. Asylum seekers and refugees are also known to fall prey to traffickers and smugglers who promise them better protection, living conditions, and economic opportunities.

Spouse and child abuse and abandonment are problems encountered by women and children in refugee and displaced persons situations. Heightened levels of domestic violence are frequent where refugees have lived for extended periods in the artificial environment of a refugee camp or reception facility, or while waiting for the decision on their asylum application. Psychological strains for husbands and adolescent boys unable to assume normal cultural, social, and economic roles can result in aggressive behavior towards wives, children, and sisters.[17]

Refugee and displaced persons camps in a number of locations house the civilian families of members of armed forces. The camps frequently serve as rest and recuperation sites. The men often bring weapons with them into the camps. Proliferation of weapons can compound the protection problems facing refugee women. In the mid-1990s some camps in what was then known as Zaire were dominated by the Hutu militias that had committed genocide in Rwanda and were continuing their armed conflict. This situation made the problem of weapons in the camps highly visible. There have been some successful efforts to separate combatants from civilians. In Zambia, for example, former combatants reside in a separate camp so they do not mix with the refugee population.

Forced recruitment of women and children into the armed forces of resistance groups is a further problem in some countries. Women and girls are often forced into sexual slavery by armed forces. In some cases, military forces recruit women and girls as soldiers. In other cases, women and children are required to carry ammunition and other supplies. Women and children are also used to clear mines. Abduction of children remains a major problem with girls often experiencing sexual abuse, as explained in the UN secretary-general's *Report on Children and Armed Conflict*: "Abducted children are subjected to brutal treatment and other egregious personal violations. In northern Uganda, the LRA [Lord's Resistance Army] has abducted thousands of children and forced them to become child soldiers and to commit atrocities. The case of the girls abducted in 1996 from Aboke secondary school has particularly brought the situation of abductions in northern Uganda to the attention of the international community. . . . While many of the children returned home within days, others remain unaccounted for, and some of the girls released have reported sexual abuse."[18] A final significant impediment to the protection of refugee and displaced women and children is the general insecurity that places humanitarian operations at risk. In modern conflict, civilians have become the targets of armed attack, not just the innocent victims of war. Also targeted are the humanitarian actors that seek to assist and protect civilians. Insecurity is by far one of the biggest impediments to securing the rights of refugee and displaced women and children, particularly when the displaced are still within their own countries or remain under the control of military forces in a country of refuge. Insecure conditions impede access to displaced populations for delivery of aid, create protection problems for aid workers as well as their clients, and make it impossible to monitor and evaluate the effectiveness of aid operations.

Such problems do not necessarily stop when the women return home. The conflict may still be continuing and, even if a peace agreement has been signed, political insta-bility, the continued presence of land mines and the destruction of the economy and infrastructure make conditions dangerous for returning women and their families. The UNHCR stresses that voluntary return must be in safety and dignity. The UNHCR *Handbook on Voluntary Repatriation* notes that "among the elements of 'safety and dig-nity' to be considered are: the refugees' physical safety at all stages during and after their return including en route, at reception points and at the destination; the need for family unity; attention to the needs of vulnerable groups; the waiver or, if not possible, reduc-tion to a minimum of border crossing formalities; permission for refugees to bring their movable possessions when returning; respect for school and planting seasons in the timing of such movements; and freedom of movement."[19] Recognizing that the protec-tion of refugee women and children may require special arrangements, the *Handbook* includes a special box reminding repatriation planners: "Make appropriate arrange-ments for the physical safety of unaccompanied women and women heads of household in departure, transit or reception centres (such as separate areas close to the relevant infrastructure with adequate security arrangements, lighting)."[20]

Access to Assistance and Self-Support

Many of Africa's refugees and internally displaced persons are dependent on interna-tional assistance for all of their material needs, including food, shelter, water, and health care. For new arrivals, this situation is not surprising. Refugees and displaced persons fleeing their homes usually cannot bring material resources with them. The clothing on their backs and perhaps a small bundle of belongings are often all that they have been able to bring with them. They may arrive in poor health, malnourished, or disabled, having experienced famine in their countries of origin and long treks through hazard-ous terrain.

That large numbers of refugees and displaced persons continue to be dependent on international assistance long after their original flight is more disturbing. In many host countries, refugees remain in care-and-maintenance camps for years, unable to return to home communities because of continued conflict and instability but denied oppor-tunities to work or access to training or income-producing activities. The refugees must rely on food rations, clothing, and shelter as provided by international donors. Of a bare subsistence nature even at the best of times, during periods of financial strain the assistance package is often inadequate to meet even the basic nutritional needs of the population. Further, there is too little coordination among the various sections of assistance—health, education, and skills training, for example—to better facilitate independence.

Access to material assistance, employment, and health care services has been re-stricted in a number of developed countries as a way of discouraging new arrivals of asylum seekers. Economic dependency, isolation, and lack of integration support may put asylum seekers, especially single women, women with children, and unaccompanied minors at a further risk of SGBV, including sexual exploitation and forced prostitution.

Refugee and displaced women are especially affected by the lack of appropriate and adequate international assistance. They and their children suffer from the inadequacies in the assistance package. Unable to obtain employment and often denied participation in training or income-generation programs, they are unable to provide for their families without international assistance. Even with it, they may still be vulnerable to sexual abuse and exploitation. And, finally, they are not adequately consulted about the programs in place nor are they permitted to participate actively in the implementation of projects ostensibly designed to assist them.

A principal contributor to heightened mortality in humanitarian emergencies is malnutrition. Malnourished people are more susceptible to disease and are more difficult to cure of illnesses. Malnourished women who are pregnant or lactating are unable to provide sufficient nutrients to their children to enable them to survive. In addition to food problems, poor sanitation and contaminated water supplies contribute to high death rates in many refugee situations.

Equal access to food and nonfood items is a key issue for refugee and displaced women and children. International organizations and host countries, often in consultation with the refugee leaders of the camps, are the ones who generally make decisions about food distribution. Refugee leadership structures, particularly at the height of emergencies, often exclude women. Yet male leaders may have little understanding of the needs and circumstances of those who cook the food or feed their families—the women. As a result, the food distribution procedures and contents may be inappropriate. Aid agencies may provide food that is inconsistent with the dietary traditions of the refugees and displaced persons. Alternatively, the food requires preparation that cannot be readily accomplished in the camp setting. These problems are further compounded by cultural practices within some refugee and displaced populations which require that men be fed first; where supplies are limited, women and children may not receive adequate food.

Since the early 1990s, there has been increased recognition that women must be involved early in the process of designing distribution systems as well as in the actual delivery of the food. The UNHCR *Guidelines on the Protection of Refugee Women* recommend that UNHCR staff "consult with refugee women regarding all decisions about food and other distribution [and] designate refugee women as the initial point of contact for emergency and longer-term food distribution."[21] World Food Program policies say that women should control the family food aid entitlement in 80 percent of WFP food distributions. The WFP guidelines also state that women should take a lead role in local decision-making committees on food aid management as well as the management of assets created through food-for-work programs.

Clean water is another essential need. Women in refugee and displaced persons camps, like many other women in developing countries, spend a great deal of time in water collection. Containers that are too heavy or pumps that are inconveniently located can make this effort more arduous. When clean water is not available, children, in particular, run the risk of life-threatening diarrheal diseases.

Collection of fuel for cooking and heating is also a task for which women are generally responsible. In a refugee or displaced persons context, however, efforts to find firewood can be not only time-consuming (if located at some distance from the camps) but dangerous (if located in mine-infested areas or the site of conflict). A 2006 report summarized the problem among displaced women in Uganda: "In northern Uganda, trees and grass are more plentiful than in Darfur, especially after the rainy season. Yet the same trees and grass that provide the means to cook also provide cover for the Lord's Resistance Army (LRA) rebels, who abduct women, and especially girls, to serve as sex slaves, cooks, porters and soldiers. The so-called 'protectors' of displaced women and girls in northern Uganda—the Ugandan army—also await women and girls collecting firewood (or water, or vegetables), and sexually exploit them by threatening to falsely expose them as LRA collaborators."[22] The report found similar problems in Darfur and Tanzania. It also assessed the alternatives to firewood collection—including distribution of firewood or other means of cooking (such as charcoal or kerosene), fuel efficient stoves, use of solar energy—as well as mechanisms to protect women while they collect firewood and to provide sources of income so they can purchase fuel. Each of these alternatives has a financial cost that the international community has been unwilling to bear in most locations, leaving women and girls to pay the cost in risk to their own lives and well-being.

A further persistent problem is the distribution of sanitary materials. Since 1996 UNHCR has required all field programs to include sanitary materials in regular budgets. A survey of fifty-two UNHCR offices found low compliance, however. The unavailability of these materials is not just an inconvenience to refugee women and adolescents. Rather, it is a major impediment to their full participation in the life of the camp society: "In both Ethiopia and Zambia girls stayed away from school and sometimes remaining [sic] in their houses because they had nothing decent to wear during monthly menstruation."[23]

The health problems refugee and displaced women and children face are similar to those of other women and children in developing countries, but many of them are compounded by the refugee experience. Nutritional problems have been discussed. Refugee women can suffer from physical disabilities resulting from their refugee experience. They may be the victims of mine explosions, for example. Loss of limbs is not uncommon both in flight and during stays in camps.

Once the emergency phase is over, a leading cause of death among refugee and displaced women of childbearing age is complications from pregnancies. Lack of trained midwives and traditional birth attendants (TBA), septic abortions, unsanitary conditions during birth, septic instruments, poor lighting during deliveries, and frequency of pregnancies all lead to difficulties.

Health complications also arise from female genital cutting, a practice in some parts of Africa that carries over into refugee and displaced persons camps. Problems include infections due to unsterilized instruments, damage to adjacent organs, obstructed menstrual flow, painful intercourse, severe blood loss, and obstetric complications.

In addition to physical health problems, some refugee and displaced women suffer from mental health problems. Becoming a refugee involves many dislocations and abrupt changes in life. At a minimum, refugee and displaced women face emotional problems and difficulties in adjustment resulting from loss of family and community support. More serious mental health problems are not uncommon, arising from torture and sexual abuse prior to or after flight. As we have seen in the section on protection issues, rape and abduction occur in many refugee situations. Depression and post-traumatic stress disorder often follow such experiences.

In contrast to their disadvantaged position regarding other goods and services, refugees sometimes are advantaged relative to their neighboring populations in access to health care services. Special programs may be implemented in refugee camps; expatriate physicians and nurses generally offer their services. Prior to recent years, however, health services for refugees and displaced persons too often overlooked female-specific needs. But an assessment of UNHCR's *Guidelines on the Protection of Refugee Women* concluded "that UNHCR and its partners have made important strides in providing reproductive health services. In contrast to a decade ago, when such services were rare, they are presently an integral part of health care delivery programs in some places."[24]

Representatives of UN agencies, nongovernmental organizations (NGOs), and governments formed the Inter-Agency Working Group on Refugee Reproductive Health (IAWG). In 1999 the IAWG produced a field manual that outlined a Minimum Initial Service Package (MISP) "designed to prevent and manage the consequences of sexual violence, reduce HIV transmission, prevent excess neonatal and maternal morbidity and mortality, and plan for the provision of comprehensive reproductive health services."[25] Several NGOs also came together as the Reproductive Health for Refugees Consortium to offer actual services for refugee and displaced women and girls.

Safe motherhood is an essential component of the MISP. In the acute stage of a humanitarian emergency, neonatal and maternal morbidity and mortality can be reduced by providing clean delivery kits to promote clean home deliveries, offering midwife delivery kits to facilitate clean and safe deliveries in health facilities, and initiating the establishment of a referral system to manage obstetric emergencies. Once conditions have become more stable, comprehensive services for antenatal, delivery, and postpartum care should be established. Also needing attention are post-abortion complications for those suffering the complications of spontaneous and unsafe abortion. To the extent possible, the needs of the local population, as well as the refugees and displaced persons, should be addressed. This is particularly important because most refugees and internally displaced persons are in countries with high maternal and infant mortality rates.

Family planning services are a second priority in reproductive health services. From the beginning of an emergency, relief organizations should be able to respond to the need for contraception, particularly the distribution of condoms. Providing a full range of family planning services may require more stable conditions. A range of contraceptives should be provided, as well as assessment of needs, counseling, information about contraceptive methods, and follow-up care to ensure continuity of services. Providers must have the technical skills to offer the contraceptive methods safely, and they must have an adequate logistics system to ensure continuity of supplies.

Programs to address sexual- and gender-based violence (SGBV) have grown along with other reproductive health services during the past decade. SGBV programs generally advocate a multisectoral approach that takes into account prevention of abuses, the physical and psychological ramifications of violence, the potential need of the victim for a safe haven, the longer-term economic needs of vulnerable populations, the legal rights of victims, the training of police and security personnel, and similar issues. For example, women in Burundian refugee camps in Tanzania undertook needs assessments which indicated that a breakdown in family, community, and government structures led to an increased incidence of violence against women. Resulting programs include a drop-in center for violence survivors, at which their critical health and protection needs are addressed; community awareness–building activities that reach out to men as well as women to discuss the prevalence and reasons for sexual- and gender-based violence; social forums for women to discuss issues affecting their lives; and training for staff of service providers in the camps to alert them to issues surrounding sexual and gender-based violence.[26]

Other health programs that developed and grew in the 1990s involve the psychosocial needs of refugees and displaced persons. Women caught in conflict experience particular stresses that can affect their mental health as well as their ability to cope. Programs for refugee women and girls tend to range from specialized mental health services to play, sports, and other recreational groups for traumatized children and to income-generation activities for traumatized women. The aims are to prevent, to the degree possible, trauma and stressors that negatively affect mental health and to strengthen the capacity of refugees to cope with the traumas and stressors when prevention fails.

The Executive Committee of the UNHCR has reaffirmed the fundamental right of refugee children to education and, at its thirty-eighth session, called upon all states, individually and collectively, to intensify their efforts to ensure that refugee children benefit from primary education. Yet the right to education continues to be abridged, particularly for girls. In 2000 fewer than 800,000 of an estimated 2.3 million children and adolescents receiving assistance from UNHCR were enrolled in schools. As a UNHCR report on education concluded: "One-third of refugee children (excluding infants) and adolescents in populations categorized as 'UNHCR assisted' are in UNHCR-supported schooling, and . . . perhaps 40 per cent are in school altogether."[27]

A UNHCR evaluation found that girls are generally underrepresented in schools. Although they represent half of all school-age children, they represent less than half of the students. As the evaluation found, "On a global basis, female refugee participation in education remains low, following patterns in countries of origin (ranging from 10 percent to 40 percent of students at the primary level, less in secondary and vocational studies, and only 25 percent of all students at the tertiary level)."[28] Poverty, which disproportionately affects women, further impedes enrollment in schools. Families may fear that adolescent girls will be subject to greater sexual harassment if they leave compounds to go to school. Lack of appropriate clothing and sanitary materials may also impede educational attainment.

Refugee and displaced women face many of the same impediments to education and skills training—inadequate resources, teachers, and classes—as do girls. In addition, women face other barriers. Traditional views of the role of women sometimes prevent them from accepting work or undertaking training that takes them out of the household. There may also be restrictions on the type of work that is considered to be appropriate for women. Practical problems also constrain enrollment, including the absence of day care and a lack of time and energy after household work, work as a wage earner, or both. Also, many skills-training programs assume some level of prior education, most notably in terms of literacy. Refugee and displaced women may not qualify for such programs, having been discriminated against in their country of origin in obtaining elementary education.

Other constraints relate to the design and contents of training programs. In some cases, programs have been too far removed from the everyday life activities of the refugee women and have therefore appeared to be irrelevant to their needs. Some vocational training programs have focused on skills that are not marketable in the refugee context or follow traditional patterns that are not sustainable for income production.

Theoretically, there are a number of ways that refugees can supplement their household income. They include employment in the local economy or with assistance agencies, agricultural activities, bartering, establishment of trades or small businesses, and participation in skills-training programs and formal income-generation projects. Women in developing countries must typically find employment in the informal sector of the economy. Refugee women in developing countries do the same. In general, refugee women who work in the local economy are within the service sector. For example, it is not uncommon to find a refugee woman supporting her family through her earnings as a domestic. Domestic employment is often a cornerstone in the household survival strategy for an extended family. Refugee women are also often involved in the tending of garden plots. In these plots surrounding the house, refugees can raise vegetables to either supplement their diet or, if they choose, sell to earn some extra cash.

Assistance agencies are an important source of employment for refugees in developing countries. Typically, these positions go to younger men who have the language skills to communicate with and relate to the expatriate staff in charge. These positions often offer a higher level of financial compensation than is usually available to refugees in the local market; relatively interesting nonmanual work (though the employees often feel they are overqualified for the position); more security; higher status; and other benefits, such as an increased chance for resettlement to a third country.

The primary area of employment with assistance agencies for refugee women is in the health sector. In a number of cultures, it is considered more appropriate for women to seek medical advice from and be examined by other women rather than by men. The employed women work in supplementary feeding programs; as traditional birth attendants; in mother-child health programs; as home visitors, particularly in public health education and outreach; as translators, and so on. Following health programs, the second largest sector for employment is "women's projects," offered by assistance agencies, including income-generation activities.

Return and Reconstruction

Refugee and displaced women are important resources for the development of postconflict countries. They have often learned skills in refugee camps that are in short supply in their home country. Yet lack of economic opportunities on return is one of the most serious assistance and protection issues facing returning women and children. War-torn societies have generally lost their capacity for economic self-support and find it difficult to recover. High rates of unemployment are found throughout these countries. When land mines prevent the resumption of agricultural activities and no urban employment is available, returnees can become desperate.

One study conducted by adolescent researchers in Sierra Leone described a too familiar outcome for women and girls: "Some young people interviewed said they had already returned home from Guinea or an IDP camp but were forced to leave again in search of work because of lack of assistance. Some former refugee girls and women said they became involved in commercial sex work for their survival and have traveled to other parts of Sierra Leone to provide services to UNAMSIL troops."[29] Increases in prostitution, including the trafficking of women and girls for the sex trade, have occurred in other postconflict states with large peacekeeping forces.

Reclaiming property is a problem that faces many returning refugees and internally displaced persons. Government authorities may have seized land. Other people, sometimes equally in need, may have moved onto the property after the refugees and displaced persons fled. Often, internally displaced persons live in housing formerly occupied by refugees. Added to the general difficulty are problems faced more specifically by women, particularly widows, in reclaiming property. The UNHCR *Handbook on Repatriation* emphasizes the need to take these issues into account in planning and carrying out repatriation programs:

> Special attention needs to be paid to the question of access to land for residential and agricultural use by returnee women heads of households. If the local legislation or traditional practice does not grant returnee women the same rights to land as returnee men, UNHCR has to draw the attention of the authorities to this problem and seek to find suitable ways to rectify the situation. If this is not done early enough, there is a danger that returnee women may lose out in the competition for land, either by not getting access or being evicted. This may in turn lead to increased vulnerability and possible internal displacement. In any case, UNHCR has to closely monitor the handling of returnees' access to land and to ensure, if necessary through intervention, that returnee women have access to land on the same footing as returnee men.[30]

Demobilization of combatants is a further issue that affects the protection of refugees and displaced persons in postconflict situations. Many combatants are adolescents who have few skills other than war making. If not given access to alternative economic opportunities, the demobilized soldiers may turn to other violent activities in order to survive. That many demobilizing women and girls have been raped only complicates the reintegration process, as it does for many refugee and displaced persons as well. In Sierra Leone, as elsewhere, "rape is often a taboo subject [and] failure to confront the issue perpetuates a culture of silence that exacerbates an already difficult recovery from these crimes. Advocacy and community sensitization work focused on preparing families and communities for their return and creating sympathy for them rather than stigmatization has only scratched the surface of what is needed."[31]

In response to the needs of women in postconflict societies, UNHCR, with the active encouragement of several donor countries, has established special women's initiatives. Although providing only a fraction of the resources needed, the Rwandan Women's

Initiatives made important contributions to helping women adjust to postconflict life. It has supported programs providing psychological support, community services, literacy and education, reproductive health education, SGBV services to women, micro-credit and income generation, skills training, capacity building of women's groups, and legal assistance.

Refugee Resettlement

Some refugees are unable to return or to remain in countries of first asylum. These may be candidates for resettlement to a third country. Resettlement in third countries is generally considered to be the least desirable solution for refugees because it moves them far from their own countries and cultures. In many situations, however, resettlement is the best solution for the individuals and groups involved, particularly when needed to provide protection or durable solutions for refugees.

Most of the refugee women and children who resettle in third countries enter as part of a complete family unit. Among some refugee populations, however, a significant number of women-headed households have resettled. In response to the difficulties faced by women at risk, UNHCR has identified the need for special Women at Risk programs for the admission of refugee women who face specific protection problems. The UNHCR *Resettlement Handbook* states: "When, despite all possible efforts, it is unlikely that the particular protection problems or related needs of a refugee woman can be adequately addressed in the country of refuge, resettlement should be actively considered."[32]

More specifically, the *Handbook* states that "in some instances resettlement may be the preferred and often only solution. This could be the case when women have been raped and when in their society and in their country of refuge a survivor of rape is ostracised. Such a situation could be aggravated when the refugee woman gives birth to a child conceived through rape. In addition to the possible serious consequences of a rape on her physical and mental health, the refugee woman may suffer lifelong rejection by her own family and community."[33]

For purposes of resettlement, the *Handbook* states,

> UNHCR considers as women-at-risk those women who have protection problems, and are single heads of families or are accompanied by an adult male who is unable to support and assume the role of the head of the family. They may suffer from a wide range of problems including expulsion, refoulement and other security threats, sexual harassment, violence, abuse, torture and different forms of exploitation. Additional problems such women face could derive from persecution as well as from particular hardships sustained either in their country of origin, during their flight or in their country of asylum. The trauma of having been uprooted, deprived of normal family and community support or cultural ties, the abrupt change in roles and status, in addition to the absence of an adult male head of family, renders some women, under certain circumstances, more vulnerable than others.[34]

Some countries have established specific women-at-risk programs—for example, Canada, Australia, and New Zealand. Other resettlement countries, such as the United

States, grant resettlement to refugee women at risk under the normal processing modalities. UNHCR also encourages special programs to help the resettled women adjust to their new lives, programs that address some of the special needs that the women at risk may have.[35] These programs are very small, however, reaching few of the women refugees who might qualify as women at risk. For example, fewer than twenty-eight hundred people have been resettled in Canada under the women-at-risk program.

Smuggling and Trafficking

A particularly troubling trend in recent years has been the emergence of professional smuggling and trafficking operations. Smuggling is defined in international law as "the procurement, in order to obtain, directly or indirectly, a financial or other material benefit, of the illegal entry of a person into a state party of which the person is not a national or a permanent resident."[36] Trafficking is defined as "the recruitment, transportation, transfer, harbouring or receipt of persons, by means of the threat or use of force or other forms of coercion, of abduction, of fraud, of deception, of the abuse of power or of a position of vulnerability or of the giving or receiving of payments or benefits to achieve the consent of a person having control over another person, for the purpose of exploitation."[37] The smuggling protocol refers only to movement across international borders, but trafficking can take place within countries as well.

Although the distinctions often blur, generally, persons who are smuggled knowingly agree to the terms under which they will be moved across borders, whereas trafficking victims have been coerced or deceived. As smuggling fees increase, and migrants find it difficult to pay all costs at once, smugglers "sell" migrants to businesses that cover the fees in exchange for indentured labor. This debt bondage can amount to virtual slavery, particularly for women and children forced into sexually exploitive occupations.

An experts meeting organized in 2002 by the UN's Division for the Advancement of Women concluded that trafficking has supply and demand dimensions. "On the supply side, factors that render persons, especially women and children, vulnerable to trafficking are development processes marked by class, gender and ethnic concerns that marginalize women, in particular, from employment and education; displacement as a result of natural- and human-made catastrophes; dysfunctional families; gendered cultural practices, gender discrimination and gender-based violence in families and communities."[38]

Areas with particularly high levels of poverty, unemployment, and limited educational opportunities are especially vulnerable to trafficking. A recent assessment of trafficking from the Iringa area of Tanzania summarized a situation faced by other African communities: "People were so poor that they would tolerate any job, even an abusive one. Very few villages have secondary schools and they are not mandatory, which contributes to the trafficking of 12-year-olds into domestic house work. Government officials reported that many young girls had been taken from Iringa to Dar es Salaam to work as prostitutes. The trafficker receives a fee of $50 for each girl. Many villages do not have teenaged girls due to trafficking."[39]

Without demand, however, there would be no market for the services of trafficking victims. The experts group concluded that the demand-driven causes are globalization that has fuelled the development of economic sectors with a woman-specific demand for cheap labour and the growth of the commercial sex industry; restrictive immigration policies and laws that are obstacles to the demand for labour being met by supply, thereby generating a market for trafficking; exploitation in the labour market, especially exploitation of illegal and unregulated work of migrants; economic and political trade offs between public officials and enforcement agencies that make trafficking a high profit low risk venture; consumerism, greed and impoverishment of values resulting in the exploitation of the vulnerability of human beings to trafficking.[40]

Generally, the flow of trafficking is from less-developed countries to industrialized nations, including the United States, or towards neighboring countries with marginally higher standards of living. Since trafficking is an underground criminal enterprise, there are no precise statistics on the extent of the problem. A 2000 report in the United States estimated that over fifty thousand trafficking victims are from Africa.[41] Trafficking is now considered the third-largest source of profits for organized crime, behind only drugs and guns, generating billions of dollars annually. Most of the victims are sent to Asia and the Middle East, Western Europe, and North America. They usually end up in large cities, vacation and tourist areas, or near military bases, where the demand is highest.

While there is no single victim stereotype, a majority of trafficked women are believed to be under the age of twenty-five, with many in their mid-to-late teens. The fear among customers of contracting HIV and AIDS infections has driven traffickers to recruit younger women and girls, some as young as seven. In extreme cases, victims of trafficking are often subjected to cruel mental and physical abuse in order to perpetuate their servitude, including beating and battering, rape, starvation, forced drug use, confinement, and seclusion. Once victims are brought to their destinations, their passports are often confiscated. Victims are forced to have sex, often unprotected, with large number of partners, and to work unsustainably long hours. Many victims suffer mental breakdowns and are exposed to sexually transmitted diseases, including HIV and AIDS. They are often denied medical care, and those who become ill are sometimes killed.

One area that has received attention and support from governments is education to combat trafficking in women.[42] Accurate, timely information about migration and trafficking that is disseminated to would-be migrants gives them the means to make an informed choice about migrating. Information is thus an important empowerment tool, diminishing the possibility of traffickers being able to exploit a lack of knowledge on the part of potential migrants.

The education campaigns are aimed at preventing the victimization of migrants, but if they do try to enter a new country, the (inadvertent) host governments must grapple with defining the standards that govern the treatment accorded to the trafficked persons. First, they must protect the trafficked persons from physical abuse at the hands of traffickers, other predators, and immigration officials. Second, they often establish witness protection and other programs for those who testify against smugglers. Often, the successful prosecution of traffickers requires the cooperation of those who have been smuggled into the country. Third, the host countries develop programs for the safe and orderly return of trafficked women to their home countries. Trafficked aliens who are stranded or apprehended often do not have the resources to return home. Abused migrants may need special help for their return. Fourth, when return is too dangerous, governments may offer continued residence to trafficking victims in the country of destination.

Ethics and the Rights of Forced Migrant Women

This chapter began with a brief discussion of the tension between cultural relativism and universal respect for the rights of women. In theory, the international community has come down firmly on the side of gender equality. As early as 1991, the UNHCR Executive Committee stressed "that all action taken on behalf of refugee and displaced women and children must be guided by the relevant international instruments relating to the status of refugees, as well as other human rights instruments, in particular, the Convention Relating to the Status of Refugees, adopted on July 28, 1951, and its 1967 Protocol, the Convention on the Elimination of All Forms of Discrimination against Women [CEDAW], and the Convention on the Rights of the Child."[43] In referencing CEDAW, the Executive Committee, composed of governments (not all of whom signed CEDAW), recognized that UNHCR would be bound by universal human rights principles in its treatment of refugee women. UNHCR's subsequent *Guidelines on the Protection of Refugee Women* reiterated that CEDAW and the other human rights instruments "provide a framework of international human rights standards for providing protection and assistance to refugee women."[44]

In practice, achieving gender equality is much more difficult. The gap between rhetoric and reality for women and girls is still very large. Women and girls remain the principal target of traffickers. They remain the civilian casualties of conflict and, with their dependent children, form a majority of the displaced. They remain the victims of sexual violence and exploitation. They remain without equal access to education and livelihoods. And cultural traditions remain a potent barrier to improving their lives.

Hence, the research discussed in this chapter raises the need for a concerted advocacy effort to break down the barriers to achieving justice and rights for women who have been forced to migrate. In an ethical world, no one would become a forced migrant. Certainly, women would not be forced to flee conflict, repression, or disasters, nor would they be vulnerable to traffickers. Advocacy for conflict and disaster prevention and mitigation, emergency preparedness that promotes coping skills in communities of origin, and the development of alternatives to displacement would help reduce forced migration. Reducing trafficking also requires advocacy in support of greater economic opportunities for women and support of education for girls. This includes the identification of ways better to promote "stay at home" development that will provide women with employment opportunities, education, health care, and other services in their home communities.

Since prevention does not always work, and because sometimes migration is a necessary response to conflict, natural disasters, and economic deprivation, advocacy in support of the following interventions would help women who have been forced to migrate:

- There should be renewed efforts to implement fully the UNHCR *Guidelines on the Protection of Refugee Women*, the UNHCR *Sexual and Gender-Based Violence against Refugee, Returnees and Internally Displaced Persons: Guidelines for Prevention and Response*, the *Guiding Principles on Internal Displacement*, and other policies and guidelines to empower refugee and displaced women and protect their rights and physical safety and security.
- Policies and programs should be adopted to enable refugee, displaced, and trafficked women to participate actively in decisions that affect them and their families.
- Improvements are urgently needed in the protection of the rights of women migrants and their safety and security. In particular, steps should be taken to help refugee and displaced women protect themselves from sexual exploitation, trafficking, involuntary prostitution, and other exploitable situations.
- Improvements are also needed in the socioeconomic status of refugee and displaced women to enable them to support themselves and their families in dignity and safety. This means improving access to employment, credit, education, and skills training as well as access to adequate and safe housing.
- Policies should ensure access of women who have been forced to migrate to primary and reproductive health care services, including programs to address sexual- and gender-based violence, trauma resulting from flight and conflict, and sexually transmitted diseases and HIV/AIDS. Such programs are needed by refugee and displaced women and victims of trafficking.
- Education programs should be implemented that inform migrant women of their rights and responsibilities under international and national laws. These programs should use an array of media techniques to reach the women in a culturally and linguistically appropriate manner.
- States should recognize that they must involve multiple sectors in the identification of trafficking victims, including but not limited to law enforcement, social service agencies, hospitals and health clinics, schools, and ethnic associations. Trafficking survivors should be given a range of options following emancipation in order to meet the specific situation in which they find themselves, including repatriation to their home country, integration in the destination country, witness protection for themselves, and the ability to bring relatives to join them if their families are likely otherwise to be targeted by the traffickers.
- The role of refugee and displaced women in the reconstruction and development of postconflict societies needs special attention to ensure their full participation in decisions on return and on their contribution to the future of their home communities and countries.
- Improvements must be made in the collection of data on internal and international migration, with particular attention to collecting gender and age disaggregated statistics.

Notes

This chapter draws heavily on research that the author conducted in the preparation of *Refugee Women*, 2nd ed. (Lanham, MD: Lexington Books, 2004), and the UN Division for the Advancement of Women's *2004 World Survey on the Role of Women in Development: International Migration* (New York: United Nations, 2005). The information has been updated for this chapter.

1. UN Division for the Advancement of Women, *2004 World Survey.*

2. Lyndsey Ellis, "A Rights-Based Approach to Development: An Exploration of Cultural Relativism and Universality in Human Rights" (Waltham, MA: Brandeis University, Heller School for Social Policy and Management, Program in Sustainable International Development, April 2006), http://www.brandeis.edu/gsa/gradjournal/2006/pdf/lyndseyellis.pdf (accessed April 6, 2007), referencing the work of Abdullahi An-Na'im, "Toward a Cross-Cultural Approach to Defining International Standards of Human Rights: The Meaning of Cruel, Inhuman or Degrading Treatment or Punishment," in *Human Rights in Cross-Cultural Perspectives: A Quest for Consensus*, ed. Abdullahi An-Na'im (Philadelphia: University of Pennsylvania Press, 1992), 21–44; Margaret Jolly, "Women's Rights, Human Rights, and Domestic Violence in Vanuatu," in *Development: A Cultural Studies Reader*, ed. Susanne Schech and Jane Haggis (Malden, MA: Blackwell Publishing, 2002), 144–54; and Ann-Belinda S. Preis, "Human Rights as Cultural Practice: An Anthropological Critique," in *Development: A Cultural Studies Reader*, 132–43.

3. Jack Donnelly, "Cultural Relativism and Universal Human Rights," *Human Rights Quarterly* 6, no. 4 (1984): 400–419.

4. Internal Displacement Monitoring Centre, *Internal Displacement: Global Overview of Trends and Developments in 2005* (Geneva: IDMC, 2005).

5. Susan Martin, "Internal Trafficking," *Forced Migration Review* 25 (May 2006): 12–13.

6. UN Population Division, *International Migration Report 2005* (New York: United Nations, 2005).

7. Susan Forbes Martin, *Refugee Women*, 2nd ed. (Lanham, MD: Lexington Books, 2004).

8. Internal Displacement Monitoring Centre, *Internal Displacement*, 5.

9. OAU Convention Governing the Specific Aspects of Refugee Problems in Africa, adopted by the Assembly of Heads of State and Government at its Sixth Ordinary Session, entry into force, June 20, 1974.

10. Female genital cutting (FGC) refers to the removal of part or all of a girl's external genitalia and, in a more radical version (infibulation), the stitching up of the vaginal opening. For more detailed description of forms of FGC, see UN Population Fund, "Frequently Asked Questions on Female Genital Mutilation/Cutting," http://www.unfpa.org/gender/practices2.htm#1.

11. UN High Commissioner for Refugees, *Guidelines on International Protection: "Gender Based Persecution" and "Membership of a Particular Social Group" within the Context of Article 1A(2) of the 1951 Convention and/or Its 1967 Protocol Relating to the Status of Refugees* (Geneva: UNHCR, May 7, 2002).

12. United Kingdom Immigration Appellate Authority. "Asylum Gender Guidelines," November 2000: 14, http://www.asylumsupport.info/publications/iaa/gender.pdf (accessed April 5, 2007).

13. UN High Commissioner for Refugees, *Guidelines on International Protection*, 7.

14. UNHCR and Save the Children UK, "Note for Implementing and Operational Partners by UNHCR and Save the Children-UK on Sexual Violence & Exploitation," February, 2002, http://www.reliefweb.int/rw/rwb.nsf/AllDocsByUNID/6010f9ed3c651c93c1256b6d00560fca (accessed April 5, 2007).

15. UN General Assembly, "Investigation into Sexual Exploitation of Refugees by Aid Workers

in West Africa: Report of the Secretary-General on the Activities of the Office of Internal Oversight Services," A57/465 Fifty-seventh Session, Agenda item 122 (October 11, 2002), 12.

16. Inter-Agency Standing Committee (IASC), *Guidelines for Gender-Based Violence Interventions in Humanitarian Settings: Focusing on Prevention of and Response to Sexual Violence in Emergencies* (New York: United Nations, September 2005).

17. Simon Turner, *Angry Young Men in Camps: International Assistance and Changing Hierarchies of Authority amongst Burundian Refugees in Tanzania*, UNHCR Working Paper No. 9 (Geneva: UN High Commissioner for Refugees, 1999).

18. UN Secretary General, *Report on Children and Armed Conflict*, A/58/546-S/2003/1053, 2003, 6.

19. UN High Commissioner for Refugees, *Handbook on Voluntary Repatriation: International Protection* (Geneva: UNHCR, 1996), section 2.4.

20. Ibid.

21. UN High Commissioner for Refugees, *Guidelines on the Protection of Refugee Women* (Geneva: UNHCR, 1991).

22. Women's Commission for Refugee Women and Children, *Beyond Firewood: Fuel Alternatives and Protection Strategies for Displaced Women and Girls* (New York: Women's Commission for Refugee Women and Children, 2006), 6.

23. Women's Commission for Refugee Women and Children, *UNHCR Policy on Refugee Women and Guidelines on Their Protection: An Assessment of Ten Years of Implementation* (New York: Women's Commission for Refugee Women and Children, 2002), 28.

24. Ibid., 30.

25. Inter-Agency Working Group on Reproductive Health in Refugee Situations, *Reproductive Health in Refugee Situations: An Inter-Agency Field Manual* (Geneva: UNHCR, 1999), 12.

26. Reproductive Health Outlook, "Refugee Reproductive Health, Program Examples," no date, http://www.rho.org/html/refugee_progexamples.htm#topofpage (accessed April 6, 2007).

27. UN High Commissioner for Refugees Evaluation and Policy Analysis Unit (EPAU), Health and Community Development Section, *Learning for a Future: Refugee Education in Developing Countries* (Geneva: UNHCR, 2002), 6.

28. Glenn Dunkley, *Review of UNHCR's Refugee Education Activities* (Geneva: UNHCR, 1997), para. 18.

29. Women's Commission, *UNHCR Policy on Refugee Women*, 33.

30. UN High Commissioner for Refugees, *Handbook on Repatriation* (Geneva: UN High Commissioner for Refugees, May 2004).

31. Women's Commission for Refugee Women and Children, *Precious Resources: Participatory Research Study with Adolescents and Youth in Sierra Leone* (New York: Women's Commission for Refugee Women and Children, April–July 2002), 25.

32. UN High Commissioner for Refugees, *Resettlement Handbook* (Geneva: UNHCR, 2002).

33. Ibid.

34. Ibid.

35. See Martin, *Refugee Women*.

36. Protocol against the Smuggling of Migrants by Land, Sea and Air, supplementing the United Nations Convention against Transnational Organized Crime (2000).

37. Protocol to Prevent, Suppress and Punish Trafficking in Persons, Especially Women and Children, Supplementing the United Nations Convention against Transnational Organized Crime (2000), http://www.uncjin.org/Documents/Conventions/dcatoc/final_documents_2/convention_%20traff_eng.pdf (accessed April 6, 2007).

38. UN Division for the Advancement of Women (DAW), *Trafficking in Women and Girls: Report of the Expert Group Meeting* (Glen Cove, NY, November 2002), 18–22.

39. U.S. Department of Justice, Civil Rights Division, *Anti-Trafficking News Bulletin*, issue 1 (August 2006): 3.

40. UN Division for the Advancement of Women, *Trafficking in Women and Girls*, 8.

41. Francis Miko and Grace Park, *Trafficking in Women and Children: The US and International Response*, U.S. Congressional Research Service Report, 98-649C (Washington, DC: CRS, May 10, 2000).

42. International Organization for Migration, *World Migration Report 2000* (Geneva: United Nations Publications, 2000).

43. UN Economic and Social Council, Resolution on Refugee and Displaced Women and Children (E/Res/1991/23), http://www.unhcr.org/excom/EXCOM/3ae69eee14.html (accessed April 6, 2007).

44. UN High Commissioner for Refugees, *Guidelines on the Protection of Refugee Women* (Geneva: UNHCR, June 1991), para. 6.

IV

Conflict, Protection, and Return

9

Human Rights, the Use of Force, and Displacement in the Great Lakes Region

Reflections on a Troubling Trend

Khoti Kamanga

This chapter is an attempt to explain the nexus between three main issues: the human right to peace, conflict, and forced displacement in the six core countries of the Great Lakes Region of Africa (GLR). Although the term "Great Lakes Region" is sometimes understood more expansively, at the core of the region are those sub-Saharan African countries located around four "great" lakes, the lakes being Victoria, Tanganyika, Albert, and Kivu.[1] The countries are Burundi, Democratic Republic of Congo (DRC), Kenya, Rwanda, Tanzania, and Uganda.

The GLR deserves attention for a host of reasons. No other geographical region on the African continent has a forced displacement problem of comparable duration or magnitude.[2] The GLR is also characterized by endemic, violent conflicts, as illustrated by the situation, particularly in Burundi, DRC, and Uganda, in the twenty-first century's first decade. The civil war (1990–1994) and the genocide (1994) in Rwanda left nearly one million dead, while the ongoing conflict in Burundi has claimed more than three hundred thousand lives since 1993. There have been cyclical genocides in Burundi too, even if rarely acknowledged. In the neighboring DRC, a civil war that began in 1996 rapidly turned into an internationalized armed conflict following the direct involvement of the armed forces of Angola, Burundi, Namibia, Rwanda, Uganda, and Zimbabwe, among others.[3] But in terms of human and natural resources, the GLR countries are among the most resource-rich countries in the world, despite their low ranking on the United Nations Development Program's Human Development Index (HDI).[4]

Duration, Magnitude, and Scope of Displacement

The GLR is deserving of attention for a host of reasons, one of which is the sheer magnitude of forced displacement. The numbers are stupendous, so much so that some of the terms used to illustrate the enormity of the problem hardly seem to capture the reality in the GLR. For instance, in order to isolate the more acute, enduring cases of forced displacement, academics and practitioners alike began using the term "protracted refugee situations"[5] to describe the presence of over one hundred thousand displaced persons for an uninterrupted period of over ten years. However, it quickly becomes evident that the "protracted refugee situation" label hardly captures the vast scope of the problem. Some other, more appropriate terminology needs to be coined, such as "global flashpoint." Tanzania has been hosting refugees from as early as 1959, and at the peak of the genocide in neighboring Rwanda, the Tanzanian refugee population stood at over one million. In the estimate of UNHCR, as of March 1, 2007, the refugee population in Tanzania alone was 280,956, which is more than twice the combined refugee populations of Germany (64,200), the United Kingdom (14,600), France (25,500), Italy (5,800), and the Netherlands (14,400).[6]

Statistics on forced displacement reveal yet another interesting trend, namely that the vast majority of displaced persons found in the GLR originated from that very region. Since the core countries of the GLR also rank among the poorest of the poor, it is safe to conclude that the brunt of the burden of hosting refugees apparently falls on the less privileged nations.[7] This observation is buttressed by the fact that all of the top sixteen countries (in a total list comprising twenty-eight) with the largest ratio of refugees to host country population are located in the Global South. Tanzania and Kenya, countries of particular concern to us, are at position 6 and 10 respectively (see table 9.1 and figure 9.1).

But is it not true also that the refugee-hosting countries in the poor South are recipients of substantive financial assistance from the industrialized nations of the North, the G8 in particular? Two sets of statistical data are pertinent. Table 9.2 lists the world's largest contributors while table 9.3 presents particular countries' donations in dollars given per person in the donating countries.

Conflict and Forced Displacement

Neither the Universal Declaration of Human Rights of 1948 nor the human rights Covenants of 1966 expressly provided for the "human right to peace." Even the most forward-looking constitutions of contemporary times, such as the Constitution of the Republic of South Africa of 1996, eschew any reference to this "third-generation" right. At the same time, the notion of "crime against the peace" is a fairly old legal concept.

Limitations on the Use of Force

The charter of the International Military Tribunal of August 8, 1945, defined "crimes against peace" as "planning, preparation, initiation or waging war of aggression, or a war in violation of international treaties, agreements or assurances, or participation in a common plan or conspiracy for the accomplishment of any of the foregoing."[8] There are several important legal developments within the body of law dedicated to the question of the legitimate use of force (that is to say, *jus ad bellum*) and the law concerned with

Table 9.1

Ratios of Refugees to Host Country Populations

Host Country	Ratio of Refugee Population to Total Population	Number of Refugees
West Bank and Gaza*	1:2	1,685,800
Jordan	1:10	609,500
Lebanon	1:13	296,800
Syria	1:21	866,300
Chad	1:35	275,500
Tanzania	1:66	549,100
Iran	1:70	994,000
Sierra Leone	1:92	60,100
Saudi Arabia	1:102	240,800
Kenya	1:117	269,300
Thailand	1:136	477,500
Venezuela	1:148	180,100
Pakistan	1:149	1,088,100
Sudan	1:173	225,900
Nepal	1:189	130,000
South Africa	1:276	169,800
Canada	1:815	39,500
Bangladesh	1:961	150,100
Germany	1:1,332	64,200
Australia	1:1,378	14,800
United States	1:1,678	176,700
European Union	1:2,006	749,500
India	1:2,142	393,300
France	1:2,380	25,500
China	1:3,696	352,700
Mexico	1:23,600	4,500
Spain	1:27,188	1,600
Japan	1:49,115	2,600

*Territories, not states.

Source: U.S. Committee for Refugees and Immigrants, *World Refugee Survey 2006,* 14.

the dual objectives of protecting victims of armed conflict and imposing limits as to the means and methods of waging warfare (in other words, *jus in bello*). The question of the use of force is set out primarily in the UN Charter, and the major provisions can be conveniently clustered into three groups.

The first is the obligation to resolve all international disputes through pacific means. These include negotiation, inquiry, mediation, conciliation, arbitration, judicial settlement, and a resort to regional organizations and arrangements.[9] The second is the prohibition on the use of force, around which there is extensive, albeit conflicting,

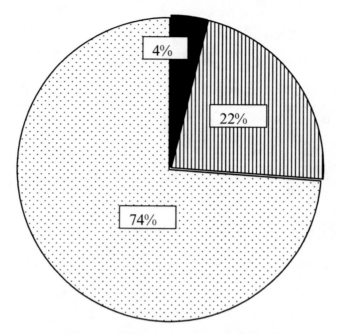

Figure 9.1 Distribution of Refugees by Host Country Income

74%—Host countries with per capita incomes below $2,000 (8,149,800 refugees)
22%—Host countries with per capita incomes between $2,001–$10,000 (2,444,400 refugees)
4%—Host countries with per capita incomes over $10,000 (416,800 refugees)
Source: U.S. committee for Refugees and Immigrants, *World Refugee Survey 2006,* 14.

jurisprudence and opinion. The pertinent part of the UN Charter reads as follows: "All [UN Member States] shall refrain in their international relations from the threat or use of force against the territorial integrity or political independence of any State, or in any manner inconsistent with the purposes of the United Nations."[10]

The third is the cluster of provisions that set out the exceptional instances in which force may legitimately be used. Key in this group is the issue of "self-defense." It includes, in part, the affirmation that "nothing in the present Charter shall impair the inherent right of individual or collective self-defense if an armed attack occurs against a Member of the United Nations, until the Security Council has taken measures necessary to maintain international peace and security."[11] There exists a vast body of jurisprudence and expert opinion on the issue of *jus ad bellum,* and much of it is not convergent. Take the example of the International Court of Justice (ICJ). In the *Nicaragua case* (1986), the Court took the view that the rule on prohibition of the use of force, as set out in Article 2 (4) of the UN Charter, constitutes a rule of customary international law and is of such legal significance as to warrant characterization as *jus cogens* (peremptory law).[12] In other words, the Court concluded that the rule is unquestionably binding and that no state or states can legislate or conduct themselves to the contrary.

Table 9.2

Top Donor Countries
(in millions of U.S. dollars)

1. United States	$600.6
2. EU	251.7
3. Sweden	132.4
4. Japan	125.9
5. The Netherlands	116.9
6. UK	115.9
7. Norway	86.6
8. Denmark	65.1
9. Germany	58.4
10. Australia	51.1
11. Canada	43.7
12. Switzerland	35.2
13. Italy	26.4
14. Finland	23.6
15. France	20.1
16. Peru	18.7
17. Belgium	17.7
18. Ireland	17.0
19. Spain	15.1
20. Guatemala	11.1

Source: U.S. Committee for Refugees
and Immigrants, *World Refugee Survey
2006*, 15.

Table 9.3

Top Donor Countries (contribution
Per Capita in U.S. dollars)

1. Luxembourg	$19.40
2. Norway	18.82
3. Sweden	14.71
4. Denmark	12.06
5. The Netherlands	7.17
6. Switzerland	4.75
7. Finland	5.54
8. Ireland	4.16
9. Australia	2.51
10. United States	2.03
11. UK	1.93
12. Belgium	1.69
13. New Zealand	1.41
14. Canada	1.36
15. Japan	0.99
16. Guatemala	0.88
17. Germany	0.71
18. Peru	0.67
19. EU	0.54
20. Greece	0.50

Source: U.S. Committee for Refugees
and Immigrants, *World Refugee Survey
2006*, 15.

However, in an advisory opinion given ten years later, the ICJ dithered in pronouncing the use or threat of nuclear weapons as contravening the UN Charter provision on the use of force.[13] Another bone of contention regards the precise meaning of "self-defense." A number of governments, particularly among the permanent members of the Security Council, tend to give Article 51 an elastic interpretation in an attempt to justify unilateral action as well as preemptive strikes and anticipatory self-defense.

Given the evident nexus between conflict and forced displacement, this approach must be questioned in favor of a restrictive interpretation. In particular, insistence should be made upon the interpretation formulated in the so-called *Caroline case,* according to which resort to the right of self-defense would be considered legitimate only when the use of force is clearly necessary and the response is proportional to the seriousness of the attack.[14] It needs to be noted that a cautious, restrictive interpretation to the right of self-defense finds support both in the practice of the Security Council[15] and also in the Panel Report by eminent persons appointed by the UN secretary-general in 2004. The report cautions against unilateralism by stating that "we all have to recognize—no matter how great our strength—that we must deny ourselves the license to do always as we please," since "no State, no matter how powerful, can by its own efforts alone make itself invulnerable to today's threats."[16]

International Law and Forced Migration

As mentioned earlier, within international law there are a number of branches pertinent to forced migration that address one major causal factor of displacement: armed conflict. Besides *jus ad bellum*, however, we need also to consider that branch which seeks to protect victims of war and regulates the conduct of belligerents.

The nexus between conflict and displacement (and, ultimately, further insecurity) in the Great Lakes Region has been described in painful detail by two important eyewitnesses to the civil war and genocide in Rwanda in the early 1990s. The accounts of Madam Sadako Ogata, then UN High Commissioner for Refugees, and Lieutenant General Romeo Dallaire, the commander of the United Nations Assistance Mission in Rwanda (UNAMIR) at the time, make it clear that had the law governing armed conflict been faithfully adhered to, the impact of the conflict on displacement would have been significantly ameliorated if not averted altogether.[17]

The rules of International Humanitarian Law (IHL) pertinent to advocates of the rights of displaced persons are to be found, first and foremost, in the four Geneva Conventions of August 12, 1949,[18] and in the two Protocols of June 1977, supplementing the Geneva Conventions.[19] Of all provisions found in the Geneva Conventions, none is as important to our topic as the one that criminalizes forcible displacement. Involuntary displacement, according to the Statute of the International Criminal Court, may be categorized, depending on the circumstances, as constituting "genocide," a "crime against humanity," or a "war crime."

According to the official commentary to the Geneva Conventions, the background to the prohibition of "forcible transfers and deportations" goes back to the deportations of World War II, and the term signifies the involuntary mass movement of persons protected by *jus in bello*, save for considerations of the population's security and imperative military reasons. In addition, unlawful deportation or transfer is an offense of a grave nature and therefore entails the most severe penal sanctions.[20] The fourth Geneva Convention prohibits the deportation and forced transfer of civilians regardless of the motive of such dislocation. The pertinent part states that "individual or mass forcible transfers, as well as deportations of protected persons from occupied territory to the territory of the Occupying Power or to that of any other country, occupied or not, are prohibited, regardless of their motive."[21] Admittedly, the Geneva Conventions do acknowledge that in exceptional circumstances it may be necessary to carry out "transfers or evacuations." According to the Conventions, this necessity could be dictated by considerations of the "security of the population" concerned or "imperative military reasons." In either case, however, there are a number of guarantees, including the obligation to return evacuees to their homes as soon as hostilities cease.[22]

This provision of the Geneva Conventions is reaffirmation of a rule in the Nuremberg Charter of 1945. Recent jurisprudence (especially in the International Criminal Tribunal for Rwanda [ICTR] and the International Criminal Tribunal for the Former Yugoslavia [ICTY]) has also stressed Article 3, common to all the Geneva Conventions, as yet another provision critical to the general standards of civilian protection during armed conflict.

On the other side are more recent legal developments that consolidate the precedents set at Nuremberg. Consistent with fourth Geneva Convention, the Statutes of the International Criminal Tribunal for the Former Yugoslavia (ICTY), as well as that of the International Criminal Court (ICC), contain provisions criminalizing deportation and transfer.[23]

The law also has provisions covering situations where displacement is occurring not as a result of a deliberate policy, as was the case during World War II, but rather as an unintended outcome of military operations. Additional Protocol I to the Geneva Conventions is quite instructive on this matter.[24] The Protocol has fairly detailed provisions concerning the precautions military commanders and other authorities must take well ahead of carrying out attacks. The general rule is to ensure that constant care is taken "to spare the civilian population, civilians and civilian objects." The Protocol imposes further explicit duties. An attack must be preceded by an assessment of the nature of the envisaged target, and there is a clear duty to distinguish civilian objects from military objectives, with only the latter constituting a legitimate target of attack and destruction. If in such an assessment it emerges that incidental, collateral damage that serves little or no military advantage whatsoever is likely to occur, commanders and planners of the anticipated attack are duty bound to refrain. More pertinently, there must be a deliberate effort to ensure that the chosen means and methods of attack avoid, or at least minimize, collateral damage to civilians and their property. Finally, there is a duty to give advance warnings of attacks likely to affect the civilian population and an obligation to protect the civilian population against "dangers resulting from military operations."

It is unfortunate, however, that the international penal tribunal of particular relevance to the Great Lakes Region, the International Criminal Tribunal for Rwanda (ICTR), has no mandate to prosecute persons responsible for the evident, large-scale deportations and transfer witnessed in Rwanda. While this indeed presents a challenge, it is mitigated by the fact that the Statute of the ICC, as noted earlier, recognizes deportation and transfer as a serious international crime such that there would be a firm ground to prosecute any future recurrence of unlawful displacement. At any rate the ICTY in the *Tadic case* (1995) made it abundantly clear that deportations and transfer in the context of a noninternational armed conflict (which is the more common type of conflict in the Great Lakes Region) constitute a serious offence, a war crime to be precise. In addition, deportation and transfer are not only punishable offences in the context of armed conflict (international or internal)—deportation is a punishable offence even when occurring outside the context of an armed conflict, and in this regard it constitutes a crime against humanity.[25] Displacement can also fall under the rubric of genocide, in particular where the deportation is done with the intent to destroy a national, ethnic, racial, or religious group or where the conditions of the displaced are such as to lead to serious risk of death and are imposed intentionally.

Implementing International Instruments

The important advocacy issue here, therefore, would seem to be a campaign to get states to ratify these international instruments and, if they have so done, to embark on the implementation and domestication of these treaties, creating the necessary policy and institutional framework for doing so. Of the six countries constituting the GLR of

Africa, Rwanda stands out for not having signed the Rome Statute of the International Criminal Court, but neither have any of the remaining GLR states satisfactorily created the legal and institutional framework required to get the statute fully operational and legally enforceable within these states' respective territorial boundaries.

Forcible transfers and deportations (and the killing of defenseless civilians) are an indisputably serious legal offense under *jus in bello*. There is a moral dimension as well to censuring such conduct. Henry Dunant's heart-rending account of one of history's bloodiest battles, the June 1859 Battle of Solferino in Italy, sets the moral backdrop to the emergence of modern-day *jus in bello*. This account was to a large extent influenced by the Calvinist thought of the time. From a quite different philosophical point of view, Jean-Jacques Rousseau's treatise *The Social Contract* (1762) challenged senseless and indiscriminate attacks, thus paving way for the subsequent legal articulation of the rule requiring that a distinction be made between "civilian objects," "noncombatants," and "military objectives." Rousseau wrote that "the object of the war being the destruction of the hostile State, the other side has a right to kill its defenders while they are bearing arms, but as soon as they lay them down and surrender they cease to be enemies or instruments of the enemy, and become once more merely men, whose lives no one has any right to take."[26]

Legal and moral tools do not exhaust the range of arsenals for advocacy. There is the cultural element, too. In recent years there has emerged the notion of "culture of peace" as a way of making the world a safer place in which to live. First articulated, and persuasively so, for UNESCO in 1989 at the International Congress on Peace in the Minds of Men in the Ivorian city of Yamoussoukro, the concept envisages a world in-spired by universal values of respect for life, liberty, justice, solidarity, tolerance, human rights, and equality and an education system promoting such a vision. Understandably, a key component of the concept "culture of peace" becomes "peace education." Such education involves schooling and other educational initiatives that enable children and others to put peace building into practice in the educational setting, using teaching and learning methods that stress participation, problem solving, and respect for differ-ences. It will draw on the knowledge of peace building that exists in the community; handle conflicts in ways that respect the rights and dignity of all involved; and main-stream an understanding of peace, human rights, social justice, and global issues into the curriculum.[27]

The plight of refugees can also be addressed by taking advantage of the vast array of institutions and instruments within the domain of human rights. Joan Fitzpatrick's trea-tise, *Human Rights Protection for Refugees, Asylum Seekers, and Internally Displaced Per-sons* (2001), is one among many valuable resource materials for advocacy.[28] Within hu-man rights discourse, controversy continues to rage as to the so-called third-generation right to peace.[29] But even those who, like Theodor Meron, acknowledge the lack of con-sensus concerning whether these third-generation rights should indisputably be con-sidered to be human rights in the same fashion as first- and second-generation rights, concede the "overriding importance of living in peace."[30] This is understandable, given the stupendous global accumulation of weapons of mass destruction, in particular nu-clear, by nations and possibly other, unidentifiable actors, held in possession covertly or overtly. As the International Court of Justice dealt with the request to provide an advisory opinion as to the legality or otherwise of the threat or use of nuclear weapons, it began by pointing out the unique characteristics of nuclear weapons, and in particular their destructive capacity, their capacity to cause untold suffering, and their ability to cause damage to generations to come.[31] But the more pertinent point to make is that a peaceful society is one in which its members do not have to vote with their feet each time there is disagreement or a dispute. Thus, the right to peace is of direct relevance to refugees, for the breakdown of peace or outbreak of war is a leading cause of flight in the Great Lakes Region, as elsewhere. Whether it is Rwanda, Burundi, or the DRC that one has in mind, the causal relationship between absence of peace and displacement is inescapable. Insecurity is also a factor that not only complicates the provision of humanitarian assistance to the displaced, but often delays repatriation of victims of armed conflicts, be they internally displaced persons (IDPs) or refugees.[32]

Causes, Consequences, and Policy Implications of Conflict

The causes of displacement are many, and an effort should always be made to differentiate the root causes from what may be termed the immediate factors, or "triggers." This is particularly important if we have to devise strategies and approaches that would allow us to deal with the challenges posed by forced migration in an effective and sustainable fashion. I have, for example, supported those who caution against the temptation to oversimplify the conflicts in our region by calling them "tribal wars," just as I have reservations about claiming poverty (or multi-ethnicity) as a factor that inevitably engenders conflict and, thus, displacement.[33]

In an attempt at explaining the origins of conflicts, Joseph Nye (citing Kenneth Waltz) identifies three factors: the individual, the state, and the international system.[34] Indeed, when we reflect on the situation in the Great Lakes Region, we see merit in this argument, although nuances must be added. The roles played by individual leaders such as Juvénal Habyarimana (Rwanda), Mobutu Sese Seko (Zaire, now the DRC), or for that matter Idi Amin (Uganda) constituted a factor of particular significance in the various policies those countries pursued and in the ensuing conflicts. At the other extreme, Tanzania's erstwhile open door policy cannot be understood without taking into account the personality and philosophy of the country's founding father, Mwalimu Julius Nyerere. If leadership is key, then we must also address the issue of governance, namely the manner in which persons assume office, their exercise of power, and their duration of tenure. In several countries in Africa (Namibia, Malawi, Nigeria, Chad, to name but a few), the incumbent leaders have attempted to amend the constitution with a view to prolonging their days in office beyond the legally permissible tenure.

In this regard, it is noteworthy that the African Union (AU) has gone some way in furthering respect for the rule of law by putting in place a mechanism for addressing those instances in which an unconstitutional change of government occurs. Several "soft law" texts are worth mentioning. The Algiers Decision of July 1999 and the Lomé Declaration of July 2000 both address the issue of AU responses in the event of an unconstitutional change of government (as by a coup d'état) in a member state. Also important is the 2002 AU Declaration, on Principles Governing Democratic Elections.

Political exclusion of certain groups based on discrimination, authoritarianism, and other forms of monopolization of power are all known to be sources of conflict. Free, fair, and regular elections constitute an important pillar of governance to the extent that they provide predictable and effective mechanisms for challenging policies and bringing about change. In so doing, they reduce the risk of resort to violent means and conflict, which all too often lead to forced migration.

As for the role of the international system and the tradition of geopolitics, Nye suggests that "location and proximity" are important factors in understanding the behavior of states. States tend to be influenced by the nature of nearby states and by developments within their neighborhood. Because of the developments of the early 1990s in the DRC, each of its neighbors found itself compelled to adopt a policy in response, even joining in the armed conflict that broke out in May 1997. Tanzania is an interesting illustration of the influence of "location and proximity" on policy. Sharing highly porous borders with DRC, Rwanda, and Burundi, all of which are conflict prone and preeminent sources of refugee movement, Tanzania has found itself ranking among the world's top countries of asylum.[35] And the Tanzanian leadership has increasingly viewed refugee presence as an unmitigated burden requiring drastic responses. As a consequence, a more restrictive refugee regime has emerged.[36]

Feeding into this new legal and policy paradigm is a reluctance to consider any benefits that a host country could gain from the presence and innovative engagement of the resident refugee population. For instance, a 2003 study revealed how one refugee-hosting location, the District of Kibondo, has registered significant achievements in the education sector. Within a span of five years (1998–2002), primary school enrollment increased from 26 percent to 88 percent, while primary school completion rates for all schoolchildren in the district shot from 58 percent to 82.6 percent, with a simultaneous fourfold decrease in the dropout rate, all within the context of a special, internationally funded assistance program. Very similar achievements have occurred in the refugee-hosting District of Ngara, where overall academic performance improved so much that the District moved from position 112 to 9 in national rankings.[37]

Besides the reluctance to acknowledge these and several other potential benefits of the presence of refugees, there is also a growing tendency to project a stereotype of foreigners and refugees as being, for lack of better term, necessarily evil. This is particularly, though not exclusively, visible in the media. In South Africa, for example, tabloid newspapers such as the *Daily Sun* perpetually churn out images of asylum seekers and refugees based on unfounded myths and stereotypes.[38] The 2003 study by the Centre for the Study of Forced Migration found that almost identical claims were being made about refugees despite the absence of any empirical data to warrant such stereotyping. Not surprisingly, the worldwide approach is increasingly to "securitize" international migration and to respond to migrants with the legislative and institutional tools designed to address criminals.[39]

In the Great Lakes Region, this negative attitude towards refugees is somewhat puzzling, given the fact that with very few exceptions (such as the Hadzabe of central Tanzania), all the remaining communities, including the largest and most prominent in the region, migrated into the region from beyond, and did so fairly recently.[40]

Conclusion

Available data on forced migration points to the Great Lakes Region as a major global flashpoint on account of both the very large numbers of forced migrants and the long duration of the displacement. These data also show that the poor countries of the world are bearing the brunt of hosting refugees, with the industrialized countries making an unacceptably modest contribution. At the same time, the contribution (monetary or otherwise) by countries of the South, the locus of many of the world's refugees, is left unacknowledged or unquantified.

There can be no doubt that the most prominent and immediate factor behind forced displacement in the Great Lakes Region is armed conflict. It explains the astounding displacement that took place in Rwanda and elsewhere in the region in the early 1990s just as it is the cause of the high level of displacement we continue to witness in Burundi and the DRC (and elsewhere in the environs).

From the legal point of view, there exists a significant body of law setting out conditions for the legitimate use of force (*jus ad bellum*). This is complemented by another branch of the law, whose dual objectives are to provide protection to victims of war (the so-called Law of Geneva) and to regulate the conduct of belligerents (the Law of The Hague). States and other actors party to existing or future conflicts need to be made aware of this body of law. For certain, liberal interpretation of self-defense should be opposed.

International law, adequate as it may be, depends for its implementation on the good will, national laws, and institutions through which states support the international system. Campaigning for the ratification and domestication of international legal instruments pertinent to the question of use of force must become a matter of heightened urgency. The "securitization" of migration that is in vogue conflicts with the human rights of many forced migrants and may even be of questionable utility. At any rate, it sits awkwardly with the historical background of the peoples of the region as themselves largely migrants, as well as their aspirations for a stronger Africa Union.

At a practical level, efforts should not be spared in working to create awareness of and capacity to exploit the existing human rights framework in advancing the cause for peace. This is a key way to aid asylum seekers, refugees, and internally displaced persons (IDPs).

Notes

The views expressed in this chapter are not necessarily those of the Centre for the Study of Forced Migration.

1. This is worth pointing out, since at times a more expansive approach is taken of the term GLR. An illustration is the international conference on the GLR initiated by the UN Security Council and launched in Dar es Salaam in November 2004. Besides Tanzania, Kenya, Uganda, Rwanda, Burundi, and the DRC (the six core countries), others sometimes included are Angola, the Central African Republic, the Republic of Congo, Sudan, and Zambia.

2. See table 9.1.

3. It earned the cliché of being Africa's First World War; for details see Mwesiga Baregu, ed., *Crisis in the Democratic Republic of Congo* (Harare, Zimbabwe: Sapes Books, 1999), and Michael Nest et al., eds., *The Democratic Republic of Congo: Economic Dimensions of War and Peace*, International Peace Academy Occasional Paper Series (Boulder, CO: Lynne Rienner Publishers, 2006).

4. The countries of the GLR are ranked as follows out of 177 countries in the 2006 Report: Burundi (169), DRC (167), Kenya (152), Rwanda (158), Tanzania (162), and Uganda (145). The *2006 Human Development Report* is available from http://hdr.undp.org/en/reports/global/hdr2006/ (accessed Feb. 28, 2008).

5. See, for example, Jeff Crisp, "No Solutions in Sight: The Problem of Protracted Refugee Situations in Africa," paper presented at the Symposium on the Multidimensionality of Displacement in Africa, Kyoto, Japan, 2002.

6. See U.S. Committee for Refugees and Immigrants, *World Refugee Survey 2006* (Washington, DC: USCRI, 2006), 5.

7. See, for example, Alex de Waal, ed., *War and Humanitarian Action in Africa* (Asmara, Eritrea: Africa World Press, 2000), 219.

8. Charter of the International Military Tribunal, Article 6 (a), http://www.yale.edu/lawweb/avalon/imt/proc/imtconst.htm (accessed April 4, 2007).

9. See UN Charter, Arts. 2 (3) and 33.

10. UN Charter, Art. 2 (4).

11. UN Charter, Art. 51.

12. International Court of Justice, "Case Concerning Military and Paramilitary Activities in and against Nicaragua (Merits)," *ICJ Reports*, 1986.

13. International Court of Justice, "Advisory Opinion of the International Court of Justice Concerning the Legality of the Threat or Use of Nuclear Weapons," *ICJ Reports*, 1996.

14. The rule was formulated by the then U.S. secretary of state Daniel Webster in correspondence with his United Kingdom counterpart in 1841 following a dispute involving an American ship, the *Caroline*, which the British had attacked and destroyed at the U.S.–Canadian border.

15. For details, see D. J. Harris, *Cases and Materials on International Law*, 4th ed. (London: Sweet & Maxwell, 1991), 848–55.

16. *A More Secure World: Our Shared Responsibility: Report of the High-level Panel on Threats, Challenges, and Change*, 2004, http://www.un.org/secureworld/report2.pdf (accessed April 4, 2007).

17. See Sadako Ogata, *The Turbulent Decade: Confronting the Refugee Crises of the 1990s* (New York: W.W. Norton, 2005), and Romeo Dallaire, *Shake Hands with the Devil: The Failure of Humanity in Rwanda* (Toronto: Random House Canada, 2003).

18. That is, the Land Warfare Convention (Geneva Convention I), Maritime Warfare Convention Geneva Convention II), POW Convention (Geneva Convention III), and Civilian Protection Convention (Geneva Convention IV), all at http://www.yale.edu/lawweb/avalon/lawofwar/lawwar .htm (accessed April 5, 2007).

19. Additional Protocol I (on International Armed Conflict), and Additional Protocol II (on civil wars), both at http://www.unhchr.ch/html/menu3/b/94.htm (accessed April 5, 2007).

20. ICRC, *Commentary to the Fourth Geneva Convention of 1949* (Geneva: ICRC, 1958), 278–80.

21. Geneva Convention IV Relative to the Protection of Civilian Persons in Time of War, Art. 49, http://www.yale.edu/lawweb/avalon/lawofwar/geneva07.htm (accessed April 5, 2007).

22. Ibid., Art. 49. This provision should be read in conjunction with Article 85 (4) (a) of Additional Protocol II, whose import is to bring deportations and transfers into the ambit of the most

serious offences under *jus in bello*. See, however, the Israeli Supreme Court judgment (reproduced in *International Legal Materials* 29 (1990):139–81) in three petitions concerning deportation orders, in which the Court offered its interpretation of Article 49 of Geneva Convention I.

23. In particular, see Statute of the International Criminal Court (the Rome Statute), Art. 6 (e), Art. & (1) (d), and Art. 8 (2) (a) (vii).

24. For further details, see Arts. 57 and 58.

25. One of the charges leveled against the late Serbian leader, Slobodan Milosevic at the ICTY.

26. Cited in Jean S. Pictet, *Development and Principles of International Humanitarian Law* (Dordrecht, Netherlands: Martinus Nijhoff, 1985), 22–23.

27. For details, see the United Nations Global Teaching and Learning Project, http://www.un .org/cyberschoolbus/peace/content2.htm (accessed April 5, 22007).

28. Joan Fitzpatrick, *Human Rights Protection for Refugees, Asylum Seekers, and Internally Displaced Persons: A Guide to International Mechanisms and Procedures* (Ardsley, NY: Transnational Publishers, 2001).

29. See, for example, Theodor Meron, ed., *Human Rights in International Law: Legal and Policy Issues* (Oxford: Clarendon Press, 1989).

30. Ibid., 99.

31. International Court of Justice, "Advisory Opinion of the International Court of Justice Concerning the Legality of the Threat or Use of Nuclear Weapons," *ICJ Reports*, 1996.

32. See, for example, Susan Martin et al., *The Uprooted: Improving Humanitarian Responses to Forced Migration* (Lanham, MD: Lexington Books, 2005), especially the chapter, "Providing Security to Forced Migrants and Humanitarian Operations," 188–225.

33. I argued this in "Refugees and Internally Displaced Persons in the Great Lakes Region," a paper presented to the International Conference on Peace, Security, and Governance in the Great Lakes Region, organized by the International Peace Academy, December, 2003. Excerpts of the paper are published in Dorina Bekoe, "Peace, Security and Governance in the Great Lakes Region," *Rapporteur's Report*, International Peace Academy, December 2003.

34. Joseph Nye, *Understanding International Conflicts*, 4th ed. (New York: Longman, 2003), 34.

35. See table 9.1.

36. For details, see Khoti Kamanga, "The (Tanzania) Refugees Act of 1998: Some Legal and Policy Implications," *Journal of Refugee Studies* 18, no. 1 (2005): 100–116, and S. S. Chaulia "The Politics of Refugee Hosting in Tanzania: From Open Door to Unsustainability, Insecurity, and Receding Receptivity," *Journal of Refugee Studies* 16, no. 2 (2003): 147–66.

37. Details can be found in the Center for the Study of Forced Migration, *The Impact of the Presence of Refugees in Northwestern Tanzania* (Dar es Salaam, Tanzania: University of Dar es Salaam, September 2003), passim.

38. National Consortium for Refugee Affairs, "Summary of Key Findings: Refugee Protection in South Africa 2006," 8–9, http://migration.wits.ac.za/RefReport2006.pdf (accessed April 5, 2007).

39. See, for an example, Brett Story, "Politics as Usual: The Criminalization of Asylum Seekers in the United States," University of Oxford Refugee Studies Center, *Working Paper* No. 26, September, 2005, http://www.rsc.ox.ac.uk/PDFs/RSCworkingpaper26.pdf (accessed April 8, 2007).

40. See the polemic of Khoti Kamanga, "Majority of Tanzanians Are Products of Forced Migration," *The Citizen*, June 21, 2005, 7.

10

Internally Displaced People, Sovereignty, and the Responsibility to Protect

David Hollenbach

In September 2005 the heads of most of the nations of the world gathered in New York for a special World Summit session of the United Nations General Assembly. At this gathering they declared: "Each individual State has the *responsibility to protect* its populations from genocide, war crimes, ethnic cleansing and crimes against humanity." The leaders stated that the wider international community shares in this responsibility and through the United Nations may use "appropriate diplomatic, humanitarian and other peaceful means . . . to help to protect populations" from these crimes. They further declared that military means may be used to exercise this responsibility if peaceful means prove inadequate.[1] The phrase "responsibility to protect" was drawn from a 2001 report with that title issued by the International Commission on Intervention and State Sovereignty. This commission had been created through the initiative of the Canadian government to consider the possible legitimacy of humanitarian intervention to prevent atrocities like the genocide in Rwanda or the ethnic cleansing in Bosnia. The International Commission cast its discussion in terms of a responsibility to protect people from these crimes, rather than in the language of the right to intervene to prevent them. It used the phrase "responsibility to protect" to describe both the duties of states toward their own citizens and the duties of the international community to prevent grave crimes when a state was unable or unwilling to do so.[2] The Commission had gone further than the 2005 World Summit by affirming that intervention could be legitimate for the more expansive cause of protecting against large-scale loss of life.

The idea of the "responsibility to protect" is directly relevant to the issue of ethical responsibilities toward forced migrants, for it was first proposed in the context of discussions in the 1990s of how to respond to the plight of internally displaced persons. In 1992 UN secretary-general Boutros Boutros-Ghali appointed Francis M. Deng as his special representative on internally displaced persons. In this role, Deng has mounted an influential argument that response to the plight of internally displaced persons means that nation-state sovereignty must be conceived as a form of responsibility to citizens rather than an absolute immunity from outside interference. "Sovereignty as responsibility" is a shorthand way of stating that national governments have the duty to protect their citizens from abuses such as internal displacement, and that if national governments fail to do so, the larger international community has a duty to come to their aid.[3] Internal sovereignty does not give states the freedom to act toward their own citizens in whatever way they choose, nor does external sovereignty mean that states abusive to their own citizens are immune from interference by outside agents. Both forms of independence are challenged by the notions of "sovereignty as responsibility" and by its corollary, the "responsibility to protect." These responsibilities also challenge the notion that states have duties only toward the well-being of their own citizens. Responsibility reaches across borders. This chapter will build upon the recent discussions of the responsibility to protect and explore some of its implications for the treatment of internally displaced persons.

The Challenge of IDPs

According to the *Guiding Principles on Internal Displacement* prepared under the guidance of the Francis Deng and presented to the UN Commission on Human Rights in 1998, internally displaced persons (IDPs) are defined as "persons or groups of persons who have been forced or obliged to flee or leave their homes or places of habitual residence, in particular as a result of or in order to avoid the effects of armed conflict, situations of generalized violence, violations of human rights or natural or human-made disasters, and who have not crossed an internationally recognized State border."[4] Because IDPs are distinguished from refugees who have been forced to cross an international border, they do not have the international protections specified in the 1951 Convention Relating to the Status of Refugees. Internally displaced people not only face the deprivation and dangers associated with being driven from their homes. They also face distinctive threats due to the fact that the government of their own country is often the source of their displacement and suffering. Former U.S. ambassador to the UN Richard Holbrooke preferred to call IDPs "internal refugees" to make clear that there is no concrete difference between the experience of an official refugee and an IDP from the point of view of the suffering they must endure.[5]

Though the *Guiding Principles on Internal Displacement* are being taken with increasing seriousness, the internally displaced do not have rights that are enforceable in "hard law." This legal difference has often led to internally displaced people being relegated to a kind of moral and political no-man's-land in which they become "forgotten people."[6] This legal vacuum means that efforts to advocate better treatment for IDPs will have to be based primarily on appeals to ethical responsibility. One hopes that such an ethical case for responsibility to protect IDPs can subsequently be translated into legal norms and politically effective action. The ethical argument that will be presented here is just the first step toward a more effective response to the plight of the internally displaced. Because both the legal and political definitions of responsibility toward IDPs are so weak, the ethical case for responsibility is a necessary step in an effort to advocate change.

The number of people displaced internally within their own countries by civil conflict and human rights violations has been rising since 1990. In December 2005 their number was estimated at 23.7 million, more than twice the number of refugees who had crossed an international border.[7] Because of the severity of the IDP crisis, the 2005 World Summit declared a commitment by both nation-states and the international community "to take effective measures to increase the protection of internally displaced persons."[8] Though the number of IDPs declined slightly in 2005, the number remains very high by historical standards. The number is disproportionately high in Africa, with more than half of the world's total in the African continent (12.1 million internally displaced people in twenty countries, with Sudan, the Democratic Republic of Congo, and Uganda alone accounting for over nine million).[9] While the number of IDPs in Africa decreased slightly over the past year due to the return of some people to their homes in southern Sudan and the DRC, both these countries and the continent at large continue to witness massive new displacements. Zimbabwe and Togo are among the countries where new displacements are occurring. These realities raise the question of whether the nation-state system based on the overriding values of national sovereignty and nonintervention can provide an adequate moral and political framework for response to these people, and this question is particularly acute in Africa.

Rethinking Sovereignty

In fact, humanitarian concern with the protection of internally displaced people has been one of the stimuli for a serious reconsideration of the meaning and implications of the sovereignty of the nation-state that has been unfolding over the past decade and a half. It will be useful to consider responsibilities to the internally displaced in light of this rethinking.

Revolutions in Sovereignty

A useful framework is provided by the work of the international political theorist Daniel Philpott, who has traced the development of two "revolutions in sovereignty" that have shaped international affairs over the past several centuries. These revolutions are transformations of what Philpott calls the "constitution of international society." This constitution is the "set of norms, mutually agreed upon by polities who are members of the society, that define the holders of authority and their prerogatives, specifically in answer to three questions: Who are the legitimate polities? What are the rules for becoming one of these polities? And what are basic prerogatives of these polities?"[10] The constitution of international society, so understood, shapes both who are acknowledged to be the legitimate actors in international affairs and also what counts as legitimate or illegitimate international political behavior. Such a constitution, therefore, is not simply a factual description of the way the international system functions. It also has an important normative component that influences or even determines what is legitimate or illegitimate international behavior, what ought and ought not be done in political interaction. This normative dimension means it contains certain ethical presuppositions, at least implicitly, even if the structure and principles of order are frequently expressed in terms of political self-interest or of international law.

Philpott's historical narrative tells the story of two fundamental changes or revolutions in the constitution of international society over the past three and a half centuries. The first was the transition from the Western medieval arrangement, in which the nation-state did not yet exist, to the modern European state system, whose beginning was marked by the Peace of Westphalia in 1648. The second was the expansion of the nation-state system to the entire globe, accomplished through the anticolonial movements that followed World War II and that culminated in the 1960 United Nations General Assembly's Declaration on the Granting of Independence to Colonial Countries and Peoples.[11]

These two revolutions created the global system of nation-states with the prerogatives of sovereignty, self-determination, and territorial integrity that we have come to take for granted. Other nation-states are bound to recognize these prerogatives by respecting the principle of nonintervention. Philpott's study seeks to show that each of these revolutions was driven primarily by the power of new ideas. In the case of the revolution that led to the emergence of the nation-state in Europe, the central ideas were theological convictions that emerged in the Protestant Reformation. These ideas led first German and then other European peoples to demand religious self-determination for themselves and freedom from religious control by the formerly dominant Holy Roman Empire. As group identities became less religiously based, these initially religious demands gradually evolved into the secular norms of self-determination, territorial integrity, and nonintervention that are central to the modern nation-state system. In an analogous way following World War II, anticolonial and antiracist ideas led to the expansion of the European nation-state system to the entire globe. The ideas that all persons are equally deserving of respect and that no racial or cultural group ought to be subordinated to another led to the affirmation of the universal right to national self-determination as a normative standard of global politics. It denied legitimacy to colonialism and empire. Philpott acknowledges that material factors such as economic and political self-interest played a role in shaping both of these revolutions. In my judgment, though, he makes a persuasive case that ideas were significant driving forces in these transformations of the international system. Since these ideas had moral content, Philpott is in effect arguing that the two major changes in the organization of the international system during the modern epoch were driven by ethical aspirations to self-determination and the equality of peoples.

Challenges to the Nation-State System Today

This history is relevant to questions of responsibility toward internally displaced people today because it shows that the nation-state system is not the only way to organize international society or to define the scope of political and ethical responsibility. Responsibility for people's well-being need not stop at national borders. Indeed, there are significant challenges to the normative status of the nation-state system under way today. These challenges are in part arising from factors such as greater global economic integration and the growing awareness of ecological interdependence across borders. Equally important are the ethical ideas and values such as human rights that energize efforts to set limits on national sovereignty. Just as the idea that people should be liberated from imperial control led to the rise and global spread of the nation-state system, today the idea that people should be free from domination is generating a movement toward the limitation of sovereignty by normative standards of human rights. In Philpott's terminology, a third revolution in sovereignty is in the making. When states fail to uphold the values of human rights, peace, and order, their legitimacy can be questioned. When they violate people's rights or threaten their lives in extreme ways, they may be subject to intervention by outside powers.[12]

Movement toward the circumscription of sovereignty has been evident in a number of post–cold war decisions at the UN, NATO, and regional intergovernmental bodies. The UN Security Council authorized intervention to stop Iraqi governmental threats to the Kurds within Iraq in 1991 and to relieve starving people within Somalia in 1992. NATO took military action in Serbia to protect the people of Kosovo in 1999. In Africa, the Economic Community of West African States (ECOWAS) intervened in Liberia in 1990 and again in Sierra Leone in 1997.[13] These actions show that the change in approaches to sovereignty has been practical as well as conceptual. Of course, this change has not been pursued in all similar cases in a consistent way. For example, the UN failed to take the actions required to prevent the 1994 genocide in Rwanda despite having dispatched a peacekeeping force to the country, in significant part due to the decisions of key permanent members of the Security Council such as France, the United States, and the United Kingdom.[14] UN peacekeepers are now present in the eastern Democratic Republic of Congo, but it is estimated that nearly four million people have already died as a result of the conflict there and the number of internally displaced people remains very high.[15] The situations faced by the internally displaced people of the Darfur region of Sudan and by the Acholi people in northern Uganda are also extremely grave, in significant part due to the actions of their own governments.[16] They are certainly not being protected by the international community in an adequate way.

Both recent normative discussion as well as actual events on the ground, therefore, suggest that exercise of the responsibility to protect internally displaced people needs to be made more effective. This will call for a more consistent revision of the international constitution. It will require, further, circumscription of sovereignty. In fact, there are some notable indicators that further movement in this direction has significant support. For example, former UN secretary-general Kofi Annan was a strong advocate of limits on sovereignty in the name of protection. In his words, "State sovereignty, in its most basic sense, is being redefined. . . . States are now widely understood to be instruments at the service of their peoples, and not vice versa. . . . When we read the [United Nations] charter today, we are more than ever conscious that its aim is to protect individual human beings, not to protect those who abuse them."[17] Full adoption of this proposed revision in the conception of sovereignty would be a revolution parallel in scope with the creation of the nation-state and the abolition of colonialism. Since revolutions can be risky business, before we sign on it will be useful to consider several reasons offered for opposing such change in the normative understanding of how we should conduct international affairs.

Opposition to Changing the Nation-State System

Opposition to such a revision takes two principal forms. One is based on the primacy of national interest in international affairs, and the other is based on concern for order of the international system.

Condoleezza Rice has advanced a national interest–based argument against redefining the scope of sovereignty. While Rice was serving as an adviser to George W. Bush during his first presidential campaign in 2000, she argued against allowing commitment to "humanitarian interests" or the interests of "the international community" to replace the national interest in the formulation of U.S. foreign policy.[18] It is no accident that in this article she places the phrase "international community" in quotes, for in effect she holds that in reality there is no such community. Rice implies that, even in the face of grave crises such as genocide or mass internal displacement in other countries, there is no duty to protect unless taking action is clearly in the national interest of the responding state. The primary objective of a country's foreign policy should be the promotion of the national interest. Bringing relief to the displaced or to others adversely affected by humanitarian crises might be a kind of side effect of pursuit of state interest, but it is not an obligation. Thus, Rice writes that "there is nothing wrong with doing something that benefits all humanity, but this is, in a sense, a second order effect."[19] This means there are no genuine "duties beyond borders," no real responsibility to protect the displaced or even those facing mass killing or genocide.[20] Rice's views seem to have influenced George Bush, for in an interview in 2000 he stated that "I don't like genocide and I don't like ethnic cleansing but I would not send our troops" to prevent another Rwanda.[21] In other words, countries have duties to their own citizens, not to the citizens of other countries.

National leaders, of course, certainly have a responsibility to protect the citizens of their country. If a government were to fail to protect its citizens, it would be derelict in its duties. Protection of one's fellow nationals can be an expression of an ethical responsibility to protect fellow humans from injustice or exploitation. Such a positive interpretation of the importance of group interest made many postindependence African leaders suspicious that humanitarian claims could easily be misused to legitimate a return to the domination of the colonial past. The line between a colonial *mission civilatrice* and humanitarian intervention can be hazy indeed. Thus, arguments for the sacredness of national boundaries have often been heard in Africa since independence. The African Charter on Human and Peoples' Rights is a strong assertion of the right of African peoples to independence from all forms of colonial or postcolonial economic domination.[22] Despite the importance of this anticolonial version of the argument from national interests, the key issue is whether the community to which both citizens and leaders are responsible is only the community of their "own" people. Does the duty to protect stop at the national border? The affirmation that there are universal human rights surely answers this question with a resounding negative. The question thus becomes how to distinguish interventions across borders that are legitimate defenses of universal human rights from those that that are illegitimate forms of domination.

Thus, until very recently, national interest has led most African countries to resist nearly all forms of intervention across borders, even for the protection of people against severe abuses by their own governments. African nations are politically and militarily weak, and this anti-interventionist stance is motivated by a desire to protect themselves from domination by the strong. In some cases, however, it has led to an excessively narrow definition of the scope of responsibility in the face of humanitarian crisis. In very recent years, many Africans have begun to recognize that responsibilities to respond to humanitarian crises and come to the aid of those threatened by them reach across borders. This is partly due to the tragic experiences of African crises such as the Rwanda genocide and the conflicts in Liberia and Sudan. It is also partly a result of a growing self-confidence among African peoples that action by regional bodies such as the African Union or the InterGovernmental Association for Development (IGAD) can help protect people facing severe humanitarian crisis or displacement without excessive risk of forms of domination analogous to colonialism. In other words, it is becoming clear that the legitimate interests of national groups increasingly reach across national boundaries. Thus, the responsibility to protect one's own citizens and the responsibility to protect the citizens of other countries can become intertwined. Following this logic, Kofi Annan has argued for the legitimacy of humanitarian intervention in the face of severe crisis. This is the basis of the African Union's efforts to aid the internally displaced people whose lives are gravely at risk in Darfur.[23]

The second main argument against limiting sovereignty in the name of protection comes from concern for the order and stability of international affairs. The international arena is often regarded as a kind of anarchy, lacking any transnational authority or government to keep it from becoming a savage contest of all against all. Against such a horizon, respect for territorial borders and national self-determination are seen as essential to averting conflict and promoting peace.[24] This is one of the principal reasons why the UN charter strongly supports sovereignty and nonintervention as preconditions of interstate peace and tranquility. Advocates of order object to intervention because they fear it will lead to greater international conflict and thus to more human suffering in the longer term. They could well point to the way George W. Bush's argument that intervention in Iraq was justified to protect the Iraqi people against oppression by Saddam Hussein would both make the Iraqis worse off and destabilize the region. Bush at times has sought to characterize the Iraq war as a form of humanitarian intervention.[25] However, the drawn-out conflict that still goes on in Iraq has confirmed the views of those who fear that such intervention is unlikely to promote either human rights or peace. A moral argument for the responsibility to protect needs to be very aware that intervention can sometimes produce negative consequences for both peace and human rights.

The UN Charter, however, is aware that nonintervention can also sometimes have unacceptable consequences. Therefore, it does not see respect for sovereignty as the *only* condition for peace in the world, and chapter 7 makes provision for limited intervention when the promotion of international peace so requires. In the same way, the argument from order can be turned around to suggest that in some circumstances, the only way to secure peace may be to intervene to protect those being subjected to grave threats such as loss of life or massive displacement.

These considerations suggest that it is misleading to formulate the issue as national interest versus humanitarian concern or as the stability of international order versus the responsibility to protect. More basic is the question of how the interests of one national community are intertwined with the interests of other communities. This means we need to explore further how the order and tranquility of one nation or region is interwoven with the order and peace of another nation or region. National boundaries are important, but they do not tell us all we need to know about the scope and limits of the responsibility to protect. This is especially true if we are considering the responsibility to protect people who are being abused by their own governments. In this situation, sovereignty is not a precondition for a government's ability to protect its own citizens, but the opposite. Large-scale internal displacement can itself also be a threat to peace and order, so protection of the displaced can in some situations become a prerequisite for the order that anti-interventionists so value. Thus, we need to consider further some recent discussions of the evolving nature of the international constitution or system and its normative foundations. We need to reflect on how sovereignty and protection are related.

New Possibilities in a Networked World

From an ethical point of view, perhaps the most attractive understanding of the relation between sovereignty and protection is found in the cosmopolitan approach to international affairs. In this approach, the common humanity of all people is seen as the basis of a worldwide moral community. The scope of political and moral responsibility is defined in terms of the need to protect and respond to the needs of all the members of this global community. Martha Nussbaum, for example, has argued that the community of all human beings has primacy over narrower communities defined in terms of nationality, ethnicity, or religion. Indeed, on one occasion she called nationality and ethnicity "morally irrelevant" characteristics.[26] Such an approach will lead to a very robust commitment to coming to the aid of displaced people, both by granting asylum to refugees and, in the extreme case, by interventionist means. Also, the duty to aid anyone in grave need, including displaced people, falls on the worldwide community as a whole.

There are strong affinities between such a secular cosmopolitan approach and that of many religious communities, including Christianity. Catholic social thought, for example, holds that all human beings are created in the image and likeness of God and thus all have a common dignity as members of a single human family. The human capacity for understanding and for freedom also reveals this shared dignity. This common membership in the single human family led Pope John XXIII to insist that "the fact that one is a citizen of a particular State does not detract in any way from his membership in the human family as a whole, nor from his citizenship in the world community."[27]

Such a vision of our common humanity can challenge the adequacy of an international system that grants near absolute moral status to international borders. John XXIII drew on that vision when, in his 1963 encyclical, *Pacem in terris*, he concluded that a system based solely on the protection of nation-state sovereignty was no longer adequate to "the task of promoting the common good of all peoples."[28] Among the reasons John XXIII gave for this conclusion was the acute suffering of refugees.[29] We could add that the plight of the internally displaced reinforces this conclusion. To remedy this situation, the pope called for an increased role for a global political organization capable of responding to issues that exceed the capacity of individual nation-states. He called for a "public authority, having worldwide power and endowed with the proper means for the efficacious pursuit of its objective," namely, the worldwide common good. John XXIII gave particular endorsement to the United Nations, with its goals of promoting peace among nations based on mutual respect and of protecting the human rights of all persons and the legitimate rights of all nations.[30] His strong focus on a possible international "public authority" suggests that something like a world government should be the main institutional vehicle that carries us forward in the face of the changing patterns of political interaction.

The issue, however, is more complex. As Kwame Anthony Appiah has pointed out, an adequate appreciation of the common humanity of all people must not only support the oneness of the human family but must also respect the differences among peoples, cultures, and nations.[31] Placing a thoroughgoing stress on what we have in common makes it more difficult to explain why being forced from home, either as a refugee or within one's own country, has such negative moral significance. Displacement is not morally objectionable solely because it is involuntary. Being able to live in one's own home is a moral value and being forced from home has a distinctive moral poignancy. Further, if responsibility to aid the displaced falls on everyone, there is danger that no one will respond. We need, therefore, a more differentiated approach than the stress on the unity of the human family alone can provide. This has been recognized in the Catholic tradition's stress on the "principle of subsidiarity," in both domestic and international affairs. This principle requires that communities and associations of less-than-global scope such as cultural and national groups must not be abolished or repressed.[32] Thus, John XXIII insisted that the "international authority" he advocated must also recognize the continuing importance of the nation-state, for the state has a continuing role in protecting the distinctive identities of local communities. Indeed, the phenomenon of failed states shows how important this role can be.

John XXIII's 1963 reflections in fact anticipated some recent proposals for restructuring the international system. Talk of subsidiarity has increasingly been heard in secular discussions of transnational and global governance. For example, the principle of subsidiarity is explicitly referred to in the treaty establishing the European Union, and it has also been invoked as a key principle for the shaping of a just world order by Anne Marie Slaughter, the dean of the Woodrow Wilson School of Public and International Affairs at Princeton University.[33] Discussion of the possible contribution of subsidiarity in a globalizing world would be clearer, however, if it began by considering how a complex network of institutions is increasingly shaping the global order. Such a transnational network of communities of many different kinds is a growing, de facto reality in the world today, so the moral argument for the relevance of subsidiarity has an empirical and social basis.

Slaughter has recommended we recognize that the international system is neither a system of entirely autonomous and independent states nor a single global community unified through a single political system.[34] Rather, it is a complex network whose strands are various parts of governments, regional and global intergovernmental agencies of different types, and numerous nongovernmental groups and agencies. Within this network, national boundaries are important, but they are not the only political structures relevant to the needs and aspirations of the people. Specifying the responsibilities to protect internally displaced persons thus requires consideration of the capacities of all the threads in the emerging network: the government of the state within which people have been displaced, the nations nearby and those more distant, regional and global intergovernmental bodies, and nongovernmental agencies as well. Picturing the world order as a complex web of overlapping networks rather than simply a system of states, of course, does not by itself tell us how to respond to the needs of displaced people of today. It does, however, open up the possibility of thinking about these issues in more productive ways. Let me make a few suggestions about the possibilities.

The interactions through transnational networks that are emerging today make it increasingly clear that those in other nations are as genuinely human as are the citizens of one's own country. When one communicates with people in other countries and cultures fairly regularly, does business with them, engages in political interaction and negotiation with them, or seeks to create joint socioeconomic arrangements with them, it becomes clear that they are fellow human beings, not members of a different biological species. The growth of transnational networks, therefore, challenges nationalist in-group, out-group divisions and supports the capacity to relate to those of other nations and cultures as persons with equal dignity. Thus, global networking both deepens awareness of transnational moral responsibilities and provides some of the institutional means needed to act upon these responsibilities.

This does not mean, of course, that one's responsibility toward all human beings is identical, or that national borders and cultural differences have no moral or political significance. In response to critics of her strong cosmopolitanism, Nussbaum acknowledged that national and cultural bonds can indeed make moral claims on us. But she rightly continues to affirm that "we should recognize, at whatever personal or social cost, that each human being is human and counts as the moral equal of every other."[35] The same point can be made in terms of universal human rights. The reality of universal rights does not deny the importance of national, cultural, or religious identity. But it does mean responsibility can reach beyond the scope of duties to one's fellow national citizens. Thus, it is meaningful to speak of being citizens of the world in a moral sense.[36] This larger "moral citizenship" can have important political implications. Let us note a few of these implications, first those that suggest negative duties to refrain from certain actions, and then some that imply positive duties to act.

Negative Duties: First, Do No Harm

Negatively, the common humanity of all persons is the basis of a fundamental responsibility not to create humanitarian crises by attacking people and placing their most basic human rights at risk. This means that all persons, groups, and especially governments have a fundamental obligation not to commit grave evils such as genocide, ethnic cleansing, religious persecution, or any other form of attack that will compel people to flee from their homes. This, of course, means governments have a duty not to force people to become refugees as defined by the 1951 Convention Relating to the Status of Refugees, that is, not to attack them in ways that can be regarded as "persecution" on the basis of race, religion, nationality, and so on. Analogous to this is the responsibility not to drive people from their homes even within the boundaries of their own countries. Thus, the government's responsibility to protect its citizens implies a duty not to create either refugees or internally displaced people. It also implies a duty not to create famine or intentionally deny people the minimum economic resources they need to survive at home. To the extent that a government violates these duties in deliberate and consistent ways, rather than as a tragic but unintentional side effect of an otherwise legitimate action such as national defense, to that extent it loses legitimacy. Truly grave and systematic violations of these duties, such as campaigns of ethnic cleaning or genocide, can undermine a government's legitimacy altogether. The 1951 Convention also strongly affirms the duty not to expel or return a refugee home if doing so would risk the returnee's life or freedom.[37] This so-called right of *nonrefoulement* places a very strong negative responsibility on states toward refugees and asylum seekers.

There are also negative responsibilities governing the use of military force in the midst of the conflicts that, especially today, have such serious humanitarian consequences. The moral tradition of just war and the norms of humanitarian law both insist that noncombatants should be immune from direct attack. These norms seek to protect innocent people from the harm of war. Their meaning needs to be developed and applied today to resist the grave harm done to large numbers of people when they are turned into refugees or IDPs. Forces conducting possibly legitimate forms of armed struggle against grave injustice, whether interstate or intrastate, have serious responsibilities not to attack civilians directly. They must also refrain from military actions that have indirect or collateral consequences that are harmful to civilians in ways that are disproportionate to the legitimate goals of a just struggle. These are standard affirmations of the moral tradition governing just and unjust forms of the use of force.

They take on added weight today because of the extraordinarily high impact of contemporary warfare on civilians, both in millions of lives lost and in the even higher numbers of those who have been displaced. In discussions of noncombatant immunity, there is a tendency to focus almost exclusively on the deaths of civilians. The displaced, however, face grave harm also; many are separated from their families, with little useful work, the women in constant danger of rape, and the near absence of any education for the children. Some might say their situation is almost as bad as death. Loss of hope and genuine despair are constant temptations for the long-term displaced. The grave harm and suffering of displaced people must also be taken into account in assessing the morality of military strategy and tactics. If we take the suffering of civilians fully into account, including the harm to many millions of displaced people, it becomes increasingly difficult to justify the use of force. Reinforcing the moral and political barriers to the use of force would itself be a significant step toward reducing the frequency of humanitarian crisis and magnitude of displacement in the world today. This also suggests that there is a serious responsibility to curtail the arms trade that feeds the fires of humanitarian conflict. Not selling arms to those who are likely to use them to conduct ethnic war or create refugees would go a considerable way toward helping reduce such evils.

Positive Duties: Sharing the Burdens

Regarding duties to respond in positive ways to humanitarian crisis, a very useful principle has been developed in a different context to help identify when persons have duties to remedy harms that they have not themselves caused. It was called the Kew Gardens Principle by the authors who developed it, for it arose from their reflection on a tragic case that occurred in the Kew Gardens section of New York City.[38] A young woman was publicly stabbed and died while thirty-eight nearby people watched and did nothing. These observers did not cause her death, just as other countries have not caused the millions of deaths in eastern Democratic Republic of Congo or the suffering of the displaced in northern Uganda and Sudan. But just as most people are deeply disturbed that none of the thirty-eight witnesses of the murder in Kew Gardens even phoned the police, we should question whether nations and other communities can legitimately claim that they have no obligation to respond to a serious humanitarian crisis because they have not caused it. There can be positive duties to aid people in danger that go beyond the obligation not to cause harm.

Reflection on the Kew Gardens case suggests that an agent has a positive ethical responsibility to respond when four conditions are present: (a) there is a critical *need*; (b) the agent has *proximity* to the need; (c) the agent has the *capability* to respond; and (d) the agent is likely the *last resort* from whom help can be expected. These criteria cannot be applied mechanically, but they are quite useful in thinking about the scope of responsibility in the face of the suffering that the vast numbers of internally displaced people in Sudan or Uganda have undergone. Clearly, the millions who have been displaced are in grave need of food, health care, safety for the women from rape, and education for the children. Above all, they need peace, justice, and an end to the conflicts that have driven them from home. Since the responsibility to respond increases when need increases, the magnitude of the need implies there is clearly an urgent duty in the face of the Sudanese and Ugandan crises.

But whose duty is it? Being near the harm increases responsibility, but proximity is not simply a geographical matter. It is connected primarily with having knowledge of the need. We are outraged with the people who failed to aid the young woman being murdered in Kew Gardens because their direct knowledge of the event involved them in it in a way that those lacking knowledge could not be involved. Further, we link responsibility with the capability to help. For example, someone who cannot swim is not expected to come to the aid of a drowning child, while a good swimmer is expected to try to help if it can be done without undue risk. In the face of the Darfur crisis, Chad is physically most proximate to the crisis and is bearing the burden of most of the refugees. Because Chad is itself a very poor country, however, it lacks the capability to carry the refugee burden alone. Even more evident is the fact that Chad lacks the resources needed to aid the more than one million displaced people inside Darfur. The responsibility thus moves to those with greater capability in the international community, namely the rich countries of the developed world. Sharing the burdens of assistance to the displaced is thus a moral responsibility for those nations with greater capacities. Pressing these nations to act on their responsibilities should be a central emphasis of advocacy on behalf of the displaced today.

Finally, the notion of last resort can be useful in simple situations of immediate need, but in complex political situations it is often difficult to determine whether someone else can be expected to act. Precisely for this reason, there is a responsibility to develop institutional means within the transnational network that will make it possible to respond to crises in a timely and effective way. Creating regional and global systems for response—such as regional peace-building agencies and a more effective international network of agencies for response to the needs of the displaced—becomes the only reliable way of assuring that the responsibility to meet many of the most urgent humanitarian needs is fulfilled. Several scholars have recently been arguing that the current collaborative approach that seeks to coordinate diverse international agencies in their efforts to assist the internally displaced needs to be replaced by a unified international body. Roberta Cohen, Susan Martin, and others who have studied the response to IDPs in depth are proposing the establishment of a United Nations High Commissioner for Forced Migrants.[39] This agency would have responsibility for both refugees and the internally displaced. Such a proposal fits well with the arguments about the limitations on sovereignty advanced above. The key issue is what institutional means will enable those who are responsible to aid the displaced effectively. If the cooperative approach fails to do so, then a high commissioner for forced migrants becomes a serious alternative.

A few suggestions will illustrate how the criteria of need, proximity, capability, and last resort can function together to help specify positive duties to respond to the issues we have been considering.[40] Probably the greatest need for positive action is for sustained efforts at building peace within nations in the midst of or threatened by humanitarian crisis. It is war and conflict that is the cause of most of the human displacement in our world today, so the need for such peace building is evident. Most often this will require concerted regional action by states that are neighbors to those experiencing conflict and displacement. When the region is politically and economically weak, however, it will also call for broader international support. For example, the IGAD countries that are Sudan's neighbors played an important role in encouraging the peace accord between the government of Sudan and the Sudan Peoples Liberation Movement/Army (SPLM/A), and the IGAD countries have received notable support in playing this role by the United States, the United Kingdom, and several other developed countries. It is unfortunate, however, that these regional and broader international initiatives did not occur until decades of war had already taken millions of Sudanese lives. Earlier action could have made the recent tragic history of Sudan very different, with significant positive effects in eastern Africa. This, in turn, could have indirectly contributed to imagining how patterns of stability could be encouraged elsewhere in the developing world. And this, in turn, could ultimately contribute to broader global peace. Such larger effects, of course, are not guaranteed, and they are likely to develop only in the long term. This means, therefore, that we need a notably more long-term focus in dealing with displacement and humanitarian policy than is common today. Short-term thinking does long-term harm.

Building peace in countries experiencing or in danger of falling into the kind of conflict that displaces large numbers of people calls for a modification of traditional concepts of national sovereignty. The internal peace of a country is a matter of legitimate moral and political concern to those outside. We have argued above that such modification of how we understand sovereignty is in fact under way. This shift raises the important issues of whether, when, and how it can be legitimate to intervene inside a country to make peace or eliminate the injustices that breed conflict.

Intervention, of course, has a number of different forms. In the briefest possible terms, I would argue that positive economic intervention to meet human needs or reduce unjust inequalities though development assistance is urgently needed. Development assistance, trade and tariff policies designed to promote development in poor countries, and granting poor countries relief from heavy transnational debts are all matters that should be pursued in their own right if the global order is to be made more just. Fulfilling such responsibilities in the domain of economic justice will also have positive consequences in helping to alleviate the conditions that contribute to forced migration. In addition, diplomatic intervention in support of peace, such as that conducted by that by the IGAD countries in the southern Sudan crisis, is both justified and can be a transnational responsibility. Such initiatives, both economic and diplomatic, are expressions of the fact that responsibilities for human well-being do not stop at national boundaries but are increasingly transnational. Serious advocacy of more effective responses is needed to grapple with the ongoing crises in Darfur, the eastern DRC, and elsewhere.

The hardest question, of course, is whether and when military intervention is justified or required in order to aid the internally displaced. The standard moral criteria governing the responsible use of force have been adapted to this question by the International Commission on Intervention and State Sovereignty. The commission concluded that military action should be "an exceptional and extraordinary measure" that is taken only when "serious and irreparable harm" is occurring or is "imminently likely to occur." They specify serious harm as genocide, ethnic cleansing, and large-scale loss of life produced by state action, state neglect, state inability to act, or failed state situations.[41] These criteria were developed in response to the tragic failure of the international community to prevent the Rwanda genocide. Just as one deeply hopes that crises such as that in Rwanda will be exceedingly rare, one can also hope that military intervention to prevent or alleviate humanitarian crisis will be rare as well. But an appropriately developed understanding of both sovereignty and transnational responsibilities means that military intervention cannot be ruled out entirely.

Finally, the responsibility to take positive action that will resolve and prevent displacement calls for significant efforts to strengthen the regional and global institutions that address this issue. Intergovernmental agencies need to be made more capable and effective in their response to intrastate conflict, refugees and internally displaced people, sustained patterns of human rights abuse, and development issues. For example, a stronger African Union and more effective cooperation through the Intergovernmental Authority on Development could surely help address the Darfur and northern Uganda crises. National governments and interstate agencies thus have responsibilities to cooperate in strengthening such interstate networks. Nongovernmental groups, such as humanitarian NGOs, church-related agencies, and indeed whole churches and religious communities, also have essential roles to play in building up these new networks of cooperation. Therefore, they have responsibilities to do so.

Thus, it is evident that the question of the scope of transnational responsibilities in the face of displacement converges with other ethical issues raised in the international arena, such as matters of the ethics of a resort to force, the meaning of economic justice in the face of globalization, and new forms of ethical responsibility toward the environment. Norms of justice and obligations to respect the dignity of all human persons are central in all of the strands of the growing global web. Though this essay has focused primarily on ethical responsibilities toward the internally displaced, I hope it sheds some light on other aspects of our more interdependent world. In this way, reflection on the tragic realities faced by internally displaced people might also have the positive effect of deepening our sense of responsibility for the entire transnational community.

Notes

1. United Nations General Assembly, 2005 World Summit Outcome Document, September 16, 2005, nos. 138–139 (emphasis added), http://daccessdds.un.org/doc/UNDOC/GEN/N05/487/60/PDF/N0548760.pdf?OpenElement (accessed May 23, 2007).

2. International Commission on Intervention and State Sovereignty, *The Responsibility to Protect* (Ottawa: International Development Research Centre, 2001), also available from http://www.idrc.ca/openebooks/960-7 (accessed June 22, 2006).

3. See Francis M. Deng et al., *Sovereignty as Responsibility: Conflict Management in Africa* (Washington, DC: Brookings Institution, 1996), esp. chap. 1; Francis M. Deng, "Trapped within Hostile Borders: The Plight of Internally Displaced Persons," in *Human Security for All: A Tribute to Sergio Vierra de Mello*, ed. Kevin M. Cahill (New York: Fordham University Press and the Center for International Health and Cooperation, 2004), 28–51.

4. *Guiding Principles on Internal Displacement*, Introduction—Scope and Purpose, no. 2. The *Guiding Principles* were prepared under the guidance of the representative of the secretary general on internal displacement, Francis Deng, and were presented to the UN Commission on Human Rights in 1998. They are available from http://www.reliefweb.int/ocha_ol/pub/idp_gp/idp.html (accessed June 22, 2006).

5. Richard Holbrooke, "A Borderline Difference," *Washington Post*, May 8, 2000, A23. Also available from http://www.reliefweb.int/rw/rwb.nsf/AllDocsByUNID/de99fa12477e37d7c12568d900505ee0 (accessed June 28, 2006).

6. Ibid.

7. Internal Displacement Monitoring Center, *Internal Displacement: Global Overview of Trends and Developments in 2005* (Geneva: Norwegian Refugee Council, 2006), 6. Also available from http://www.internal-displacement.org (accessed June 22, 2006).

8. United Nations General Assembly, 2005 World Summit Outcome Document, no. 132.

9. Internal Displacement Monitoring Center, *Internal Displacement*, 51.

10. Daniel Philpott, *Revolutions in Sovereignty: How Ideas Shaped Modern International Relations* (Princeton, NJ: Princeton University Press, 2001), 12.

11. General Assembly Resolution 1514 (XV) of December 14, 1960. Available from http://www.unhchr.ch/html/menu3/b/9.htm (accessed June 28, 2006).

12. Philpott, *Revolutions in Sovereignty*, 41.

13. Ibid., 42. For discussion of post–cold war military interventions in Africa, including those by ECOWAS, see Susan F. Martin, Patricia Weiss Fagen, Kari Jorgensen, Lydia Mann-Bondat,

and Andrew Schoenholtz, *The Uprooted: Improving Humanitarian Responses to Forced Migration* (Lanham, MD: Lexington Books, 2005), 196–204.

14. See Alison Des Forges et al., *"Leave None to Tell the Story": Genocide in Rwanda* (New York and Paris: Human Rights Watch, International Federation of Human Rights, 1999), esp.18–26, 595–691; "Report of the Independent Inquiry into the Actions of the United Nations during the 1994 Genocide in Rwanda," December 15, 1999, http://daccessdds.un.org/doc/UNDOC/GEN/N99/395/47/IMG/N9939547.pdf?OpenElement (accessed June 29, 2006).

15. Benjamin Coghlan, Richard J Brennan, Pascal Ngoy, David Dofara, Brad Otto, Mark Clements, and Tony Stewart, "Mortality in the Democratic Republic of Congo: A Nationwide Survey," *Lancet* 367 (January 7, 2006–January 13, 2006): 44–51. This article reports a study conducted by the International Rescue Committee.

16. See Roberta Cohen and William G. O'Neill, "Last Stand in Sudan?" *Bulletin of the Atomic Scientists* 62 (March–April 2006): 51–58. See Olara A. Otunnu, "The Secret Genocide," *Foreign Policy*, no. 155 (July–August 2006): 45–46, and Civil Society Organizations for Peace in Northern Uganda, "Counting the Cost: Twenty Years of War in Northern Uganda," March 30, 2006, http://www.oxfam.org.uk/what_we_do/issues/conflict_disasters/downloads/csopnu_nuganda .pdf (accessed June 30, 2006).

17. Kofi A. Annan, "Two Concepts of Sovereignty," *The Economist*, September 18, 1999, 49.

18. Condoleezza Rice, "Promoting the National Interest," *Foreign Affairs* 79, no. 1 (January–February, 2000): 47. During the 2000 campaign and also during his presidency before September 11, 2001, George W. Bush also held this view. As Bush put it in an interview on January 23, 2000, "We should not send our troops to stop ethnic cleansing and genocide in nations outside our strategic interest." Cited in Ivo H. Daalder and James M. Lindsay, *America Unbound: The Bush Revolution in Foreign Policy* (Washington, DC: Brookings Institution Press, 2003), 37. Both Rice and Bush changed their stances in the period immediately following the attacks of September 11, 2003.

19. Rice, "Promoting the National Interest," 47.

20. The phrase "duties beyond borders" is Stanley Hoffmann's. See his *Duties beyond Borders: On the Limits and Possibilities of Ethical International Politics* (Syracuse, NY: Syracuse University Press, 1981).

21. See Samantha Power, "Genocide and America," *New York Review of Books*, March 14, 2002. Power indicates that Bush may have had a change of heart on this issue and subsequently indicated that he would not stand by in the face of another Rwanda.

22. See my "Human Rights and Development: The African Challenge," in *The Global Face of Public Faith: Politics, Human Rights, and Christian Ethics* (Washington, DC: Georgetown University Press, 2003): 218–30.

23. See Kofi Annan's lecture on "Intervention," delivered in 1998 at the Ditchley Foundation, http://www.ditchley.co.uk/news/news_supplement97-98.htm (accessed August 4, 2004). For reports on AU involvement in the Darfur crisis, "The Situation in the Darfur Region of Sudan," http://www.africa-union.org/DARFUR/homedar.htm (accessed February 27, 2005).

24. For a discussion of order and stability as reasons for supporting Westphalian sovereignty, see the International Commission on Intervention and State Sovereignty's supplementary volume, *The Responsibility to Protect: Research, Bibliography, Background* (Ottawa: International Development Research Centre, 2001), 131–33.

25. President George W. Bush, Address to the General Assembly of the United Nations, New York City, September 23, 2003, http://www.whitehouse.gov/news/releases/2003/09/20030923-4 .html (accessed August 4, 2004).

26. Martha C. Nussbaum, "Patriotism and Cosmopolitanism," in *For Love of Country*, ed. Joshua Cohen (Boston: Beacon Press, 2002), 5. Nussbaum subsequently qualified this statement

by acknowledging that nationality and ethnicity might be granted some moral value as long is it does not override the more fundamental values linked with the common humanity of all people.

27. Pope John XXIII, *Pacem in terris*, no. 25.

28. Ibid., no. 135.

29. Ibid., no. 103.

30. Ibid., nos. 135–38.

31. Kwame Anthony Appiah, *Cosmopolitanism: Ethics in a World of Strangers* (New York: W. W. Norton, 2006), xiv–xviii.

32. Pope John XXIII, *Pacem in terris*, nos. 135–45.

33. Anne-Marie Slaughter discusses the principle of subsidiarity as essential for her vision of a just future in *A New World Order* (Princeton, NJ: Princeton University Press, 2004), 255–57, and she quotes the use of subsidiarity in the treaty establishing the EU in chap. 6, n. 95, 256.

34. Ibid., 5.

35. Nussbaum, "Reply," in *For Love of Country*, p. 133.

36. See Pope John XXIII, *Pacem in terris*, no. 25, cited above.

37. 1951 Convention Relating to the Status of Refugees, art. 33.

38. The discussion of the "Kew Gardens Principle" is based on John G. Simon, Charles W. Powers, and Jon P. Gunnemann, *The Ethical Investor: Universities and Corporate Responsibility* (New Haven, CT: Yale University Press, 1972), 22–25.

39. See Susan Martin et al., *The Uprooted: Improving Humanitarian Responses to Forced Migration* (Lanham, Md.: Lexington Books, 2005), chap. 3, and Roberta Cohen, "Strengthening Protection of IDPs: The UN's Role," *Georgetown Journal of International Affairs* 7 (Winter–Spring, 2006), 101–9.

40. Some of the suggestions mentioned here, as well as others, are more fully developed in the following: Gil Loescher, *Beyond Charity: International Cooperation and the Global Refugee Crisis* (New York: Oxford University Press, 1993), chaps. 7 and 8; Arthur C. Helton, *The Price of Indifference: Refugees and Humanitarian Action in the New Century* (New York: Oxford University Press, 2002); United Nations High Commissioner for Refugees, *Agenda for Protection*, 3rd ed (Geneva: UNHCR, 2003).

41. International Commission on Intervention and State Sovereignty, *The Responsibility to Protect* (Ottawa: International Development Research Centre, December 2001), esp. 31–37. I have not presented the full set of norms developed by the commission. For a parallel but slightly different approach that limits just cause for military humanitarian intervention to genocide and ethnic cleansing, see J. Bryan Hehir, "Military Intervention and National Sovereignty," in *Hard Choices: Moral Dilemmas in Humanitarian Intervention*, ed. Jonathan Moore (Lanham, MD: Rowman and Littlefield, 1998), 29–54.

11

Internally Displaced Persons in Northern Uganda

A Challenge for Peace and Reconciliation

Lam Oryem Cosmas

For the last twenty years Joseph Kony and his rebel group, the Lord's Resistance Army (LRA), have waged a war against the government of Uganda (GoU) and its military, the Ugandan People's Defense Forces (UPDF). While Kony claims that he is leading a spiritual rebellion against the GoU for the Acholi people in northern Uganda, his agenda remains unclear. It is clear, however, that the rebels lack the support of the people of northern Uganda. The LRA has committed numerous atrocities against the communities of that region, including the abduction of nearly twenty thousand children. The problem of internally displaced persons (IDP) in Uganda arose chiefly out of this LRA rebel insurgency in the north and northeast of the country and from the activities of another rebel group, the Allied Democratic Forces (ADF), in the western Rwenzori region. In eastern Uganda, in the Teso subregion, IDPs were also created as a result of violent cattle raids and killings by armed Karimojong herdsmen, a pastoralist people in northeastern Uganda clustered with the Turkana and Pokot of Kenya and the Toposa and Dindinga of southern Sudan. These communities are characterized by the practice of violent raids and counter-raids.

In northern Uganda, the IDPs came into existence due to the LRA's violent atrocities, mass killings, and abductions in 1995 and 1996 and from the response of Uganda's government to the rebellion. Those abducted were mainly children who were forcefully recruited into the rebel ranks. The girls, besides becoming combatants, were also used as "sex slaves" by the rebel commanders.

Overview of the IDP Situation

About 1.5 million people lived in camps throughout north and northeastern Uganda at the height of the insurgency between 2002 and 2004. The IDP phenomenon has had grave effects, especially on traditional social structures. In the Acholi culture, clear roles are assigned to the male head of household, his wife or wives, and children ranked by age and gender. The male head of the family has the responsibility to provide for and protect the members of his household. Similarly, households are identified and assigned within the hierarchies of traditional communities on the basis of their assets, such as land, cattle, and other tangible indicators of wealth. But the economic breakdown in northern Uganda has disrupted these patterns.

As a result of displacement, most heads of households have been unable to provide for family needs. This has contributed to the high number of woman-headed households as families are forced apart for economic and security reasons. This disruption of family roles and community status hierarchies, combined with feelings of disempowerment by heads of households, has resulted in a marked increase in cases of domestic violence, spousal and child abuse, and broken marriages. As people have been forced off their land to live in camps, land tenancy has become increasingly ambiguous for the affected population. Prior to the war, individuals clearly knew what land they owned, as it was passed down the family lineages, known as customary tenure. These individuals cultivated their land on a daily basis and could easily see if someone was encroaching on their property. While disputes may have arisen within families or neighbors, arguments were usually minor and settled by the clan leaders.

At the beginning of the internal displacement in northern Uganda, the UPDF forced people to leave their villages and move to what were initially called "protected villages." Since the army could not adequately protect the population scattered in the vast areas of Acholiland, it was hoped that bringing them together in a few selected areas would improve the provision of security, which to a large extent it did, as the rebels were deprived of opportunities for mass abductions. It is imperative to note that at this juncture the LRA's favored method of recruitment was abduction. The major targets for abduction have been children and young people whom the LRA would indoctrinate and easily retain in its ranks. This situation led to the phenomenon of "night commuters"—in which fear of abductions caused children to flock to urban centers in Gulu, Kitgum, Lira, and Pader at night and return to their homes in the morning.

The government of Uganda's enforced confinement to camps in northern Uganda has gone on since the mid-1990s. It was an emergency measure, intended at first to restore security. No advance planning preceded the establishment of the IDP camps, however, and thus they lack almost all the basic social infrastructure and amenities; for example, health centers and schools are overcrowded and sanitation is overburdened. The IDPs became even more vulnerable to rebel attacks than they had been before their resettlement, because the population overwhelmed the number of soldiers whose task was to protect them. In most cases, the military detachments were situated in the middle of the camps, raising the question of who was protecting whom. The Lord's Resistance Army has displaced people not only in Uganda but in south Sudan as well.

Attempts to Address the Needs of IDPs

In 2001 and 2002 the Justice and Peace Commission of the Archdiocese of Gulu, together with the Acholi Religious Leaders Peace Initiative (ARLPI), published two studies: *Let My People Go: The Forgotten Plight of the People in the Displaced Camps in Acholi*,[1] and *Seventy Times Seventy: The Implementation and Impact of the Amnesty in Acholiland*.[2] The first study underscored the circumstances of displacement in northern Uganda and the wishes of the affected communities. The second statement assessed the impact of the amnesty law in Uganda and its contribution to justice, reconciliation, and peace. It was clear from the study by the ARLPI that the displacement of people in the north was both partly forceful and partly voluntary. It was forceful, especially at the start, in that people always resist any abrupt change to their normal life. However, when abductions by the LRA increased, coupled with the fact that people in the camps were being provided with food, people started moving voluntarily. Most IDPs, of course, will find it difficult not to go back to their original homes. At the same time, confinement in camps due to internal displacement in northern Uganda has caused major disruptions in people's lives:

- overcrowding, leading to poor sanitation and constant outbreak of diseases, especially cholera and other water-borne diseases
- food shortages, making displaced persons dependant on the UN World Food Program (WFP)
- free movement of rebels in the uninhabited parts of the vast Acholiland

As we look toward resettlement, the same mixture of involuntary and voluntary movement is likely to repeat itself.

Because one of the main challenges to the IDPs is inadequate food supplies, in May 2003 the government of Uganda proposed what is known as the "Security and Production Programme" (SPP). The proposal aimed at settling IDPs nearer to arable land for food cultivation. Security would be provided in the new settlements. There was a lot of resentment against this proposed government policy. People felt that it was a way of creating separated settlements like South African townships such as SOWETO (South West Township). The introduction of the Security and Production Program document states:

> SPP is a strategic plan for solving the insecurity in Acholi region. It will work through beefing up local defense using community youth volunteers who are recruited and trained specifically to secure the production areas in which they live. They would train under the Uganda People's Defense Force (UPDF) and be supervised by the local Uganda Police under the community-policing programme. *There is minimal crop production on adjacent land because of constant expectation to move back home and produce from their former homes. Whereas production from home would be a familiar practice, the security conditions in the region cannot allow the population back to the villages in the face of LRA's position to abduct their children and kill them. Providing security through cultivation of land surrounding the camp is the only practical solution for current food and security crisis.*[3]

In 2004 the government began implementing a "decongestion policy," which meant that larger camps would be divided into smaller units. This policy was a response to the challenges posed by problems within the large camps. The first IDP camp to be decongested was that of Pabo, situated about thirty kilometers northwest of Gulu town in northern Uganda and was the largest in the country, with a population of about sixty-eight thousand people. Decongestion involved movement to a place south of Pabo called Geng Gari. Other areas of Acholiland were also "decongested" by May 2006. In Amuru District, the IDPs of Abera, Jengari, and Olong were decongested from the main Pabo IDP camp. Langol was decongested from Alero and Alokolum, while Palukere was decongested from Atiak and Kona Nwoya from Anaka IDP camp. In Kitgum district, the IDP camps of Lokung, Putika A and B, and Ngomoromo were decongested to Madi Kilok. In Gulu district, Adak was decongested from Opit, Cetkana from Coope, Kona Ayula from Lalogi, Lukodi from Coope, and Omel from Paicho. In Pader district, decongested camps are located in Kokil, Ligiligi, Opyelo, Olung, Olupe, Toroma, Lamiyo Achol Pii, Paula, and Acuru in Agago and Dure in Aruu counties respectively. All the newly created camps have common features. They lack nearby water sources and mature grass for thatching the huts. Schools and health centers are not functioning. Food is lacking, so people walk back to the camps for relief supplies. There is also apparently no assistance for resettlement in the new camps. People moving to them leave their children behind in the old camps, so they can continue going to school there and because of uncertainty about the children's security. Therefore, there are two types of IDP camps in Acholiland: the original large settlements, and those that have been subdivided into smaller units under the decongestion policy, as in the case of decongestion from Pabo to Geng Gari and Otong.

Introducing the *Guiding Principles on Internal Displacement*, the UN secretary-general's representative on internally displaced persons, Francis M. Deng, stated the challenge clearly: "The international community is confronted with the monumental task of ensuring protection for persons forcibly up-rooted from their homes by violent conflicts, gross violation of human rights and other traumatic events, but who remain within the borders of their own countries. Nearly always, they suffer from severe deprivation, hardships and discrimination."[4]

In response to this challenge, in August 2004 Uganda passed a National Policy for Internally Displaced Persons. The policy was officially launched in February 2005. It has been translated into the local languages that are spoken in the affected communities of Acholi, Lango, and Teso. The policy specifies that international and regional human rights instruments ratified by the government as well as the *Guiding Principles* must be taken into account in its implementation. The policy sets out the rights of IDPs and designates responsibilities for upholding these rights to national and local government authorities, in conjunction with humanitarian and development agencies. Its stated objectives are "to minimize internal displacement; to minimize the effects of internal displacement by providing an enabling environment for upholding the rights and entitlements of IDPs; to promote integrated and coordinated response mechanisms to address the causes and effects of internal displacement; to assist in the safe and voluntary return of IDPs; and to guide the development of sectoral programs for recovery through rehabilitation and reconstruction of social and economic infrastructure in support of the return and re-settlement of IDPs."[5]

However, almost none of these principles have been adequately addressed, and the IDPs in Uganda and those in the north of the country have generally remained vulnerable to all kinds of deprivation, trauma, and gross violation of their rights as human persons. The policy relies on existing government structures to carry out implementation, either by assigning new responsibilities or by bringing together government officials in new committees. At the national level, the responsible authorities are the Office of the Prime Minister's Department of Disaster Preparedness and Refugees, which is charged with coordinating, monitoring, and supervising the implementation of the policy.

Uganda's decentralized system of governance devolves to district level officials the primary responsibility for implementing disaster management and coordinating humanitarian response. It designates the District Disaster Management Committees (DDMCs) as the lead agencies for protection and assistance of IDPs. The policy tasks them with the responsibility of planning, identifying, and designing responses to disasters. Unfortunately, there has been inadequate IDP participation in forming the policy and subsequently little awareness of its existence. Besides, the DDMCs do not have the resources and capacity to implement the policy.

Challenges for the Reintegration of Displaced Peoples

Commissioned by the Office of the Uganda Prime Minister in 2005, the Institute for Applied International Studies based in Oslo, Norway, undertook a study of internally displaced persons in northern Uganda.[6] It was conducted against the background of the assumption that all conflicts and wars, however long they take, eventually come to an end. It was therefore important that the government, its development partners, and all stakeholders started considering scenarios of what will happen when the conflict ends and people have to return to their original homes. All in all, the study highlighted three fundamental questions related to the challenges of the return of peace.

- Will people move at once if peace returns tomorrow?
- Will people return gradually?
- Will it be difficult to convince people to return home?

The study showed that there was little displacement before 1995 and that 55 percent of the population in Gulu was displaced between 1995 and 1996, while only 30 percent was displaced in 2001. The decline was the effect of "operation iron fist," launched in March 2001. The protocol signed between the governments of Uganda and Sudan provided that the Ugandan army would go into southern Sudan in pursuit of the LRA, which had bases there. The result was that the LRA, dispersed from Sudan by the UPDF, came into Uganda and caused much havoc.

The increased violence by the LRA resulting from the effects of the operation caused further displacement, especially in Pader district (Acholiland), Lango, and Teso. However, it also provided an opportunity to meet some of the commanders and engage them in dialogue. Several of these commanders surrendered and benefited from the amnesty law in place. Others were captured or killed by the UPDF. Those who were displaced more recently are more ready to return to their original homes than those who have been displaced for more than ten years. The probable reason is that those displaced earlier have settled in better locations than those more recently displaced and have adjusted to camp life within and outside the Acholi subregion in northern Uganda.

A number of IDPs walk long distances toward their original homes. They cultivate along the roads en route because they are denied land ownership and access. However, some of them are discouraged from cultivating their gardens because rebels loot the food. In terms of income, the IDPs have almost nothing. However, a few, particularly in the major town of Gulu, have means of obtaining food and therefore sell off some of the relief supplies. For the most part, it is difficult to make money in the IDP camps. Most IDPs are victims of violent crimes. No police are in the camps. The IDPs live in fear both within and outside the camps and so cannot go out to fetch firewood for their personal cooking. They are still pessimistic about the future and would not be ready to return home.

Since 2006, rebel attacks have declined in number following the departure of the rebels to Garamba in the Democratic Republic of Congo (DRC) and to Sudan. Attacks have also declined because the rebels now are militarily very weak. However, a small group of marauding rebels has often attacked civilians who venture to their gardens to cultivate some food. These attacks perpetuate a level of insecurity that does not allow the full-scale resettlement of Acholi people to their original homes. Therefore, whereas the process of resettlement in Lango and Teso has begun, about one million people (90 percent of the population) in Acholiland still remain in about one hundred camps for internally displaced persons.

Returning IDPs, Justice, and Peace: A Delicate Balance

There has been much debate concerning what is most needed in northern Uganda: peace or justice? Most people have urged the "peace first" side of the coin and have used it in particular to oppose the indictment of the LRA's five top commanders by the International Criminal Court (ICC). However, I think the quest should be that of "peace" and "justice" together, and thus the delicacy of the matter. The "peace versus justice" debate does not take the preferences of the primary victims of the conflict into consideration. In a survey by the International Center for Transitional Justice and the Human Rights Center at the University of California, Berkeley, researchers found 76 percent of the population believed that war criminals should not go unpunished.[7]

All local, civil, religious, cultural, and political leaders must act in concert to develop a strategy of confidence building to give hope to the IDPs. In 2005 I worked with the community in Atiak to prepare the population for the tenth anniversary of the massacre of 250 people by the LRA in 1995. The theme for the event was "Working towards Effective Re-Integration: Reconciliation." We chose to focus on giving opportunity and space for the direct victims and survivors to "tell their stories," hence providing an opportunity for the community to reflect on these stories and play appropriate transformational roles. It was hoped that in the process, some individuals who had been involved in the massacres would eventually come forward to complete the process of healing and reconciliation.

The Justice and Peace Council (JPC) of the Ecclesiastical Province of Gulu, formed by the Gulu Archdiocese (Acholiland), the Nebbi and Arua dioceses (West Nile), and the Lira Diocese (Lango) in northern Uganda has adopted "restorative justice" as its main orientation for justice, reconciliation, and peace. We should apply restorative justice principles based on the three central pillars.

- It focuses on harms and needs. Its concern for victims and their needs seeks to repair the harm as much as possible, both concretely and symbolically. A victim-oriented approach to justice requires concern about victims' needs even when no offender has been identified or apprehended.
- Wrongs or harms result in obligation. This emphasizes offender accountability and responsibility. Perpetrators should begin to comprehend the consequences of their behavior. They have a responsibility to make things right as much as possible.
- It promotes engagement and participation. This suggests that the primary parties affected by the conflict—victims, perpetrators, and members of the community—are given significant roles in the healing process.

Howard Zehr of Eastern Mennonite University's Center for Justice and Peacebuilding (CJP) has defined and described restorative justice as requiring, at the minimum, that we address victims' harms and needs; hold offenders accountable to put right those harms; and involve victims, offenders, and communities in the process.[8]

Conclusion

The IDP phenomenon resulting from the activities of the LRA is not limited to northern and northeastern Uganda, but includes southern Sudan. A number of communities in the Eastern and Central Equatoria regions of Sudan have been displaced by the LRA. Addressing issues of displacement, peace building, and reconciliation will therefore require cooperation and collaboration across common borders, not only of Uganda and Sudan, but also the border of Uganda with the Democratic Republic of Congo. On August 1 and 2, 2006, we had a "Collaborative Cross Border (Northern Uganda-South Sudan) Peace Building Meeting for Religious and Cultural Leaders" in Juba in the southern Sudan. It was organized by the Archdiocese of Juba, the Forum for Cultural Leaders of South Sudan, and Totto the Chan Trauma Center (in southern Sudan), in conjunction with the Ker Kwaro Acholi (or the Acholi Traditional Institution) and the Justice and Peace Council of the Ecclesiastical Province of Gulu in northern Uganda. Participants mentioned that IDPs were not involved, that the LRA was not in attendance, and that many avoided acknowledging guilt. These factors have significant bearing on justice, peace, and the return of IDPs in the region.

The traditional justice system, from which most of the principles for restorative justice have evolved, hinges on the offenders accepting responsibility and thus being accountable for the crimes they have committed. In most communities in Uganda, notably among the Acholi, Lando, Madi, and Teso, the criminal justice system was based on amicable resolution of conflicts. In these communities, unlike the contemporary Western criminal justice system, criminal responsibility is based on the principle of collective responsibility for a crime committed by a member of the group (family, clan, or tribe). The group assumes both the moral and legal responsibility for such a crime. The rationale for this is that a person who carried out a wicked act did so because the clan failed to exercise due diligence to ensure that he or she was brought up in a proper way. The clan was therefore considered as the custodian of good morals and thus responsible for the development of the character and personality of all its members. Crimes, especially murder, were considered abominations. The intentional killing of a fellow human being was regarded as a very wicked and unacceptable act. A person who kills another became an outcast in the community. Such a person would undergo cleansing in order to be readmitted into the fellowship of the clan. There was, however, no death penalty. Compensation was the punishment, not imprisonment. In a rare case of a person refusing to cooperate with the clan in resolving matters, he or she could be banished from the community.

Therefore, the lack of remorse, especially by the LRA leadership, is an obstacle to the peace and reconciliation process. It will remain a big challenge for community healing, reconciliation, and peace if the LRA continues to avoid taking responsibility for its acts. At the Juba community meeting referred to above, each of the groups agreed on some action points:

- Regarding northern Uganda, hold meetings of victims of violence to provide space for LRA and Karamojong input and participation; convene meetings of district leaderships and members of parliament to develop consensus, coalition building, and interaction among religious, cultural, and civic leaders.
- To more broadly encourage mass community mobilization and sensitization for peace actions, such as spiritual, social, and cultural responses aimed both at the elimination of small arms and light weapons and at demilitarization of the mind.
- The South Sudan group formed a thirteen-member coordinating committee and planned to have a series of consensus-building workshops.

An alternative system of justice is being proposed to serve in the transitional period from violent conflict to peace in northern Uganda. Such a system would be a hybrid of traditional and contemporary elements. It would assure all victims, perpetrators, and stakeholder communities that their needs and concerns are being adequately addressed in the search for a comprehensive solution to the complexity of the LRA conflict.

I believe that reconciliation and peace must be a long-term group effort. Therefore, it calls for active community engagement and dialogue to provide understanding and the possibility of harmonious coexistence.

Notes

1. *Let My People Go: The Forgotten Plight of the People in the Displaced Camps in Acholi*, an assessment carried out by the Acholi Religious Leaders' Peace Initiative and the Justice and Peace Commission of Gulu Archdiocese (Gulu, Uganda, July 2001), also available from http://www.archdioceseofgulu.org/JPC/LET_MY_PEOPLE_GO.pdf (accessed February 28, 2007).

2. *Seventy Times Seventy: The Implementation and Impact of the Amnesty in Acholiland*, an assessment carried out by Acholi Religious Leaders' Peace Initiative, Caritas Gulu Women's Desk and the Justice and Peace Commission of Gulu Archdiocese (Gulu, Uganda, May 2002).

3. Security and Production Programme (SPP), unofficial document privately circulated, May 2003.

4. Francis M. Deng, "Introductory Note," in *Guiding Principles on Internal Displacement* (New York: United Nations, 2004), also available from http://www.unhcr.org/protect/PROTECTION/43ce1cff2.pdf (accessed March 14, 2007).

5. The Brookings Institution–University of Bern Project on Internal Displacement, Workshop on the Implementation of Uganda's National Policy for Internally Displaced Persons, Kampala, Uganda, July 3–4, 2006, "Background Paper," 45, http://www.brook.edu/fp/projects/idp/conferences/Uganda_Workshop2006_rpt.pdf (accessed March 18, 2007).

6. Morten Bøås and Anne Hatløy, Northern Uganda IDP Profiling Study (Uganda: Office of the Prime Minister, Department of Disaster Preparedness and Refugees, September 2005), also available from http://www.fafo.no/ais/africa/uganda/IDP_uganda_2005.pdf (accessed February 28, 2007).

7. International Center for Transitional Justice and the Human Rights Center, University of California, Berkeley, "Forgotten Voices in a Population-Based Survey on Attitudes about Peace and Justice in Northern Uganda," July 2005, http://www.ictj.org/images/content/1/2/127.pdf (accessed March 14, 2007).

8. See Howard Zehr, *Little Book on Restorative Justice* (Intercourse, PA: Good Books, 2004).

12

Justice and Peace

Reintegration and Reconciliation of Returning Displaced Persons in Postconflict Situations

Stephen J. Pope

This chapter deals with the relation between peace and justice in various efforts to promote postconflict reconciliation. It focuses on the particular case of the ongoing conflict in northern Uganda, a situation that former UN undersecretary-general for humanitarian affairs Jan Egeland described as the "world's worst and most forgotten humanitarian crisis."[1] I refer primarily to the Acholiland in northern Uganda. Ideally, internally divided civil societies move toward peace when they establish conditions of justice that protect human rights and that enable their citizens to overcome mutual alienation and to interact within relatively unified political communities. Peace, in other words, is properly based on justice and reconciliation. The complexities and historical legacy of the conflict in northern Uganda, however, constitute a daunting challenge to the implementation of this ideal. Some parties argue that establishing peace, and more precisely the ending of hostilities, ought to precede the pursuit of justice against perpetrators of crimes, while others insist that retributive justice must precede, and can even establish the basis for, a peace that lasts. This chapter argues that international agents and institutions ought to honor the prevailing desire in northern Uganda for peace based on restorative justice.

This chapter begins by defining the key terms in this debate and then briefly rehearses four significant historical precedents established in reconciliation efforts in Latin America and South Africa. It then examines some of the key proposals for how the transition from conflict to peace within northern Uganda ought to be pursued. Insights from a few prior peacemaking efforts elsewhere in the world shed light on key ethical concerns, particularly accountability and reconciliation, though whether or how they might be relevant is not necessarily either simple or direct. The heart of this chapter focuses on proposals that give a priority to the pursuit of peace, especially via restorative justice, and to the opposing view that insists on giving priority to retributive justice. These considerations lead to the suggestion that peace and justice can be pursued simultaneously in processes that focus on restorative justice rather than re-tributive justice.

Conceptual Distinctions

I will speak about northern Uganda. However, I would like to begin by providing a brief description of the meaning of certain key categories and distinctions relevant to this set of topics.

The term "justice" has classically been understood to include a variety of subcategories, including (a) "distributive justice," the giving of what is due from the whole of a community to its constituent parts; (b) "commutative justice," the giving of what is due from one part of a community to another; (c) "legal justice," or "general justice," the giving of what is due from constituent parts to the whole; and, finally, (d) "retributive justice," which rectifies the imbalance of an unjust situation by rendering appropriate punishment to perpetrators.[2] In addition to these four classical forms of justice, we speak about "transitional justice" and "restorative justice." The former involves legal responses to offenders during processes of political transition from repressive to more democratic regimes, and the latter constitutes a response to offenses that seek to restore the losses suffered by victims, hold perpetrators responsible for the harm they have done, and establish harmony within a particular relationship or community.[3]

Restorative justice attempts to move beyond the purely punitive approach associated with retributive justice. The proportionate punishment of retributive justice constitutes a morally preferable alternative to revenge and unrestrained retaliation, but it tends to focus on the harm done by the offender to the state. Restorative justice, in contrast, encourages the offender to understand the damage that he or she has done to particular victims and to make proper restitution. It is facilitated by victim-offender mediation, family group conferencing, community restorative justice boards, and sentencing circles (also called "peacemaking circles"). These programs have shown significant success in reducing recidivism, but they are unsuitable to cases in which victims refuse to participate or where offenders deny responsibility or fail to express remorse for their conduct. As we will see, this emergent ethic has some degree of overlap with traditional African approaches to justice that are importantly related to peacemaking in northern Uganda.

Peace is attained when alienated parties are truly reconciled. Reconciliation in conditions following civil war or insurrection includes the reintegration of combatants or other hostile parties into their original communities. Those in need of reintegration are typically either soldiers or guerillas involved in the use of lethal force, sometimes against their own community members, as well as girls and women abducted for use as "wives." It also includes the reintegration of refugees or internally displaced persons (IDPs) forced to flee either by the actual use of armed force or by the fear of imminent harm. A critically important question in northern Uganda concerns how to reintegrate former perpetrators and victims into the same communities.

Reconciliation can be pursued along a broad spectrum of contexts from the micro, interpersonal level to the macro, intersocietal level. The primary analogue is interpersonal: a person guilty of wrongdoing comes to an understanding of his or her personal guilt, feels remorse, asks the victim for forgiveness, compensates for the harm that has been done (inasmuch as possible), and makes a commitment not to engage in harmful behavior in the future. Reconciliation is hard enough to attain in interpersonal friendships, let alone on a massive scale that involves traumatized populations. Social or collective reconciliation—the forgiveness and acceptance of one large group by another—is by all accounts more difficult to attain than interpersonal reconciliation. The severity of the challenge is amplified when the reconciliatory efforts must proceed against mutual suspicion and bias or when each group believes that the other is the aggressor and while it, on the other hand, acts only defensively. In some cases tolerance and coexistence can be considered moral accomplishments despite falling short of reconciliation.[4]

Historical Precedents

In the last thirty years the international community has experienced many attempts, some successful and others less so, to move to peace, justice, and reconciliation after intense forms of internal conflict. Argentina, Chile, South Africa, and El Salvador present four of the most important cases of attempted postconflict reintegration.

Argentina

Between 1976 and 1983, the Argentine ruling junta "disappeared" at least fourteen thousand people (and probably closer to 30,000) in the period of massive state terror known as the "Dirty War."[5] After democracy was established in December 1983, civilian authorities moved to put some of those responsible for human rights abuses on trial. Those convicted of crimes included five generals who received sentences ranging from 4.5 years to life imprisonment. President Raul Alfonsin created the National Commission on Disappeared Persons (CONADEP) to investigate the fate of the disappeared; its findings were published in a final report called *Nunca Mas*.[6] Alfonsín also worked to repeal an amnesty law put in place by the military to protect itself, and he installed a judicial regime based on respect for human rights and the rule of law. However, a fierce backlash from the armed forces in the mid-1980s and the threat of a military coup d'état led the National Congress, at Alfonsin's urging, to pass legislation to limit and then to stop further prosecutions. The "Full Stop" Law (*funto final*) of 1986 held that there would be no more military prosecutions except for individuals charged with rape, theft, and kidnapping children. The Law of "Due Obedience" of 1987 declared that all but the highest level of military officers should be presumed to have been following orders from superiors and are therefore not legally culpable for their actions. This law granted automatic immunity to all members of the armed forces, except in the cases of rape, kidnapping, and falsification of civil status (irregular adoptions). Alfonsin defended his compromise with the military on the grounds that those who insisted on prosecution and retributive punishment were ignoring the more primary good of social peace.[7] Feeling pressure from the military, Alfonsin's successor, President Carlos Menim, went on to pardon previously convicted high-ranking officers who had not already been freed. In December 1990 he pardoned all members of the junta who were originally convicted in 1985.

Much to the approval of human rights activists, however, the last few years have seen some holes punched in the wall of impunity in Argentina. In August 2003, Argentina's legislature annulled both amnesty laws, a decision that was ratified in June 14, 2005, by a 7 to 1 majority of the Argentine Supreme Court. The Court cited a previous decision rendered by the Inter-American Court of Human Rights on the Barrios Altos case in Peru which ruled that a set of amnesty laws passed by the Fujimori government were in violation of the American Convention on Human Rights. Human rights NGOs predicted that the Argentine judicial decision to follow the Barrios Altos precedent might provide a basis in international law for future prosecutions in places like Chile.[8] Following this Supreme Court decision, former high-ranking police official Miguel Osvaldo Etchecolatz was convicted and sentenced to life imprisonment for eight cases of illegal arrest, torture, and homicide during the Dirty War.[9] At the present time about three thousand Argentine military officers (including three hundred on active duty) could be subjected to prosecution.[10]

Chile

Chilean general Augusto Pinochet seized power in a coup d'état on September 11, 1973, and established a dictatorship that lasted until he was defeated by civilian Patricio Aylwin in a 1988 plebiscite. Pinochet presided over a regime that "disappeared" over three thousand people and that tortured tens of thousands more. A month after he assumed office, Alywin created the Truth and Reconciliation Commission, or Rettig Commission, to investigate and communicate the truth about the most serious crimes of the Pinochet regime, to identify its victims, and to recommend legal reforms for the sake of national reconciliation. Critics objected that the Rettig Report named victims but not perpetrators and that it listed those who were murdered or "disappeared" but not the victims of torture, forced exile, or other human rights abuses. Despite the public record, however, an amnesty law enacted during the Pinochet regime in 1978 made it impossible to prosecute offenders.

Yet as in Argentina, recent years have brought some success in legal battles to break through the wall of impunity. The National Commission on Political Imprisonment and Torture Report presented its findings to President Ricardo Lagos on November 11, 2004. It found that more than 18,000 people had been tortured by agents of the state during the four months after the September 1973 coup and another 5,266 people tortured between January 1974 and August 1977. It recommended that the government of Chile give victims symbolic and material reparations as well as resources to provide for their mental health.

Since the end of the Pinochet regime, Chilean courts have convicted 109 police officers and military men for various crimes, including disappearances. As of October 31, 2006, thirty-five high-ranking military officers have either been sentenced or are awaiting trial for various abuses of human rights. Pinochet himself was detained in London in 1998 while British courts reviewed a Spanish request for extradition. British judges eventually decided Pinochet was too ill to undergo extradition and trial, so he was permitted to return to Chile on March 2, 2000. In December of that year, though, he was stripped of parliamentary immunity from criminal prosecution. Though Pinochet was initially disqualified from prosecution on grounds of health, in October 2005 a court-ordered panel of psychiatrists judged him mentally fit to stand trial. He died of a heart attack on December 6, 2006, while under house arrest and facing the possibility of criminal prosecution for tax evasion as well as for human rights abuses. Chilean president Michele Bachelet, like Argentine president Nestor Kirchner, believes that national peace can best be established by the pursuit of criminal justice for former abusers of human rights. Argentina and Chile embody resurgent justice following a period of immunity.

South Africa

South Africa, a third case, represents the most well-known attempt to pursue both justice and peace.[11] The Truth and Reconciliation Commission (TRC) was charged with restoring the moral order to a society torn apart by violence. It understood peace-building to be a process that only begins with the cessation of armed hostilities. The TRC offered amnesty for perpetrators on the condition that they speak the truth about their past behavior; failure to disclose the truth made them vulnerable to criminal and civil prosecution. Some of the TRC hearings involved emotionally powerful confessions of guilt by offenders and generous offers of forgiveness from victims, and especially from the families of deceased victims. Yet others (such as Steve Biko's family) complained that the TRC process neglected justice for the sake of national reconciliation. They and others argue further that the TRC did not in many cases generate true healing and authentic reconciliation. Continued socioeconomic injustice indicates how far South African society is from genuine peace and justice.[12]

Proponents, however, maintain that the TRC played a valuable role in allowing open discussion of the trauma of the past, enabling victims to tell their stories and to be publicly acknowledged as victims, assembling a public record of many of the atrocities and other crimes of the state against innocent people, and helping some perpetrators understand the impact their aggression had on their victims. The TRC helped to discredit defenses of the apartheid system and its racist ideological legitimation. Yet for all its accomplishments, journalist Antjie Krog writes, few South Africans think the TRC process achieved reconciliation, and in fact most believe that "people are further apart than ever before."[13]

El Salvador

If Argentina and Chile moved to accountability through criminal prosecution and South Africa through the Truth and Reconciliation Commission, El Salvador, the final case, represents secure impunity for perpetrators. The Salvadoran civil war generated a scale of horror that in twelve years led to seventy-five thousand dead and nearly two million displaced persons. The settlement of 1992 brokered by the United Nations required the establishment of a Truth Commission to investigate and report on the brutalities of both the Right and Left in the civil war and to recommend legal and administrative reforms to prevent a recurrence of similar violence in the future. The UN Truth Commission report, *From Madness to Hope: The Twelve-Year War in El Salvador*, provides a clear public record of the most egregious violations of human rights and, in one significant blow to the culture of impunity, published the names of more than forty high-ranking military officers guilty of grossly violating human rights.[14] The report's findings led to the dismissal of over one hundred military officers, revealed the truth about the brutality of the armed forces (the report found that 95 percent of the abuses came from the military and associated death squads), and issued recommendations for the reform of the courts and for demilitarizing Salvadoran security forces.

The UN Commission was intended to play a broad role in the transformation of Salvadoran political, legal, and military institutions, but many observers doubt its full effectiveness. Almost immediately after its publication, the report was denounced by President Alfredo Christiani on the grounds that it "failed to meet the Salvadoran people's yearning for national reconciliation."[15] The Salvadoran legislature passed a General Amnesty Law five days after the report was published.[16]

The assignment of accountability in El Salvador was initially more robust than what happened in Chile and Argentina, but it is not clear that the process significantly contributed to either justice or reconciliation. There have been no public apologies by offenders and no efforts to provide reparations payments. The amnesty shields perpetrators behind a wall of impunity. The government of El Salvador lacks the political will to pursue justice, so it ignores the standard of international law that individuals who commit crimes against humanity and war crimes cannot be subject to amnesty. Still marked by a wide inequality between landowners and land-deprived populations, Salvadoran society renders distributive justice as elusive as true peace.

This is not to say that former human rights abusers are completely immune from prosecution. On September 3, 2004, Judge Oliver Wanger of the Eastern District of California in Fresno ruled that California resident Alvaro Saravia must pay $10 million in damages to a relative of Oscar Romero for his involvement in Oscar Romero's 1980 assassination.[17] On January 6, 2006, the United States Court of Appeals in Atlanta upheld an earlier verdict ordering former Salvadoran minister of defense Carlos Eugenio Casanova and General Jose Guillermo Garcia to pay $54 million to three survivors of torture during the civil war.[18] This judgment was particularly important in upholding the relevance of the Alien Tort Statute and the Torture Victim Protection Act to human rights abusers who are foreign nationals resident in the United States. This conviction was obtained because the offenders resided in the state of Florida, but impunity obtains for all offenders who reside in El Salvador.

Difficulties of Transitional Justice

These four cases exemplify some of the difficulties of transitional justice. Impunity for offenders is the rule and prosecution the exception, typically confined to punishment for a few paradigmatic cases. This is especially the case when powerful figures from former authoritarian regimes square off against large segments of societies engaged in the process of democratization. After the cessation of armed hostilities, governments offer amnesty to create conditions for transition and national reconciliation. Yet amnesties bury the truth, allow perpetrators to continue to function as if they had done nothing wrong, and even sometimes allow the intellectual authors of massive atrocities to remain in positions of economic or even political power. The need for healing and reconciliation is ignored. Authorities appeal to "reconciliation" but generally prefer "forgetting" based on implicit impunity to "forgiving" based on accountability, contrition, and making amends. "Peace" is usually reduced to "coexistence" rather than to national reconciliation based on forgiveness and accountability. Disputed issues concern whether justice must include punishment as well as other forms of accountability and whether retributive justice contributes to the healing of victims and social reconciliation. In any case, human rights activists insisting on enforcement of international law are often set against pragmatic politicians emphasizing the need for peace.

The Ugandan Situation

We now turn to the current debate over the relation of peace and justice in northern Uganda. Ruti Teitel asks, "How should societies deal with their evil past?"[19] The Ugandan people face the question, "How should societies deal with their evil present?" The government of Uganda has been fighting the Lord's Resistance Army (LRA) in the north in a twenty-year war that has cost one hundred thousand lives and involved the abduction of approximately twenty thousand children.[20] Fighting between the LRA and government military forces led to the displacement of more than 1.6 million people into so-called (and misnamed) protected villages, where about one thousand individuals die each week as a result of violence and from lack of basic necessities.

The Amnesty Acts of 2000 sought to reduce the rebel ranks by offering amnesty for any members of the LRA who leave the bush, turn in their weapons, and renounce rebellion. This amnesty differs from those granted in Argentina, Chile, South Africa, and El Salvador because it was offered to facilitate a cessation of ongoing hostilities. Unlike the South African amnesty, it is not conditioned on any form of public testimony.[21] Such public acknowledgement of guilt is sought by the International Criminal Court (ICC). In the first case since its founding in 2002, the ICC in October 2005 took the controversial action of issuing arrest warrants for Joseph Kony, the leader of the LRA, and four of his top commanders. In November 2007 the UN Security Council issued a nonbinding statement supporting the peace talks but also asserted the need for Kony to face justice.

Kony and his deputies have been ensconced for some time in the Garamba National Park in northeast Democratic Republic of Congo. The Ugandan government claims to be in control of northern Uganda. As of December 2007, however, the situation there was fluid. The Cessation of Hostilities Agreement was signed by the Government of Uganda and the LRA in August 2006 and renewed in November 2006. At the time of this writing in December 2007, the parties are negotiating over the technical details that must be settled before formal peace talks can be resumed in Juba, Sudan.[22]

Peace First

Those who advocate a "peace first" position hold that peace can only be achieved through negotiation preceded by amnesty.[23] "Peace first" proponents criticize the ICC's response to the northern Ugandan situation as simplistic, legalistic, abstract, individualistic, and "Western." "Peace first" proponents regard a military solution as either unworkable, on the grounds that the LRA will never be defeated in the field of battle, or too costly, particularly when one takes into account the costs exacted by harsh LRA retaliation against local populations in the wake of government incursions. The army's Operation Iron Fist attack on the LRA in Sudan was followed by harsh LRA retaliatory attacks on civilians, the ferocity of which was attributed to an LRA desire to punish "traitors" who worked for the military in civilian militias. Military actions and other government efforts have not succeeded in defeating the LRA. The government army of around one hundred thousand strong has not been able to conquer what in May 2005 was speculated to be a force of about three thousand individuals, of whom only about eight hundred are fighters.[24] The LRA seems more vulnerable since the withdrawal of support for them by the government in Khartoum in 2002, and the amnesty of 2000 has generated significant numbers of defections.

Some advocates of "peace first" regard the amnesty itself as a form of justice because it has the greatest potential to end the violence and save lives.[25] "Justice" here refers not to a narrow notion of retributive justice assigned to individual perpetrators, but in a broad sense the well-being of the entire community. It is forward-looking rather than backward-looking. Deterrence—the benefit attributed to prosecution—bears little relevance to the concrete situation in northern Uganda; if anything, threats of retribution fuel the cycle of violence that has plagued Uganda since independence. The associated demand for compensation from perpetrators is also suspect: nothing can truly compensate people who are mutilated, raped, or murdered. The urgent and immediate need to end killings and other crimes trumps the compelling claims of retributive justice enshrined in international law, and particularly in the Rome Charter that guides the ICC.

"Peace first" advocates object to the ICC arrest warrants. Delegations of the Lango, Acholi, Iteso, and Madi communities actively lobbied the ICC not to undermine the credibility of the amnesty and the prospects for negotiation by threatening prosecution. They argued that the warrants provide an added incentive for the LRA leaders to remain in the bush and so threaten both justice and peace. Long-term justice is best promoted by preventing the further loss of life and other kinds of social destruction. Ugandans' popular approval of the amnesty testifies to their exhaustion after twenty years of brutal warfare and the massive dislocation it has caused, as well as to a widespread popular reluctance to support a war against child soldiers.

As will be seen below, "justice first" proponents regard the amnesty offer as objectionable on legal and moral grounds. Legally, human rights lawyers argue that international conventions on human rights take precedence over national amnesty laws that would protect violators. Morally, "justice first" proponents maintain that amnesty re-victimizes the abused and creates a culture of impunity that increases the likelihood of future outrages.

Advocates of the "peace first" position argue that the government's persistence in waging war against the LRA gives the impression that the offer of amnesty has only been a ruse for disarming its opponents. They are highly sensitive to the drawbacks of the military approach because innocent people are usually caught in the crossfire between these forces. If the government is interested in a military solution to the insurgency, then the amnesty could be calculated to drain Kony of followers so that he will be weak enough to be either killed in action or captured and sent to the ICC for prosecution and punishment.

One major challenge facing northern Uganda concerns the reintegration of former rebel soldiers into their home communities. This process sometimes involves reestablishing a communal relationship between perpetrators and victims and at least a minimal level of social coexistence and basic civility. Reintegration also has to include attempts to reestablish ties between refugees and IDPs and those whose acts have led to their displacement. Advocates of "peace first" do not make the simplistic assumption that peace begins when armed insurrection ends, nor do they assume that amnesty suffices for either peace or justice. The fundamental issue concerns how to help heal the wounds caused by a horrific and prolonged period of terror and how to the repair a badly damaged civil society. Amnesty is thus the first step in a long journey to peace. The fact that roughly sixteen thousand former combatants have renounced the rebellion and come in from the bush is taken as an indication of the degree to which most inhabitants of northern Uganda want the war to end and to return to their homes.[26]

The traditions of northern Uganda pursue reconciliation when transgressors are reincorporated into their communities through undergoing "cleansing rituals."[27] People who have been away from a village for a long time engage in an Acholi ritual known in the Luo language as *Nyono Tonggwenko ki Opobo*. This ceremony, which includes the act of stepping on a fresh egg and an Opobo branch, cleanses individuals from whatever wrongdoing they have done while away.[28]

The traditional Acholi reconciliation ceremony called *Mato oput* facilitates communal reconciliation through a process in which perpetrators accept responsibility, express contrition and remorse for the actions, ask the community for forgiveness, and offer to compensate for the damage they have caused. It is symbolized in the act of "drinking the bitter root," or *mato oput*.[29] This ritual has been performed as a way of reincorporating children who were abducted and then forced to commit atrocities by the LRA. The event includes offenders giving their testimony before the community, expressing confession of wrongdoing, sharing a meal with their victims, and hearing the reflections of the paramount chief and other notable guests.

Ritualized means of reconciliation promote justice in requiring both communal accountability and the appropriate payment of compensation. The natural desire for vengeance, especially by family members of deceased victims, is not completely eliminated in all cases, but the ceremony allows the perpetrators to be seen as human beings who are remorseful for their wrongdoing and who desire to be forgiven and accepted back into their communities. The fact that so many LRA soldiers were initially abducted as children allows them to be viewed as victims as well as perpetrators, which facilitates forgiveness. Justice can thus be understood as restorative. What Joanna Quinn calls the "Politics of Acknowledgement" provides an important ingredient for both small-scale interpersonal healing and large-scale reestablishment of social cohesion.[30]

The difficulties facing the "peace first" position are daunting, however. Seasoned human rights authorities like Richard Goldstone argue that not only does peace not always have to precede justice, but that the latter in fact provides the proper condition for the former. The International Criminal Tribunal for the former Yugoslavia was established during the ongoing war there over the objections of those who believed that threatening prosecution would make it more difficult for the Bosnian Serbs to surrender. Some observers worried that prosecution would undermine the chances to obtain a negotiated peace, but Goldstone, on the contrary, argues that in fact the tribunal was instrumental for creating conditions for the true and durable peace.[31] The International Criminal Tribunal for the former Yugoslavia's prior indictment of Radovan Karadzic and Ratko Mladic, coupled with knowledge of the massacre at Srebenica, contributed to the isolation of these Bosnian Serb leaders by the international community and helped to bring pressure on Slobodan Milosevic to cooperate with the Dayton peace process. The indictment led to the exclusion of Karadzic and Mladic from the negotiating process, which in turn created an opening for a more worthwhile and reliable negotiating process based on a greater level of mutual trust and commitment than would have otherwise been possible.[32]

"Peace first" advocates, however, might respond that the Balkan war is a poor analogy to northern Uganda. The question is not whether there are historical cases in which justice can precede peace, but whether such a sequence is actually attainable at the present time in Uganda. Yet several difficulties face the "peace first" position. One can wonder if the unprecedented level of damage done to the social network of villages by moving people into IDP camps can be addressed by traditional means. The depth and the scope of the transgressions, moreover, extend well beyond the kind of small-scale violations for which traditional mechanisms are typically suited. One report explains, for example, that children "are forced to fight, some to carry bags, others to have sex with the fighters. By way of initiation, many are obliged to club, stamp, or bite to death their friends and relatives and then to lick their brains, drink their blood, and even eat their boiled flesh."[33] This level of violence calls into question whether dialogue with Kony and his deputies would not be another case of "shaking hands with the devil," as Romeo Dallaire described his experience in Rwanda,[34] and it also raises a question of what it means to be "healed" in such cases. One can also wonder whether traditional mechanisms of reconciliation can be applied to groups of perpetrators who come from outside victimized communities and have no previous relationships with victims that can be repaired. The damage to people caused by life in IDP camps implies that peace must include an effort to reconstitute whole communities.[35] The challenge is thus not to reintegrate offenders into intact communities, but to reestablish communities comprised of victims and perpetrators.

Justice First

International human rights groups like Amnesty International and Human Rights Watch argue that justice has to come to Uganda before it can have genuine peace.[36] The "justice first" position insists that the government renounce the offer of amnesty, particularly for those whose objectionable conduct has not come in acts of war but in gratuitous violence against civilians or prisoners.[37] It advocates prosecution of those who have engaged in a deliberate and sustained campaign to violate human rights. This includes Kony and the leaders of the LRA, but also government officials guilty of their own crimes against the residents of northern Uganda. Those defending the International Criminal Court arrest warrants for Kony and his deputies appeal both to a retrospective rationale for the Court's decision, that criminals deserve punishment for their acts, and to a prospective justification, the value of deterrence against future unjust aggression.[38] Human rights are best promoted in the long term, the warrants' defenders argue, by the juridical pursuit of retributive justice. They maintain that this agenda can be pursued before, during, and after the cessation of hostilities.

This position makes a principled argument that genuine and lasting peace can only be based on justice advanced through the pursuit of accountability for past crimes against humanity, war crimes, and other gross violations of human rights. It criticizes the habitual tendency of governments to favor pragmatism and expediency over ethical principles, and it rejects the offer of amnesty that allows even the most heinous crimes to go unpunished and even unacknowledged. Accountability demands public recognition of wrongdoing as well as the assignment of appropriate retributive punishment to guilty parties. Durable peace depends on the creation of political, economic, and social institutions marked by justice; these include respect for the rule of law, protection of human rights, and the establishment of democracy.

Prosecution can contribute to genuine and long-term peace by providing a public record of the truth (and thereby offer a counternarrative to popular misunderstandings), an official acknowledgment of the unjust harm done to the victims, and some form of accountability for criminal behavior. Assignment of individual blame also helps to counter the attribution of collective guilt which fuels forms of group hatred that set the stage for future recrimination.

"Justice first" argues that the failure of the international community to uphold the rule of law, either out of political expediency or for other long-term goals, inevitably contributes to a culture of impunity. It would thus seem to concur with the ICC's arrest warrants for top leaders of the LRA, though some might object that there are other and more effective ways to pursue justice. It also promotes "reintegration" of rank-and-file members but not the leaders of the LRA. It would allow for the return of soldiers and would put to use the established traditional mechanisms of psychological and social rehabilitation for former abductees and former combatants. It seeks peace and justice but takes a non-negotiable, deontological stance regarding prosecution of those who lead campaigns of horror against innocent people.

"Reconciliation" might be possible between most people caught up in the war, but "justice first" proponents would be especially reluctant to endorse forgiving the prime instigators of attacks, mutilations, and murders. Their concern rests on the need to punish these transgressors as a necessary support for the rule of law and the culture of human rights. This position assigns priority to rendering retributive justice to the leaders and promotes restorative justice, rehabilitation, and education for less powerful parties as well as to their victims. Even if the lines of command are not always so clear-cut, the just prosecution of the primary authorities, as at Nuremburg and Tokyo after World War II, makes an important symbolic point.

"Justice first" appeals to an elemental human revulsion at the prospect of impunity given to gross violators of human rights. Unfortunately, most effective work against abusers of human rights seems to be done ex post facto, for example, in the trial and conviction of some Argentine police officers, some Salvadoran soldiers involved in assassinations, and some Chilean authorities. In the practical order, however, it is not clear that amnesty is always the last word heard by offenders. High profile cases in Chile and Argentina suggest that, under some circumstances, government-granted amnesties and pardons can be overturned when more progressive regimes assume power. Former Chilean officials have been prosecuted for disappearances as "ongoing crimes" extending beyond the amnesty window, and Argentines have been punished for kidnapping children of the disappeared. Thus, even if the Ugandan government grants amnesty, one can expect "justice first" advocates to work through a variety of legal channels for the criminal or civil prosecution, or both, of former LRA leaders.

The "justice first" position depends heavily on cooperation between key powers in the international community. International leadership has an obligation to mobilize efforts against criminals engaged in flagrant and systematic violation of human rights. As Goldstone points out, "Pursuit of justice has to be accompanied by the firm resolve of the international community to put an end to the conflict effected through the use of economic, diplomatic and military sanctions."[39] He might argue that while it may not always be sufficient, retributive justice is a necessary element in the removal of injustice.

Considerations

This chapter closes with a set of considerations rather than with firm conclusions, an approach dictated by the complexity of the current situation in northern Uganda. The general direction of this chapter is to endorse the essentials of the "peace first" position. This orientation reflects a primary concern to accord respect to the perspectives of the people in northern Uganda, who have suffered the most from the civil war and who have the most to gain from both peace and justice in the region. This is by no means to suggest that justice in the form of criminal prosecution of offenders is morally inappropriate or socially unnecessary, but only that the perspective of the victims ought to be given a high priority in the interpretation of their relevance to concrete circumstances in northern Uganda.

The peace process faces an unsettling number of ambiguities. The Acholi Religious Leaders Peace Initiative has repeatedly called for some form of dialogue between the government and the LRA as offering the best hope for ending warfare and establishing stable and long-lasting peace. Yet some observers question whether the Ugandan government is politically motivated to attain peace with the LRA, and others wonder whether Kony's apocalyptic spiritualism motivates him to engage in political dialogue or provides a clear enough set of policy goals for practical negotiation.

Local leaders rightly complain about the timing of the ICC arrest warrants and resent the potential obstacle they present to ongoing efforts at peacemaking. A policy that pursues restorative justice within the peace process meets both the goal of accountability, in the form of recognition of harm done, and the goal of justice, understood as that which promotes community reintegration and reduces the chances of further violence. A natural desire for some form of vengeance (personally rendered retaliation) or at least retribution (socially sanctioned punishment) is still held by many Acholi people.[40] The question is whether traditional methods of reconciliation will provide some reasonable satisfaction of these legitimate desires. Far from abandoning justice, customary mechanisms of reincorporation pursue justice in a more comprehensive sense. Civil Society Organizations for Peace in Northern Uganda hold that "the Acholi justice system . . . is based on compensation, reconciliation, and reintegration. The main objective of the justice system is to integrate perpetrators into their communities with their victims, through a process of establishing the truth, confession, reparation, repentance and forgiveness. . . . The ICC system of justice is based upon western-style legal systems, which in many cases contradict traditional justice procedures."[41]

The victims themselves should have the greatest weight in determining what means are most likely to contribute to healing wounds, righting wrongs, and rebuilding communities. The long-range desire to undercut impunity, to build an international respect for human rights, and to show the efficacy of the ICC are all laudable goals, but they should not be pursued against the wishes, and at the expense, of the people who have already suffered so much after two decades of brutal violence. It is not, however, easy to determine what these wishes actually are at any given point in time.[42]

This leads to a question about the wisdom of the timing of the ICC arrest warrants. Because they were instigated at the personal request of President Yoweri Museveni, the warrants are often regarded as a manipulation of the ICC by a government whose actions, particularly regarding its military conduct in the north, are also deserving of ICC attention. "Justice first" proponents—including the Argentine public prosecutor Luis Moreno-Ocampo, who prosecuted "Dirty Wars" offenders—regard the ICC as providing an opportunity to make a long-term correction of the culture of impunity that so often protects perpetrators after their own abusive regimes have been replaced by democracies.

The relevant question here concerns whether it is necessary to set international law against customary justice. An alternative way of relating these two sets of norms would be for the ICC to recognize the legitimacy of traditional Acholi means of pursuing accountability within the reconciliation process. Leading Ugandan peace advocates have pleaded for the ICC to withdraw its indictments; the government itself has offered amnesty to all perpetrators. Helena Cobban proposes that the government of Uganda give official legal status to the Acholi reconciliation process, add a condition to the amnesty that all offenders who seek forgiveness must go through *mato oput*, and then petition the ICC to rescind the indictments on the ground that justice has been served through the means provided by the Ugandan legal system.[43] This scenario, of course, does anything but guarantee a solution to the problem presented by Kony, but it has the advantage of providing a more satisfactory solution than the alternatives—either continued stalemate and warfare or a blanket amnesty that requires neither accountability nor compensation.

The Refugee Law Project suggests rightly that, once hostilities are definitively concluded, the people of Uganda would benefit from something like a South African TRC.[44] Whether it would apply also to the major leaders of the LRA—and whether they could be reincorporated into northern Ugandan communities—should be a point for discussion and practical judgment. In any case, a TRC would encourage victims to speak about their own suffering and enable them to hear from perpetrators of violence. Amnesty could be given to those who testify to their crimes, and prosecution retained as an option for those who refuse to testify. It would promote some degree of accountability, even if not what would be pursued in a legal trial followed by retributive punishment. There are, of course, significant disanalogies with South Africa—for example, reconciliation is perceived as a regional problem and amnesty has already been granted, among other things—and, furthermore, critics point out that even the South African TRC was more successful at discovering truth than in accomplishing reconciliation.[45] Reconciliation is the goal of forgiveness, and forgiveness is given by victims in response to the expression of genuine contrition by perpetrators. Unfortunately, perpetrators involved in the Latin American cases noted previously—Argentina, Chile, and El Salvador— have either denied all involvement in any atrocities or have justified their actions on the basis of national security. The same might happen in Uganda.

The level of the LRA's viciousness raises questions about the possibility of genuine reconciliation between the Acholi people and the leaders of the LRA campaign that employed extraordinarily cruel methods. However, the same alienation also marks the relation between the Acholi and the government of Uganda. The army drove the people into the unhealthy and unsafe IDP camps, and its conduct has repeatedly violated the human rights of the people it is charged with protecting. The undisciplined and predatory conduct of soldiers has also contributed significantly to the misery of the people of northern Uganda, and especially of women. Human Rights Watch and other NGOs report that agents of the government routinely engage in illegal detentions, torture, rape, and extrajudicial executions.[46] Kony and his deputies are no more prone to admit fault than are the government and the army. They show no signs of remorse over their heinous actions and in fact justify them as necessary means of social purification.

If Uganda cannot meet the standard set by the South African TRC, perhaps the international community could fund and organize a less ambitious independent truth commission of the kind established by the United Nations in El Salvador. The commission could investigate major crimes and publish an official report, something akin to what was produced by the UN Salvadoran Truth Commission's report, *From Madness to Hope*, that would establish a public record of crimes, give a degree of validation to victims, and make suggestions for future reforms. The report could highlight the fact that the conflict is not just a problem of northerners in Uganda but involves the entire country. Zachary Lomo of the Refugee Law Project at Makerere University argues that "the truth needs to be known before reconciliation can start."[47] Acknowledgment is one critically important aspect of justice. Since the leaders of both sides of the Ugandan conflict have been guilty of atrocities, they may have a shared interest in impunity and silence. A truth commission might be able to produce what will not be forthcoming from perpetrators.

A complementary set of recommendations regarding institutional reforms of the Ugandan government and economic and symbolic reparations would also contribute to long-term peace. Justice requires compensation for victims, even if it will always be inadequate. Some effort to repair the massive damage done to society as a whole and to individuals, families, and communities ought to follow the establishment of the initial conditions of peace.

Conflict and reconciliation constitute two ends of a long spectrum. The harm done in northern Uganda has been so profound and grievances are so deeply seated that co-existence might be the only achievable collective goal at this time, at least if one is referring to the macro level. Taking concrete steps to make possible the return of abducted children and former LRA members to their villages would contribute significantly to the movement away from conflict and toward reconciliation, even if it falls short of the latter. The government's forced settlement of 1.6 million villagers into compounds without adequate food, water, health care, or even physical security from rebel intruders has had a devastating effect on their lives, on the economy of the region, and on the social cohesion of village life.[48] The state will have to make it possible for internally displaced people to return to their homes.[49] "Justice first" and "peace first" positions agree that the current government policy of combining amnesty with pursuit of military victory is both practically unworkable and ethically bankrupt. Most fundamentally, they agree that the current policy fails to address the deeper causes of the conflict that must be addressed and resolved if durable peace is to be attained. Long-term and meaningful peace can only be promoted by establishing more just social institutions governed by the rule of law for all of the people of Uganda, regardless of their ethnic identity, economic class, or geographical location. Genuine peace in Uganda must be based on a healthy civil society and democratic institutions.[50]

Notes

1. "A Voice for Peace in Northern Uganda: An Interview with John Baptist Odama," *America*, March 27, 2006, 17.

2. See Brian Berry, *Theories of Justice* (Berkeley: University of California Press, 1989); John Rawls, *A Theory of Justice* (Cambridge, MA: Harvard University Press, 1971); and Michael Walzer, *Spheres of Justice* (New York: Basic Books, 1983).

3. See Ruti G. Teitel, *Transitional Justice* (New York: Oxford University Press, 2000), on transitional justice, and Howard Zehr, *Changing Lenses: A New Focus for Crime and Justice* (Scottdale, PA, and Waterloo, Ontario: Herald Press, 1990), on restorative justice.

4. See Wilheim Verwoerd and Tudy Govier, "Trust and the Problem of National Reconciliation," *Philosophy in the Social Sciences* 32, no. 2 (2002):178–205.

5. See Argentina's National Commission on Disappeared People, *Nunca Mas Never Again* (Boston: Faber and Faber, 1986), and Marguerite Feitlowitz, *Lexicon of Terror: Argentina and the Legacies of Torture* (New York: Oxford, 1999).

6. Argentina's National Commission on Disappeared People, *Nunca Mas Never Again.*

7. See Raul Alfonsin, "'Never Again' in Argentina," *Journal of Democracy* 4 (1993):15–19.

8. See "Argentina: Amnesty Laws Struck Down," June 14, 2005, *Human Rights Watch*, http://hrw.org/english/docs/2005/06/14/argent11119.htm (accessed March 21, 2007).

9. See "Trial Watch: Miguel Osvaldo Etchecolatz," http://www.trial-ch.org/en/trial-watch/profile/db/context/miguel-osvaldo_etchecolatz_583.html (accessed February 13, 2007). See the sentencing at http://www.youtube.com/watch?v=88dt2UAcAsc.

10. See "Argentine Amnesty Laws Scrapped," BBC, June 15, 2005, http://news.bbc.co.uk/2/hi/americas/4093018.stm (accessed March 21, 2007).

11. See Lyn S. Graybill, *Truth and Reconciliation in South Africa: Miracle of Model?* (Boulder, CO: Lynne Rienner Publishers, 2002).

12. See Amnesty International and Human Rights Watch, "Truth and Justice: Unfinished Business in South Africa," Amnesty International Index: AFR 53/001/2003,http://www.amnesty.org/library/index (accessed February 9, 1907). See also Rosemary Nagy, "Reconciliation in Post-Commission South Africa: Thick and Thin Accounts of Solidarity," *Canadian Journal of Political Science* 35, no. 2 (June–July 2002): 323–46. On the success of the TRC in overcoming the legacy of apartheid, see the study by James L. Gibson, *Overcoming Apartheid: Can Truth Reconcile a Divided Nation?* (New York: Russell Sage Foundation, 2004).

13. Antjie Krog, *Country of My Skull* (New York: Three Rivers Press, 2000), 385.

14. See *From Madness to Hope: The 12-Year War in El Salvador: Report of the Commission on the Truth for El Salvador*, UN Doc. S/25500, Annex, 1993, reprinted in United Nations, *The United Nations and El Salvador: 1990–1995* (New York: United Nations, 1995), 290–414. Also available from http://www.usip.org/library/tc/doc/reports/el_salvador/tc_es_03151993_toc.html (accessed March 21, 2007).

15. Martha Doggett, *Death Foretold: The Jesuit Murders in El Salvador* (Washington, DC: Georgetown University Press, 1993), 266.

16. See Margaret L. Popkin, *Peace without Justice: Obstacles to Building the Rule of Law in El Salvador* (University Park: Pennsylvania State University Press, 2000).

17. See the documents on *Doe v. Saravia* at the website of the Center for Justice and Accountability, http://www.cja.org/cases/romero.shtml (accessed February 27, 2007).

18. See *Romagoza v. Garcia* (S.D. Fla. July 23, 2002) (No. 99-8364-CV), http://www.cja.org/cases/romagoza.shtml (accessed February 27, 2007).

19. Ruti G. Teitel, *Transitional Justice* (New York: Oxford, 2000), 3.

20. BBC, "Country Profile: Uganda," http://news.bbc.co.uk/2/hi/africa/country_profiles/1069166.stm (accessed February 16, 2007).

21. See the official South Africa Truth and Reconciliation website, http://www.doj.gov.za/trc (accessed March 21, 2007). See also Charles Villa-Vicencio and Fanie Du Toit, eds., *Truth and Reconciliation in South Africa: 10 Years On* (Claremont, South Africa: David Philip, 2006).

22. For periodic updates, see http://www.ugandacan.org.

23. This chapter employs a distinction between a "peace first" and "justice first" position that is useful despite its excessive simplicity. The issue concerns temporal priority (first stop the fighting and then deal with correction) but also moral priority (loss of life is a more urgent problem than correction). These positions also differ over how to interpret "correction," that is, whether it should involve restorative justice, retributive justice, or both. On "peace first," see Refugee Law Project, "Peace First, Justice Later: Traditional Justice in Northern Uganda," Refugee Law Project Working Paper No. 17, July 2005, 1–57, http://www.refugeelawproject.org/resources/papers/workingpapers/RLP.WP17.pdf (assessed March 16, 2007). See also Refugee Law Project, "Whose Justice? Perceptions of Uganda's Amnesty Act 2000: The Potential for Conflict Resolution and Long-term Reconciliation," Refugee Law Project Working Paper No. 15, http://www.refugeelawproject.org/resources/papers/workingpapers/RLP.WP15.pdf (accessed March 21, 2007). See also Adam Branch, "International Justice, Local Injustice," *Dissent*, Summer 2004.

24. See "Hunting Uganda's Child Killers; Justice versus Reconciliation," *The Economist*, May 7, 2005, 41.

25. See Refugee Law Project, "Peace First, Justice Later," 31.

26. See ibid.

27. See ibid., 22–23 and ff.

28. See Amy Colleen Finnegan, "A Memorable Process in a Forgotten War: Forgiveness within Northern Uganda" (MALD thesis, Tufts University, 2005), 2 ff.

29. Ibid., 43.

30. Lucy Hovil and Joanna R. Quinn, "Peace First. Justice Later: Traditional Justice in Northern Uganda," *Refugee Law Project Working Paper Series*, no. 17 (July 8, 2005):7–8.

31. Richard J. Goldstone, "Bringing War Criminals to Justice during an Ongoing War," in *Hard Choices: Moral Dilemmas in Humanitarian Intervention*, ed. Jonathan Moore (Lanham, MD: Rowman and Littlefield, 1988), 195–210.

32. Ibid.

33. "Hunting Uganda's Child Killers; Justice versus Reconciliation," *The Economist*, May 7, 2005, 41.

34. Romeo Dallaire, *Shake Hands with the Devil: The Failure of Humanity in Rwanda* (Toronto: Vintage Canada, 2003).

35. See Médecins Sans Frontières, "Life in Northern Uganda: All Shades of Grief and Fear," December 2004, http://www.globalpolicy.org/security/issues/uganda/2004/1200msf.pdf (accessed March 21, 2007).

36. See Human Rights Watch, "The Lack of Accountability," 2005 Report on Uganda, http://hrw.org/reports/2005/uganda0905/6.htm (accessed August 5, 2006). The general "justice first" position is advanced by Aryeh Neier, *War Crimes: Brutality, Terror, and the Struggle for Justice* (New York: Time Books–Random House, 1998).

37. See Médecins Sans Frontières, "Life in Northern Uganda."

38. Tim Allen, *Trial Justice: The International Criminal Court and the Lord's Resistance Army* (London: Zed Books, 2006).

39. Goldstone, "Bringing War Criminals to Justice," 208–9.

40. See Allen, *Trial Justice*; and Hovil and Quinn, "Peace First. Justice Later."

41. Civil Society Organizations for Peace in Northern Uganda (CSOPNU), *The International Criminal Court Investigation in Northern Uganda: A CSOPNO Briefing Paper*, cited in Finnegan, "A Memorable Process," 27.

42. Authorities differ on what the people of northern Uganda want. Tim Allen argues that they want the ICC prosecution but Adam Branch believes they advocate a "peace first" approach. See Allen, *Trial Justice*, and Adam Branch, "Neither Peace nor Justice: Political Violence and the Peasantry in Northern Uganda, 1986–1998," *African Studies Quarterly* 8, no. 2 (Spring 2005), also available from http://web.africa.ufl.edu/asq/v8/v8i2a1.htm.

43. See Helena Cobban, "Uganda's Challenge to the ICC," *Transitional Justice Forum*, August 27, 2006, 12, also available from http://tj-forum.org/archives/002087.html (accessed March 21, 2007).

44. Zachary Lomo and Lucy Hovil, *Behind the Violence: The War in Northern Uganda*, Institute for Security Studies, no. 99 (Pretoria, South Africa: South Africa Institute for Security Studies, 2004), 47.

45. See Trudy Govier and Wilhelm Verwoerd, "Trust and the Problem of National Reconciliation," *Philosophy of the Social Sciences* 32, no. 2 (June 2002):178–205, and Rosemary Nagy, "Reconciliation," 323–46.

46. See, for example, Human Rights Watch, "State of Pain: Torture in Uganda," March 2004, http://hrw.org/reports/2004/uganda0404 (accessed March 21, 2007), and Human Rights Watch, "Uganda: Anti-Terror Unit Allegedly Electrocuted Detainee," July 26, 2006, http://hrw.org/english/docs/2006/07/25/uganda13812.htm (accessed March 21, 2007).

47. Refugee Law Project, "War without End? Behind the Violence in Northern Uganda," Refugee Law Project Working Paper No. 11, http://www.refugeelawproject.org. Also in *Review of African Political Economy* 39, no. 99 (March 2004):142–44.

48. Acholi Religious Leaders, "Let My People Go: The Forgotten Plight of the People in Displaced Camps in Acholi" (Gulu, Uganda: ARLPI, July 2001), also available from http://www.unight.org/Documents/Let%20my%20People%20Go_ARLPI_%20July%202001.pdf (accessed March 16, 2007).

49. See Refugee Law Project, "Only Peace Can Restore the Confidence of the Displaced," 2nd ed. (Geneva and Kampala, Uganda: Internal Displacement Monitoring Center and Refugee Law Project, 2006), also available from www.refugeelawproject.org/resources/seminars/RLPNRClaunch.htm (accessed March 21, 2007).

50. Refugee Law Project, "Peace First, Justice Later," 20–21.

V

Ethics and Rights
in Practice

13

Key Ethical Issues in the Practices and Policies of Refugee-Serving NGOs and Churches

Agbonkhianmeghe E. Orobator

Humanitarian nongovernmental organizations (NGOs) and churches constitute a permanent feature of refugee camps in eastern Africa. From Lukole (Tanzania) to Rhino Camp (Uganda) and Kakuma (Kenya), they provide a variety of services to communities of displaced people.[1] The cast of faith-based, refugee-serving organizations includes the Jesuit Refugee Service (JRS), the Lutheran World Federation (LWF), the Tanganyika Christian Relief Services (TCRS), the National Council of Churches of Kenya (NCCK), and the different national affiliates of Caritas Internationalis. A variant of this involvement exists in the form of international church-related organizations, like the World Council of Churches (WCC), the Pontifical Council for the Pastoral Care of Migrants and Itinerant People, and the All Africa Conference of Churches (AACC), which focus on international advocacy and policy issues on behalf of uprooted people, occasionally producing critical reflections on forced migration and ethical responsibilities towards refugees.[2] In addition to this variety of refugee-serving NGOs, there exists a plethora of missions and mandates internal to each organization, the perception of which determines how each one views the ethical issues generated by forced migration and its preferred advocacy framework. This chapter examines some divergences arising from the mandates of refugee-serving NGOs.

To date the subject of refugee-serving, faith-based NGOs and churches has attracted remarkably scant scholarly attention. By way of introduction, some reminders are relevant. First, refugee assistance predates the international refugee regime; it did not commence only with the regime's adoption. Second, prior to this regime, the bulk of care and assistance was provided by religious agencies.[3] Third, and most important, Christian ethics and practice of refugee assistance have firm foundations in Scripture and theology. Both ethics and practice draw upon the "memory of exile" encapsulated in the Jewish religious tradition and the archetypal forced migration of Joseph, Mary, and Jesus to Egypt, which combine to keep the community called church "attuned to the plight of refugees and migrants today."[4]

This chapter presents and analyzes some ethical issues that arise in the practices and policies of NGOs, faith-based organizations, and churches seeking to come to the assistance of refugees and assesses how such analysis may serve a broader project of effective advocacy. It assumes that faith-based organizations bring a unique perspective to the care and assistance of forced migrants that should neither be subsumed hastily under a generalized category nor facilely exempted from the strict ethical standards required of humanitarian actors.

Problems of Perception and Principles of Neutrality and Impartiality

Leaving aside the difficulty of producing a definition of "forced migration" that fully satisfies the interests, objectives, and expectations of all the actors, including forced migrants themselves, contemporary literature is divided on the nature and perception of the refugee crisis. Three partly overlapping and partly antithetical "angles of perception" can be distinguished. They raise ethical issues for humanitarian NGOs and churches.

Forced Migration as a Political Problem

Gil Loescher expresses the first position succinctly when he asserts that "the global refugee problem is not a humanitarian problem requiring charity, but a political problem requiring political solutions."[5] Although Loescher's main concern is with international agencies and governments responsible for oversight of the international refugee regime, an extreme form of his position would consider a purely humanitarian or charitable response, such as prioritized by some faith-based NGOs, to be suspect, because this approach attends to symptoms, rather than dealing with underlying political issues. What is required, Loescher argues, is "multilateral cooperation" that would compel a host of international organizations to effect institutional, legal, administrative, and structural reforms of the international refugee regime. Hence, he concludes, "to deal with political problems requires efforts that well exceed the scope of humanitarian organizations."[6]

An approach that prioritizes political solutions has ethical implications for the policies and practices of humanitarian NGOs. First, one cannot ignore issues of protection and human rights violations in the context of forced migration. Second, the practice of charity, if delinked from other structural and institutional concerns (such as reform of the international refugee regime), is essentially ineffectual. And, third, it is a disservice to uprooted people not to see beyond charity in attempting to address their needs and concerns.

To limit refugee assistance to charity contradicts the fundamental truth that forced migrants are victims of a violation of basic human rights. Whether in Kakuma, Ngara, Adjumani, or elsewhere, a refugee is a person who has been denied his or her rights by a constellation of political actors. While there is room for emergency response to their immediate needs, the overarching concern should be how to respect and restore those rights. As Mervyn Frost argues, such people "ought to be seen not as supplicants deserving charity but as people whom we need to establish as citizens in democratic free states in order to secure our own freedom."[7] Documentary evidence suggests that this is not a shared assumption among humanitarian NGOs, some of which continue to conceive of refugee assistance "in terms of charity rather than as a means of enabling refugees to enjoy their rights."[8]

Forced Migration as a Human Rights Problem

Following upon the assertion that human rights violations lie at the root of displace-ment, a second approach sees forced migration as essentially a human rights problem.[9] In light of this approach, the fundamental goal of care and assistance should be the monitoring and reporting of violations of the human rights of displaced populations in view of securing more adequate protection for them. Often, the social context of these human rights violations is characterized by lawlessness, arbitrariness, and impunity. Hence, some authors speak of "spaces" or "zones" of exception, which not only facilitate abuses, but also excuse moral accountability and stigma of guilt for atrocities commit-ted against refugees.[10]

Protection can be understood at many levels. Establishing adequate and functional legal and policy instruments to guarantee the rights of forced migrants represents one level. Another is the oversight of human rights situations in camps to prevent abuses. Each level calls for an appropriate response. Humanitarian NGOs, especially faith-based organizations, argue with reason that their very presence also constitutes an effective form of protection. By their presence in refugee camps, NGO personnel provide both protective humanitarian and political cover for displaced populations. Such cover serves as a deterrent to violators of human rights. Nearly all observers agree on the ef-fectiveness of this form of refugee protection. Firm evidence also shows that religious or faith-based organizations are best placed to provide this cover, since they are more likely to remain in areas where international agencies maintain little or no significant presence and may enjoy the confidence of refugees as "natural 'social partners.'"[11] Faith-based NGOs tend to take a longer view of the refugee situation than other NGOs and commit resources to the lifespan of refugee crises. The fundamental ethos and experi-ence of JRS amply illustrate these points.

JRS adopts a three-prong approach to refugee assistance: accompaniment, service, and advocacy. Accompaniment presupposes "being with" forcibly displaced or uprooted populations; it does not make sense from a distance: "It is by *being with* refugees that one discovers how to serve them. Similarly, accompanying refugees leads spontaneously to defending their cause."[12] Besides, JRS recruits a balanced mix of international, na-tional, and local staff. Taken as a whole, one sees how the presence of such humanitarian workers can serve as a deterrent to human rights violations and abuses. It also facilitates advocacy, because the latter presupposes "withness."[13] Seen in this optic, the kind of as-sistance implied by "accompaniment" transcends superficial responses to the problem of forced migration. The matter, however, is not as unproblematic as this analysis of accompaniment might suggest. There is a critical ethical issue here: Is accompaniment (or "withness") simply a passive experience? Of what value is this act if it does not trans-late into an active advocacy against human rights violations and the defense of rights of displaced people? In addressing these questions, it is important that we understand advocacy as a multifaceted reality that assumes various concrete forms besides the defense of human rights. The guaranteeing of conditions such as education, microcredit schemes, income-generating projects, skills acquisition, and women's empowerment, all of which further the socioeconomic development of displaced populations, are among the different facets of advocacy.

The issues that surface here concern neutrality and impartiality—fundamental in the ethos of humanitarian action in the midst of conflict and complex emergencies. On these issues controversies have raged between those who espouse the inviolability of neutrality and impartiality and those who advocate political solidarity (or taking sides with victims of human rights violations), respectively categorized by Thomas Weiss as "classicists" (keep politics and humanitarian action apart) and "political humanitarians" (keep them together).[14] This is not the place to rehash the debate, some elements of which have clear ethical implications for refugee-serving NGOs. The crucial question facing the latter is what to do in the event of abuse: when accompanying forced migrants, do neutrality and impartiality attenuate the obligation to monitor, document, report, and denounce acts that violate their rights? No easy solutions exist for these ethical problematics, but the following considerations help situate them within a larger analytical framework.

First, it has become commonplace to link "protection," as a political duty, with "assistance," as a humanitarian option. From the perspective of the subject of forced migration, the two are inseparable: the refugee in need of assistance is the same one whose rights are being violated. There are not two realities at stake here, writes Elizabeth Ferris: "Protection and assistance are, of course, closely linked. If refugees do not receive the assistance they need to survive, they will seek it elsewhere. Women will turn to prostitution to feed their families, young people will be recruited to join rebel forces when there are no educational or other opportunities in refugee camps, and refugees may turn to crime—which often brings reprisals."[15] The tendency for some authors to frame this issue in terms of conflicting alternatives does not obscure the fact that we are not dealing with mutually exclusive options. Both options essentially overlap; each humanitarian crisis entails a political consequence and unfolds within a highly politicized space. The concomitant responsibility toward forced migrants, while not absolutely tied to specific political goals, need not become an excuse for political inaction.[16]

Second, if political action or human rights activism and humanitarian assistance overlap, they do not simply merge into one and the same reality, certainly not in the context of forced migration. Any confusion of roles can have deleterious consequences. An unguarded statement, hasty conclusions, and unfounded allegations can jeopardize access to and assistance for crisis-affected people, especially in situations, such as a remote refugee camp, where accurate reporting and independent confirmation are not readily available. Former International Committee of the Red Cross president Cornelio Sommaruga makes a salutary point when he stresses the need to correctly identify and distinguish the roles of the different players in crisis situations.[17] In the context of forced migration, for example, these roles can span the gamut of protection, assistance, relief aid, publicizing abuses, human rights advocacy, policy formulation, and so on. Humanitarian workers operate on the basis of a clear mission to provide relief and material assistance. Their inability to monitor comprehensively the climate of human rights in refugee camps need not lessen the validity of their roles. Nevertheless, it bears repeating that a situation of *forced* migration points to violations of human rights. Humanitarian organizations cannot but confront the situation. As I have mentioned above, and many authors concur, humanitarian and faith-based NGOs are often the only ones in close proximity to displaced populations in situations where budgetary constraints hinder adequate protection by UNHCR, thereby compelling them to meet the multifaceted needs—including protection and defense of human rights—of displaced populations.[18]

Third, a useful rule of thumb would require humanitarian NGOs to make their presence count beyond offering palliative care and assistance to refugees. Rather than maintain strict silence and passivity in the name of neutrality, which ultimately could amount to complicity, they need to identify collaborators and dialogue partners and establish strategies and protocols for reporting abuses while at the same time preserving the humanitarian space that would allow them to continue to serve the needs of crisis-affected people.[19]

Forced Migration as a Problem of Charity

A third and final angle of perception sees the refugee problem as a problem of charity. The only appropriate response from this perspective is to give refugees handouts. Today, given the multifaceted nature of forced migration, it would be hard to defend this approach in its pure form. This form, if ever it existed, would correspond to what Weiss has condemned as "visceral charity"[20]—superficial at best and inhumane at worst. In both cases, this kind of charity easily excuses nonengagement in critical issues of human rights and justice.

From an ethical perspective, charity as virtue (as opposed to visceral charity) manifests a different dynamic in the context of forced migration. As a motivation for humanitarian action, charity is neither blind to political implications nor uncritical of acts of injustice that may exist in any given humanitarian space, such as a refugee camp. Those such as Weiss who have published the obituary of charity need to understand the difference between a merely charitable response and a comprehensive one. As the approach adopted by JRS suggests, and Sommaruga argues, caritative assistance forms part of a whole; it defines a point of entry rather than a terminus that imposes an embargo on justice-related and political issues. While this approach may eschew direct political action, it neither denies the critical need for a comprehensive framework for assuming ethical responsibilities towards forced migrants, nor does it fail to recognize the advantages of a long-term focus over short-term and largely symbolic solutions.[21] Whether as a primary motivation or an operational principle for refugee assistance, "charity alone" hardly ever survives the lifespan of an emergency. Charity has an expiry date: generosity wanes in inverse proportion to the protraction and prolongation of refugee crises; aid progressively diminishes as donor fatigue or compassion fatigue sets in and grows.

I have chosen the term "angles of perception" to designate the foregoing approaches because, as I shall indicate later, they represent essentially complementary approaches to forced migration that are more effective when integrated and coordinated rather than absolutized and compartmentalized.

Humanitarians and Military: Strange Bedfellows or Allies for Good?

Without denying the presence of socioeconomic and environmental factors, forced migration is almost always associated with armed conflicts. The refugee populations of Kenya, Uganda, and Tanzania can be accounted for by decades of political instability and armed conflicts in the neighboring countries of Sudan, Ethiopia, Eritrea, Somalia, the Democratic Republic of Congo (DRC), Rwanda, and Burundi. This situation raises some ethical questions relative to the policies and practices of refugee-serving NGOs and churches. Divergent positions have emerged relating to the appropriate relationship between humanitarian actors and both political and military agents in the context of forcibly displaced people. This issue relates to some of the considerations raised above. Before looking at some of the positions, a few remarks are in order.

First, a military presence in refugee camps takes different forms. For example, in Adjumani, the Uganda People's Defense Force (UPDF) has maintained, on occasion, some presence, especially at the height of the Lord's Resistance Army's campaign of terror against defenseless refugees and nationals in the early 2000s. In Tanzania the government has threatened to use military force to dislodge elements of Burundian rebel militias of Hutu extraction active in camps close to the border; it actually used the army to forcibly repatriate refugees and arrest political activists.[22] Anecdotal evidence indicates that besides low-level intimidation of refugees and recruitment of youth, rebel elements residing in camps extorted money from impoverished refugees, ostensibly to support the war effort and facilitate their speedy return to Burundi.

Second, a related question is the use of the police in the context of forced migration. When refugees cross the border, their first encounter with security operatives is with the police. Urban-dwelling refugees live in perpetual fear of harassment and intimidation by the police. Barbara Harrell-Bond writes that "another local institution that has direct contact with refugees from the moment they enter a country and throughout their stay is the police force. They play an enormously important role in determining the extent to which refugees' rights will be upheld."[23] If a country lacks a functioning legal and security framework or there is ignorance of the international refugee regime, the interaction between the police and refugees could result in atrocious consequences for the latter. This question, however, does not fall within the scope of this essay.[24]

Third, although refugee camps are nominally under the government of UNHCR, the overall administration falls under the jurisdiction of commandants appointed by the internal or home affairs ministry. They control access to camps, maintain security, and enforce discipline. A close observation of camp administration reveals the military style in which they are run. For example, the "Rules and Regulations" for Rhino Camp Refugee Settlement prohibit all meetings and public gatherings "save the usual religious congregations," except with the camp settlement commandant's (CSC) permission. Movement is strictly regulated; no refugee is allowed to leave the settlement without the CSC's written permission, which requires a clear statement of reason, destination, and duration. The rule book concludes: "Like it, hate it; it works. And therefore adhere to it."[25]

One approach, typically advanced by military personnel, considers the use and presence of the military as benign and beneficial. The military's roles in their view are to support emergency or disaster relief efforts, to be used for so-called humanitarian intervention, and to deliver aid when the security situation precludes the presence of humanitarian workers. In these instances, Rupert Wieloch sees the military as a "force for good," with a proviso that it operate in close collaboration with civilian and humanitarian actors and, where possible, even be subject to their overall direction. Wieloch concludes that "NGOs who still deny that troops can do anything humanitarian at all are in danger of perpetuating ill-informed and out-of-date opinions."[26]

Some authors adopt a more cautious position and point to the clash of the humanitarian ethos (neutrality, impartiality, and independence) with that of the military (*"force for good"*). The possibility exists of the former becoming tainted and compromised by association with the latter, in particular if the military resorts to physical force.[27]

Besides the risk of compromising the principles of humanitarian action, refugee-serving NGOs face the question of whether and when having recourse to military or police force in the physical sense of the term becomes ethically tenable among displaced populations. It is important to avoid dogmatic and ideologically fixed positions because of the complexity of this ethical dilemma. Without ruling out its use a priori, given the unpredictability of refugee-causing armed conflicts with regard to timing or outbreak, scope, and intensity, "one can also hope," David Hollenbach has stated, "that military intervention to prevent or alleviate humanitarian crisis will be rare as well."[28]

A much more intractable problem occurs when elements of armed rebel militias and nonstate actors establish an amorphous but potentially lethal presence among civilian refugees, as was the case in the eastern DRC and western Tanzania. These groups compound an already ethically charged environment by reason of their lack of a clear objective or political agenda, their use of unconventional means, and the often ambiguous relationship between them and the civilian refugees. Clearly lacking the political power (that is, force) to separate belligerents and human rights violators from genuine refugees, and given the inability and unwillingness of the host state to assume this task, NGOs and churches face the added dilemma of whether to give or withhold aid. The key ethical question becomes whether *to engage or not to engage.* Either way, refugees stand to lose the most. To provide assistance in view of relieving short-term needs risks aiding and abetting the atrocities of "refugee warriors" who have infiltrated the camps and, therefore, prolonging the violence and crisis, which in the long run could generate more refugees. To withhold assistance in the short term in view of preventing long-term suffering caused by rebels in the camps risks compounding the present and real misery of refugees, who are manipulated and intimidated by the "refugee warriors." This second option resembles a calculated attempt to starve out the refugee warriors, and it presupposes their inability to identify other sources of survival. This, however, is rarely the case. For example, in western Tanzania, Hutu rebels imposed a clandestine levy on refugees.[29]

On the use of the military, often the situation of insecurity in a refugee camp could necessitate their presence to protect humanitarian workers. This is understandable where conflict is still occurring, but it raises questions where conflict has ceased and refugees direct their hostility at humanitarian workers. The underlying question relates to the relationship between beneficiaries of aid and givers of aid. Tension arises when refugees perceive humanitarian workers as exploiters profiting from the predicament of forced migrants.

As a general principle, we may assert that a great deal of sensitivity is required in the context of forced migration: an inordinate use of or association with the military could damage further the already brutalized psyche of refugees. Among refugee populations are to be found people who have experienced torture at the hands of armed groups or who have witnessed myriad atrocities inflicted on family members, relatives, and fellow refugees. A military presence constitutes a potential source of psychological trauma for such refugees.

Overall, the issues raised by the interaction between humanitarian NGOs and military actors in the context of forced migration require recourse to long-standing traditions of morality and ethics. I shall address this point below.

Finance and Accountability: Who Pays the Piper?

The term "humanitarian aid" evokes notions of altruism and philanthropy; it is construed as help freely given to a needy population—a true but barely functional notion of humanitarian aid. There is no such thing as free aid; aid costs money. International agencies and NGOs devote a considerable portion of their time and energy to soliciting donations from multiple sources to guarantee both their institutional survival and humanitarian activities. The assertion that there is "no such a thing as free aid" is also true in another sense. Donors routinely impose strict conditions on the use of their funds in terms of various issues: Who gets the money? Where and how should it be spent? What may or may it not be used for? How must it be accounted for? Frequently, the relationship of dependency and asymmetry between NGOs and their beneficiaries parallels that between the NGOs and their donors. How and where to find sufficient money is a constant preoccupation of aid agencies. This preoccupation carries significant ethical implications for policies and practices of refugee-serving NGOs and faith-based organizations. Various factors affect and inform such ethical dimensions and implications.

UNHCR, the body responsible for overseeing the enforcement of the international refugee regime, does not command an automatic guarantee of funds from the constituent UN countries. The countries' financial obligation is essentially voluntary, which compels UNHCR to provide justification for increases in expenditure and circumscribes its freedom in applying donor funds to the crisis of forced migration. Loescher rightly asserts that "the most significant institutional weakness of the UNHCR is its dependence on voluntary contributions to carry out its programs."[30] As mentioned above, UNHCR engages in partnerships with various humanitarian organizations as "implementing partners," relying on them to operate programs partly funded by UNHCR. Examples include several partnerships between UNHCR and JRS: Radio Kwizera in Ngara; secondary education in Adjumani; and psychosocial programs in Kakuma. It is now commonplace for governments to channel bilateral aid either directly through international NGOs or national aid agencies. One example is Norwegian People's Aid (NPA), which has been active in Ngara, providing health care and various forms of community services for refugees.

Donor Impact on Humanitarian Priorities

The conditions attached to the use of private and public funds can be ethically problematic. A donor's strategic interests come into play in various circumstances, with the result that while some "high-level" crises (like the refugee crisis in Kosovo in 1999) might either be particularly fancied or considered strategically important, other, "low-level" crises (like the refugee situation in Adjumani or Kakuma) suffer serious financial shortfalls. According to Lluís Magriñà, the international director of JRS: "The donors, particularly the private ones, prefer that their donations go to the refugees they see on television or that they have perhaps read about in the papers, in spite of the fact that occasionally, situations can arise when too much money and too many humanitarian agencies are directed towards one country that has generated media interest, resulting in a complete absence of resources in more needy areas."[31]

It is no secret that, as Loescher states, "UNHCR's dependence on voluntary contributions forces it to adopt policies that reflect the interests and priorities of the major donor countries. Politics and foreign policy priorities cause donor governments to favor some refugee groups over others."[32] Besides, it is not inconceivable that government agencies wielding substantial financial leverage would claim immunity to allegations of malpractice and corruption in their refugee work, albeit tacitly. Evidence suggests that while refugees in countries of the Global North can rely on far better aid and assistance than refugees in the Global South, where conditions of living hardly ever meet minimum standards required for safe and dignified living. Loescher reports that "according to one researcher, during the 1980s, individual refugees from the Ogaden, Cambodia, and Afghanistan received a sum of perhaps $10 to 20 per year; Angolan and Eritrean refugees received only about half this amount. On average, a Third World refugee received around 5 cents a day through the UNHCR during the last decade. In most cases this meager sum was supposed to cover not only food, water, and shelter, but also transport, logistical support, and medium- to long-term development assistance for both refugees and the host population."[33] This situation becomes more acute given the geographical shift of the refugee crisis, which began as a European problem, to poor countries mainly in Africa, Asia, and Latin America.

This consideration brings to the fore a critical ethical question: is one group of refugees more deserving of aid than another? A clear need exists to affirm the moral equivalence of all refugees, which would hold that no one refugee is more valuable than another, and that therefore, all refugees, irrespective of where they are, deserve equal treatment. David Hollenbach makes the same point earlier in the volume, echoing the views of Martha C. Nussbaum, in his analysis of "transnational good" and the duty to protect refugees and IDPs.[34] The quality of refugee protection, care, and assistance depends largely on how well donors follow this ethical principle.

In general, we can suppose that what affects UNHCR also affects humanitarian NGOs. The latter often face a thornier ethical issue, because they adopt ethical perspectives vis-à-vis emergency relief based on the mandate received from their religious congregations (for example, JRS from the Society of Jesus) and church leadership (for example, Catholic Relief Services [CRS] from the United States Conference of Catholic Bishops). One concern relates to the sources of funds and whether or not these sources guarantee the NGOs' freedom with regard to the basic humanitarian ethos of the work with crisis-affected people. As with UNHCR, the choices that humanitarian NGOs face can be stark: "either become subservient to the policies of powerful donors or become immobilized."[35] It could mean the difference between conditioned engagement and radical nonengagement, either of which portends serious consequences for NGOs' institutional survival and for the intended beneficiaries of aid—in this case, refugees.

However, one can argue that NGOs, including faith-based organizations, remain free to solicit donations from whomever they want and, therefore, are immune to promoting, overtly or covertly, donor interests that may contradict their humanitarian goals or mission. As Kenneth Hackett, president and CEO of CRS, puts it, "we are not obliged to take money, and certainly we do not take funds for something we disagree with."[36] This principle seems undeniably correct, yet in reality, it might prove too challenging for a host of humanitarian organizations. An increasingly fierce competition among too many NGOs to tap a gradually shrinking pool of donations, such as is the case in refugee assistance, confronts them with a real temptation to alter or slant their identity and mission to suit the donors' strategic interests and conditions.

Formulaic repetition of clichés or mantras ("the one who pays the piper dictates the tune" or "an agency is only as independent as its source of funding") does not substitute for a critical analysis of this ethical quandary. We need to raise a different set of key questions that could elucidate the ethical implications at stake here. Given the foregoing considerations, the debate over accepting funds in controversial circumstances will depend on how the questions are framed and what factors are deemed primary:

- Do the urgent needs of crisis-affected people constitute an attenuating factor in the quest for donor funds when the donor's geostrategic interest conflicts with the principles and values of humanitarian organizations?
- Is there such a thing as tainted money when it comes to delivering mercy to people whose very survival depends on the limited available funds? In other words, does the end (delivering critical relief and assistance to crisis-affected people) justify the means (accepting funds from sources deemed to be morally compromised or compromising)?
- In light of the minimalist principle of "do no harm," what degree of harm would accepting or refusing funds cause or avoid, and how should this be measured?
- Whose interest is paramount: the donor's, the institution's, or the refugees'?
- Does an organization's decision to accept funds undermine its overall independence and moral responsibility to challenge publicly larger structural issues that relate to the conditions of beneficiaries of the funds? For example, if the funds are for refugee assistance, does the organization remain free to challenge donor countries and other sources whose politics and policy priorities might be aggravating on-the-ground realities relative to peace and security of refugees? "It is not enough," according to

Fr. Fred Kammer, "to feed more and more hungry families; we must also raise the public question about why so much hunger persists . . . and how that condition might be changed."[37]

- Does the opportunity created by particular sources of funding open up wider opportunities for engaging issues of critical importance to the welfare and well-being of crisis-affected people such as forced migrants?

Establishing Ethical Accountability for Humanitarian NGOs

A somewhat related question to that of the financial accountability and independence of humanitarian NGOs is the issue of ethical behavior, as much adverted to today as it was ignored in the past. What norms of professional accountability should govern the behavior of humanitarian agents in their interaction with crisis-affected people? How should their behavior be ethically evaluated?

Recent revelations of gross abuses of crisis-affected people in refugee camps in the DRC and Liberia implicate a cast of humanitarian agents (peacekeepers, UNHCR protection officers, various cadres of NGO staff), despite their professed commitment to moral probity. The intricacies of power in the social context of refugees create an ideal situation for abuse, intimidation, and impunity: "On the whole, we are dealing with the groups that habitually occupy 'higher' positions [that is, 'big men'] in the social world of the refugee camps."[38] As demonstrated by Harrell-Bond's phenomenology of power in charitable giving, the underlying consideration here is that, in the context of forced displacement, humanitarian agents wield real power over their clients, the exercise of which can be debasing and inhumane.[39]

An often-repeated criticism of humanitarian organizations is their apparent reluctance to adopt mechanisms of institutional and operational accountability, an attitude that "can mask institutional or political goals which are unrelated to the needs of individual refugees or displaced persons."[40] This charge may not be overstated, given the fact that a growing emphasis on impact assessment, scrutiny, and evaluation has placed humanitarian action under the spotlight and led to the emergence of "'a culture of evaluation' . . . a culture that is based on some common principles (such as a commitment to transparency and the introduction of innovative evaluation techniques) and which cuts across the institutional boundaries and turf wars that all too frequently characterize the international humanitarian system."[41] Several instruments and mechanisms of institutional evaluation, regulation, and standards now exist or have gained renewed significance.[42]

One instrument of special relevance to the purposes of this essay is the Sphere Project, an interagency initiative that in 1997 adopted the *Humanitarian Charter and Minimum Standards in Disaster Response*.[43] The *Humanitarian Charter* presupposes and draws upon key international instruments and decades of experience in humanitarian action. Of particular salience is the fact that these standards go beyond a simple evaluation of financial accountability and adherence to stipulated goals and objectives; they also address beneficiaries' concerns. Questions remain, however, about the standards' binding force, independent monitoring of compliance, and the ground staff's overall knowledge of these instruments.[44]

With respect to the *Humanitarian Charter*, for example, it is not inconceivable that, given the proclivity of humanitarianism for relieving clear and present suffering, NGOs would be strongly oriented toward identifying and providing the material needs of crisis-affected people: water supply and sanitation, nutrition, food aid, shelter and site planning, and health services—what Loren Landau describes as using "kilograms, litres, or square meters" to "provide for humanity's basic animal functions" in his essay on self-settled refugees in urban environments.[45] Meeting these tangible conditions, however, ought not to absolve humanitarian organizations from their responsibility and accountability for some key ethical intangibles: respect for the dignity of crisis-affected people; prioritization of their interests; and consideration of their views and opinions. No charitable endeavor, no matter how noble, may substitute for the assurance, delivery of, and accountability for these ethical intangibles. On this question the Humanitarian Accountability Partnership might offer some useful correctives, precisely because it envisages with particular comprehensiveness the role of crisis-affected people in evaluating the quality of care and assistance provided by NGOs.[46]

One important ethical consideration that should inform the behavior of humanitarian organizations is the moral priority of crisis-affected people. This means that the primary goal of humanitarian action should be always to serve the interest of the beneficiaries. In other words, NGOs are morally accountable to the crisis-affected populations that they serve and on whose account they solicit donations. No initiative, no matter how laudable, can compensate for the subversion of this principle. This does not undermine the validity of humanitarian organizations' accountability to a variety of donors and to themselves as goal-oriented and objective-driven institutions.

It helps to keep in mind the simple reality that, notwithstanding their crisis-induced limitations, vulnerabilities, and disadvantages, beneficiaries of aid distribution can distinguish good NGOs from bad ones. As Koenraad Van Brabant has said, "Crisis-affected people themselves may also hold benchmarks, perhaps more implicit than explicit."[47] Thus, a corollary of the principle that humanitarian organizations are first and foremost morally accountable to their beneficiaries is the ethical imperative to adopt participatory models of assessment, evaluation, and standards, which empower crisis-affected people such as refugees to have a say about how their cause is being served by these organizations. Reluctance to solicit *and* consider the input of refugees leaves refugee-serving NGOs open to the charge of stereotyping refugees as helpless, dependent, and ignorant, effectively disempowering them.

The Way Forward: An Agenda for Advocacy

This chapter has identified key ethical issues relating to policies and practices of refugee-serving humanitarian organizations and faith-based organizations. The issues are more than just definitional; they raise substantial matters relative to ethical responsibilities toward forced migrants and the formulation of an effective framework for advocacy. In light of the foregoing considerations, the following priorities for advocacy suggest themselves.

A Holistic, or Integrated, Approach

Decades of debate over the meaning, scope, objective, and effectiveness of humanitarian action have produced unhelpful compartmentalizations. Given the ever-evolving phenomena of migration with regard to categories (forced or voluntary migrants), direction of flow (toward poor countries of the global South or toward rich countries of the global North), and causative factors (wars, natural disasters, ethnic tension, human trafficking, and so on), there is little hope of a simple consensus on the problem of defining forced migration. Again, the issues at stake transcend definitional niceties. The arguments have turned on whether forced migration is primarily a problem of ethics, technique, justice, politics, economics, culture, religion, or charity. This debate resembles that over the proverbial elephant (a trunk, a rope, a wall, a spear?)—an exercise in futility that portends little or no benefit at all for displaced populations. Even the briefest stint in a refugee camp reveals how messy the social context of humanitarian assistance can be—so messy, in fact, that it precludes absolutist, reductionist, and exclusivist conceptualizations, policies, and practices. A clear ethical imperative exists to think outside the box of entrenched positions, admit that no one approach suits all situations, and adopt a multisectoral strategy for advocating ethical responsibilities towards forced migrants. A multisectoral strategy recognizes the presence and validity of various refugee-serving actors, each of whom approaches the problem of forced migration from a unique perspective, possesses a comparative advantage, and makes meaningful contributions to the overall goal and duty to protect the rights of displaced people. Effective advocacy should seek to represent these constituent approaches or sectors as complementary aspects of a complex truth that function best when held together in a wider ethical synthesis.

Objective Needs and Subjective Voices

As indicated above, too often humanitarian actors cast displaced people in the mould of objects—victims of a calamity who need to be helped by generous and charitable outsiders. There is no denying the fact that displaced people are victims of gross violations of human rights. These violations are not only retrospective but ongoing. We must avoid the fallacy that refugees are merely objects of charitable concerns that constitute interesting statistics; rather, we must recognize that they are moral subjects—bearers or holders of rights, as William O'Neill demonstrates convincingly in his chapter in this volume on the rights of refugees and IDPs. Beyond material needs and wants, responsibilities towards forced migrants include ethical intangibles. It seems almost axiomatic that, as subjects of displacement, refugees ought to have a say in how their rights denied should be restored (for example, in exploring alternatives to traditional solutions of the refugee crisis) and ways of avoiding future violations of those rights (for example, global governance, an international refugee regime, and proactive, positive interventions). Abebe Feyissa and Rebecca Horn's firsthand account in this volume of the effects of long stays in refugee camps is a poignant demonstration of the value of listening to the voices of crisis-affected people like forced migrants. Thus, focusing on refugees as subjects rather than objects ought to constitute an aspect of effective advocacy for a just treatment of forced migrants.

Expanded Ethical Framework and Communities of Discernment

Mervyn Frost argues convincingly the case for "thinking ethically about refugees."[48] The question then is, what ethics or ethical principles? Classical *operational* principles such as neutrality, impartiality, and independence have served well the cause of humanitarianism. But they are often confused with *ethical* principles. Effective advocacy needs to distinguish the two sets of principles. We begin with the assumption that the goal of humanitarian action, particularly in the context of forced displacement, is variously conceived of as preservation of the sanctity of life, defense of human dignity, and protection and promotion of human rights, all of which transcend narrow preoccupation with geopolitical sovereignty and national interest. In that case, the ethical principles that inform the effective attainment of this goal include more than just practical operational principles, identified by Weiss as "second order principles." Specifically ethical principles or categories, which are less discussed, except in closed religious circles, need to be explicitly incorporated into the overall agenda of humanitarian assistance. These principles are common good (assistance contributes to the attainment of just social conditions for forced migrants); lesser of two evils (assistance can entail options of asymmetrical consequences for victims of forced displacement); and double effect (assistance carries unintended consequences, not always beneficial to victims of forced displacement).

Each one of these principles is far too complex to be addressed in this relatively short essay. By way of illustration I offer a brief explanation of one of them (the principle of double effect) in the context of ethical responsibilities toward forced migrants.

Experience shows that refugee assistance does not always produce a univocal and unambiguous effect. While the intention or objective remains the alleviation of the refugees' suffering, assistance is not immune to other, less desirable and less salutary unintended consequences or results. Refugee-serving organizations need to take seriously into account the unpredictability of the refugee situation. This implies a readiness to execute some requisite ethical procedures rather than merely settling for operational convenience or expediency in their work. The kind of ethical procedure envisaged here involves weighing the intention and objective of alleviating the suffering of forced migrants against the unintended effect of unwittingly perpetuating refugee-producing factors such as conflict itself, for example, in particular instances where rebel elements who have infiltrated refugee camps also benefit from relief assistance meant for innocent civilian refugees. Although unintended, this less desirable, indirect effect may carry less moral weight when related to the weightier ethical responsibility of assisting and protecting forcibly displaced and vulnerable people.

A related scenario appears in cases where refugee-serving NGOs, particularly faith-based organizations, might be compelled to tolerate, cooperate with, or have recourse to the "*force* for good" provided by the military, for example, to protect humanitarian workers or dislodge refugee-warriors from civilian camps. As indicated above, the presence and use of the military can provoke some deleterious effects among refugees. In the scenario under consideration, these concomitant effects are indirect and unintended, the more direct and intended good being the guarantee and delivery of critically needed aid to refugees in life-threatening situations. Thus, cooperation with the military, rather than amounting to an unequivocal endorsement of the use of force, appears as a necessary indirect evil effect, avoided when possible and morally permitted *only* when the intended direct and good effect, in this case protecting and saving the lives of vulnerable, crisis-affected people like refugees, outweighs the negative consequences in a proportionate way.

Making these choices is never easy, but attaining clarity about and determining how and where these ethical principles apply represent an important dimension of ethical responsibilities toward forced migrants among refugee-serving NGOs and require a new understanding of humanitarian organizations as "communities of discernment,"[49] committed to a just resolution of the crisis of forced migration. To suggest a communitarian discernment of ethical principles and policies among a disparate and often competing cast of organizations appears a daunting task. Perhaps herein lies a distinctive contribution of faith-based organizations, namely their ability to act as catalysts for the creation of ethical frameworks, guidelines, and consensus for advocacy, as in the Sphere Project, the international coalition on detention of refugees and asylum seekers, and the Christian Relief and Development Association (CRDA) in Ethiopia.

Finally, it is helpful to distinguish genuine humanitarian crisis from surreptitious attempts to provide cover for political inaction or to promote harmful geostrategic interests and interventions. Effective advocacy operates within an expanded ethical framework and creates communities of discernment in promoting the cause of forced migrants.

Conclusion

The word "humanitarianism" delineates an overcrowded and intensely contested space—nowhere more so than in a refugee camp. It is not unusual for refugee-serving NGOs and churches to demarcate the physical space of a refugee camp into distinct spheres of interest and zones of operation. This can create multiple kinds and levels of tension and generate ethical dilemmas and quandaries. Many refugee-serving humanitarian organizations approach the crisis of forced migration from a faith perspective. A critical evaluation of their roles serves the important theoretical project of identifying some key ethical issues and establishing a framework for effective advocacy. This essay does not answer all the questions, but it allows us to make some remarks and suggestions about implications for advocacy; the justice versus charity debate in relation to forced migration; and the distinctive contribution of faith-based, refugee-serving organizations.

In the first place, advocacy delineates a long-term commitment extending beyond the lifespan of any humanitarian crisis. In this sense, advocacy constitutes the antithesis of the "CNN effect," which focuses on humanitarian crises for as long as audience ratings can be guaranteed. As an effective tool for conflict transformation, particularly in the context of forced migration, advocacy entails a watchfulness that monitors potential flashpoints, devises and deploys early warning mechanisms, and assesses potential for the escalation of refugee-generating conflicts. We need, therefore, to conceive of advocacy in proactive rather than reactive terms. Herein lies an important ethical obligation for faith-based organizations for whom charity—often limited to relief assistance—carries more priority than promoting measures that diffuse tension and ensure de-escalation of refugee-producing conflicts. As mentioned above, charity can have a very short lifespan; it is more effective when integrated into proactive, long-term strategies on behalf of forced migrants.

The justice-charity debate opens up new vistas for advocacy and policy in relation to forced migrants. Of particular salience is the need to avoid hardening the divergent positions into normative, absolutist, and reductionist definitions. Adopting a charitable approach toward refugee assistance ought not to be a transient, selective, and superficial response but a comprehensive approach that equally promotes other aspects of refugee assistance, like long-term development and rehabilitation programs. On the other hand, perceiving and approaching refugee service from a justice perspective ought not to become a narrow and rigid focus on legalistic provisions or guarantees of basic human rights. On the present evidence, each approach has its limits.

In principle, a faith-based humanitarian organization like Catholic Relief Services admirably combines both perspectives, albeit the relationship sometimes can be fraught with tension and ambiguities—hence the need for flexibility in correlating both principles and perspectives.[50] Jesuit superior general Peter-Hans Kolvenbach underscores this point when he affirms that

> the Church discovered only very slowly that charity is not sufficient if there is no justice. What has to be done by JRS is not just charity but also justice. If you really love, you will do justice. You will not do justice out of justice, but out of love. That is quite difficult because if someone speaks only about justice, he could be terribly unjust. The Romans here already knew about this, that the best justice could become the most profound injustice. If you stick only to what is legal, juridical justice, you can come up with unjust measures. We see this in the way the immigrants, the refugees are treated by the laws in Europe. This is the reason that the Pope (John Paul II) and also Father Arrupe (founder of JRS) spoke about justice as the incarnation of love, the concrete way to love. . . . One can say charity just to do something but it is very clear all these people have their rights which need to be attended to. They have the right to go back to their country. They have the right to join in a just society. JRS is called to help do this, not out of legal or juridical motivations but out of Christian love.[51]

In general, it helps to recall that charity and justice represent wide principles, neither of which can be easily or completely exhausted in any given situation. Attaining some clarity about each particular perspective in relation to an organization's mandate constitutes a crucial methodological requirement, as is an acknowledgement of the interface between these principles, as demonstrated in this chapter. The upshot of this double dynamic is that, while respecting the focus of an individual internal mandate, which may place an accent on one or the other principle, advocacy can be enhanced via strategic alliances, partnerships, networks, and coalitions built on the relative strengths and comparative advantages of the various cooperating organizations. A recent example is the JRS-led international coalition on detention of refugees and asylum seekers.

This brings us to the final remark. In light of the foregoing considerations and consistent with the central premise of this essay—that many refugee-serving NGOs are faith based and church related—some additional comments are in order on their distinctive contributions from the perspective of ethical responsibilities toward forced migrants. The aim, however, is not to isolate them and therefore impede their capacity to collaborate with secular NGOs.

Unsurprisingly, the mission and mandate of faith-based organizations are heavily informed by ethical and ultimately spiritual norms. Much has been said in this essay about the mission of JRS: accompaniment, service, and advocacy. These broad categories are generally underpinned and animated by ethical principles proper to the larger ecclesial community. Perhaps the best illustration of this is Catholic Relief Services, which defines itself as the official international relief and development agency of the U.S. Catholic community. As such, "the policies and programs of the agency reflect and express the teaching of the Catholic Church. At the same time, Catholic Relief Services assists persons on the basis of need, not creed, race or nationality."[52] The policies and programs of CRS, like those of JRS, "draw upon a rich tradition of Scripture and Catholic social teaching," a tradition that prioritizes recognizing the God-given basic dignity of each human person, advancing the value and equality of all human beings, promoting the common good, practicing a preferential option for the poor, and fostering solidarity and interdependence, among other principles.[53]

Although explicitly espoused and promoted by a religious organization, in reality these principles create a common platform and framework for far-reaching collaboration and partnership with other religious and secular groups. This collaboration is noticeable "in programs and projects which contribute to a more equitable society" rather than isolate the organization itself and exclude others from its operational ambit.[54]

Proximity and presence represent yet another distinctive feature of faith-based, refugee-serving organizations. As a quick tour of refugee camps in eastern Africa would reveal, the refugee situation there hardly qualifies as "high profile"; some of the refugee populations seem to count for little in the eyes of the international community. In this kind of situation, available evidence shows that faith-based organizations like JRS, TCRS, and LWF are more likely than secular organizations to focus on the needs of "forgotten" populations of refugees, in places like Rhino Camp, Adjumani, Kibondo, and others, trying in difficult circumstances with limited resources to respond to unmet needs.

Finally, international faith-based organizations find a ready constituency of local partners in realizing their goals and objectives. This is often facilitated by their access to a network of local church communities and church-related organizations with compatible or shared values. The advantages of this kind of local partnership are multiple. They include ensuring local participation, fostering local ownership, and guaranteeing the sustainability of various assistance, rehabilitation, and development projects beyond the temporal mandate of the initiating international organization, as demonstrated by the report in this volume on the work of Joint Commission on Refugees among the Burundian refugees in western Tanzania.

Notes

1. I have described and analyzed this phenomenon in my *From Crisis to Kairos: The Mission of the Church in the Time of HIV/AIDS, Refugees and Poverty* (Nairobi, Kenya: Paulines, 2005). Besides the United Nations High Commissioner for Refugees (UNHCR), there is a plethora of international and governmental agencies and nongovernmental organizations that occupy the highly populated humanitarian space of refugee assistance. See Gil Loescher, *Beyond Charity: International Cooperation and the Global Refugee Crisis* (New York and Oxford: Oxford University Press, 1993), 130–31; and Mark Raper, "Changing Roles of NGOs in Refugee Assistance," in *Refugees and Forced Displacement: International Security, Human Vulnerability, and the State*, eds. Edward Newman and Joanne van Selm (Paris: United Nations University Press, 2003), 350. How these humanitarian actors relate to UNHCR is the subject of ongoing debate. In the context of refugee assistance, most NGOs operate as "implementing partners" of UNHCR and assume responsibility for an estimated 50% of UNHCR's programs of assistance. Elizabeth G. Ferris, "The Role of Non-Governmental Organizations in the International Refugee Regime," in *Problems of Protection: The UNHCR, Refugees, and Human Rights*, eds. Niklaus Steiner et al. (New York and London: Routledge, 2003), 125–26.

2. For example, World Council of Churches, "A Moment to Choose: Risking to Be with Uprooted People," Statement on Uprooted People, September 22, 1995; Pontifical Council for the Pastoral Care of Migrants and Itinerant People, *Refugees: A Challenge to Solidarity* (Nairobi, Kenya: St. Paul Publications, 1992); *The Three Consultations of 1998 for a More Coordinated Pastoral Response of the Church in Africa to the Present Refugee Crisis: The Official Texts with Commentary* (Vatican City, 1999); All Africa Conference of Churches, *The Refugee Problem "A Time Bomb in Africa"* (Nairobi, Kenya: AACC, 1992); *Too Many, Too Long . . . : Refugees in Africa and the Churches' Response* (Nairobi, Kenya: AACC, n.d.).

3. Ferris, "The Role of Non-Governmental Organizations," 117–22.

4. Drew Christiansen, "Movement, Asylum, Borders: Christian Perspectives," *International Migration Review* 30, no. 1 (Spring 1996): 2.

5. Loescher, *Beyond Charity*, 130, see also 150; *The UNHCR and World Politics: A Perilous Path* (Oxford: Oxford University Press, 2001), 16–18.

6. Loescher, *Beyond Charity*, 151.

7. Mervyn Frost, "Thinking Ethically about Refugees: A Case for the Transformation of Global Governance," in *Refugees and Forced Displacement*, eds. Newman and van Selm, 129.

8. Barbara Harrell-Bond, "Can Humanitarian Work with Refugees Be Humane?" *Human Rights Quarterly* 24 (2002): 52–53. In this same article Harrell-Bond presents a critical phenomenology of "charitable giving" in refugee camps that, besides creating an asymmetrical relationship of power between refugees and humanitarian workers, debases human dignity.

9. Cf. Loescher, *The UNHCR and World Politics*, 3; World Council of Churches, "A Moment to Choose," 2–3.

10. Michel Agier and Françoise Bouchet-Saulnier, "Humanitarian Spaces: Spaces of Exception," in *In the Shadow of 'Just Wars': Violence, Politics and Humanitarian Action*, ed. Fabrice Weissman (Ithaca, NY: Cornell University Press, 2004), 298–304; Stephen John Stedman, "Conclusions and Policy Recommendations," in *Refugee Manipulation: War, Politics, and the Abuse of Human Suffering*, eds. Stephen John Stedman and Fred Tanner (Washington, DC: Brookings Institution Press, 2003), 169–72.

11. Agier and Bouchet-Saulnier, "Humanitarian Spaces," 311–12; see also Ferris, "The Role of Non-Governmental Organizations," 131–32; Raper, "Changing Roles of NGOs," 356–57; Thomas G. Weiss, "Principles, Politics, and Humanitarian Action," *Ethics and International Affairs*

13 (1999): 13; Cornelio Sommaruga, "Humanity: Our Priority Now and Always: Response to 'Principles, Politics, and Humanitarian Action,'" *Ethics and International Affairs* 13 (1999): 26–27; Theresa Baldini, "The House of Prayer and Peace," in *Another Day in Paradise: International Humanitarian Workers Tell Their Stories*, ed. Carole Bergman (Maryknoll, NY: Orbis, 2003), 164–70.

12. Jesuit Refugee Service, *God in Exile: Towards a Shared Spirituality with Refugees* (Rome: Jesuit Refugee Service, 2005), 108. Emphasis in original.

13. I make a distinction between "withness" (a discreet but active presence in connection with humanitarian assistance), as practiced by the JRS, and (in)direct "witness," or *témoignage* (explicit documentation of abuses in connection with political action), as practiced by Médecin Sans Frontières. See Eric Dachy, "Justice and Humanitarian Action: A Conflict of Interest," in *In the Shadow of "Just Wars*," ed. Weissman, 314–24; Joelle Tanguy and Fiona Terry, "Humanitarian Responsibility and Committed Action: Response to 'Principles, Politics, and Humanitarian Action,'" *Ethics and International Affairs* 13 (1999): 32.

14. Weiss, "Principles, Politics, and Humanitarian Action," 1–22.

15. Ferris, "The Role of Non-Governmental Organizations," 128.

16. Weiss, "Principles, Politics, and Humanitarian Action," 20–21; Tanguy and Terry, "Humanitarian Responsibility," 33; David Rieff, "Moral Imperatives and Political Realities: Response to 'Principles, Politics, and Humanitarian Action,'" *Ethics and International Affairs* 13 (1999): 35–42.

17. Sommaruga, "Humanity: Our Priority Now and Always," 24.

18. Ferris, "The Role of Non-Governmental Organizations," 129–31.

19. Mark Raper has described the usefulness of such an approach in the collaboration between the JRS and Human Rights Watch (HRW) in the specific instance of refugee camps in eastern Africa. "Changing Roles of NGOs in Refugee Assistance," 357–59.

20. Weiss, "Principles, Politics, and Humanitarian Action," 14.

21. Cf. David Hollenbach, "Humanitarian Crises, Refugees, and the Transnational Good: Global Challenges and Catholic Social Teaching" (unpublished paper prepared for the Expert Seminar, "Scrutinising the Signs of the Times and Interpreting Them in Light of the Gospel," Katholieke Universiteit Leuven Centre for Catholic Social Thought, Leuven, Belgium, September 9–11, 2004): 30–33.

22. See Liisa Malkki, *Purity and Exile: Violence, Memory, and National Cosmology among Hutu Refugees in Tanzania* (Chicago and London: University of Chicago Press, 1995), 263 ff. In some cases, Tanzanian camp authorities have used the army to enforce payment of taxes imposed on refugees. Ibid., 121–28.

23. Harrell-Bond, "Can Humanitarian Work with Refugees Be Humane?" 83.

24. Ibid., 83–84.

25. "Rules and Regulations for the Settlements, Issued by the Office of the Prime Minister (OPM), Rhino Camp Refugee Settlement, March 2000" (photocopied).

26. Rupert Wieloch, "The Humanitarian Use of the Military," *Forced Migration Review* 18 (September 2003): 32, 33. The use of the military in heavy logistical operations such as emergency airlifts of large refugee populations and airdrops of food and relief materials would count as examples of the military acting as a "force for good."

27. See Antonio Donini, "Taking Sides: The Iraq Crisis and the Future of Humanitarianism," *Forced Migration Review* 19 (January 2004): 38. On military-civilian humanitarian issues, see Arthur C. Helton, *The Price of Indifference: Refugees and Humanitarian Action in the New Century* (Oxford: Oxford University Press, 2002), 216–21; Ferris, "The Role of Non-Governmental Organizations," 133–34.

28. Hollenbach, "Humanitarian Crises, Refugees, and the Transnational Good," 32.

29. The ethical scenarios briefly presented here are dealt with extensively in Stedman and Tanner, *Refugee Manipulation*.

30. Loescher, *Beyond Charity*, 131; see also Helton, *The Price of Indifference*, 207–10.

31. *Refugees in the 21st Century: Can We Find a Solution?* (Barcelona: Cristianisme í Justicia, 2006), 26.

32. Loescher, *Beyond Charity*, 137.

33. Ibid., 136.

34. See David Hollenbach, "Humanitarian Crises, Refugees, and Transnational Good."

35. Ibid., 138.

36. Kenneth Hackett, "Public Funds, Catholic Mercy: Fulfilling the Promise of the Church in the World," Rome, Italy, November 21, 2003 (photocopied).

37. Quoted in ibid.

38. Agier and Bouchet-Saulnier, "Humanitarian Spaces: Spaces of Exception," 299; see Stedman "Conclusions and Policy Recommendations," 169.

39. Harrell-Bond also documents a variety of power relationships that degrade, stereotype, infantilize, and dehumanize refugees, in "Can Humanitarian Work with Refugees Be Humane?" 56 ff; cf. Malkki's idea of the "refugee camp as a 'technology of power,'" in *Purity and Exile*, 236–38.

40. Helton, *The Price of Indifference*, 210; Koenraad Van Brabant, "Benchmarks and Yardsticks for Humanitarian Action: Broadening the Picture," *Forced Migration Review* 17 (May 2003): 45.

41. Jeff Crisp, "Thinking Outside the Box: Evaluation and Humanitarian Action," *Forced Migration Review* 8 (August 2000): 5.

42. See Van Brabant, "Benchmarks and Yardsticks," 43–45.

43. The Sphere Project, *Humanitarian Charter and Minimum Standards in Disaster Response* (Geneva: The Sphere Project, 2004).

44. One senior staff member of a refugee-serving, faith-based NGO interviewed as part of the research for this chapter had never heard of The Sphere Project and the *Humanitarian Charter and Minimum Standards*.

45. See Loren B. Landau, "Protection as Capability Expansion: Practical Ethics for Assisting Urban Refugees," in this volume.

46. Formerly known as the Humanitarian Accountability Project and Humanitarian Ombudsman Project. Available from http://www.hapinternational.org/en/ (accessed June 28, 2006).

47. Van Brabant, "Benchmarks and Yardsticks," 44.

48. Mervyn Frost, "Thinking Ethically about Refugees: A Case for the Transformation of Global Governance," 129.

49. I have borrowed this term from Drew Christiansen, "Sacrament of Unity: Ethical Issues in Pastoral Care of Migrants and Refugees," in *Today's Immigrants and Refugees: A Christian Understanding*, Office of Pastoral Care of Migrants and Refugees (Washington, DC: National Conference of Catholic Bishops, 1988), 101–2.

50. See "Mission Statement," http://www.crs.org/about_us/who_we_are/mission.cfm (accessed December 26, 2006).

51. Address to Jesuit Refugee Service International Meeting, Santa Severa, Italy, May 25, 2006.

52. "Mission Statement," http://www.crs.org/about_us/who_we_are/mission.cfm.

53. "Guiding Principles," http://www.crs.org/about_us/who_we_are/what_we_believe.cfm (accessed December 26, 2006).

54. "Mission Statement," http://www.crs.org/about_us/who_we_are/mission.cfm.

Contributors

Lam Oryem Cosmas is a consultant and adviser to the Justice and Peace Council (JPC) of the ecclesiastical province of Gulu in northern Uganda. He served as coordinator for an interfaith peace organization in northern Uganda, the Acholi Religious Leaders Peace Initiative (ARLPI). He holds a master's degree in conflict transformation and peace building from Eastern Mennonite University's Center for Justice and Peacebuilding (CJP), Harrisonburg, Virginia.

Abebe Feyissa was born in Ethiopia in 1965. Ten years after completing secondary school in Addis Ababa, he attended Addis Ababa University to study educational psychology. When political change took place in Ethiopia, his life was put in danger by the ethnic-based politics of the new government. He fled Ethiopia to Kenya in 1991 and has lived in a refugee camp for the last sixteen years. He is still living in Kakuma Camp in northwest Kenya.

John Guiney, SJ, is regional director of Jesuit Refugee Service (JRS) in eastern Africa. He coordinates the work of JRS in Tanzania, Uganda, Sudan, Kenya, and Ethiopia. The JRS work in eastern Africa covers education, psychosocial services, pastoral care, peace and reconciliation, and urban emergency programs for refugees and internally displaced persons.

David Hollenbach, SJ, is director of the Center for Human Rights and International Justice and holds the University Chair in Human Rights and International Justice at Boston College. His principal interests are in the areas of human rights, religion in social and political life, and issues facing refugees and displaced people. His most recent book is *The Global Face of Public Faith: Politics, Human Rights, and Christian Ethics* (2003). He has regularly been visiting professor at Hekima College in Nairobi, Kenya.

Rebecca Horn is a psychologist from the United Kingdom. Her background is in forensic psychology, but since 2003 she has been working with people affected by conflict in Africa. She spent three years working with the Jesuit Refugee Service in Kakuma, northern Kenya, and has also worked in Kitgum, northern Uganda, and in Sierra Leone.

Lucy Hovil has spent the previous seven years initiating and implementing research agendas in forced displacement, conflict, and related areas at the Refugee Law Project, Faculty of Law, Makerere University, Uganda. She previously completed her doctorate at London University's School of Oriental and African Studies, which focused on the relationship between violence and identity in South Africa in the period leading up to the country's first democratic elections.

The *Joint Commission for Refugees* (JCR) is a commission of the Burundi and Tanzania Roman Catholic Episcopal Conferences. It oversees pastoral programs for the Burundian refugees in Tanzania and internally displaced people in Burundi. It was formed in 2002 at the initiative of Bishop Paul Ruzoka of Kigoma, Tanzania, in conjunction with the pastoral workers in the camps for Burundian refugees in the Kigoma and Rulenge dioceses of Western Tanzania.

Khoti Kamanga is the coordinator, Centre for the Study of Forced Migration, University of Dar es Salaam in Tanzania, and secretary, International Association for the Study of Forced Migration. He studied law in Moscow and Amsterdam. At the University of Dar es Salaam he teaches public international law, refugee law, and international humanitarian law. His publications are in the areas of refugee law and policy, security, and regional integration. He sits on the editorial boards of the *Journal of Refugee Studies* (Oxford) and the *African Yearbook on International Humanitarian Law* (Johannesburg).

Loren B. Landau is director of University of Witwatersrand's Forced Migration Studies Programme in Johannesburg, South Africa, and is executive committee chair for the Consortium of Refugees and Migrants in South Africa (CRMSA). A political scientist by training, his research has explored migration and state power in rural Tanzania and southern African cities.

Susan Martin holds the Donald G. Herzberg Chair in International Migration and serves as the director of the Institute for the Study of International Migration in the School of Foreign Service at Georgetown University in Washington, D.C. She is the author of *Refugee Women*, 2nd ed (2004), and serves as the president of the International Association for the Study of Forced Migration.

Binaifer Nowrojee heads the Open Society Initiative for East Africa, a grant-giving and advocacy organization based in Nairobi, Kenya. She is also a lecturer at Harvard Law School. Earlier, Ms. Nowrojee worked as legal counsel with the Women's Rights and Africa divisions of Human Rights Watch and with the Lawyers Committee for Human Rights. Ms. Nowrojee has documented abuses throughout the African continent and is the author of a number of reports and articles on human rights issues.

Moses Chrispus Okello is head of the Research and Advocacy Department at the Refugee Law Project at the Faculty of Law, Makerere University, Uganda. He holds a master's degree in international human rights law from the American University in Cairo and has research interests in conflict resolution, human rights, transitional justice, and forced displacement. He is coauthor or editor of a number of Refugee Law Project research reports available from www.refugeelawproject.org.

William O'Neill, SJ, is a professor of social ethics at the Jesuit School of Theology at Berkeley and a visiting professor of ethics at Hekima College in Nairobi, Kenya. His writings include a book on ethics and hermeneutics, *The Ethics of Our Climate: Hermeneutics and Ethical Theory* (1994), and articles on human rights, social reconciliation, conflict resolution, and refugee and immigration policy.

Agbonkhianmeghe E. Orobator, SJ, is a Jesuit priest from Nigeria. He teaches theology and religious studies at Hekima College Jesuit School of Theology and Peace Studies in Nairobi, Kenya, where he is also rector. He is author of several books, including *From Crisis to Kairos: The Mission of the Church in the Time of HIV/AIDS, Refugees, and Poverty* (2005).

Stephen J. Pope is professor of theology at Boston College. He received his PhD in theological ethics from the University of Chicago. He has written *Human Evolution and Christian Ethics* (2007) as well as editing *Solidarity and Hope: Jon Sobrino's Challenge to Christian Theology* (2008). He is currently working on a book on political forgiveness and social reconciliation.

John Burton Wagacha is chief operating officer and cofounder of Mapendo International, an agency providing medical care and protection to at-risk and overlooked refugees. He previously worked in refugee health with Gesellschaft für Technische Zusammenarbeit (GTZ), UNHCR, and the International Office for Migration in Kenya and across Africa. Wagacha holds an MD and an MA in sociology.

Index